Ludwig Grote and the Bauhaus Idea

Edition Bauhaus 53

Edited for the Bauhaus Dessau Foundation
by Peter Bernhard and Torsten Blume

ERNST VON SIEMENS
KUNSTSTIFTUNG

Contents

Appendix

Acknowledgments

This publication was generously supported by the Ernst von Siemens Kunststiftung, which had already sponsored the cataloging of Ludwig Grote's papers in the Germanisches Nationalmuseum in Nuremberg. We thank them very much for that. We would also like to thank the Germanisches Nationalmuseum as well as two other places where Grote was once active—the Anhaltische Gemäldegalerie in Dessau and the Württembergischer Kunstverein in Stuttgart—for kindly providing illustrations at no cost. Last but not least, we wish to thank Thomas Altmann for his helpful research work and of course the authors, who have contributed to the success of this volume.

Peter Bernhard
Torsten Blume

Fig. 1 Ludwig Grote in his official residence in Dessau, ca. 1927

Ludwig Grote: A Conservative Friend of the Bauhaus

Peter Bernhard and Torsten Blume

A glance at the list of Ludwig Grote's publications makes it clear: As an art historian, he published his most extensive texts and books primarily on the art of the early modern period and the painting of German Romanticism.[1] By contrast, he expressed himself about the Bauhaus more in connection with specific occasions, in lectures, in the context of exhibitions—of which he organized and curated several[2]—and in newspaper articles. Nevertheless, Grote's texts, and even more so the activities associated with them, and his commitment to the Bauhaus influenced the history and reception of that college. For Grote, who, as recently appointed Landeskonservator (state conservator) of Anhalt and consultant on art to Mayor Fritz Hesse, vehemently advocated for the Bauhaus moving to Dessau and after 1945 organized exhibitions that were pioneering for their reception in West Germany, was an important figure in art and cultural policy. From the time of his encounter with the Bauhaus in Dessau, Grote spent the rest of his life working as a supporter of and propagandist for this school in his posts and functions and in the networks that developed as a result (fig. 1). For that reason, Grote's relationship to the Bauhaus was less that of a scholar than that of a facilitator and supporter. In his speech at the celebration of Grote's eightieth birthday, the Swiss art historian Christoph Bernoulli remarked that his friend and colleague of many years had made the Bauhaus as an idea his own to such an extent that one had to note: "Wherever he goes, the Bauhaus goes along."[3]

It seems strange that an overall account of Grote's "Bauhaus path" has yet to be published and that his role in the history of the Bauhaus has been treated largely in footnotes. For during his engagement as an agent for art and culture for the City of Dessau and above all in the context of the state-supported programs of the young Federal Republic of Germany, Grote managed to come up with a Bauhaus narrative that is still influential today. The present book is an attempt to show how the Bauhaus was tied to Grote's career as a mediator in the art world and that it was ultimately possible for his interpretation of the Bauhaus to continue shaping how it was perceived well beyond his own lifetime. To that end, for the first time the essays compiled in this book are dedicated to all of Grote's essential Bauhaus stations without leaving out the years of National Socialism during which, although he could no longer operate as a promoter of aesthetic modernism, he nevertheless continued to work as an art historian and art dealer.[4] In the end, the goal is to show that Grote's commitment to the Bauhaus was not only interrupted by the National Socialist system and in a sense paused for a time but also how he readjusted it thereafter under the conditions of the cultural politics of postwar West Germany.

In the process it becomes clear that there are consistent motifs in Grote's descriptions of the Bauhaus. One of these is his effort to interpret the Bauhaus as *a whole*, that is, as a school that despite all the internal conflicts and external upheavals was always permeated by a common artistic spirit that was represented above all by the painters who taught there. For that reason, he ultimately saw the Bauhaus as a school of artists. Thus he remarked already in 1928: "Anyone who sees in the Bauhaus only the technical research institute and the workshops for developing standardized equipment sees only the outward" and not the artistic behind it that is the "driving force" there.[5] He argued that above all the teaching in the preliminary course by Wassily Kandinsky and Paul Klee had made it possible to "expose the sources of artistic design"[6] and showed the students how to examine analytically "the *elements* of art"[7] that only then could form the foundation of a functional design practice. Only by means of this ground of all Bauhaus design could the spaces designed at the Bauhaus become, according to Grote, "modern" in a way that begins to make sense.[8]

That modern design and architecture needed a deeper meaning or a spiritual foundation and that it could be found in modern art was one of Grote's basic convictions and was essentially based on the ideas of the Lebensreform (Life Reform) movement and the visions of Lebensphilosophie (Life Philosophy) that had influenced him intellectually in his youth and during his studies. He had been an ardent support of the nationalist-conservative wing of the Wandervogel (Migratory Bird) movement. Above all, however, while studying archaeology in Jena Grote connected to the Serakreis (Sera Circle), which was a gathering point in the publishing house of Eugen Diederichs for the city's intellectual and cultural elite, which saw itself in the tradition of the early Romantic circle in Jena around Friedrich and Wilhelm Schlegel. It not only discussed the neo-Romantic literature being published by Diederichs (by Hermann Hesse and Ricarda Huch, for example) and texts by John Ruskin and Friedrich Nietzsche but also and above all the utopian designs for a new culture on the basis of the arts.[9]

Clearly, Grote understood the Bauhaus, which he had supported from 1927 onward, also with commissions and exhibitions in his role as director of the Anhaltische Gemäldegalerie, as an enterprise that could be described in connection with the visions of the artistic renewal of culture and life of the sort he had encountered in the Serakreis. He also saw similarities between the Bauhaus and German Romanticism, which he had researched as an art historian,[10] which, according to Grote, developed "the idea that the experience of art communicates values that are among the greatest and most profound of humanity and that [should be] bestowed not only on connoisseurs and the especially privileged but also as much as possible on all people."[11] Accordingly, he also idealized the avant-garde school as a place where Walter Gropius had "assembled forces that pressed ahead from Expressionism, from the subjective, toward a new objective order."[12] In this way, all his life Grote related his Bauhaus interpretation to the art of Romanticism and to the "desire for a renewal of culture" expressed in that art.[13] He thus described the Bauhaus painters above all as modern Romantics whose art was concerned not only with a "synthesis of reason and emotion, with mastery and spiritualizing of the means of expression of painting."[14] Through their art they had also opened up paths and hence founded a new unity of all design. Such descriptions of the Bauhaus recall the expectations of totality or desires for order and unity of German Romanticism in which by means of art the individual's sense of feeling lost in an increasingly rational, technologically and economically influenced world should be overcome or spiritually sublated in a new national unity. Grote believed that the unity of art and technology that Gropius had advocated in 1923 could be understood as almost the quintessence of the Bauhaus as an idea and as a summary of the Bauhaus "epoch" of the "first four years in which the turn to [...] constructivism" occurred[15] that provided the Bauhaus with its intellectual foundation. From 1919 to 1923, artists such as Kandinsky and Klee had, in his view, established the principles of a totalizing, idealistic program for the Bauhaus.

In that spirit, Grote believed he could also say, especially after 1945: "The Bauhaus was an idea,"[16] and hence really always more than a school as well: "not an institute, a spiritual, creative movement."[17] So Grote described the Bauhaus above all as a program that was remote from any specific politics whose ideas and projects were rooted in a realm that, like that of the Romantics of the nineteenth century, was in essence not of this world. That in the process—especially in Dessau in his function as a civil servant of the city that was financing the Bauhaus—he always also emphasized—and had to emphasize—the importance of the Bauhaus as an institution developing and designing for industry did not represent a contradiction for Grote. After all, with his descriptions he also managed to lend an artistic and idealistic change to the architecture of the Bauhaus buildings in Dessau. For, according to Grote, the "roots" of all Bauhaus architecture lay in a "idea of space" previously developed by the painters—they had "turned away from the delimited, measurable, static, and rational space of the Renaissance and developed a dynamic, irrational space"; that had made it possible in the first place that it was no longer "heavy, oppressive wall masses or sculptural volumes" that form the building but rather light "planes of glass and metal" that were hung freely in a "pictorial structure by Feininger" that they "seem to float."[18]

Grote's texts present the image of a conservative protagonist of modernity and a cultured citizen who sees himself as apolitical. Yet he probably saw the Bauhaus as above all a project of the aesthetic modernization of Germany and not as a manifestation of the democracy of the Weimar Republic. That is at least suggested by the following sentences, which Grote put to paper with a fateful enthusiasm in a letter to his wife, Maud, in 1940: "A people that manages to do something like winning this war has demonstrated such power and such will that it has earned a claim to a share in ruling the world. Hitler's greatness is growing into the legendary, the larger-than-life. [...] A large gate to the future is being opened for our children."[19] Did Grote see in National Socialism a movement that could finally have realized the ideas of a superiority of the German nation that were cultivated by the nationalist-conservative bourgeoisie? Such sentences do not, in any case, seem to fit with the propagandist of an internationalist Bauhaus who in 1965 described modern architecture as "the most powerful weapon of the democracy" of the free West.[20] Nor do they seem to fit the supporter of the Bauhaus who had friendships, some of them lifelong, with a whole series of members of the Bauhaus[21]—but the fact that the second director of the Bauhaus, Hannes Meyer, was not one of them does. For Grote had rejected Meyer not because of the latter's critique of an artistic foundation for the Bauhaus but above all because of his profession of Marxism and the Soviet Union. That was why he had played a role in Meyer's dismissal in 1930[22] and also in his later lectures, publications, and exhibitions ignored his contribution to the history of the Bauhaus almost entirely. As late as 1968—now in the context of the Cold War of the free West against the "dictatorships of the east"[23]—Grote wrote of

Meyer: "his scientific marxism narrowed his views. He wanted to give the bauhaus a scientific, political character and wanted to deprive it of its cultural climate."[24]

As a civil servant and cultural politician, Grote had legitimized—and felt obliged in the spirit of the Bauhaus as he interpreted it as an artistic institution—to push for Meyer's dismissal. At the same time, he also understood the latter's demission as a defense of the Bauhaus as idealized by him as a neo-Romantic school of art and design. As a conservative modernist, he felt called upon to defend—also in the exhibitions he conceived and in his numerous articles and lectures—the Bauhaus as an apolitical school, which in his view could take root only in an artistic sphere that stands above all political developments, against all kinds of culturally reactionary attacks.[25] Just how important the Bauhaus was to Grote, in part for his self-image as a mediator for the arts, is evident by quoting his diary from 1931, when he noted about a conversation with the mayor that his "activity in D. would only made sense together with the Bauhaus."[26]

The summer of 1932 marked the end for Grote of the "golden times of Dessau,"[27] in which his work on behalf of the Bauhaus increased his own significance as a figure in cultural policy. For on August 22, the NSDAP faction in the Gemeinderat (Municipal Council) pushed through the closing of the school on October 1. He was outraged; he sought the aid of influential National Socialists who were open to aesthetic modernism to preserve the Bauhaus as an apolitical, modern institution that as a *German* Bauhaus could adapt to the Nazi system as well and become useful to it.[28] It was not yet possible to foresee the future of modernism in Germany, especially as several leading National Socialists, including Joseph Goebbels, wanted to make Expressionism the national art.[29] From Grote's perspective, the Constructivism of the Bauhaus would not be in contradiction with that, since it could also be understood as an aesthetic modernization of Expressionist principles of design.

Grote's attempt to save the Bauhaus failed, and it moved to Berlin, where in April 1933 it was searched by request of the attorney general of Dessau and then sealed. That same month, Grote accepted early retirement in order to avoid imminent dismissal under the Gesetz zur Wiederherstellung des Berufsbeamtentums (Law for the Restoration of the Professional Civil Service).[30] The fact that he joined the SA (Sturmabteilung) in 1934 suggests that even thereafter he was continuing to come to terms with the new circumstances.[31] After Hitler had declared at the Nuremberg party conference in September 1934 that all supporters of modernism were enemies of tradition and at the latest when preparations for the *Entartete Kunst* exhibition began in 1937, which opened soon thereafter in Munich, all hopes for Grote to be able to continue to pursue in some form his ambitions concerning aesthetic modernism were shattered. He therefore sought out other fields of activity in an art world ruled by National Socialism.

Like many art historians of his era in Germany, after 1945 Grote held back with statements about his activity during National Socialism. In a tabular curriculum vitae on these years he noted only: "1933: Dismissal by the National Socialists. Up to 1951: Worked freelance as a writer on art."[32] After working as a consultant on stone restoration in the 1930s, in 1940 Grote was hired by the Galerie

Fig. 2 *Der Blaue Reiter* (The Blue Rider), view of the exhibition, 1949
Fig. 3 Ludwig Grote and Theodor Heuss at the exhibition *Die Maler am Bauhaus* (The Painters at the Bauhaus) at the Haus der Kunst, Munich, 1950

Fig. 4 Lauritz Lauritzen (Federal Minister of Housing and Urban Planning), Walter Gropius, and Ludwig Grote (*from left*) at the opening of the exhibition *50 jahre bauhaus* (50 years bauhaus), May 4, 1968, in Stuttgart

Zinckgraf, which had resulted from the forced sale of the renowned Jewish-owned Galerie Heinemann the previous year. Even if Grote himself had not been involved in this "Aryanization," in the numerous letters he wrote to his wife while working there he does not mention at all that he found the history of the gallery's origin problematic or regarded it critically in any way. He complained rather than he was no longer in a managing position and as an employee could not work very independently.[33]

The urgency for action that Grote developed after the Nazi regime collapsed was all the greater as a result. "De-Nazified" by the American Allies already at the end of 1946, very quickly he was able to put himself in a position as aspirant for new tasks in art and cultural policies as a representative of the Bauhaus and as a modern gallerist. The so-called reeducation program proved helpful in that effort. For in that program, with which the American cultural authorities in particular were supporting the de-Nazification of the young Federal Republic by means of democratic educational work, the culture and art of the Weimar Republic that had been condemned by the National Socialists was considered the role model for a new, liberal, democratic Germany. In that context, Grote was at the start also able to use the experiences he had gained in the art field and, for example, participate in an exhibition in 1948 that included works by Kandinsky at the Moderne Galerie, recently founded by Otto Stangl. In July 1949 the founding of the Gruppe der "Gegenstandslosen" süddeutschen Maler (Group of Nonobjetive Southern German Painters) took place there as well. Grote supported that group, which in late 1949 renamed itself ZEN 49, and to which the early Bauhaus student Fritz Winter belonged, among others, above all through lectures at their exhibition openings. Moreover, Grote established contacts to Allied cultural functionaries, such as Stefan P. Munsing, who from 1947 was director of the Amerikahaus in Munich and of its Central Collecting Point for art plundered by the Nationalist Socialists. Above all, however, Grote tried constantly after 1945 to take up the torn threads to former members of the Bauhaus, just as former members of the Bauhaus sought contact to him.[34] In a letter to Josef Albers, Grote regretted that he had "not left" during the Nazi period and emigrated to the United States. Grote was concerned that for that reason he might have been forgotten as an ally of the Bauhaus and that it had also been a mistake to have said too little about his "services to the Bauhaus," indeed that without him it "would not have come to Dessau"—only to add self-confidently: "In fact, I did more for the Bauhaus than Schardt or Dorner[35] or other museum directors who at most purchased a few paintings from the painters."[36]

Yet this concern would prove to be unfounded. Already in 1948 Grote was invited by Eberhard Hanfstaengl to curate the first exhibitions of modern art that had been condemned by the National Socialists in the former Haus der Deutschen Kunst, which had been opened by Adolf Hitler in 1937 (fig. 2). Hanfstaengl, who in 1940 had connected Grote to the position at the Galerie Zinckgraf was now director of the Bayerische Staatsgalerie für Moderne Kunst in Munich. In the end, Grote was able with Munsing's support to curate the first significant Bauhaus exhibition at the Haus der Kunst in Munich, which was by then considered de-Nazified: *Die Maler am Bauhaus* (The Painters at the Bauhaus).

Thanks to the success of these exhibitions, Grote soon established connections to other important cultural decision makers, including Martin Keim, a senior governmental official in the Bavarian State Ministry of Education and Culture, who advocated Grote's appointment as artistic director of the Haus der Kunst. Nevertheless, Grote, who certainly felt he had a higher calling, wrote to Keim in 1950: "I mention, parenthetically, that I have a path to Heuss via C. G. Heise"[37] (fig. 3). That same year, Theodor Heuss arranged for Grote to be appointed director of the Germanisches Nationalmuseum in Nuremberg—a position that ultimately also qualified Grote to be a member of the committee for the Foreign Ministry's exhibitions abroad as well as commissioner of the German exhibitions for the Bienal de São Paulo, which was founded in 1951. To make this new director's position in the civil service possible, Heuss summarily retroactively declared Grote's membership in the SA, which Grote had not mentioned in the de-Nazification process, to be void.[38]

As a museum director in Nuremberg, too, Grote continued to be a protector of and spokesman for the Bauhaus legacy. Almost as soon as he was in office, he wrote Fritz Hesse, former mayor of Dessau: "In Nuremberg, they have long been searching for a new mayor; my favorite would be the old Dessau one. Then we could build Bauhauses together again."[39] Hesse did not go to Nuremberg. Nevertheless, with the reconstruction of and addition to the Germanisches Nationalmuseum based on ambitious modern designs by Sep Ruf that he had initiated, Grote still believed he could influence architecture in the spirit of the Bauhaus tradition.[40] Grote hoped, moreover, that the "Bauhaus archive" that he wanted to establish would find a home in the new building.[41] He was able to gain support for this idea from many of the former members of the Bauhaus who remained in Germany during World War II, who remembered him as a Bauhaus mentor. It was therefore to a great extent taken for granted that he was "the collecting point [...] for everything connected with the bauhaus."[42] People were also grateful that he took on this task. "It would, of course, be very nice if all bauhaus things could be collected at your institution,"[43] wrote Willi Hauswald, the former master of crafts in the sculpture workshop, for example. Grote also wanted to persuade personally the former members of the Bauhaus living in the United States of his plan. "On my ninety-day study trip through America [...] I saw more or less all of the former Bauhaus members again. [...] I used the opportunity to speak to everyone about my intention to collect all of the objects, memoirs, etc., of the Bauhaus at the Germanisches National-Museum [*sic*],"[44] he reported to the former managing director of the Bauhaus, Margarethe Sachsenberg. Grote was not able to pursue his project with the intensity he wished, however: He did manage to bring together the initial archives and works by members of the Bauhaus, but in the end something else more urgent always came up, above all the planning and overseeing of the extensive construction measures at the Germanisches Nationalmuseum, the organizing of its hundredth anniversary in 1952, and his involvement in the Bienal de São Paulo, though in the biennials of 1953 and 1959 presentations of the legacy of the Bauhaus played an important role.[45] Because these activities and projects meant that Grote could scarcely find time to continue the collecting and archiving of the Bauhaus heritage that he had begun, and Gropius had in the meanwhile selected the young art historian Hans Maria Wingler to tend to the legacy of the Bauhaus; the Bauhaus-Archiv was ultimately founded in Darmstadt in 1960 with the latter as its director.[46] Grote retired two years later, which for him marked the beginning of a period of lively activity with exhibitions, publications, and lectures, many of which had connections to the Bauhaus. Its ultimate culmination was the exhibition *50 jahre bauhaus* (50 years bauhaus) that opened in Stuttgart in 1968 (fig. 4).[47]

Whereas as a municipal agent of art and culture under the Weimar Republic Grote had still advocated the Bauhaus as an idealized, apolitical school, at which in the spirit of a modern revival of Romanticism art is "the source of all design work"[48] and permeates "all spheres of life,"[49] as a function of the art and culture policies of the Federal Republic in the first decades after 1945 he increasingly depicted the Bauhaus as a historical example of an exemplary school of democracy. In his lectures and articles, he now emphasized how much Gropius had structured the Bauhaus as an "open form" that the students could help shape: "The Bauhaus was the epitome of creative education, and the students were collaborators in the building of a new universal culture."[50] The Bauhaus had therefore been a type of school in which ultimately the "students and not the teachers" realized the program,[51] that is to say, could work democratically to help shape it.

The exhibition *50 jahre bauhaus*, for which Grote as project director collaborated with Herbert Bayer, Dieter Honisch of the Württembergischer Kunstverein, and Wingler, was described by its patron, Gropius, as a successful illustration of *his* "Bauhaus idea." This show, which was financed by the Institut für Auslandsbeziehungen and thus by the German government, was not just the most extensive exhibition on the Bauhaus presented up to that point. After opening in Stuttgart, it also reached an audience of millions as an international traveling show over fourteen years—thus even after Grote's death. For the last stop on his "Bauhaus path," Grote was once again able to present the Bauhaus as an essential neo-Romantic, artistic, and in essence timeless concept of creativity. Not least because of the many current works by former members of the Bauhaus who were still alive at the time, he had produced a picture of the Bauhaus purged of contradictions, conflicts, and deficits that is still influential today. One sign of this picture of the Bauhaus that was especially concise visually was the basic geometric forms of the circle, triangle, and square. Grote made these forms, which Kandinsky had emphasized above all in his teaching at the Bauhaus in Weimar, representations of the artistic principles of the school and of his idea of the Bauhaus. Bayer not only used them to design posters and the catalog but also presented them three-dimensionally as sphere, cone, and cube prominently in the exhibition's entrance. The exhibition of 1968 is surely also to thank for many people thinking of the Bauhaus when they see combinations of triangle, circle, and square.

Such compressed images of the Bauhaus that Grote crucially helped form continue to have an influence today, as does his narrative of a *whole* Bauhaus, which is particularly attractive in popular accounts of the Bauhaus and its history. "Thinking the World Anew"—the motto under which the Federal Republic of

Germany celebrated 2019 as the centenary of the Bauhaus—could have been from a text by Grote. But even if the *Bauhaus100* program was just as much supported by the state as the Bauhaus exhibition of 1968, the program in 2019 was of quite different character. Whereas the celebration of the fiftieth anniversary of the founding of the Bauhaus largely served to idealize, canonize, and instrumentalize it as an export product for its cultural policy, the centenary jubilee of the Bauhaus was much more about writing the history of the contradictions and complexity of the legacy of the Bauhaus and reflecting on it in the context of the international networks of the avant-gardes. Today, moreover, there is a consensus among Bauhaus scholars that there was not just *one* idea of the Bauhaus and that at no point in its fourteen-year existence was this school seen and interpreted by those involved, the teachers, and the students in a unified way but also in very different ways. It is also accepted as fact that the school and its actors were enmeshed in complex political and cultural processes.

The exhibition *50 Jahre nach 50 Jahre Bauhaus 1968* (*50 Years after 50 Years of the Bauhaus 1968*)—which was held at the Württembergischer Kunstverein in Stuttgart in 2018, and hence in the same place as Grote's large Bauhaus project—was also the attempt to reflect on and counteract the omissions from the show it had organized. For example, it addressed the fact that the continuity of a fifty-year (West German) history of the Bauhaus suggested in the 1960s ignored the fact that no small number of former members of the Bauhaus had, like Grote, certainly come to terms with the Nazi system. Moreover, that exhibition, unlike its precursor in 1968, treated facets and aspects of a complex, international modernism in art and design. That also included projects in which the Bauhaus was taken up as inspiration beyond the Bauhaus ideals sketched by Grote, such as the *Bauhaus Imaginiste* of Asger Jorn[52] or the program to renew, in terms of scholarship as well, the Bauhaus pedagogy at the Hochschule für Gestaltung in Ulm, which closed in 1968. It turned out to be an irresolvable "dilemma" for the curatorial team that gaining a critical perspective on the history of the reception of the Bauhaus meant having to "co-narrate anew."[53] Against that backdrop, the present volume also dedicates itself to the narratives of the Bauhaus that Grote drew up between 1925 and 1968 and repeated varied and changed in the contexts of cultural policy in which he was working.

1 See the bibliography of Ludwig Grote's work in the present volume.
2 See the list of exhibitions organized by Ludwig Grote in the present volume.
3 Christoph Bernoulli, "Ludwig Grote (1973)," in *Beiträge zur Rezeption der Kunst des 19. und 20. Jahrhunderts: Im Gedenken an Ludwig Grote*, ed. Wulf Schadendorf (Munich: Prestel, 1975), 7–8, esp. 7. Christoph Bernoulli (1897–1981) received his doctorate in 1921 with a dissertation on the music of Romanticism as an expression of the Romantic worldview, worked as an art dealer in Switzerland in the 1930s and 1940s, and as a guest curator at the Kunsthalle Basel in 1950 helped arranged for the *Der Blaue Reiter* exhibition that Grote curated at the Haus der Kunst in Munich in 1949 to travel there.
4 He was also able to publish during this period what is probably his most important work of scholarly research: *Die Brüder Olivier und die deutsche Romantik* (Berlin: Rembrandt-Verlag, 1938).
5 Ludwig Grote, "Rede anlässlich der Eröffnung der Ausstellung *Junge Bauhausmaler* in Halle/Saale," 1928, manuscript, GNM, DKA, NL, Grote, Ludwig (hereafter "NL Grote"), 1368; see "Opening Speech of the Exhibition *Young Bauhaus Painters* (1928)" in the present volume, esp. 74.
6 Ibid., 75.
7 Ibid.
8 Ibid., 74.
9 There was also dancing, singing, performing plays, reading, and hiking in order to practice a new Romantic culture of life that was supposed to open up the limitations of traditional bourgeois life. The Serakreis that Eugen Diederichs (1867–1930) founded in 1904 had grown out of evening get-togethers for tea at his home and started to fall apart when World War I began and then dissolved entirely in the early 1920s. Whereas the Romantic experiment of Diederichs, who from 1920 was editor of the nationalist-conservative journal *Die Tat*, brought him close to anti-Semitic, German Christian, and ultimately National Socialist circles, other former members of the Serakreis, such as Rudolf Carnap (1891–1970), moved in leftist, Enlightenment, progressive directions; see Meike G. Werner, *Moderne in der Provinz: Kulturelle Experimente im Fin de Siècle Jena* (Göttingen: Wallstein, 2003).
10 See Peter Bernhard, "Grote's Bauhaus Idea," in the present volume.
11 Ludwig Grote, "Zur Geschichte der Anhaltischen Gemäldegalerie," in *Führer durch die Anhaltische Gemäldegalerie 1929* (Dessau: Anhaltische Gemäldegalerie, 1929), 12.
12 Ludwig Grote, "Lyonel Feininger zum 60. Geburtstag," *Museum der Gegenwart* 2, no. 2 (1931): 41–49, esp. 48.
13 Ludwig Grote, "Vom Bauhaus," in *Die Maler am Bauhaus*, exh. cat. (Munich: Prestel, 1950), 6–10, esp. 6.
14 Ludwig Grote, "Der Weg zum 'Blauen Reiter,'" in *Der Blaue Reiter*, exh. cat. (Munich: Haus der Kunst, 1949), 14–17, esp. 15.
15 Grote, "Vom Bauhaus" (see note 13), 7.
16 Ludwig Grote, "Zum Vortrag 'Das Bauhaus—eine Schule schöpferischer Erziehung,'" January 26, 1966, Akademie der Bildenden Künste, Nuremberg, central Franconia, typescript, NL Grote, 1448.
17 Grote, "Vom Bauhaus" (see note 13), 6.
18 Grote, "Feininger" (see note 12), 49.
19 Ludwig Grote to Maud Grote, 20 June 1940, NL Grote, 61. His wife, Maud, reported of his participation in the war that he had been conscripted into the Wehrmacht in October 1941. In May 1942, having been promoted to Oberleutnant (first lieutenant), his task was to accompany transports of troops within Germany. That same year, after being on leave, he was ordered to Russia to take on similar tasks behind the front lines that Maud Grote described as a kind of "policing function." Promoted to Hauptmann (captain) in 1943, Grote was then "honorably" discharged in September 1944 because of a myocardial insufficiency; see Gertrud Maud Grote, "Lebenserinnerungen und biographische Aufzeichnungen zu Ludwig Grote" (ca. 1910–90), NL Grote, ASS 2, and "Unterlagen zum Militärdienst von Ludwig Grote," NL Grote, 992.
20 Ludwig Grote, "Funktionalismus und Stil," in *Historismus und bildende Kunst*, ed. Ludwig Grote, Studien zur Kunst des 19. Jahrhunderts 1 (Munich: Prestel, 1965), 67–72, esp. 67.
21 See Grote's correspondence, which in some cases continued for decades, with Anni and Josef Albers; Walter Allner; Alfred Arndt; Eugen Batz; Herbert and Irene Bayer; Hannes Beckmann; Max Bill; Hermann Blomeier; Hinrich Bredendieck; Marcel Breuer; Roman Clemens; Howard Dearstyne; Lyonel, Laurence, and Julia Feininger; Albert Flocon; Ise and Walter Gropius; Gustav Hassenpflug; Otto Hofmann; Wilhelm Imkamp; Elisabeth and Gerhard Kadow; Wassily and Nina Kandinsky; Lily and Paul Klee; Hermann Klumpp; Fritz Kuhr; Frida Leischner; Margaret Leiteritz; Ludwig Mies van der Rohe; Lucia Moholy; Georg Muche; Helene Nonné-Schmidt; Lilly Reich; Alexander (aka Xanti) Schawinsky; Lou Scheper-Berkenkamp; Hinnerk Scheper; Helena (aka Tut) Schlemmer; Gunta Stölzl; Hans Thiemann; and Fritz Winter. Later, these would be joined by correspondence with members of the Bauhaus from the Weimar period, including Marianne Ahlfeld-Heymann, Gerhard Marcks, Mordekay Ardôn, Hans Haffenrichter, Johannes and Anneliese Itten, Peter Keler, Ida Kerkovius, Karl Peter Röhl, Lothar Schreyer; and Ré Soupault, in NL Grote. Grote's wife, Maud—"die Grotin" (the Grotinesse), as some of the Bauhaus members called her, to whom she sometimes felt "unreserved friendship" (Getrud Maud Grote, "Lebenserinnerungen und biographische Aufzeichnungen zu Ludwig Grote," see note 19)—also participated actively in Bauhaus life and was even briefly a member at Bauhaus, albeit only as an auditor; see Folke Dietzsch, "Die Studierenden am Bauhaus: Eine analytische Betrachtung zur strukturellen Zusammensetzung der Studierenden zu ihrem Studium und Leben am Bauhaus sowie zu ihrem späteren Wirken," PhD diss. (A), Hochschule für Architektur und Bauwesen Weimar, 1991, vol. 2, 166. Accordingly, Grote's archive also has a rather extensive correspondence of hers with Marcel Breuer, Julia Feininger, Lucia Moholy, Lilly Reich, Gunta Stölzl, the Kandinskys, the Schepers, the Alberses, and the Klees. Against that backdrop, it is unsurprising that their son, who was born in 1931, was considered "Bauhaus damaged," because he was surrounded in his childhood and youth by constant "talk about the Bauhaus"; Christian Grote, interview by Christian

Eger, under the headline "Das Bauhaus salutierte," *Mitteldeutsche Zeitung* (August 28, 2019).
22 See "'It's not working with Hannes Meyer any longer,'" in the present volume.
23 Ludwig Grote, "basic form and functionalism," in *50 Years Bauhaus: German Exhibition*, exh. cat. (London: Royal Academy of Arts, 1968), 18–20, esp. 18.
24 Ibid., 20.
25 See Nadine Willing-Stritzke, "Ludwig Grote in Dessau," in the present volume.
26 Ludwig Grote, diary entry, January 22, 1931, NL Grote, 31.
27 Ludwig Grote to Fritz Hesse, 18 December 1951, NL Grote, 351.
28 See Christian Eger, "The Politics of Depoliticization," in the present volume.
29 See Michael Tymkiw, *Nazi Exhibition Design and Modernism* (Minneapolis: University of Minnesota Press, 2018).
30 See Elisabeth Kremer, "The First Exhibition of 'Degenerate Art' in Germany," in the present volume.
31 See Eger, "The Politics of Depoliticization" (see note 28), 101.
32 "Zum wissenschaftlichen Lebenslauf von Ludwig Grote," NL Grote, 1128.
33 See Birgit Jooss, "Ludwig Grote and the Galerie Zinckgraf (formerly Heinemann) in the Years 1940–1946," in the present volume.
34 See, for example, Ludwig Grote to Josef Albers, 1 April 1948, NL Grote, 702.
35 Alois Jakob Schardt (1889–1955) and Alexander Dorner (1893–1957) were German art historians and museum directors who had supported modern art from early on.
36 Ludwig Grote to Josef Albers, 22 February 1947, NL Grote, 702, the final sentence is crossed out in the typescript of the letter.
37 Ludwig Grote to Walter Keim, 21 May 1950, NL Grote, 1192. Grote had known the art historian and museum director Carl Georg Heise (1890–1979) from youth and university. When Grote was working with Heise on articles for art historical journals in Berlin in 1935, he also met Theodor Heuss, who belonged to Heise's circle of friends.
38 See Eger, "The Politics of Depoliticization" (see note 28), n. 62, 104.
39 Ludwig Grote to Fritz Hesse, 18 December 1951, NL Grote, 351. Immediately following the war, Grote was already thinking about the possibility of a new Bauhaus. Thus he wrote to Josef Albers: The "incredible scale of destruction all but [necessitates] for the reconstruction institutes such as the Bauhaus, where coursework and teaching are combined with specific tasks for household items. [...] You would be the right man" for that; Ludwig Grote to Josef Albers, 22 February 1947, NL Grote, 702.
40 See Irene Meissner, *Sep Ruf, 1908/1982* (Berlin: Deutscher Kunstverlag, 2013), 188–200.
41 Ludwig Grote to Margarethe Sachsenberg, 4 March 1953, NL Grote, 620.
42 Helene Nonné-Schmidt to Ludwig Grote, 4 January 1949, NL Grote, 427. Grote had the idea of a central collecting point for all Bauhaus material even before he was appointed museum director.
43 Willi Hauswald to Ludwig Grote, 8 February 1948, NL Grote, 1249.
44 Grote to Sachsenberg (see note 41).
45 When, in preparation for the second Bienal in 1953, the Foreign Office was asked by the Brazilian organizers to make a special exhibition of Paul Klee's work the center of the German contribution, it entrusted Grote with the task of arranging it. Its justification read: "The increasing influence of his work, which seems almost lost for Germany as result of the unfortunate political developments of the past, will, if this plan should succeed, be of crucial importance to Germany's cultural reputation abroad"; Dr. Wolf of the Foreign Office to Ludwig Grote, 17 June 1953, NL Grote, 1802. The special exhibition at the fourth Bienal de São Paulo—*Bauhaus: Meister und Schüler* (Bauhaus: Masters and Students)—in 1957, also organized by Grote, had a similar significance. See Susanne Neubauer, "Ludwig Grote and Brazil's Interest in the Bauhaus," in the present volume.
46 See Claus Netuschil, ed., *Bauhaus-Archiv Darmstadt: Bilanz und weltweite Wirkung 1960 bis 1970* (Darmstadt: Kunst-Archiv Darmstadt, 2019).
47 See Torsten Blume, "From Stuttgart into the World," in the present volume.
48 Grote, "Rede anlässlich der Eröffnung der Ausstellung *Junge Bauhausmaler*" (see note 5).
49 Ludwig Grote, "Das Weimarer Bauhaus und seine Aufgaben in Dessau," *Anhaltische Rundschau*, no. 78 (March 19, 1925).
50 Ludwig Grote, *Deutsche Kunst im zwanzigsten Jahrhundert*, 2nd ed. (Munich: Prestel, 1954), 56.
51 Ludwig Grote, "Zum Gestaltwandel des Bauhauses" (1961), in *von dürer bis gropius: Aufsätze zur deutschen Kunst* (Munich: Prestel, 1975), 127–34, esp. 127.
52 Mouvement International pour un Bauhaus Imaginiste (IMIB), 1954–57.
53 See the interview with Hans Christ and Iris Dressler in the present volume.

Fig. 1 Cover of Grote's essay collection *von dürer bis gropius* (from dürer to gropius), 1975

Grote's Bauhaus Idea

Peter Bernhard

All his life, Ludwig Grote remained a convinced advocate and propagandist of the Bauhaus idea—as he understood it: In August 1948 he wrote to Walter Gropius on the subject: "I recently gave a lecture on the Bauhaus as creative education that I want to repeat in various cities.[1] From the very title, you will gather that I have not understood the Bauhaus as a rigid, time-bound teaching system; on the contrary, I have shown that it constantly transformed, that it was driven by a living idea [...], and I believe that I thereby also grasp the intention that moved you when founding and directing the Bauhaus."[2] This self-confident assessment was based on Grote's conviction that he had been not just a close contemporary but a direct participant. He surely also intended it for himself when looking back at the Bauhaus he declared with full emphasis: "It was [...] the birth of an idea, and anyone who has experienced it can know how every individual was encouraged, lifted above himself, that he is a cocreator and codiscoverer of a new world."[3] Grote was certainly able to claim such a role for himself, since he was crucially involved in the school's continuation in Dessau, where he supported it in diverse ways in his various functions: as Landeskonservator (state curator) of Anhalt, as director of the Anhaltische Gemäldegalerie, as vice managing director of the Freunde des Bauhauses, and as chairman of the Dessauer Kunstverein.[4] Many members of the Bauhaus therefore considered him a patron or at least as a someone with expert knowledge about the school. Not coincidentally, both Joost Schmidt and Josef Albers turned to him when they saw danger looming for the Bauhaus as a result of Hannes Meyer's behavior;[5] Oskar Schlemmer also contacted him to sound out the possibility of his return to the Bauhaus;[6] and even after World War II, Grote was the first person to whom several former members of Bauhaus turned when they wanted him to win him over as editor of a planned book on the Bauhaus,[7] as did Max Bill, who surely had the former constellation from Dessau in mind when he wanted to interest Grote in a position as museum director in Ulm, as he himself was in the process of becoming director of a newly founded Bauhaus.[8] In circles of art historians at the time, he was already considered "a primary source for the Bauhaus."[9]

Grote's relationship to the founder of the Bauhaus, Walter Gropius, must also be seen against this backdrop. Without a doubt, he felt sympathy for the conciliatory man of the world and great respect for the creator of the avant-garde school that so fascinated. Nevertheless, to judge from the tone of a correspondence lasting over forty years,[10] all of his life he saw him as an equal. That may be because, among other reasons, professionally he was never either dependent on or in competition with him. In relation to the Bauhaus, however, in addition to this formal independence surely one that can be called "intellectual" was more important, which derived from Grote's understanding of the Bauhaus as an idea that one could make one's own independently, separated from its creator. In terms of this idea of the Bauhaus, Grote could even imagine he had an advantage over Gropius, since he was involved in the Bauhaus of all three directors and hence in the whole scope of the formation of this idea. Moreover, the art historian with a doctorate surely had a deeper understanding, compared to these three directors, of the not insignificant production of art by members of the Bauhaus (and with his preliminary diploma in architecture did not lack an understanding of that field either).[11]

What was the Bauhaus idea according to Grote? Apparently, his understanding was shaped by his own experience and professional specialization. He had experienced the avant-garde school under all its different leaders and, of course, seen that it had been different "under Gropius [...] [than] under Hannes Meyer [...], only to obtain yet another form with Mies van der Rohe."[12] He admitted that "Gropius [had] instilled the idea of the Bauhaus of his creation as spiritual energy."[13] Be that as it may, it was for him a certainty that the core idea only emerges when one has an overview of the whole, that is, "when the organization of the Bauhaus in 1919 is compared with that of 1932"[14] (that is, the first program with the one that can be seen as the last, in light of the fact that the reorganization in Berlin no longer brought results). And what it reveals, he argues, is not a specific content tied to a particular time but a timeless form or, more precisely: a method that was supposed to consist in repeatedly adapting without reservation to the requirements of the time[15]—in Grote's words: "The willingness to try out new materials, new possibilities, uninfluenced by historical solutions, creating the form by returning to the function, from the root, as it were—that was the attitude that the Bauhaus protected from any rigidity in the fourteen years of its existence."[16]

Grote's specialty was Romanticism.[17] With that background, he was certain that the Bauhaus should be seen as a child of Romanticism. He observed apodictically: "The Romantic tone echoes through the whole manifesto"[18] of the Bauhaus: "the memory of the masons' lodge at the foot of the great cathedrals of the Middle Ages is evoked. As then, the isolated, separated arts should once again enter the service of architecture and construct the great *Gesamtkunstwerk*, the cathedral."[19] "Since Ruskin and Morris, the ideal of the Gothic cathedral stands behind—or, better, in front of—all reform movements that strive for a cultural renewal. All human desire this side of the Alps since Romanticism has gathered in this dream."[20]

It was, however, not just the Bauhaus manifesto and its title page, with Lyonel Feininger's woodcut *Kathedrale* (fig. 2), that according to Grote announced that "the spiritual principles of the Bauhaus" can "be traced back to Romanticism."[21] "The word Bauhaus *also* contains Romantically idealized ideas of medieval craft. As a result of the academies, artists have become alienated from the people and lost solid ground—they should return to the craft and place themselves in the service of architecture."[22] "The founding of the Bauhaus was thus accompanied by a complex of Romantic ideas."[23]

The links to Romanticism should not be limited to the statements of the Bauhaus: as Grote noted, Gropius followed them with corresponding actions. He believed that the director of the Bauhaus had clearly recognized that, as already in Romanticism, in the modern era painters had a pioneering role[24] and acted entirely in that spirit: "with the exception of the sculptor gerhard marcks, gropius appointed painters as teachers. gropius based this approach on the fact that since the beginning of the century painting had taken the lead among the arts and had created a new aesthetic which should govern the structuralism principles of the architecture of the future if humanity was to be joined henceforth in a compre-

Fig. 2 Walter Gropius (text), Lyonel Feininger (print), cover of *Manifest und Programm des Staatlichen Bauhauses Weimar* (Manifesto and Program of the State Bauhaus in Weimar), 1919

Fig. 3 Illustrated report on the exhibition *Die Maler am Bauhaus* (The Painters at the Bauhaus) at the Haus der Kunst, Munich, from the illustrated insert of the *Neue Zeitung*, May 20–21, 1950

hensive cultural unity."[25] On top of that, Grote found diverse connections to Romanticism in most of the painters who were appointed early. For example, Lyonel Feininger's paintings are "unfathomable and mysterious-Romantic"[26] and related to "those of Caspar David Friedrich";[27] in Paul Klee's paintings, Grote finds "irony—it is the Romantic irony, which had found its painterly fulfillment in his work";[28] and Wassily Kandinsky's work is "Russian mysticism" tied to "ideas from German Romanticism"[29] and thus permeated by "mystical-Romantic lines of thought."[30] Clearly, Grote assumed these diverse connections to Romanticism were passed down through art, because on the occasion of an exhibition on the students of the painting classes at the Bauhaus he observed that "all young bauhaus painters have an unmistakable penchant [...] for a romanticism."[31]

Grote was thus able to imagine he was in agreement with Gropius in considering that fine art was essential for the Bauhaus; not coincidentally, the first Bauhaus exhibition he organized after World War II was dedicated to the painters (fig. 3).[32] But even during the Bauhaus era, Grote was already emphasizing the importance of art, especially painting, for the first college of design.[33] Surely deliberately, he underscored in the *Bauhaus* journal the position already expressed there by Klee that artistic, irrational intuition was indispensable for Bauhaus work as a complement to rational, constructive thinking.[34] Because the artist left the Bauhaus that year, Grote was thus making it clear once again "what klee meant for the intellectual stance of the bauhaus"[35] and retrospectively justified in this way the dismissal of Hannes Meyer (which he had helped initiate),[36] whom he made responsible not only for Klee's departure[37] but also for the general artistic hemorrhaging of the Bauhaus.[38] Later, Grote would sum it up: Meyer "did not attribute to art any role in giving form and believed the best solution could be found solely through calculation. [...] His successor, Mies van der Rohe, returned art and freedom, which had been suppressed by the dictatorship of Marxist dogmas, to their rights."[39]

In one central point, however—in assessing the concept of style—Grote was at odds with all three directors of the Bauhaus but also with many of his fellow art historians. For example, Georg Schmidt declared in the catalog to the traveling Bauhaus exhibition in 1930: the "crucial thing is the goal of the Bauhaus today. But this goal cannot be described more correctly than with the formula: 'Overcoming of style.' One can only say it even more drastically: the goal is 'lack of style'! Just as the plow or the airplane is without style and yet—or perhaps for precisely that reason, among others, for example, in addition to its simple utility—also beautiful, so too are our cities, our houses, our furniture, and our equipment!"[40] He was describing here a broad consensus within the avant-garde. Ludwig Mies van der Rohe had already proclaimed in 1923: "Form as goal is formalism; and we reject that. Nor do we strive for a style."[41] And, as director of the Bauhaus, Meyer emphasized: "we are not seeking a bauhaus style,"[42] only to report after his dismissal of his "tragicomic situation [...]: As Director of the Bauhaus I fought against the Bauhaus style."[43] Because he had to see this as an attack on his leadership of the Bauhaus, he emphasized that same year in the twelfth volume of the Bauhausbücher (Bauhaus books) series: "the goal of the bauhaus is not a 'style,' [...] a 'bauhaus style' [...] would mean regressing to academic stagnation,"[44] only to remark again in a lecture given in 1934: "shortly before the swing in germany i was busy writing a book 'against the bauhaus style.'"[45] Grote remained unimpressed by all these pronouncements, however. For him, it was certain: "Gropius and Le Corbusier advocate the view that the 'Modern Movement' has nothing to do with style in the historical sense. They do not want to think about style any more than engineers. The word was not used at the Bauhaus; it meant manner, stylization, template, rigidity, turning away from life and its changing challenges. But a style is determined not from theories and program but solely from designs."[46] He therefore insisted "that the 'Modern Movement' is a stylistic phenomenon."[47] Yet he did not want to see the term as limited to the Modern Movement.[48] Already during the Bauhaus era, he placed the school in the tradition of the old idea of reform "that a style results not from ornament but has to rise up from deeper roots. From that grew the demand for … modern style."[49] Grote probably did not want to distance himself all that far from the doctrine. After all, Gropius had used the term "idea" early on to characterize his vision of the Bauhaus,[50] which was quickly taken up by others[51] and became established with a different connotation, to the point of Mies van der Rohe's now famous lapidary employment of it.[52] Against that backdrop, it seems an effort to reach to come to a compromise when Grote declared the Bauhaus was striving to realize a "stylistic idea."[53]

1 Grote's archive does indeed have a series of lecturer manuscripts whose titles are slightly varying the Bauhaus as places of "creative education" (see DKA, NL Grote, Ludwig [hereafter "NL Grote"], 1440, 1441, 1444, 1448, 1468). Grote had, however, presumably also given this lecture under a different title. He thus reported to Ise Gropius the following year: "On April 30, I am speaking in Frankfurt on 'The Bauhaus as Idea and the Evolution of Modern Architecture'" (Ludwig Grote to Ise Gropius, 31 March 1949, NL Grote, 814); no manuscript of the lecture survives.

2 Ludwig Grote to Walter Gropius, 20 August 1948, NL Grote, 360.

3 Ludwig Grote, "Vorträge zum Bauhaus," drafts, single pages, and incomplete typescripts with handwritten notes that cannot be associated with any lecture, n.d., NL Grote, 1467.

4 See Elisabeth Kremer, "The First Exhibition of 'Degenerate Art' in Germany," in the present volume. Grote tried to support the Bauhaus even after his time in Dessau, for example, by arranging for funds to be allocated by the Moses-Mendelssohn-Stiftung; see the minutes of the meeting of the Bauhaus advisory council of December 20, 1932, SBD, I 8383/1-2 D. This enlisting of an organization dedicated to the memory of the Jewish philosopher shows how little Grote himself was convinced by the notion of the "German Bauhaus" that he presented to the National Socialists when trying to prevent the closure of the school in Dessau; see Christian Eger, "The Politics of Depoliticization," in the present volume.

5 See Ludwig Grote to Helene Schmidt-Nonne, 17 March 1965, NL Grote, 811; Josef Albers to Maud and Ludwig Grote, 25 May 1930, NL Grote, 701.

6 See Oskar Schlemmer to Ludwig Grote, 19 December 1931, NL Grote, 810. In the summer of 1929, Schlemmer had gone to the Staatliche Akademie für Kunst und Kunstgewerbe in Breslau, which was, however, closed on April 1, 1932, as a consequence of the rigid cost-cutting measures in the wake of the Great Depression.

7 They included Helene Schmidt-Nonne, Joost Schmidt, Gustav Hassenpflug, Hinnerk Scheper, and presumably Lou Scheper-Berkenkamp; see Ludwig Grote to Josef Albers, 1 April 1948, NL Grote, 702. The book was delayed, initially because of the generally difficult conditions of the immediate postwar period, but also because of problems getting adequate illustrations; see Ludwig Grote to Josef Albers, 1 May 1948, NL Grote, and Grote to Gropius, 20 August 1948 (see note 2); for Grote, this project receded into the background for a time after he was appointed director of the Germanisches Nationalmuseum in 1951, although he did not abandon the project entirely. Shortly after his retirement, he wrote to Josef Albers: "If I were to find time, I would like to write a history of the Bauhaus" (Ludwig Grote to Josef Albers, 31 October 1963, NL Grote, 702), but by that time the gap in the German-speaking world had already been filled by the Bauhaus book of Hans Maria Wingler; see Torsten Blume, "From Stuttgart into the World," in the present volume.

8 See Max Bill to Ludwig Grote, 30 May 1950, NL Grote, 1001; on the Hochschule für Gestaltung Ulm as a successor institution to the Bauhaus, see Christiane Wachsmann, *Vom Bauhaus beflügelt: Menschen und Ideen an der Hochschule für Gestaltung Ulm* (Stuttgart: Verlag für Architektur und Design, 2018).

9 Nikolaus Pevsner, in Pevsner et al., "Diskussion," in *Historismus und bildende Kunst: Vorträge und Diskussion im Oktober 1963 in München und Schloss Anif*, ed. Ludwig Grote (Munich: Prestel, 1965), 73–106, esp. 73.

10 See NL Grote, 360, 814.

11 See Grote's biography in the appendix of the present volume.

12 Ludwig Grote, "Zum Gestaltwandel des Bauhauses" (1961), in *von dürer bis gropius: Aufsätze zur deutschen Kunst* (Munich: Prestel, 1975), 127–34, esp. 127.

13 Ludwig Grote, "Zum Vortrag 'Von Weimar nach Dessau: Zum Gestaltenwandel des Bauhauses,'" January 30, 1963, Darmstadt, typescript, NL Grote, 998. It is indeed noteworthy that when Grote cited Schlemmer's observation that "[t]he unique structure of the Bauhaus can be perceived in the person of its director"—Oskar Schlemmer, "Diary, June 1923," in *The Letters and Diaries of Oskar Schlemmer*, ed.
Tut Schlemmer, trans. Krishna Winston (Middletown, CT: Wesleyan University, 1972), 139—he replaced "eigentümlich" (unique) with "eigentlich" (actual); see Grote, "Zum Gestaltwandel des Bauhauses" (see note 12), 134. But whether one should conclude from that that he was a "very orthodox Gropiusian" who did "everything for his Bauhaus master"—Bernd Polster, *Walter Gropius: Der Architekt seines Ruhms* (Munich: Carl Hanser, 2019), 550—seems doubtful, not least because Grote also cited the immediate continuation of Schlemmer's sentence: "flexibility, adherence to no dogma," which makes it clear that Grote was more interested in emphasizing the ability to transform that the origin of this quality. Nevertheless, this mistake surely also betrays Grote's conviction that he had thereby grasped the heart of the matter.

14 Grote to Gropius, 20 August 1948 (see note 2).

15 In emphasizing the teaching method as the central specific quality of the Bauhaus, Grote was perhaps influenced by two theories from his immediate vicinity in Dessau: first, Theodor Blum, the department head for colleges, professional, and technical schools of the State of Anhalt (and hence the governmental official state authority to whom the Bauhaus directors reported), who had already tried to influence the mood in Dessau even before the Bauhaus moved there with his article "Das Bauhaus—eine pädagogische Tat," *Anhalter Anzeiger*, no. 65 (March 18, 1925); excerpt translated in Hans M. Wingler, *The Bauhaus, 1919–1933, Weimar, Dessau, Berlin, Chicago*, 2nd ed. (Cambridge, MA: MIT Press, 1981), 102–3—and then after World War II once again emphasized the exemplary pedagogy of the Bauhaus in his essay "Das Dessauer Bauhaus"—*Berufsbildung: Zeitschrift für das berufliche Bildungswesen* 2, no. 8 (1948): 10–13—a copy of which is found in Grote's archive as no. 2176, and, second, Gerhard Heine, the director of the Friedrich-gymnasium in Dessau, who put the Bauhaus in the tradition of reform pedagogy (with the Gartenreich of Friedrich Franz von Anhalt-Dessau and the Philanthropin of Johann Bernhard Basedow: see Gerhard Heine, "Ministerialrat Dr. Arndt: Ein Dessauer Schulmann," *Anhalter Anzeiger*, no. 176 (June 30, 1932). Heine was included among the people by whom Grote "was assisted" (Ludwig Grote to Fritz Hesse, 11 January 1964, NL Grote, 351) when writing fake "responses to negative statements in the press" (ibid.) in the run-up to the Bauhaus move to Dessau; see "The Bauhaus Comes to Dessau," in the present volume.

16 Grote, "Zum Gestaltwandel des Bauhauses" (see note 12), 133.

17 See Grote's magnum opus, *Die Brüder Olivier und die deutsche Romantik* (Berlin: Rembrandt, 1938). Even before his professional specialization, Grote had a penchant for Romanticism, as his commitment to the youth movement and above all to the Serakreis (Sera Circle) shows (where he participated in, among other things, a "call to collect German folk dances"; see Claudia Selheim, "Der Wandervogel—eine Quelle der Volkskunde," in *Aufbruch der Jugend: Deutsche Jugendbewegung zwischen Selbstbestimmung und Verführung*, ed. Selheim and Ulrich Grossmann, exh. cat. (Nuremberg: Verlag des Germanischen Nationalmuseums, 2013), 92–97, esp. 94; and Maud Grote, "Erinnerungen zu Kindheit, Jugend und Studium von Ludwig Grote, typescript, NL Grote, 249; on the neo-Romantic Serakreis, see Sigrid Bias-Engels, *Zwischen Wandervogel und Wissenschaft: Zur Geschichte von Jugendbewegung und Studentenschaft, 1896–1920* (Cologne: Verlag Wissenschaft und Politik, 1988), 126–32. Grote maintained contact with many acquaintances from this period later as well; see Hans Herzfeld, *Aus den Lebenserinnerungen*, ed. Willy Real (Berlin: De Gruyter, 1992), passim. Grote also found an active fellow activist for the Bauhaus in the Dessau publisher Karl Rauch, who was involved in the youth movement; see "The Bauhaus Comes to Dessau" in the present volume (see note 15).

18 Ludwig Grote, "Zu einem Vortrag über das Neue Bauen, insbesondere Entstehung, Geschichte und Inhalte des Bauhauses," typescript with handwritten annotations, n.d., NL Grote, 1462.

19 Grote, "Vorträge zum Bauhaus" (see note 3).

20 Ibid. Grote was thanks to his position very familiar with the Romantic worship of the Gothic, which found an echo that was as late as it was emphatic in Gropius's evocation of a "volcanically erupting new 'Gothic' worldview"—Walter Gropius, "Beantwortung der Frage: Wie kann Weimar zu neuer Blüte gelangen?," *Die Schatzkammer: Sammelblätter für Kunst, Wissenschaft, Leben* 2, no. 4, series I, no. 2 (1921): 89—because it originated in the park grounds in Wörlitz of Prince Franz von Anhalt-Dessau, which Grote managed

as Landeskonservator of Anhalt; see Ludwig Grote, "Zur Wiederentdeckung der Gotik" (1929), in Grote, *von dürer bis gropius* (see note 12), 69–71. The Romantic rediscovery of the Gothic is alluded to by the title and cover of *von dürer bis gropius*, a collection of Grote's essays and lectures, which featured portraits of Dürer and Gropius, supplemented by that of Caspar David Friedrich, positioned between them, symbolizing the mediation of the two (fig. 1).

21 Grote, "Vorträge zum Bauhaus" (see note 3); see also Grote, "Die Kathedrale—eine romantische Idee," typescript with handwritten notes, NL Grote, 2055.

22 Grote, "Vorträge zum Bauhaus" (see note 3) (italics added).

23 Grote, "Vortrag über das Neue Bauen" (see note 18).

24 See Ludwig Grote, "Moderne Bildwirkereien," *Die Form: Zeitschrift für gestaltende Arbeit* 5, no. 10 (1930): 256–62.

25 Ludwig Grote, "walter gropius and the bauhaus," in *50 Years Bauhaus: German Exhibition*, exh. cat. (London: Royal Academy of Arts, 1968), 9–11, esp. 9 (lowercase original).

26 Ludwig Grote, "Lyonel Feininger zum 60. Geburtstag" (1931), in Grote, *von dürer bis gropius* (see note 12), 121–23, esp. 123.

27 Ibid.

28 Ludwig Grote, "Erinnerungen an Paul Klee" (1959), ibid., 118–20, esp. 119.

29 Ludwig Grote, "Zum 'Blauen Reiter'" (1949), ibid., 112–14, esp. 112. The extraordinary significance of Romanticism for German intellectual history was doubtless a reason for Grote to emphasize the Romantic links of the members of the Bauhaus. That made it possible to counter the accusations against the avant-garde school as being considered "alien" and "culturally bolshevist," which was particularly necessary in the Weimar Republic but also in the young Federal Republic of Germany. For that reason, he was careful not to emphasize too directly "the German essential character"—Grote, "Vorträge zum Bauhaus" (see note 3). This is clear from his deleting the sentence: "[F]or that very reason, the Bauhaus was exemplarily German and is also viewed as German from abroad" (ibid.) in his lecture manuscripts. A comparable intention must be attributed to Grote's friend Wilhelm Adolf Fahrenholtz, who wrote a letter to Lyonel Feininger in March 1933—that is, at a time when it was reasonable to assume that the letter was being read by the authorities—addressing the artist as the "Romantic of our time" and emphasizing how close that made him to Germanness (in the letter, which is slightly more than one typewritten page, the word "Romantic" occurs seven times); see Wilhelm Adolf Fahrenholtz to Lyonel Feininger, 19 March 1933, NL Grote, 2357.

30 Ludwig Grote, "Zu Wassily Kandinskys 'Rückblick, 1901–1913'" (1955), in Grote, *von dürer bis gropius* (see note 12), 115–17, esp. 117. Kandinsky would surely have agreed with Grote's analysis; as early as 1925 he wrote: "Today there is 'Neue Sachlichkeit' [New Objectivity]—there should by all means be a (or the) new Romanticism. [...] It is especially interesting the Germans in particular are so afraid (a-f-r-a-i-d!) of this word. And the Russians too. On this point, one can feel one's way through sometimes-hidden inner connection of the two peoples"; Wassily Kandinsky to Will Grohmann, 21 November 1925, in Wassily Kandinsky, *Briefe, Texte, Schriften aus der Zeit am Bauhaus*, ed. Alexander Graeff (Weimar: Weimarer Verlagsgesellschaft, 2016), 96–99, esp. 97.

31 Ludwig Grote, "junge bauhausmaler," brochure published by the Hallescher Kunstverein on the occasion of the eponymous exhibition in 1929, unpaginated, SBD I 9344 L; reprinted in the present volume.

32 See the exhibition catalog *Die Maler am Bauhaus*, comp. Leonie von Wilckens, text by Ludwig Grote (Munich: Prestel, 1950).

33 It seems apt to Grote's view that Helene Schmidt-Nonne later reproached him: "It is a real shame that you never had contact with the members of the Bauhaus in Dessau but limited yourself only to the 'great old masters'"; Helene Schmidt-Nonne to Ludwig Grote, 10 March 1965, NL Grote, 811. Indeed, the Grotes "were in the habit of celebrating New Year's Eve with Klee and Kandinsky" —Grote, "Erinnerungen an Paul Klee" (see note 28), 119—and would "regularly inspect the new paintings"—Gertrud Maud Grote, "Lebenserinnerungen und biografische Aufzeichnungen zu Ludwig Grote," ca. 1910–1990, typescript with handwritten notes, February 23, 1980, and 1990, NL Grote, ASS 2—as guests in the homes of various members of the Bauhaus. In his reply, however, Grote sought to make it clear that this "was by no means the case [...,] on the contrary" his "real friends [had been] Breuer, Schepers, and Albers"; Grote to Schmidt-Nonne, 17 March 1965 (see note 5); the surviving correspondence in Grote's archive seems to confirm this; see ibid., 384, 426, 701–4, 708–12.

34 See Paul Klee, "Exact experiments in the realm of art," in *Bauhaus Journal, 1926–1931: Facsimile Edition, with Commentary and English Translation*, ed. Lars Müller, trans. Eva Gaida and Jana Mainel (Zurich: Lars Müller, 2019), 42, and Ludwig Grote, "to paul klee," ibid. 105. Grote's assessment was no doubt correct: Klee's "article had a programmatic character in the bauhaus's former intellectual situation" (ibid.), aimed at the course by the new director, Hannes Meyer, with whom the "curses" had arrived "Romanticism! Cosmicism! Mysticism!"—Klee, "Exact experiments," 42). Apparently, the promotional value of the artist's name was more important to Meyer than the differences that became clear in the article, which is why he included excerpts from the text in the "provisional prospectus" he "compiled in a great hurry"—Hannes Meyer, "situationsbericht, 1.9.1929," in *hannes meyer 1889–1954: architekt, urbanist, lehrer*, exh. cat. Bauhaus-Archiv, Berlin; Deutsches Architekturmuseum, Frankfurt am Main; and Museum für Gestaltung, Zurich (Berlin: Ernst & Sohn, 1989), 168–70, esp. 169: *junge menschen, kommt ans bauhaus!*; facsimile in *Hannes Meyer und das Bauhaus: Im Streit der Deutungen*, ed, Thomas Flierl and Philipp Oswalt (Leipzig: Spector, 2018), 5–52. By contrast, it was probably precisely these differences that moved Gropius—or perhaps the editor of the brochure, Herbert Beyer, who had left the Bauhaus with Gropius when Meyer took over as director—to permit the inclusion of an excerpt from the essay in the exhibition catalog for the German section of the Werkbund exhibition in Paris in 1930, perhaps hoping for the side effect of winning over the French public, with which Klee had a good reputation; see Walther Fuchs and Osamu Okuda, "Paul Klees 'Exakte Versuche im Bereich der Kunst' im Katalog der Werkbund-Ausstellung von 1930 in Paris," *Die Zwitscher-Maschine: Zeitschrift für internationale Klee-Studien*, no. 7 (2019): 55–57.

35 Grote, "to paul klee" (see note 34).

36 Grote's role in and motivation for Meyer's dismissal had long since been the subject of public debate by this point. For example, Meyer let it be known via the Marxist journalist Fritz Schiff that "the Landeskonservator of Anhalt, Dr. Grote, [had been] an opponent of Meyer. For what was to become of 'high art' if the students [of the Bauhaus] were assigned the task unworthy of a student to build apartments for the proletariat. It was also this Grote" who, together with "a petty-bourgeois and Social Democratic clique" called for Meyer's dismissal; Fritz Schiff, "Gespräch mit Hannes Meyer," *Berlin am Morgen* (August 17, 1930).

37 Gerhard Marcks assessed the situation very similarly: "When Gropius left, Hannes Meyer came, a Swiss, party-line Communist, totally unartistic, hostile to art. Klee went to Düsseldorf"; Gerhard Marcks to Friedrich Henkel, 4 March 1963, in *Durchs dunkle Deutschland: Gerhard Marcks, Briefwechsel 1933 bis 1980*, ed. Jens Semrau (Leipzig: E. A. Seemann, 1995), 325–27, esp. 326.

38 See Peter Bernhard, "'It's not working with Hannes Meyer any longer,'" in the present volume. László Moholy-Nagy, whom Grote admired so much that he wanted to acquire a painting for the Anhaltische Gemäldegalerie despite resistance from Fritz Hesse—see Helga Heise, "Die ersten Jahre der Anhaltischen Gemäldegalerie unter Ludwig Grote," in *Verrat an der Moderne: Die Gründungsgeschichte und das erste Jahrzehnt der Anhaltischen Gemäldegalerie Dessau 1927–37*, ed. Norbert Michels, exh. cat. (Dessau: Anhaltische Gemäldegalerie, 1996), 51–79, esp. 65–66—had difficulties with Meyer's hostility to art. After a vehement debate, he wanted to quit without notice already in January 1928; see Anthony Fontenot, "Streit um die Bauhauskonzeption: Hannes Meyer gegen László Moholy-Nagy," in *Hannes Meyers neue Bauhauslehre: Von Dessau bis Mexiko*, ed. Philipp Oswalt (Basel: Birkhäuser, 2019), 57–71; the conflict between Meyer and Moholy-Nagy escalated after the latter accused the former of being a Romantic (see ibid., 60), but, at Gropius's request, Moholy-Nagy remained until the end of the semester, at which point not only he but also Herbert Bayer and

Marcel Breuer left the Bauhaus; they were followed by Schlemmer, Marianne Brandt, and, finally, Klee.

39 Ludwig Grote, "Zum Vortrag 'Das Bauhaus—eine Stätte schöpferischer Erziehung,'" presented at the Deutsches Haus, Paris, NL Grote, 1440. Grote admired the new director of the Bauhaus not only for his advocacy of the *Baukunst* (building art) that had been scorned by Meyer—see Ludwig Mies van der Rohe, "Baukunst und Zeitwille," *Der Querschnitt* 4, no. 1 (1924): 31–32, translated as "Building Art and the Will of the Epoch!," in Fritz Neumeyer, *The Artless Word: Mies van der Rohe on the Building Art*, trans. Mark Jarzombek (Cambridge, MA: MIT Press, 1991), 245–47, and Neumeyer, "Autobahnen als baukünstlerisches Problem," *Pariser Zeitung: Das Organ für Europäische Zusammenarbeit* 7, no. 4 (1932): 1, translated as "Expressways as an Artistic Problem," in ibid., 313. Full of praise and impressed, Grote, who himself tended to see things "from a philosophical, ideological perspective—Grote, "Vorträge zum Bauhaus" (see note 3)—emphasized "In addition to architecture, he [Mies van der Rohe] was interested in philosophy. Especially Thomas Aquinas, scholasticism. I repeatedly witnessed conversations in which he brilliantly mastered philosophical terminology"; Ludwig Grote, "Von Weimar nach Dessau: Zum Gestaltwandel des Bauhauses," typescript for a lecture at the Bauhaus-Archiv, Darmstadt, January 30, 1963, NL Grote, 998, 35.

40 Georg Schmidt, *Bauhaus-Wanderschau 1930*, Wegleitungen des Kunstgewerbemuseums der Stadt Zürich 94a (Zurich: Kunstgewerbemuseum, 1930), 14; see the facsimile in Flierl and Oswalt, *Hannes Meyer und das Bauhaus* (see note 34), 77–92.

41 Ludwig Mies van der Rohe, "Building" (1923), in *G: An Avant-garde Journal of Art, Architecture, Design, and Film, 1923–1926*, ed. Detlef Mertens and Michael Jennings, trans. Steven Lindberg with Margareta Ingrid Christian (Los Angeles: Getty Research Institute, 2010), 105.

42 Hannes Meyer, "bauhaus and society" (1929), in *Bauten, Projekte und Schriften / Buildings, Projects, and Writings*, trans. D. Q. Stephenson (Teufen, Switzerland: Niggli, 1965), 99–101, esp. 101.

43 Hannes Meyer, "My Expulsion from the Bauhaus: An Open Letter to Lord Mayor Hesse of Dessau," in Wingler, *The Bauhaus* (see note 15), 163–65, esp. 164. Ernst Kállai, whom Meyer brought to the Bauhaus, polemicized much more vehemently against the supposed Bauhaus style; see Ernst Kállai, "Zehn Jahre Bauhaus," *Die Weltbühne*, January 21, 1930, translated as "Ten Years of Bauhaus," in *Form and Function: A Source Book for the History of Architecture and Design, 1890–1939*, ed. Tim and Charlotte Benton with Dennis Sharp (London: Crosby Lockwood Staples, in association with the Open University Press, 1975), 172–75. By contrast, the art critic Peter Meyer observed that in the era of Hannes Meyer as well there was "the chimera of style that does not want to be a style still stands behind all works of the Bauhaus"; Peter Meyer, "Bauhaus-Wanderschau im Kunstgewerbemuseum Zürich," *Das Werk: Schweizer Monatszeitschrift für Architektur, freie Kunst, angewandte Kunst* 17, no. 9 (1930): XXXI.

44 Walter Gropius, *bauhaus buildings dessau*, trans. Helen Ferguson (Zurich: Lars Müller, 2021), 10 (lowercase original); Gropius also emphasized there (p. 9) the importance of the paintings for the Bauhaus project.

45 Walter Gropius, "bilanz des neuen bauens" (1934), lecture manuscript, in *Ausgewählte Schriften*, ed. Hartmut Probst and Christian Schädlich (Berlin [East]: VEB Verlag für Bauwesen, 1987), 152–65, esp. 155 (lowercase original).

46 Ludwig Grote, "Funktionalismus und Stil" (1965), in *von dürer bis gropius* (see note 12), 135–39, esp. 135.

47 Ibid., 137–38. In this view, Grote had on his side the young team that was in the process of forming the Museum of Modern Art in New York—Henry-Russell Hitchcock, Philip Johnson, and Alfred Barr—which was enthusiastic about the Bauhaus and would establish the concept of the "International Style" in the field of architecture; see Wolfgang Thöner, "1932: Austreibung des Funktionalismus und Ankunft im Stil; Von der Ausstellung zum Buch 'The International Style,'" in *Bauhausstil zwischen International Style und Lifestyle*, ed. Regina Bittner (Berlin: Jovis, 2003), 108–28. In connection with the Bauhaus, he received unexpected support much later. For example, Eckhard Neumann explained that Hans Maria Wingler of all people, whom Grote did not especially respect, put an end with his Bauhaus book to "the false halo of the nonexistent 'Bauhaus style'"; Eckhard Neumann, "Literaturbericht: Hans M. Wingler, 'Das Bauhaus,'" *Das Kunstwerk* 16, no. 10 (1963): 33.

48 Grote had a very broad concept of style in general, which included "[e]verything designed by human beings, the whole culture of an era—religion, customs, morality, politics, science, economics, technology"; Ludwig Grote, *Deutsche Stilfibel* (Leipzig: L. Staackmann, 1936), 6.

49 Ludwig Grote, *Das Land Anhalt* (Halle: Waldersee, 2008; orig. pub., Berlin: Deutscher Kunstverlag, [1929]), 224.

50 See Walter Gropius, "Idee und Aufbau des Staatlichen Bauhauses," in *Staatliches Bauhaus Weimar, 1919–1923*, ed. Staatliches Bauhaus in Weimar (Munich: Langen, 1923), 7–18.

51 See Carl August Emge, *Die Idee des Bauhauses: Kunst und Wirklichkeit* (Berlin: Pan, [1924]), and Peter Bernhard, "Carl August Emge: Ein philosophischer Propagandist des Bauhauses," in Bernhard, ed., *bauhausvorträge: Gastredner am Weimarer Bauhaus, 1919–1925* (Berlin: Gebr. Mann, 2017), 311–16.

52 In his speech on the occasion of the seventieth birthday of Walter Gropius on May 18, 1953, Mies van der Rohe said: "The Bauhaus was an idea, and I believe that the influence the Bauhaus had in the world was due to the fact that it was an idea." Ludwig Mies van der Rohe, quoted in Neumeyer, *The Artless Word* (see note 39), 329.

53 Grote, *Das Land Anhalt* (see note 49), 224.

On the Bauhaus Idea as "Open Form"

Torsten Blume

When Ludwig Grote remarked in his speech for the opening of the exhibition *50 jahre bauhaus* (50 years bauhaus) that "the Bauhaus was [...] an idea,"[1] he was explicitly referring to Ludwig Mies van der Rohe, who had said precisely that on Walter Gropius's seventieth birthday (May 18, 1953). Yet Grote had long since been familiar with this thought Gropius had formulated as early as 1923 that the Bauhaus was an idea that signified more than a specific historical institution.[2] He had also experienced personally in the 1950s how Gropius increasingly depicted the Bauhaus as a total idea of reconciling architecture, art, technology, and economy or as a "path to the unity of artistic design,"[3] in part in order to defend against accusations that he, Gropius, or the Bauhaus stood for a dogmatic, rationalist style. In keeping with that, too, was Gropius's only vaguely defined totality of the Bauhaus idea, whose object was "realizing a modern architectonic art, which like human nature was meant to be all-embracing in its scope."[4] It suited Grote's art-oriented interpretation of the Bauhaus that Gropius repeatedly pointed out that at the Bauhaus he had always been interested in a balance "between the soulful-dreamy and the mental-logical."[5] In the end, however, in 1968 Ludwig Mies van der Rohe—who a year earlier had responded to a loan request from Grote by saying "I have absolutely nothing to do with the Bauhaus"[6]—had become a chief witness to and defender of a mythical narrative of the Bauhaus as a timelessly valid idea. The full quotation from the speech by Mies van der Rohe that Grote cited is: "The Bauhaus was an idea, and I believe that the influence the Bauhaus had in the world was due to the fact that it was an idea. Such a resonance one cannot obtain with organization alone nor with propaganda. Only an idea has the forcefulness to spread to such an extent."[7] But, despite Mies van der Rohe's statement, "propaganda" had indeed contributed to the spread of the Bauhaus as an idea.

Already in the founding manifesto of the Bauhaus in 1919, Gropius had made the Bauhaus seem like a project that was supposed to be much larger than the school that was in fact established in Weimar, which initially had just over one hundred students, few teachers, and hardly any workshops. From the outset, the Bauhaus was conceptually vague but charged with imaginary, utopian surplus value, like "bring[ing] together all creative effort into one whole," a "new architecture," and the vision of a "unified work of art," which was supposed to be a "crystal symbol of a new faith."[8] In this way, the term "Bauhaus" combined with a dimension of ideas that could be projected onto all of the images and products produced by it or starting from it. With Roland Barthes, it could be said that the Bauhaus had since its founding been expanded by a "second semiological system"—or by myths in which all specific projects and real details ultimately can always point to an overarching whole of ideas.[9] In what was probably his most important program text, "Idee und Aufbau des Staatlichen Bauhauses" (Idea and Structure of the State Bauhaus), Gropius formulated this in a particularly convincing way and identified the basic elements of his Bauhaus construction already in the title: the spiritual-mystical "idea" and the practical-concrete "structure."[10] In their interplay and conflict, Gropius could develop and describe the Bauhaus as at once vision, brand, and symbol as well as school and workshop. By describing all the Bauhaus's activities and projects as components of a

Fig. 1 “painting class w. kandinsky still life herman röseler photo: marwits, bauhaus,” illustration for the article “junge bauhausmaler” (young bauhaus painters) by Ludwig Grote in *bauhaus* 2, nos. 2–3 (1928): 31.

Fig. 2 Cover of the exhibition catalog *Die Maler am Bauhaus* (The Painters at the Bauhaus) at the Haus der Kunst, Munich, 1950

whole, which are ultimately obliged to nothing less than a new “idea of today’s world,” Gropius could then also write: “Nothing exists in itself any longer; every form becomes a simile of a thought that forces its way out of us into the design; every work, a manifestation of our inner essence.”[11] Already during the fourteen years of its existence in Weimar, Dessau, and Berlin, the Bauhaus had been able to design itself as a legendary structure, a mythological construction, and hence as a brand, as a holistic entity in which an idea of modernity is manifested exemplarily. With manifestos, the Bauhaus books, the *bauhaus* journal published in Dessau, extensive journalistic work, and programmatic exhibition projects, the historical Bauhaus worked intensely to interpret, mythologize, itself, and from the outset presented itself as an already historical phenomenon. Karin Wilhelm has described this sort of “production of myths that knows how to attribute to commodities—that is, to objects and ideas—seemingly magical functions” as a “marketing mechanism typical of the capitalist economy” that “at the end of the nineteenth century and in the early twentieth century was discovered and applied by architects and artists as well.”[12]

In that sense, the Bauhaus was from the beginning in part a paradigmatic space of thinking and designing that was always intended to be more than a specific pedagogical institution that is defined by concrete teaching practices, methods of learning, and practical results. So, under the headline “the bauhaus idea” in the *bauhaus* journal in 1928, the kreis der freunde des bauhauses (circle of friends of the bauhaus), which Grote codirected, courted new members thus: “the bauhaus idea has led to a great spiritual movement to which important personalities from all cultured nations and from all creative fields belong. [...] you, too, can participate in the movement!”[13] In the same issue, the first one of Hannes Meyer’s directorship, one could also read “interviews with students,” in which they were asked whether for them the “meaning of the new design” lies “only in the practically useful” or whether they considered “even today a purely spiritual attitude”—that is, in essence, the idea of the Bauhaus—to be still “possible or necessary.”[14] Whereas Otti Berger replied: “the practical-useful cannot be separated from the purely spiritual design,”[15] Max Bill believed: “i conceived the bauhaus as larger than it is in reality: picasso, jacobi, chaplin, eiffel, freud, stravinsky, etc., really belong to the bauhaus as well.”[16] Hubert Hoffmann, too, saw the Bauhaus as something larger, namely, more “in the will to continue creating something than in what is actually created [...] in influencing the environment through this will.”[17] The statement by Fritz Kuhr concludes almost euphorically: “the world only has a meaning if it is a ‘bauhaus.’ ‘the whole world a bauhaus.’”[18] Grote, who in the same issue wrote about the exhibition of Kandinsky’s painting class that he had organized in the Anhaltischer Kunstverein and the planned exhibition on “bauhaus painters,” surely read such student statements as a confirmation of his idea of the Bauhaus as an open, artistic idea (fig. 1). He had, moreover, perceived at the Bauhaus a growing interest in free painting after, in the early Dessau years, “the practical, purely rational” had been “entirely in the foreground at first.”[19] This reinforced Grote’s assumption that now “the artistic” would become “free again,” which “alone signifies the driving force for living development and prevents ossifying into construction and technology."[20] It was also in keeping with that that, as reported in the news section of the journal, after the departure of Gropius, Herbert Bayer, Marcel Breuer, and László Moholy-Nagy, "new forces [regard] the work of predecessors [...] as a necessary and courageous beginning that needs a living development,"[21] and that Ernst Kállai, as the journal's editor, addressed in his editorial a "basic idea of the bauhaus" that is "strong enough [...] not to become formless and aimless even in its greatest extensions."[22] The very next issue of *bauhaus* that Kállai edited already had no mention at all of a Bauhaus idea. And very much to Grote's disappointment, this issue opened with the article "modest painting,"[23] in which Kállai, without mentioning the names Klee and Kandinsky, wrote of a "vanished relevance of those webs of color that easily get caught up in the boundless" and of "disappointed hopes" for a "return of the spiritual in art."[24]

Gropius, who had gone to Berlin in the spring of 1928 to work as a freelance architect, claimed the idea of the Bauhaus for himself alone and presented himself as its only legitimate owner. So he not only remained, along with Moholy-Nagy, the editor of the bauhausbücher (bauhaus books) series but also used the so-called German Werkbund exhibition in Paris in 1930 to present the Bauhaus.[25] One particular climax in this focus on the Gropius Bauhaus and its imparting as an ideal image of a new unity of art and technology that was presented above all by tubular steel furniture and cubic buildings with flat roofs, large windows, and white facades from the early Dessau phase was the exhibition *Bauhaus, 1919–1928* at the Museum of Modern Art (MoMA) in 1938. Because of the political situation in Germany, it largely had to fall back on works by former members of the Bauhaus who were then living in the United States, but also conceptually it was a constricted, reduced picture in the spirit of Gropius's interpretation of the Bauhaus. Moreover, its structure was largely based on that of the exhibition in Weimar in 1923, which presented his idea. Accordingly, in the foreword to the exhibition catalog the director of MoMA, Alfred H. Barr, declared that "the fundamental character of the Bauhaus had already been established under Gropius's leadership."[26]

In the 1950s Gropius had then once again fundamentally increased his efforts to present the Bauhaus as an idea essentially formed by him, not least in order to defend against increasing criticism of the Bauhaus and a stylistically dogmatic modernism associated with it. One culmination of this was a debate triggered by the architect Rudolf Schwarz in the journal *Baukunst und Werkform*, in which he accused the Bauhaus and also Gropius directly for being partially responsible for a cold, materialist rationalism in architecture and urban planning that he claimed negated the traditions of Western architecture and encouraged a soulless, technical functionalism. Gropius had become the target of such criticism not least because in 1947 he had been sent to Germany as a special envoy of the United States government on issues of urban and architectural development and thus claimed a leading role in the West German debates on reconstruction. In numerous lectures and interviews, he had, as he had previously in the 1920s, radically rejected all use of historical forms for contemporary architecture. He presented a series of projects produced in the United States and promoted Germany adopting American urban planning concepts, because the Neues Bauen of the 1920s, whose principles had been developed at the Bauhaus, had developed into the "International Style" in the United States. Criticism, like that of Schwarz, was therefore aimed not only at the urban concepts of Gropius but also at the Bauhaus as the founding place of a supposedly economistic, technical, and formally dogmatic architecture movement. Gropius responded to this with a complex defense strategy in which the myth of the Bauhaus as a humanistic, democratic idea played a central role: He emphasized that the Bauhaus had been hated, condemned, and exiled by the National Socialists especially because of its ideas and its liberal, modern character. For that reason, it was part of the resistance to Hitler and Nazi Germany and had to be understood as their victim. Because he and several other important members of the Bauhaus, such as Bayer, Breuer, and Josef Albers but also Mies van der Rohe, had immigrated to the United States, he claimed that the Bauhaus as idea lived on there and could also continue to evolve. Anyone who attacks the Bauhaus now and criticizes its members was ultimately acting like the National Socialists had back then and thus presumably wanted to prevent the Bauhaus vision of democracy and resistance from returning to Germany.[27] Moreover, the Bauhaus had matured in his new American homeland more than ever into the symbol of the liberal Western world and could therefore serve as a countermodel to the dogmatic art policy of Eastern countries. This argumentation was initiated by Gropius and also disseminated through a network of authors who were his friends or allies. In its result, the Bauhaus was ultimately regarded more than ever as a heroic act by Walter Gropius, who was stylized into a "figurehead of modernity" (fig. 5).[28] What was left out of this narrative of the members of the Bauhaus that had been closed by the National Socialists in 1933 who then condemned, persecuted, exiled, and even murdered them was that there had also been former members who had been able to successfully continue their professional development even in a fascist Germany. For example, before emigrating to the United States in 1938, Bayer had continued to stand out as a graphic designer with modern, visually attractive advertising and exhibition designs for various propaganda projects of the Nazi regime. Wilhelm Wagenfeld, too, established himself as an industrial designer in the Nazi state. Ernst Neufert and other less well known early members of the Bauhaus found positions in architecture or design firms, coming to terms with the National Socialist system and for a time even operating as its convinced supporters.[29] Even Gropius and Mies van der Rohe had continued to hope until the time of their emigration that they could continue to work in architectural competitions in National Socialist Germany with designs adapted to the needs of those now in power. Like many other technicians and engineers, several former Bauhaus members also believed that they could work purely as specialists in the Nazi system. But unlike Fascist Italy, which was modernist in inclination, in Nazi Germany artistic modernism was rejected as a "Jewish-Bolshevist" movement and combatted as harmful to German culture. Only by emphasizing this rejection and saying nothing about specific, ambiguous biographies of former members of the Bauhaus who continued to work in and with the Nazi regime could the Bauhaus as defined above all by Gropius be presented after 1945 as a humanistic educational ideal.

Part of putting this Bauhaus myth, which was now also regarded as a liberal, open counter-model to the dogmatic policies for art and culture of the East, into service was Gropius's push to have his successor, Hannes Meyer, expunged from the history of the Bauhaus. Gropius had already done so as early as 1938 for the exhibition at the Museum of Modern Art (MoMA), but now it was further reinforced in that he alleged that his great, holistic, open idea of the Bauhaus had been betrayed by Meyer as a Communist hostile to art and a dogmatic Marxist. All the rationalist and materialist constrictions of the concept of the Bauhaus and of modern architecture were therefore the fault of Meyer and not him.[30] Gropius noted that in 1927 Meyer had deceived him about his political stance and presented himself as a "radical petit bourgeois."[31] Ludwig Grote was entirely in agreement with this assessment of Meyer; as a Bauhaus advisor to the mayor of Dessau in 1930, after all, he himself had worked intensely to get Meyer dismissed as director. In the exhibition catalog *50 jahre bauhaus*, Grote wrote about Meyer that "his scientific marxism" narrowed his views, and that he therefore wanted to "give the bauhaus a scientific, political character and wanted to deprive it of its cultural climate," since "to him the bauhaus was not an artistic idea, but a 'social phenomenon'"; for that reason, there could have been no "greater contrast from a human as well as an artistic point of view"[32] between Gropius and Meyer. Although Meyer's teaching of architecture at the Bauhaus could certainly be acknowledged as a service, especially his projects on "determining basic data for houses and communities," Grote could not recognize Meyer as a representative of the Bauhaus idea, because for him design had "no aesthetic factor"; form was "a product of arithmetic"; and the minimum dwelling and the "furnishings" should therefore be built demonstratively cheaply and scantly under his directorship at the Bauhaus.[33] Only after Meyer's dismissal "a new artistic spirit returned to the bauhaus"[34] with Mies van der Rohe.[35] Grote was also convinced that Gropius had influenced the character of the Bauhaus above all by appointing abstract and Constructivist painters. In many lectures and finally again in 1968 in the *50 jahre bauhaus* exhibition, Grote wanted to show precisely that and make it clear how "out of the essence of modern art" and a "strangely irrational [...] sense of space"[36] conveyed by it a new unity of design could emerge. Because the students in the painter's courses had been able to experience the "assimilating power"[37] of modern art and had also been introduced to the artistic "spiritualizing of material and of abstract," the school not only obtained an essential artistic foundation but could also develop a special "impartiality" and "freedom with respect to the material."[38] And only in that way had the Bauhaus been able to unfold its extraordinary power to renew architecture and design (figs. 2–4).[39]

Because this "artistic spirit" had been adopted again at the Bauhaus with Mies van der Rohe after Meyer's dismissal, the former could certainly be considered a continuer and defender of the Bauhaus, whose "essence" Gropius had, after all, designed as an "open form."[40] For much more than Gropius, Grote had in mind the years of his own influence at the Bauhaus, from 1922 to 1933, and was at the same time trying to synchronize and har-

Fig. 3 Herbert Bayer (exhibition design), "architektur 2, gestaltung" (architecture 2, design) section of the exhibition *50 jahre bauhaus* (50 years bauhaus) in Stuttgart, 1968

Fig. 4 Herbert Bayer, cover of the exhibition catalog *50 jahre bauhaus* (50 years bauhaus), 1968

Fig. 5 Cover of the exhibition catalog *walter gropius: ein weg zur einheit künstlerischer gestaltung* (a path to the unity of artistic design), 1952. Preface by Ludwig Grote.

monize his interpretation with that of Gropius. That only seemed possible to him if he described the Bauhaus as an idea of an "open form" that has a "living spiritual power," that "is capable of constantly changing its form without losing its essence."[41] Following Gropius, who expressed the same opinion that "the Bauhaus did not have [...] a fixed program,"[42] Grote observed: "The Bauhaus possessed no permanent structure, no rigid program, no systematic organization [*Aufbau*]."[43] With an eye to his own Bauhaus experiences, however, he took this further: "It was different in its first three years in Weimar than in the last two; after the Dessau period under Gropius, it adopted a different form under Hannes Meyer, only to obtain yet another form with Mies van der Rohe. The protean is part of the essence of the Bauhaus; it is the most fruitful of the qualities that Walter Gropius gave it."[44] For, according to Grote: "life was to flow freely through it, it was to be intimately related to time and its problems and not become the victim of schematism."[45] As an "open form," the Bauhaus could therefore constantly change, could expand its teaching and its production, but also allow many members of the Bauhaus to participate in a democratic way. In the face of the international student protest, which culminated in 1968, as well in the face of the students' resistance to the closing of the Hochschule für Gestaltung in Ulm that same year, Grote probably believed it was necessary to point to the exemplarily democratic character of the Bauhaus. So he repeatedly addressed "the question of co-determination by the students which is so hotly contested today," only then to give an account of a participation of Bauhaus students that Gropius had set up in a way he regarded as exemplary: "gropius was always on the side of the students. he was always interested in what they planned, he supported their endeavours and procured contracts for them."[46] For that reason, student codetermination had been a matter of course at the Bauhaus: "from the very beginning the students had two representatives in the council of masters. if fundamental questions were involved general meetings were held in which all the teachers and students participated and which then resulted in vehement discussions."[47] Gropius, he argued, had taken into account criticism from the young people, just as he had transferred the direction of the workshops in Dessau to former students as "young masters" from 1925 onward. As proof of this, Grote cites Oskar Schlemmer, who had written to his friend the painter Otto Meyer that nothing was so ill received, "by Gropius as well as the students, as a suggestion that comes from one of the masters, once he no longer sticks to theoretical neutrality [...]. The students want to do everything themselves."[48]

According to Grote, "the aggregate state of the Bauhaus" could be called a permanent revolution: as it changed, "the new Bauhaus retained [...] essential features of the old one. [...] The willingness to try out new materials, new possibilities, uninfluenced by historical solutions, creating the form by returning to the function, from the root, as it were—that was the attitude that the Bauhaus protected from any rigidity in the fourteen years of its existence. The departure of Gropius, Moholy, Bayer, and Breuer; the subsequent era of Hannes Meyer—and finally the great form that Mies van der Rohe lent the Bauhaus—everything required transformations in structure, teaching materials, objective, and production. The artistic, spiritual forces of the time always met at the Bauhaus, and always it remained the young people who introduced these forces, and who were urged to critique the whole and their own work. From the young people, Gropius heard the voice of the future speaking; he entrusted the Bauhaus to them—and yet knew how to guide it at the same time. His conception for the founding of the Bauhaus was the ability to change while faithfully preserving the essential core; a quality that distinguished it from all other schools and academies.”[49]

At the same time, however, this remained an essentially historical matter for Grote. He was interested hardly at all in schools and projects such as the Hochschule für Gestaltung in Ulm founded by Max Bill in 1953 or the Bauhaus imaginiste initiated by the Danish artist Asger Jorn in 1954. Whereas the Hochschule in Ulm ultimately could scarcely have come into question for Grote as a successor to the Bauhaus because of its increasing orientation around the social sciences and technology, Jorn’s decidedly artistically ambitious Bauhaus imaginiste was truly in its spirit a project that wanted to preserve the Bauhaus as artistic inspiration. It is unknown whether Grote was even aware of Jorn’s certainly anarchic project, which for a time even lead to the founding of a “mouvement international pour un Bauhaus imaginiste contre un Bauhaus imaginaire.” After World War II, Grote was in general much more concerned with the open Bauhaus of the 1920s and the appreciation of its protagonists and scarcely with contemporaneous artistic developments any longer.

Grote’s Bauhaus hagiography and his narrative of “open form,” with which he tried to imagine the historical Bauhaus, with its complex abundance of upheavals and contradictions, as a model of “creative freedom”[50] and at the same time to give it a specific, essential core still encourages today primarily clichés of a Bauhaus. Above all in popular depictions, of which there were many in 2019, the year of the Bauhaus centenary, its history is frequently apprehended as a creative, highly ambitious fermentation process that had been started by Gropius. For example, the motto of the campaign for the pan-German cooperation *Bauhaus100*, “die Welt neu denken” (Thinking the World Anew) was in essence a paraphrase of the dictum Gropius formulated in 1923 of a Bauhaus obliged to the “idea of today’s world.”[51] Even today, many of the works of art, studies, architectures, and design objects presented in the *50 jahre bauhaus* exhibition as typical of the Bauhaus are now considered canonical and hence suitable examples for illustration of the Bauhaus as an idea that led to diverse forms of expression.

By characterizing the Bauhaus idea as an “open form,”[52] Grote had found in 1968 an effective formula with which he managed to harmonize his idealizations of the school from the 1920s, when he had characterized the Bauhaus as a neo-Romantic program for the renewal of design and the world by means of abstract art, with cultural policy in West Germany. Moreover, that formulation was well suited to the way Gropius had, already since the 1950s, been revising *his* Bauhaus as a school of democracy, teamwork, and a generalist design. In the 1920s Grote had explained the importance of the Bauhaus above all in terms of a holistic, spiritual foundation established by the abstract art of the Bauhaus painters and with the “irrational, mysteriously vibrating, floating, tension-filled dynamic space"[53] concepts of space that it made possible. In the 1950s and 1960s Grote then wrote that the liberal, democratic character of teaching at the Bauhaus meant "creative education" and "responsibly working together with the culture as a whole."[54] Now he regarded the "spiritual, artistic freedom" that marked the Bauhaus as an "open form" to be "the most powerful weapon of democracy."[55] This interpretation of the Bauhaus was well suited to taking the Bauhaus condemned by the National Socialists and rediscovered in the Federal Republic of Germany as part of a new liberal and democratic culture and putting it into service as a trademark for a new, better Germany. In 1951 Grote was a member of the committee for exhibitions abroad of the Foreign Office of the Federal Republic and became commissioner of the German exhibitions of the Bienal de São Paulo, which had been founded that same year.[56] Thanks especially to those positions, he was repeatedly able to present the Bauhaus worldwide as part of a new and open national culture of West Germany—he did so successfully for the last time, and particularly effectively, with the traveling exhibition *50 jahre bauhaus*.[57]

Can Grote's attempt to grasp the Bauhaus as an "open form" still inspire us today, even though until 1968 he had, as a conservative art historian and art and culture functionary for the young Federal Republic helped to present the Bauhaus as a symbol of Western freedom and democracy, honored Gropius as the eternal "Mr. Bauhaus," and installed himself as a participant in the history of the Bauhaus? Could Grote's efforts to sum up the heterogeneous history of the Bauhaus from a programmatic perspective be preserved, perhaps with a new twist? In any case, as a participant in and contemporaneous eyewitness to the design school, he had seen its contradictory coexistences as a complex inscrutability and tried to describe it: as a juxtaposition and interweaving of craft and expressive art, of Constructivist formalism and industrial mass production, of faith in the artistic genius and technocratic enthusiasm for the machine, of autonomous spirituality and market conformity, of political moderation and revolutionary, socialist, and liberal but also nationalistic convictions. Could Grote's idea of the Bauhaus as an "open form" be helpful in a new way if it is accepted less as a description of a heroic foundational vision but is instead interpreted as a sober observation of an interested process of searching? Then one could perhaps discover in Grote's presentations of the Bauhaus that the instabilities of the Bauhaus are much more interesting and inspiring than its certainties.

1 Ludwig Grote, “Ansprache zur Eröffnung der Ausstellung *50 Jahre Bauhaus*,” in *50 Jahre Bauhaus: Ansprachen zur Eröffnung der Ausstellung am 4. Mai 1968 im Kleinen Haus der Württembergischen Staatstheater*, ed. Württembergischer Kunstverein (Stuttgart: Cantz, 1968), 16–26, esp. 16.
2 Nevertheless, Grote himself often preferred the term *Geist* (spirit, mind) to *Idee* (idea), speaking, for example, of Gropius having lent the Bauhaus a particular “spirit [...] as a living breath”; Ludwig Grote, “Laudatio,” *Verleihung der Würde eines Ehrensenators an Professor h.c. Walter Gropius* (Berlin: Hochschule für bildende Künste, 1963), n.p.
3 “Walter Gropius: Ein Weg zur Einheit künstlerischer Gestaltung” (A Path to the Unity of Artistic Design) is also the title of an exhibition organized by the Institute of Contemporary Art, Boston, and the Smithsonian Institution, Washington, DC, that toured Germany and which Grote showed at the Fränkische Galerie in Nuremberg from October 19 to November 9, 1952, shortly after taking his post as director of the Germanisches Nationalmuseum; Grote also wrote a foreword for the catalog.
4 Walter Gropius, *Scope of Total Architecture* (New York: Harper, 1955), 7.
5 Walter Gropius, “Zur Eröffnung der neuen Gebäude der ‘Hochschule für Gestaltung’ Ulm,” September 1955, Bauhaus-Archiv Berlin, NL Walter Gropius, Mappe 26, inv. no. 12000/1596-99.
6 Herbert Bayer, quoting Ludwig Mies van der Rohe, in a letter to Walter Gropius, December 8, 1967, quoted in Reginald Issacs, *Gropius: An Illustrated Biography of* the *Creator of the Bauhaus* (Boston: Little, Brown and Company, 1991), 305.
7 Ludwig Mies van der Rohe, speech on May 18, 1953, Chicago, on the occasion of the seventieth birthday of Walter Gropius, in Fritz Neumeyer, *The Artless Word: Mies van der Rohe on the Building Art* (Cambridge, MA: MIT Press, 1991), 329.
8 Walter Gropius, “Program of the Staatliche Bauhaus in Weimar” (1919), in *The Bauhaus: Weimar, Dessau, Berlin, Chicago*, ed. Joseph Stein, trans. Wolfgang Jabs and Basil Gilbert (Cambridge, MA: MIT Press, 1978), 31–33, esp. 31–32.
9 Roland Barthes, *Mythologies*, trans. Annette Lavers (London: Vintage, 2000), 136; see Karin Wilhelm, “Der Bauhaus-Mythos: Strategien der Erinnerungspolitik,” in *Brasilia, Auschwitz, Hiroshima: Weltkulturerbe im 20. Jahrhundert; Modernität und Barbarei*, ed. Walter Prigge (Berlin: Jovis, 2003), 50–60.
10 See Walter Gropius, “Idee und Aufbau des Staatlichen Bauhauses,” in *Staatliches Bauhaus, Weimar, 1919–1923*, ed. Staatliches Bauhaus in Weimar (Munich: Langen, 1923), 7–18.
11 Ibid., 7.
12 Wilhelm, “Der Bauhaus-Mythos” (see note 9), esp. 51.
13 “die bauhaus-idee,” *bauhaus: zeitschrift für gestaltung*, 2, nos. 2–3 (1928): 33.
14 Ibid., 24.
15 Ibid.
16 Ibid., 26.
17 Ibid., 28.
18 Ibid., 29.
19 Ludwig Grote, “junge bauhausmaler,” *bauhaus: zeitschrift für gestaltung*, 2, nos. 2–3 (1928): 31. Grote’s opening speech, which was published in the exhibition catalog, is reprinted here as an appendix.
20 Ibid.
21 “bauhausnachrichten,” *bauhaus: zeitschrift für gestaltung*, 2, nos. 2–3 (1928): 32.
22 Ernst Kállai, “das bauhaus lebt!,” *bauhaus: zeitschrift für gestaltung*, 2, nos. 2–3 (1928): 1–2, esp. 2.
23 Ernst Kállai, “bescheidene malerei,” *bauhaus: zeitschrift für gestaltung* 2, no. 4 (1928): 1–2, esp. 1.
24 Ibid. Kállai is referring here to Kandinsky’s *Das Geistige in der Kunst* of 1913.
25 The German Foreign Ministry had passed on an invitation to participate in the Parisian salon of the Société des Artistes Décorateurs, the French association of interior designers, to the Deutscher Werkbund, which commissioned Gropius to conceive the exhibition. Along with Bayer, Breuer and Moholy-Nagy were part of the design team for the Section allemande. Gropius used the opportunity to present the Bauhaus internationally from his perspective for the first time since leaving the Bauhaus.
26 Alfred H. Barr, “Preface,” in *Bauhaus, 1919–1928*, ed. Herbert Bayer, Ise Gropius, and Walter Gropius, exh. cat. (New York: Museum of Modern Art, 138), 7–9, esp. 8–9.
27 See Winfried Nerdinger, “Das Bauhaus zwischen Mystifizierung und Kritik,” in *Die Bauhaus-Debatte 1953: Dokumente einer verdrängten Kontroverse*, ed. Ulrich Conrads et al. (Braunschweig: Vieweg, 1994), 7–8.
28 Winfried Nerdinger, *Walter Gropius: Architekt der Moderne, 1883–1969* (Munich: C. H. Beck, 2019), 327.
29 This was possible because in the Nazi system modernist design in propaganda and advertising—with new attributes in certain areas—was by all means appreciated, just as there continued to be fields of application for modern, rationalized architecture as well. Kurt Kranz (1910–1997) drew pictures for war propaganda and for a time, like Otto Umbehr (1902–1980), produced photographs and advertising graphics used in Nazi propaganda, as it did trade exhibitions designed by Lilly Reich (1885–1947) until 1937. During the war, Hubert Hoffmann (1904–1999) worked as a regional planner for the German army and, like Neufert, was a member of Albert Speer’s staff. Whereas such activities allowed many former members of the Bauhaus to earn a living, Hans Martin Fricke (1906–1994) was active as a Nazi cultural functionary as the director of the Reichskammer der Bildenden Künste for the Weser-Ems region, and Fritz Ertl (1908–1982) was a member of the Waffen-SS (the military branch of the Schutzstaffel) and helped design the Auschwitz-Birkenau concentration camp; see Winfried Nerdinger, *Bauhaus-Moderne im Nationalsozialismus: Zwischen Anbiederung und Verfolgung* (Munich: Prestel, 1993); Patrick Rössler, “Exil daheim: Die *neue linie* und der braune Geist; Beobachtungen zur Avantgarde im Nazi-Deutschland,” in *Deutsche Publizistik im Exil, 1933 bis 1945: Personen, Positionen, Perspektiven; Festschrift für Ursula E. Koch*, ed. Markus Behmer (Münster: LIT, 2000), 261–83; Laura Rosengarten, “Bauhaus und Nationalsozialismus,” in *100 Jahre Bauhaus: Vielfalt, Konflikt und Wirkung*, ed. Bernd Hüttner and Georg Leidenberger (Berlin: Metropol, 2019), 73–86; Adina Seeger, “Vom Bauhaus nach Auschwitz: Fritz Ertl (1908 bis 1982); Bauhausschüler in Dessau, Mitarbeiter der Auschwitzer

Bauleitungen, Angeklagter im Wiener Auschwitzprozess—Stationen und Kontexte eines Werdegangs zwischen Moderne und Nationalsozialismus," thesis, Universität Wien, 2013.
30 See Nerdinger, *Gropius* (see note 28), 334–35.
31 Ibid., 347 and n. 58, 387.
32 Ludwig Grote, "basic form and functionalism," in *50 Years Bauhaus: German Exhibition*, exh. cat. (London: Royal Academy of Arts, 1968), 18–21, esp. 20.
33 Ibid.
34 Ibid.
35 As early as 1950, Grote had written about Meyer: "As an adherent of a doctrinaire materialism, he interpreted the concept of function narrowly and mechanically and restrained the part of art"; Ludwig Grote, "Vom Bauhaus," in *Die Maler am Bauhaus*, exh. cat. (Munich: Prestel, 1950), 6–10, esp. 10.
36 Ludwig Grote, "Zum Vortrag 'Von Weimar nach Dessau: Zum Gestaltwandel des Bauhauses,'" January 30, 1963, Darmstadt, typescript, GNM, DKA, NL Grote, Ludwig (hereafter "NL Grote"), 998.
37 Ibid.
38 Ibid.
39 See Grote, *Die Maler am Bauhaus* (see note 35), 12: "The very presence and participation of personalities as great as Kandinsky und Klee, whose art influenced the era, represented a productive abundance and vital wealth even beyond their coursework."
40 Ludwig Grote, "walter gropius and the bauhaus," in *50 Years Bauhaus* (see note 32), 9–11, esp. 10.
41 Grote, "Ansprache zur Eröffnung" (see note 1), 16.
42 Walter Gropius, "Ansprache zur Eröffnung der Ausstellung *50 Jahre Bauhaus*," in ibid., 27.
43 Ludwig Grote, "Zum Gestaltwandel des Bauhauses" (1961), in Grote, *von dürer bis gropius: Aufsätze zur deutschen Kunst* (Munich: Prestel, 1975), 127–34, esp. 130.
44 Ibid.
45 Grote, "walter gropius and the bauhaus" (see note 40), 9.
46 Ibid.
47 Ibid.
48 Oskar Schlemmer to Otto Meyer-Amden, 13 February 1924, in *The Letters and Diaries of Oskar Schlemmer*, ed. Tut Schlemmer, trans. Krishna Winston (Middletown, CT: Wesleyan University, 1972), 150.
49 Grote, "Zum Vortrag 'Von Weimar nach Dessau'" (see note 36).
50 Grote, "walter gropius and the bauhaus" (see note 40), 9.
51 Gropius, "Idee und Aufbau" (see note 10), 7.
52 See Grote, "walter gropius and the bauhaus" (see note 40).
53 Ludwig Grote, "Rede anlässlich der Eröffnung der Ausstellung *Junge Bauhausmaler* in Halle/Saale," 1928, manuscript, NL Grote, 1368; see "Opening Speech of the Exhibition *Young Bauhaus Painters* (1928)" in the present volume, esp. 75.
54 Grote, "Vom Bauhaus" (see note 35), 9.
55 Ludwig Grote, "Funktionalismus und Stil," in *Historismus und bildende Kunst*, ed. Ludwig Grote, Studien zur Kunst des 19. Jahrhunderts 1 (Munich: Prestel, 1965), 67–72, esp. 67.
56 See Susanne Neubauer, "Ludwig Grote and Brazil's Interest in the Bauhaus," in the present volume.
57 See Torsten Blume, "From Stuttgart into the World," in the present volume.

Fig. 1 Fritz Hesse (1881–1973), 1930

The Bauhaus Comes to Dessau: A Chronology

Peter Bernhard

"The relocation of the entire Bauhaus to the small ducal seat with no more than 40,000 residents is one of the miracles of the Golden Twenties."[1]

That was how Ludwig Grote later assessed the action to bring Germany's most controversial avant-garde school to Dessau—not without self-praise, he was, after all, surely the most important figure in this coup, along with the local mayor, Fritz Hesse (fig. 1). Just twelve weeks passed from the first, spontaneous proposal to the deciding vote in favor by the Gemeinderat (Municipal Council) of Dessau. The sequence of events was correspondingly rapid.[2]

Everything had begun at the turn of the year from 1924 to 1925, when Franz von Hoesslin, the director general of music of the Friedrich-Theater, suggested to Hesse during a phone call that the Bauhaus be taken in by Dessau. Hoesslin had gotten this idea after reading in an article in the *Berliner Tageblatt* that the school in Weimar should be considered closed as of March 31, 1925.[3] Hesse, who had also read that article and already briefly considered the possibility of adopting it, was now encouraged by Hoesslin's proposal to become truly active in the matter. The very next day, he discussed it with the outside expert Grote, who immediately declared himself willing—unofficially and on a kind of secret mission[4]—to travel to Weimar to explore the feasibility of this project. Walter Gropius and his wife, Ise, were on vacation in Italy at the time, so that László Moholy-Nagy led the negotiations from there. Grote later reported "on my first visit to the Bauhaus, during which Moholy handed me a telegram from Gropius with the words: 'Dessau impossible!'"[5] The basis for Gropius's negative attitude is not known, but certainly this "industrial city which seems smaller than Weimar but is actually bigger"[6] did not have all that good a reputation in general. Nevertheless, already during this exploratory conversation the attractiveness of Dessau's offer became clear in that it was prepared to accept all of the teachers without exception. Most of the latter surely shared Oskar Schlemmer's view on this, namely, that "the enticing prospect of keeping the good students and masters together" made Dessau "worth considering."[7] For his part, within a few days after his trip to Weimar, Grote was able to tell Moholy-Nagy that Hesse agreed to the stated conditions. At the meeting of the Meisterrat (Council of Masters) that had been scheduled in response,[8] the Bauhaus masters had responded positively to the offer from Dessau, so that Moholy-Nagy was in a position to ask Grote to come with the mayor for an inspection (fig. 2).[9] During this visit, which by agreement took place on February 12, the two men from Dessau were taken on a tour of the classrooms by Wassily Kandinsky and Lyonel Feininger and of the workshops by Moholy-Nagy and Georg Muche. A few days later, Muche announced to Grote a visit from Weimar in return, consisting of himself, Kandinsky, and their two wives.[10] Immediately after their return from this investigatory trip, there was a meeting of all the masters, a talk by Kandinsky and Muche about Dessau. The visit there of the men, with their wives, had gone splendidly, highest satisfaction on all points. [...] They telegraphed Dessau today to say that we agree in principle,"[11] as Feininger summed it up. Shortly before that, Schlemmer had told his fellow artist Otto Meyer: "The German cities' dance around the Golden Bauhaus is drawing to a close. The lukes have

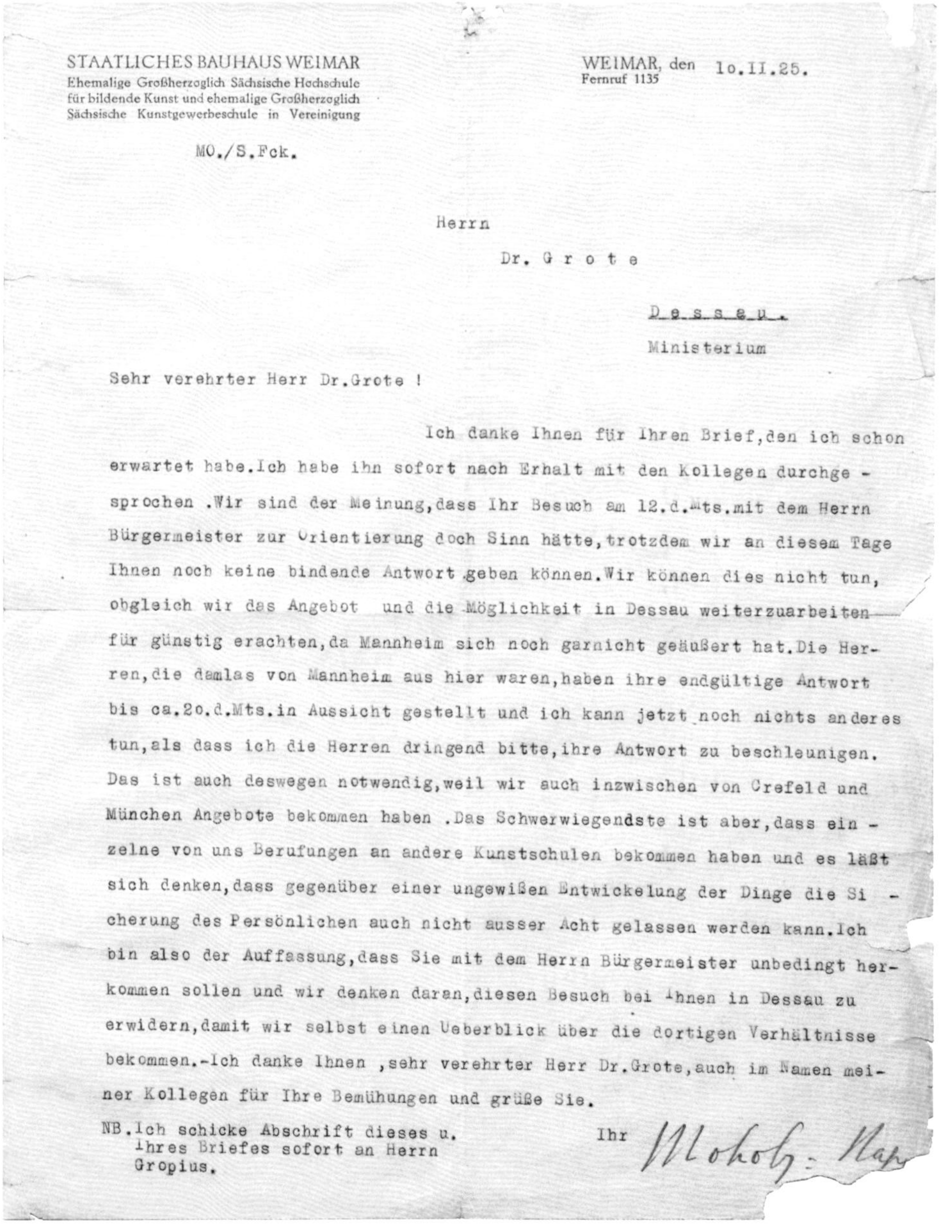

STAATLICHES BAUHAUS WEIMAR
Ehemalige Großherzoglich Sächsische Hochschule
für bildende Kunst und ehemalige Großherzoglich
Sächsische Kunstgewerbeschule in Vereinigung

WEIMAR, den 1o.II.25.
Fernruf 1135

MO./S.Fck.

Herrn

Dr. G r o t e

D e s s a u .

Ministerium

Sehr verehrter Herr Dr.Grote !

Ich danke Ihnen für Ihren Brief,den ich schon erwartet habe.Ich habe ihn sofort nach Erhalt mit den Kollegen durchge - sprochen .Wir sind der Meinung,dass Ihr Besuch am 12.d.Mts.mit dem Herrn Bürgermeister zur Orientierung doch Sinn hätte,trotzdem wir an diesem Tage Ihnen noch keine bindende Antwort geben können.Wir können dies nicht tun, obgleich wir das Angebot und die Möglichkeit in Dessau weiterzuarbeiten für günstig erachten,da Mannheim sich noch garnicht geäußert hat.Die Herren,die damlas von Mannheim aus hier waren,haben ihre endgültige Antwort bis ca.2o.d.Mts.in Aussicht gestellt und ich kann jetzt noch nichts anderes tun,als dass ich die Herren dringend bitte,ihre Antwort zu beschleunigen. Das ist auch deswegen notwendig,weil wir auch inzwischen von Crefeld und München Angebote bekommen haben .Das Schwerwiegendste ist aber,dass ein - zelne von uns Berufungen an andere Kunstschulen bekommen haben und es läßt sich denken,dass gegenüber einer ungewißen Entwickelung der Dinge die Si - cherung des Persönlichen auch nicht ausser Acht gelassen werden kann.Ich bin also der Auffassung,dass Sie mit dem Herrn Bürgermeister unbedingt herkommen sollen und wir denken daran,diesen Besuch bei Ihnen in Dessau zu erwidern,damit wir selbst einen Ueberblick über die dortigen Verhältnisse bekommen.-Ich danke Ihnen ,sehr verehrter Herr Dr.Grote,auch im Namen meiner Kollegen für Ihre Bemühungen und grüße Sie.

NB.Ich schicke Abschrift dieses u. Ihres Briefes sofort an Herrn Gropius.

Ihr Moholy-Nagy

Fig. 2 Letter from László Moholy-Nagy to Ludwig Grote, February 10, 1925
Moholy-Nagy writes to Grote that he and his Bauhaus colleagues “consider the offer and the opportunity to continue working in Dessau to be promising.” He also mentions, however, inquiries and offers that the Bauhaus has received from Mannheim, Crefeld (now Krefeld), and Munich. A Bauhaus visit requested by Grote and Fritz Hesse to Weimar should, in his view, definitely take place soon as well as a subsequent return visit by the Bauhaus members to Dessau.

parted company with the warms, the hots with the scaldings. This leaves Dessau (this in confidence)."[12]

Now the task was to persuade the committee that would decide on Dessau's side: the Gemeinderat. With high probability, it would be met with resistance there, since, after all, it meant converting an institution that had thus far been funded by the state into a municipal one and thus also taking over the costs entirely. In order to reduce this increased burden, Hesse wanted to integrate the Bauhaus into the existing Kunstgewerbe- und Handwerkerschule (Crafts and Artisans School), for which expansion efforts were already underway. The crucial opinion leaders and decision makers of Dessau were to be won over by a visit to the Bauhaus after Gropius had returned. On March 2 Muche was finally able to report to Grote that the director was expected back in Weimar on March 4,[13] and so the delegation from Dessau could come the following day. Then Hesse appeared himself on March 6, initially alone, to plan in detail the scheduled tour. And already on March 7 "at the Dessau train station [...] the members of Dessau's Gemeinderat had arrived and with them the minister president of Anhalt, Dr. Weber, and, as a representative of the government, the councilor of schools, Professor Blum.[14] The Handwerkskammer [Chamber of the Trades and Crafts] had sent its syndic, Dr. Rausch, who was also participating in this trip in his capacity as a member of the Gemeinderat and chairman of the Stadtverordnetenversammlung [Assembly of City Councilors], which he had been commissioned to represent. Appearing for the Handwerkskammer, were its syndic, Dr. Seiss, who was also a member of the Gemeinderat, and its president, master joiner August Wagner. The editors-in-chief of the Dessau newspapers had also come along on the journey, at the invitation of the Magistrat [Municipal Administration]."[15]

Ise Gropius reported in her diary on this: "Gentlemen from Dessau here to inspect the Bauhaus. The impression on both sides was a very good one, and one can certainly hope that something comes of the matter. The mayor seems to be a very adroit and clever person. Democrat. The majority has already been won over, but the goal is a unanimous resolution to take over the Bauhaus. Afternoon tea at the Bauhaus with all the masters and their wives participating."[16] Feininger reported shortly thereafter, however: "Gropi is a little reserved about Dessau—the atmosphere is favorable and the prospects are for very good development later—but, for the time being things are not quite as rosy as we had first envisioned. ... And also the housing problem is not yet clear. Only one third of the million is available for our buildings—and even that third has not been given willingly by the city representatives to us outsiders when they are not allowed to build for themselves."[17] The very next day, Gropius traveled to Dessau, accompanied by his wife, where he was to stay two nights to talk through all the details. Ise Gropius wrote of this: "Discussions with Overhoff of the planning department, who has a very favorable stance on G. They are looking at building new workshops by the autumn. So a new Bauhaus under one roof with the mechanical engineering school and the architecture school. A very nice idea. Afternoon car trip through the environs of Dessau. Evening discussion at Hesse's with Overhoff, Schmetzer,[18] Grote. Overhoff proposed entrusting G. with the directorship of the architecture school as well."[19] That day, the headline of the first supplement to the *Anhalter Anzeiger* was "Ein neues Kulturinstitut für Dessau" (A New Cultural Institution for Dessau).[20] The report was flanked by a journalistic double beat in order to win broad support for the project right away: an article by Gropius titled "Das Staatliche Bauhaus"[21] and one by Grote titled "Das Weimarer Bauhaus und seine Aufgaben in Dessau" (The Weimar Bauhaus and Its Tasks in Dessau).[22] This propaganda was certainly necessary, since the very next day Ise Gropius reported: "Hell has broken out here again in the form of the 'yellow brochure,' which is already in everyone's hands. It appears to have been sent from Weimar and distributed in Dessau by the arts and crafts school. Now, the disclaimers and explanations are starting again, and in the end something does indeed stick. G. is very depressed about the whole thing, which is very capable of causing the whole plan to fail again, since the city councilors will probably react very dismissively now."[23] The "yellow brochure" probably refers to a diatribe published in March 1924 under the title *Das Staatliche Bauhaus Weimar und sein Leiter* (The State Bauhaus in Weimar and Its Director), which had been written in December 1922 by Hans Beyer, a former syndic of the Bauhaus who had been dismissed for incompetence. The pamphlet would have an unfavorable effect on the negotiations on the Bauhaus budget in the Landtag (State Parliament) of Thuringia in May 1924—an official proceeding taken by the Bauhaus was won but only thereafter.[24]

As an immediate measure to counter this agitation, a promotional lecture by Gropius was scheduled to be held already on the following Saturday (fig. 3). So the Bauhaus director had just enough time to return to Weimar to inform the masters about the state of affairs[25] before heading for the capital of Anhalt again. Under the heading for March 14, one can read in Ise Gropius's diary: "Departure for Dessau. [...] Evening Gropius lecture. Very good success, despite the many foes. Afterward, large reception at the mayor's. The trades—incited by Weimar—are acting disapprovingly."[26] The local opponents of the Bauhaus had indeed teamed up; on the evening of the lecture, a leaflet titled "Der Bauhaus-Spuk" (The Bauhaus Nightmare) was being distributed (fig. 4). From this point forward, critical voices reported daily in the local newspapers. Grote later remarked on this that he operated "in the background,"[27] that is to say: in his "office, responses to negative statements in the press were written."[28] Concretely, that meant: "As soon as an article against the Bauhaus appeared in some Dessau newspaper, our office wrote an article in favor. And it went like this—we always did it under a different name—once we said 'retailers are writing us'—that was us! Then came 'From the world of banking we learn'—that was us. 'From the book trade we hear'—it was always us. And so every blow against was answered with one in favor."[29] With this campaign carried out with military precision, Grote and several comrades in arms were completely dedicated to the move of the avant-garde school, so that even the "battle-weary mayor" ultimately asked: "should I really bring the Bauhaus to Dessau for you six?"[30]

The Gemeinderat was scheduled to make a decision at its meeting on March 19. The closer that date came, the more the vote threatened to turn against the Bauhaus. The government of Thuringia had in the meanwhile finally come to the decision not to reject the

Am Sonnabend, den 14. März 1925, abends 8 Uhr, hält im großen Saale des „Evangelischen Vereinshauses“

Herr Professor Dr. Walter Gropius-Weimar,

der Leiter des staatlichen Bauhauses in Weimar, dessen Übersiedelung nach Dessau geplant ist, einen Lichtbilder-Vortrag über

„Die Ziele des Bauhauses“.

Zu diesem Vortrage und einer anschließenden zwanglosen Aussprache beim Glase Bier in den Räumen des städtischen Messelhauses (Kavalierstraße 33) beehre ich mich hierdurch namens der Stadtverwaltung ergebenst einzuladen.

Antwort unter Benutzung der beiliegenden Karte bis zum 13. März abends erbeten. Die vorbestellten Karten (nummerierte Saalplätze) liegen am 14. März vormittags von 9 bis 12 Uhr im Stadtsekretariat (Rathaus, Zimmer Nr. 30) zur Abholung bereit.

Dessau, den 11. März 1925.

Hesse,
Bürgermeister.

Ich nehme

a) an dem Vortrag des Herrn Professor Dr. WALTER GROPIUS am 14. März im Evangelischen Vereinshause teil / ~~nicht teil~~ und bitte, ... Eintrittskarten für mich zurückzulegen,

b) an dem anschließenden zwanglosen Beisammensein in den Räumen des städtischen Messelhauses teil / ~~nicht teil~~.

D. d. 11.III.25 — Dr. Grote

Ort und Datum. — Unterschrift.

Fig. 3 Invitation card from Mayor Fritz Hesse to Gropius's lecture "Die Ziele des Bauhauses" (The Goals of the Bauhaus) in Dessau on March 14, 1925, with Ludwig Grote's confirmation of participation on the verso.

Bauhaus as a whole but only its masters of form. Ise Gropius noted: "Weimar was now spreading the message that the Bauhaus proper would remain in Weimar, while Dessau would only get the useless part of its teaching staff":[31] "The masters of the crafts appear to have negotiated privately with the Thuringian government. They want to open up their own Bauhaus."[32] Moreover, "the Dessauer [...] are being flooded with leaflets, with letters, with the old Weimar [yellow] brochure against the Bauhaus. All these writings and also the personal appearance of envoys from Weimar aim to prevent the plan that benefits us, and at the moment we find ourselves desperate in the most difficult position as a result of all these machinations,"[33] Moholy-Nagy reported to Edwin Redslob, together with a request that he, in his capacity as Reichskunstwart (Imperial Protector of Art), "write Mayor Hesse a letter immediately in which you assure him that, despite all the intrigues and slanderous actions, moving the Bauhaus [...] to Weimar is desirable for the city and for the whole of German culture,"[34] in order to give Hesse something, since it was to be feared that "now even members of his own party, the Democrats, [could] leave [him] in the lurch."[35] Unfortunate circumstances, however, presented Moholy-Nagy's letter from reaching Redslob in time.[36]

In this uncertain situation, Hesse postponed the Bauhaus agenda item to the meeting on March 23. On that date, the follow motion was finally proposed: "The Gemeinderat agrees to the integration of the Weimar Bauhaus into the municipal Kunstgewerbe- und Handwerkerschule. [...] The joint direction of the Kunstgewerbe- und Handwerkerschule and of the Bauhaus will be [conferred on] Professor Gropius."[37] The next day, Moholy-Nagy wrote Redslob: "The municipal parliament of Dessau passed a resolution yesterday afternoon to relocate the Bauhaus with 26 versus 15 votes."[38] The five members of the Magistrat and the Town Councilors of the SPD (Social Democratic Party of Germany), KPD (Communist Party of Germany), and the DDP (German Democratic Party) voted in favor of it, and the so-called Einheitsliste (Unity List), a coalition of the bourgeois and conservative parties, voted against it. With that, the new location of the Bauhaus was officially sealed. In the night from March 28 to 29, the Letzter Tanz (Last Dance) final party was held at the Ilmschlösschen in Oberweimar; on April 1; Gropius moved into his new office in the accommodations of the Kunstgewerbe- und Handwerkerschule in Dessau; and on May 1, teaching began at the Bauhaus Dessau (fig. 5). It knew what it had in Grote, as a thank-you letter to him demonstrates (fig. 6).

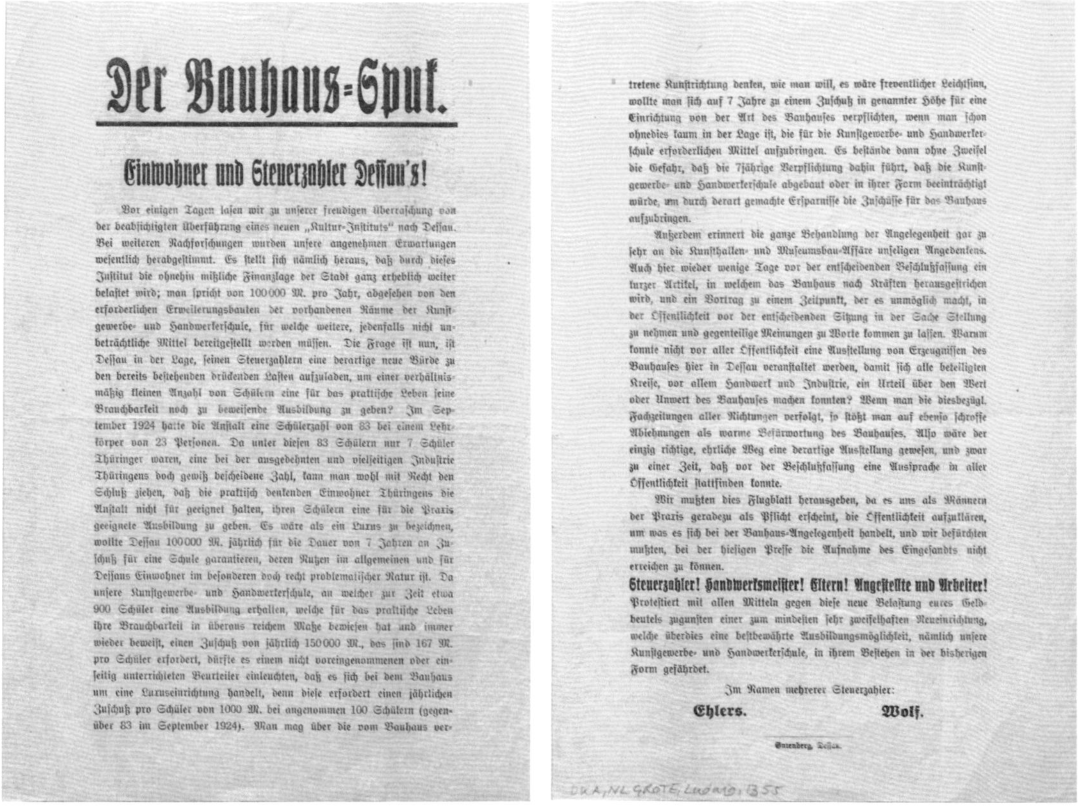

Der Bauhaus-Spuk.

Einwohner und Steuerzahler Dessau's!

Vor einigen Tagen lasen wir zu unserer freudigen Überraschung von der beabsichtigten Überführung eines neuen „Kultur-Instituts" nach Dessau. Bei weiteren Nachforschungen wurden unsere angenehmen Erwartungen wesentlich herabgestimmt. Es stellt sich nämlich heraus, daß durch dieses Institut die ohnehin mißliche Finanzlage der Stadt ganz erheblich weiter belastet wird; man spricht von 100000 M. pro Jahr, abgesehen von den erforderlichen Erweiterungsbauten der vorhandenen Räume der Kunstgewerbe- und Handwerkerschule, für welche weitere, jedenfalls nicht unbeträchtliche Mittel bereitgestellt werden müssen. Die Frage ist nun, ist Dessau in der Lage, seinen Steuerzahlern eine derartige neue Bürde zu den bereits bestehenden drückenden Lasten aufzuladen, um einer verhältnismäßig kleinen Anzahl von Schülern eine für das praktische Leben seine Brauchbarkeit noch zu beweisende Ausbildung zu geben? Im September 1924 hatte die Anstalt eine Schülerzahl von 83 bei einem Lehrkörper von 23 Personen. Da unter diesen 83 Schülern nur 7 Schüler Thüringer waren, eine bei der ausgedehnten und vielseitigen Industrie Thüringens doch gewiß bescheidene Zahl, kann man wohl mit Recht den Schluß ziehen, daß die praktisch denkenden Einwohner Thüringens die Anstalt nicht für geeignet halten, ihren Schülern eine für die Praxis geeignete Ausbildung zu geben. Es wäre als ein Luxus zu bezeichnen, wollte Dessau 100000 M. jährlich für die Dauer von 7 Jahren an Zuschuß für eine Schule garantieren, deren Nutzen im allgemeinen und für Dessaus Einwohner im besonderen doch recht problematischer Natur ist. Da unsere Kunstgewerbe- und Handwerkerschule, an welcher zur Zeit etwa 900 Schüler eine Ausbildung erhalten, welche für das praktische Leben ihre Brauchbarkeit in überaus reichem Maße bewiesen hat und immer wieder beweist, einen Zuschuß von jährlich 150000 M., das sind 167 M. pro Schüler erfordert, dürfte es einem nicht voreingenommenen oder einseitig unterrichteten Beurteiler einleuchten, daß es sich bei dem Bauhaus um eine Luxuseinrichtung handelt, denn diese erfordert einen jährlichen Zuschuß pro Schüler von 1000 M. bei angenommen 100 Schülern (gegenüber 83 im September 1924). Man mag über die vom Bauhaus vertretene Kunstrichtung denken, wie man will, es wäre freventlicher Leichtsinn, wollte man sich auf 7 Jahre zu einem Zuschuß in genannter Höhe für eine Einrichtung von der Art des Bauhauses verpflichten, wenn man schon ohnedies kaum in der Lage ist, die für die Kunstgewerbe- und Handwerkerschule erforderlichen Mittel aufzubringen. Es bestände dann ohne Zweifel die Gefahr, daß die 7jährige Verpflichtung dahin führt, daß die Kunstgewerbe- und Handwerkerschule abgebaut oder in ihrer Form beeinträchtigt würde, um durch derart gemachte Ersparnisse die Zuschüsse für das Bauhaus aufzubringen.

Außerdem erinnert die ganze Behandlung der Angelegenheit gar zu sehr an die Kunsthallen- und Museumsbau-Affäre unseligen Angedenkens. Auch hier wieder wenige Tage vor der entscheidenden Beschlußfassung ein kurzer Artikel, in welchem das Bauhaus nach Kräften herausgestrichen wird, und ein Vortrag zu einem Zeitpunkt, der es unmöglich macht, in der Öffentlichkeit vor der entscheidenden Sitzung in der Sache Stellung zu nehmen und gegenteilige Meinungen zu Worte kommen zu lassen. Warum konnte nicht vor aller Öffentlichkeit eine Ausstellung von Erzeugnissen des Bauhauses hier in Dessau veranstaltet werden, damit sich alle beteiligten Kreise, vor allem Handwerk und Industrie, ein Urteil über den Wert oder Unwert des Bauhauses machen konnten? Wenn man die diesbezügl. Fachzeitungen aller Richtungen verfolgt, so stößt man auf ebenso schroffe Ablehnungen als warme Befürwortung des Bauhauses. Also wäre der einzig richtige, ehrliche Weg eine derartige Ausstellung gewesen, und zwar zu einer Zeit, daß vor der Beschlußfassung eine Aussprache in aller Öffentlichkeit stattfinden konnte.

Wir mußten dies Flugblatt herausgeben, da es uns als Männern der Praxis geradezu als Pflicht erscheint, die Öffentlichkeit aufzuklären, um was es sich bei der Bauhaus-Angelegenheit handelt, und wir befürchten mußten, bei der hiesigen Presse die Aufnahme des Eingesandts nicht erreichen zu können.

Steuerzahler! Handwerksmeister! Eltern! Angestellte und Arbeiter!

Protestiert mit allen Mitteln gegen diese neue Belastung eures Geldbeutels zugunsten einer zum mindesten sehr zweifelhaften Neueinrichtung, welche überdies eine bestbewährte Ausbildungsmöglichkeit, nämlich unsere Kunstgewerbe- und Handwerkerschule, in ihrem Bestehen in der bisherigen Form gefährdet.

Im Namen mehrerer Steuerzahler:

Ehlers. **Wolf.**

Gutenberg, Dessau.

Fig. 4. "Der Bauhaus-Spuk" (The Bauhaus Nightmare): a leaflet addressed to the "residents and taxpayers of Dessau." The authors criticize the planned—but not yet publicly discussed—transfer of the Bauhaus from Weimar to Dessau as a great burden on the city budget. They cry "Taxpayers! Master craftsman! Parents! Salaried employees and workers!": "Protest with all means this new burden [...] in favor of an—at the least—highly dubious new establishment, which [...] endangers our arts and crafts school in its existence in its current form."

Bauhaus Dessau

Hochschule für Gestaltung

Das bisherige „Staatliche Bauhaus in Weimar" setzt als Städtisches Institut in Dessau seine Arbeiten auf breiter Grundlage fort:

I. Gestaltungslehre: Vorlehre – Handwerkslehre (Gesellenbrief) – Baulehre

II. Versuchsarbeit für die Praxis – Herstellung von Modellen für Handwerk und Industrie – Hausbau und Einrichtung

Leitung: Walter Gropius

Lehrkräfte: L. Feininger, W. Kandinsky, P. Klee, L. Moholy-Nagy, G. Muche, O. Schlemmer J. Albers, H. Bayer, M. Breuer, J. Scheper

Werkstätten: Bildhauerei – Metallwerkstatt – Tischlerei – Wandmalerei – Weberei – Druckerei (Typographie, Reklame, Kunstdruck)

Die Vorlehre ist für jeden obligatorisch. Beginn für Neueintretende am 1. Mai d. J. Aufnahme vom 17. Lebensjahr ab. Anmeldung sofort unter Beifügung von Arbeiten, die Begabung nachweisen, und eines Lebenslaufes mit Photographie an die Geschäftsstelle des Bauhauses: Dessau, Mauerstr. 36.

Auch ausgebildete Handwerker, Techniker, Mechaniker, Architekten werden aufgenommen.

Vorlehre pro Semester Mark 30.–, Aufnahmegebühr Mark 10.–, Werklehre frei.

Fig. 5 Bauhaus advertisement in *Junge Menschen*, no. 6 (May 5, 1925). From the content: "The former 'State Bauhaus in Weimar' continues its work on a broad basis as the municipal institute in Dessau." In addition to "design theory," the "experimental work for practice—production of models for craft and industry—house construction and furnishings" is emphasized.

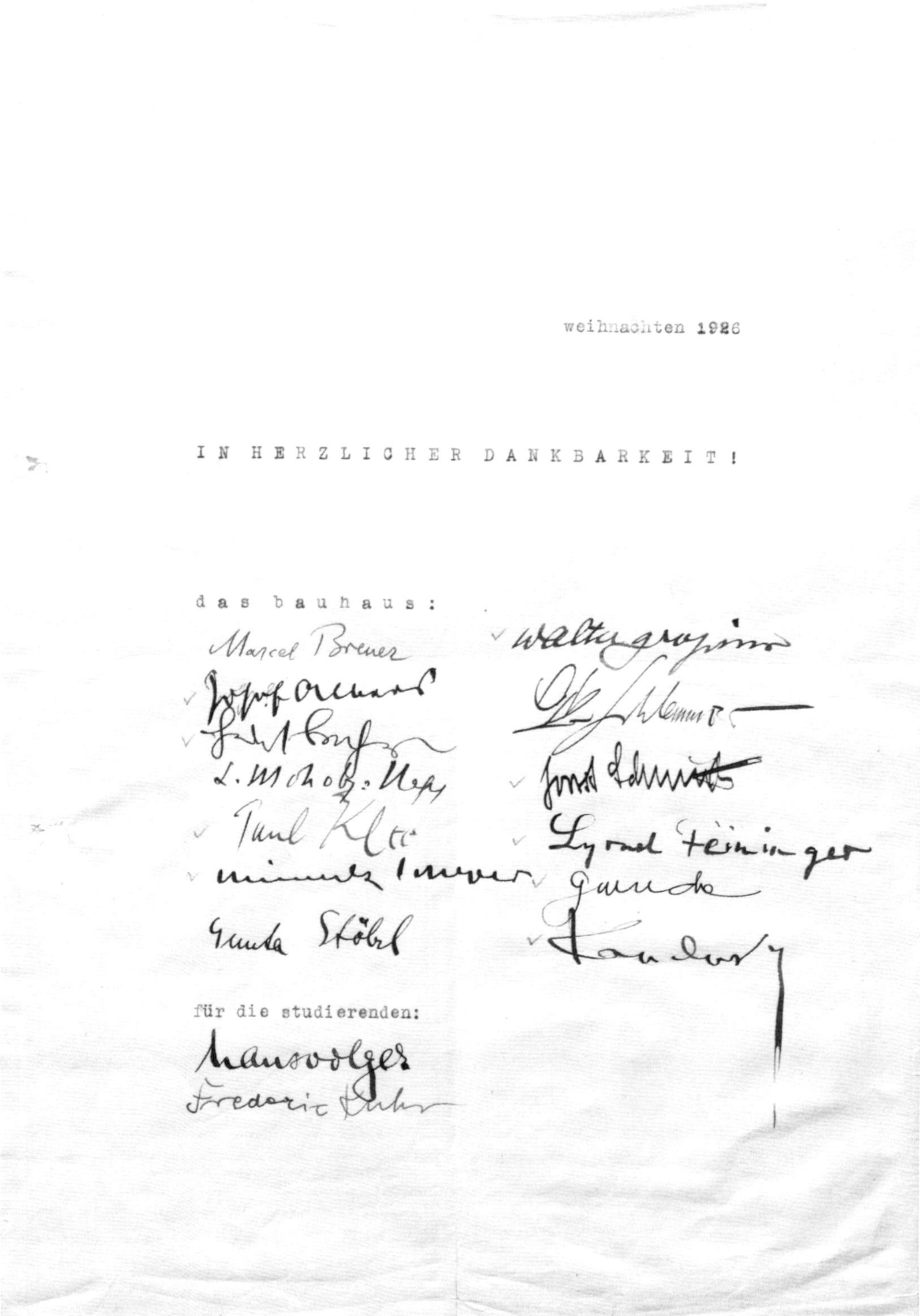

weihnachten 1926

I N H E R Z L I C H E R D A N K B A R K E I T !

d a s b a u h a u s :

für die studierenden:

Fig. 6 Letter of thanks from the Bauhaus members to Ludwig Grote, Christmas 1926. Signed by the Bauhaus masters Marcel Breuer, Josef Albers, László Moholy-Nagy, Herbert Bayer, Paul Klee, Hinnerk Scheper, Gunta Stölzl, Walter Gropius, Oskar Schlemmer, Joost Schmidt, Lyonel Feininger, Georg Muche, and Wassily Kandinsky as well as by Hans Volger and Frederic Kuhr "for the students."

1 Ludwig Grote, "Zu einem Vortrag über das Neue Bauen, insbesondere Entstehung, Geschichte und Inhalte des Bauhauses," typescript, n.d., DKA, NL, Grote, Ludwig (hereafter "NL Grote"), 1462.
2 On the summary that follows, see Fritz Hesse, *Erinnerungen an Dessau*, vol. 1, *Von der Residenz zur Bauhausstadt* (Bonn: the author, 1990), 195–207, and Reginald Isaacs, *Gropius: An Illustrated Biography of the Creator of the Bauhaus* (Boston: Little, Brown, 1991), 119–25.
3 See "Ende des Weimarer Bauhauses," *Berliner Tageblatt und Handels-Zeitung*, no. 613, December 27, 1924, morning edition. The declaration of the Bauhaus masters on the dissolving was reprinted in several newspapers; a more detailed version from the *Weimarischen Landeszeitung "Deutschland"* may be found in Hans M. Wingler, *The Bauhaus, 1919–1933, Weimar, Dessau, Berlin, Chicago*, 2nd ed. (Cambridge, MA: MIT Press, 1981), 93. In his memoirs—Hesse, *Erinnerungen* (see note 2), 195—Hesse mistakenly dates the article to January 1925, possibly confusing it with another note published in the *Berliner Tageblatt* that cites an announcement by "students, pupils, journeymen, and apprentices" as follows: "We inform the [Thuringian] government that we employees at the Staatliches Bauhaus will leave the Bauhaus with the forced departure of its leading figures. [...] The last opportunity to continue 'our Bauhaus' in Weimar has been taken away once and for all with our departure"; "Die Bauhäusler verlassen Weimar," *Berliner Tageblatt und Handels-Zeitung*, no. 28, January 17, 1925, morning edition. In a lecture he gave in the early 1960s, Grote even spoke in this context of an article from October 1924—surely another confusion—in this case with the call to support the Bauhaus, "which the Thuringian government and the Landtag intend to dissolve" ("Das staatliche Bauhaus in Weimar," *Berliner Tageblatt und Handels-Zeitung*, no. 512, October 28, 1924, morning edition) by joining the newly founded Kreis der Freunde des Bauhauses (Circle of Friends of the Bauhaus); see Ludwig Grote, "Zum Vortrag 'Von Weimar nach Dessau': Zum Gestaltenwandel des Bauhauses," lecture, January 30, 1963, Darmstadt, typescript, NL Grote, 998.
4 With an eye to their acceptance by the public, Hesse wanted to inform it only when concrete plans to achieve it could be shown.
5 Ludwig Grote to Fritz Hesse, 11 January 1964, NL Grote, 351.
6 Oskar Schlemmer to Otto Meyer-Amden, April 1925, in *The Letters and Diaries of Oskar Schlemmer*, ed. Tut Schlemmer (Middletown, CT, Wesleyan University Press, 1972), 163–64, esp. 163.
7 Oskar Schlemmer to Otto Meyer-Amden, 17 February 1925, in ibid., 161–62, esp. 161; see also Feininger's statement: "But remaining in a body together is for all of us the most important consideration and a great comfort"; Lyonel Feininger to Julia Feininger, 13 February 1925, in Wingler, *The Bauhaus* (see note 3), 97. Taking over the teaching staff without exception was, apparently, not welcomed by all of the students. Grote later reported that on his first visit to Weimar the husband of a Bauhaus student advised him not to offer a contract to Moholy-Nagy or Georg Muche; see Grote, "Zum Vortrag 'Von Weimar nach Dessau'" (see note 3).
8 See the invitation to the Meisterrat meeting on February 6, 1925, in Volker Wahl, ed., *Die Meisterratsprotokolle des Staatlichen Bauhauses Weimar, 1919 bis 1925* (Weimar: Böhlau, 2001), 348; all that survives, however, is the invitation, not the minutes.
9 See László Moholy-Nagy to Ludwig Grote, 10 February 1925, NL Grote, 1354.
10 See Georg Muche to Ludwig Grote, 16 February 1925, NL Grote, 1354.
11 Lyonel Feininger to Julia Feininger, 20 February 1925, in Wingler, *Das Bauhaus* (see note 3), 108.
12 Schlemmer to Meyer-Amden, 17 February 1925 (see note 7), 161.
13 See Georg Muche to Ludwig Grote, 2 March 1925, NL Grote, 1354.
14 The Bauhaus in Dessau was to become a municipal institute, but the state had a right to supervise educational institutions on the communal level, which is why Hesse was concerned to "interest the state authorities who come into consideration in the project as early as possible"; Hesse, *Erinnerungen* (see note 2), 198.
15 Ibid., 200.
16 Ise Gropius, diary, March 7, 1925, Bauhaus-Archiv Berlin, NL Walter Gropius, inv. no. 1998/55. Ise speaks here of twenty and Hesse in his *Erinnerungen* of fifty visitors from Dessau. This discrepancy can perhaps be explained by the fact that Ise Gropius first joined them at the concluding tea she mentions, in which perhaps not everyone from Dessau participated in light of the fact that the return journey took two hours.
17 Lyonel Feininger to Julia Feininger, 9 March 1925, in Wingler, *The Bauhaus* (see note 3), 96.
18 Theodor Overhoff (1880–1963) and Friedrich Wilhelm Schmetzer (1876–1952) were architects in the planning department of Dessau and Schmetzer a member of the Magistrat with voting rights in the Gemeinderat.
19 Ise Gropius, diary (see note 16), March 10, 1925.
20 See *Anhalter Anzeiger*, no. 58, March 10, 1925.
21 Walter Gropius, "Das Staatliche Bauhaus," *Anhalter Anzeiger*, no. 58, March 10, 1925. Muche had been asked by the *Dessauer Zeitung* already in February for an article on the Bauhaus, but on Grote's advice did not fulfill that request; see Georg Muche to Ludwig Grote, 24 February 1925, NL Grote, 1354.
22 See Ludwig Grote, "Das Weimarer Bauhaus und seine Aufgaben in Dessau," *Anhalter Anzeiger*, no. 58, March 10, 1925. The Landeskonservator (State Curator) had been provided by the Bauhaus with information material several weeks earlier; see Georg Muche to Ludwig Grote, 23 March 1925, NL Grote, 1354; the unabridged original typescript (NL Grote, 1355) is reprinted here as an appendix.
23 Ise Gropius, diary (see note 16), March 11, 1925.
24 Beyer was not identified as the author in the brochure, which was rather signed by the Weimar master metalworker Arno Müller as "responsible for the content"; see *Das Staatliche Bauhaus Weimar und sein Leiter* (Weimar: Hof-Buchdruckerei, [1924]), NL Grote, 1363. Beyer had already made publicly many of the same objections to Gropius expressed in it, who initiated a libel action against him in response. A notice in the newspaper reporting on the outcome of that procedure, which was decided for Gropius, is pasted into the copy of the brochure found in Grote's

archive (see NL Grote). Just how damaging the yellow brochure was taken to be can be judged from the fact that its distribution in Dessau became the subject of a debate in the Landtag of Thuringia; see the excerpts from the minutes of the final debate on the budget proposal of the Staatliches Bauhaus in the session of the Landtag of Thuringia of March 19, 1925, in Volker Wahl, *Das staatliche Bauhaus in Weimar: Dokumente zur Geschichte des Instituts 1919–1926* (Cologne: Böhlau, 2009), 475–98.

25 Lyonel Feininger to Julia Feininger, 12 March 1925, in Wingler, *The Bauhaus* (see note 3), 97.

26 Ise Gropius, diary (see note 16), March 14, 1925; for reports on Gropius's lecture and the objections of the opponents of the Bauhaus, see "Der Kampf um das Bauhaus," *Anhaltische Rundschau*, no. 75, March 16, 1925; "Um das Weimarer Bauhaus," *Volksblatt für Anhalt*, no. 58, March 16, 1925; and "Die Ziele des Bauhauses," *Anhalter Anzeiger*, no. 64, March 17, 1925.

27 Grote to Hesse (see note 5).

28 Ibid.

29 Grote, "Zum Vortrag 'Von Weimar nach Dessau'" (see note 3). In Grote's papers, there are two letters to Hesse, 18 March and 23 March 1925, allegedly written by the "construction industry" and by "manufacturers of artistic lighting fixtures," respectively, both of which end with the sentence "We submit these lines to you, dear mayor, to use as you please" (NL Grote, 1354); they may be two of the fake texts discussed here.

30 Grote, "Zum Vortrag 'Von Weimar nach Dessau'" (see note 3). Of the five other people, Grote mentions the entrepreneur Heinrich König (1889–1966), who would soon become the general representative of the Bauhaus GmbH; the Dessau SPD city councilor Gerhart Seger (1896–1967); the publisher Karl Rauch (1897–1966), who ran the Kunst- und Bücherstube (Art and Books Parlor), which was later frequented by members of the Bauhaus; and the director of Friedrichsgymnasium in Dessau, Gerhard Heine (1867–1949), who was an advocate of pedagogical reform who would later propose that Gropius write an article on the Bauhaus for the yearbook he edited; see Walter Gropius, "Das Bauhaus in Dessau," *Heimatliches Jahrbuch für Anhalt* (Dessau: C. Dünnhaupt, 1926), 15–22.

31 Ise Gropius, diary, March 14, 1925 (see note 16), see "Vorsicht, Dessau!—s' 'Bauhaus' spukt!," *Anhalter Woche*, no. 11, March 15, 1925; the distinction between artisans and artists made by opponents of the Bauhaus is also the basis of a joke about Weimar recorded by Grote: "The masters of the crafts provide training [*Ausbildung*]; the masters of form provide vanity [*Einbildung*]"; Grote, "Zum Vortrag 'Von Weimar nach Dessau'" (see note 3).

32 Ise Gropius, diary, March 16, 1925 (see note 16). Feininger reported on such negotiations already in mid-February; see Lyonel Feininger to Julia Feininger, 11 February 1925, in Wingler, *The Bauhaus* (see note 3), 96–97. The Thuringian Staatsminister (Minister of State) Richard Leutheuser declared accordingly: "the Weimar Bauhaus is not going to Dessau but, at most, just Mr. Gropius"; excerpt from the minutes of the final debate on the budget proposal of the Staatliches Bauhaus (see note 24), 486. The masters of the craft did indeed choose not to move to Dessau.

33 László Moholy-Nagy to Edwin Redslob, 19 March 1925, Bauhaus-Archiv Berlin, NL Walter Gropius Papers II, 652 (with sincere gratitude to Jan Willem Kort for this reference).

34 Ibid.

35 Ibid.

36 Edwin Redslob to Walter Gropius, 26 March 1925, Bundesarchiv Berlin, Bestand Reichskunstwart, R32/60, fol. 207, and Reichskunstwart Edwin Redslob to Mayor Fritz Hesse, 26 March 1925, ibid., fols. 209–10. What did reach Hesse in time and "favorably influence[d] the whole state of affairs"—according to László Moholy-Nagy to Reichskunstwart Edwin Redslob, 24 March 1925, ibid., fol. 208—was a telegram of support (possibly initiated by Grote) from the Zehnerring (Ring of Ten), a group of ten members of the Bund Deutscher Architekten (Association of German Architects), to which Peter Behrens, Otto Bartning, Hugo Häring, Ludwig Mies van der Rohe, Bruno Taut, Hans Poelzig, and Erich Mendelsohn belonged; see ibid. and "Die Übernahme des Bauhauses beschlossen," *Anhalter Anzeiger*, no. 71, March 25, 1925; the contents of the telegram were published in *Volksblatt für Anhalt*, no. 69, March 23, 1925, and *Anhalter Anzeiger*, no. 70, March 24, 1925.

37 Report on the meeting of the Dessau Gemeinderat on March 24, 1925, *Anhalter Anzeiger*, no. 71, March 25, 1925, reprinted in Wingler, *The Bauhaus* (see note 3), 103; see "Das Weimarer Bauhaus kommt nach Dessau!," *Volksblatt für Anhalt*, no. 70, March 24, 1925.

38 Moholy-Nagy to Redslob, 24 March 1925 (see note 36).

Das Weimarer Bauhaus (The Bauhaus Weimar) (1925)

Ludwig Grote

The typescript printed here can be found in Grote's estate under the call number 1355. A shortened version of the text was published with the heading "Das Weimarer Bauhaus und seine Aufgaben in Dessau" ("The Bauhaus Weimar and Its Tasks in Dessau") in two daily newspapers: in the Anhalter Anzeiger on March 10 and in the Anhaltische Rundschau on March 11, 1925. In the run-up to the planned takeover of the school by the City of Dessau, it was supposed to have a positive influence on the general mood, especially with regard to the still pending decisive vote in the Dessau municipal council.

So here is an information and an advertising leaflet. In keeping with the 1919 Manifesto, Grote describes the Bauhaus as a new type of school that bridged the gap between applied and fine arts by focusing all teaching on building—comparable to the cathedral huts of the Middle Ages. In this way alone it is possible to "fertilize modern life artistically"—and this for society as a whole, because since one does not oppose industrial production methods, the production of both aesthetically demanding and affordable mass products is now realistic. Dessau could benefit in particular from the settlement of the school, not only in terms of cooperation with local industry—Grote mentions the wagon factory and the Junkers works as examples—but also in terms of the prospect of inexpensive construction of "settlements and apartments for the workers and employees" under the guidance of the Bauhaus. In addition, Grote points out that the "Bauhaus stage workshop [...] shows the stage art new ways, so that [...] new possibilities arise for the artistic development of our Friedrichtheater"; in general, the establishment of the Bauhaus Dessau would "place it at the forefront of the artistic development of Germany" and would have a positive influence "on the cultural and intellectual life" of the city. Regarding the fact that the school had to leave the old location, he explains: "The Bauhaus in Weimar has become a victim of intrigues that came from academy professors who were dismantled when the Bauhaus was founded. They succeeded in disastrously mixing up the questions of art with politics and in getting the state government to dismiss the Bauhaus masters." Regardless of this, the Bauhaus finds support and recognition everywhere, be it from recognized organizations such as the Federation of German Architects, the Werkbund or the Central German Industry Association, be it from well-known personalities such as the architect Peter Behrens, the writer Gerhardt Hauptmann or the physicist Albert Einstein. Dessau can therefore count itself lucky among the many competitors for the takeover of the school—Grote names Mannheim, Munich, Frankfurt am Main and Cologne—to have been awarded the contract, the main reason being its location in the prosperous industrial landscape of Central Germany. Grote tries to dispel any concerns that still exist: with regard to worries about the financial burden, he points out that the merger with the already existing arts and crafts school would not result in additional costs and he dispels the fears of the local handicrafts by pointing out that the Bauhaus does not have its own production aim, but see itself as a laboratory which designs models for industry.

DAS WEIMARER BAUHAUS.

Aus der Erkenntnis, daß die verhängnisvolle Zersplitterung der Kunst in Einzelkünste, in freie und angewandte Kunst überwunden werden kann, wenn die Idee des Baues wieder die Führerstellung einnimmt, ist das staatliche Bauhaus in Weimar entstanden. In den starken und einheitlichen Stilwillens war die Architektur die Mutter aller Künste, ihr dienten sie alle, von ihr empfingen sie Nahrung und mit ihr entwickelten sie sich.

das Bauhaus hat sich zum Ziel gesetzt die bisher vom praktischen leben isolierte Kunsterziehung mit den wirklichen Forderungen heutigen Lebens in Einklang zu bringen. Zu diesem Zweck hat es die Einheit der theoretischen und der Werkstattarbeit in sein Erziehungsprogramm unter dem Gesichtspunkt eingeführt, daß heute eine ganze Reihe isoliert neben ein anderstehender Spezialberufe oder schöpferischer Leistungen letzten Endes auf das Bauen gerichtet ist. Als Ideal steht im Hintergrunde die Mittelalterliche Bauhütte der großen Kathedralen und Dome.

Keineswegs handelt es sich bei der Bauhausidee um Wirklichkeitsferne, romantisch-rückschauende Wiedererweckung handwerklicher Tradition. Im Gegenteil unterscheidet gerade die völlig unsentimentale, rational-praktische Methode das Bauhaus von den Kunstgewerbeschulen alten Schlages. Diese sind entstanden durch Ablehnung der Maschine und brachten ein Kunsthandwerk hervor, daß abseits vom eigentlichen Lebensstrome stand und seine sicher sehr reizvollen und künstlerisch wertvollen Erzeugnisse für eine sehr kleine Zahl vermögender, verständnisvoller Menschen schuf. Das Bauhaus hat die Schwächen des modernen romantisch-sentimentalen Kunstgewerbes erkannt. Die Maschine ist das Mittel, in die Masse des Volkes zu dringen mit künstlerischen Leistungen. Nicht gegen die Maschine, sondern mit der Maschine gilt es zu arbeiten, wenn ich das moderne Leben künstlerisch befruchten will. Die Vergeistigung der industriellen Arbeit hat sich das Bauhaus und gemeinsam mit ihm der Deutsche Werkbund zum Ziele gesetzt.

Die große Masse des Bürgertums und der Arbeiterschaft ist für seine Bedürfnisse an Mobiliar und Hausgerät auf maschinelle Produkte angewiesen. Das Bauhaus hat sich zur Aufgabe gestellt, diese notwendigen

notwendigen Dinge so zu gestalten, daß sie von Maschinen in Massen hergestellt werden können und den ästhetischen Anforderungen genügen. Aber diese Gestaltung wird, wie schon gesagt, vom Bau bestimmt. Eine völlig neue Auffassung vom Wesen der Architektur liegt zu Grunde: Die verschiedenen Elemente des Baues erfahren eine neue Deutung. Unter Verzicht auf jegliches Ornament, das als Maskerade, als Sentimentalität empfunden wird, soll die reine Form herauskristallisiert werden, sollen ihre bildenden Kräfte ungehemmt zur Auswirkung kommen.

So bringen alle Schöpfungen des Bauhauses – Haus, Wohnung und jedes Gerät – eine Idee zum Ausdruck, die sie zu einer überzeugenden Einheit zusammenschließt. Alle Werke machen den Eindruck von Typen; frei von jeder Phantastik, von jeder Gefühlsduselei und Sentimentalität wirken sie in ihrer Gestaltung unbedingt notwendig und klar wie Kristall. Das Bauhaus steht mit diesen Schaffensprinzipien keineswegs allein; es ist für Deutschland der Anführer geworden in dem Kampfe um die Kunst der Zukunft. Nach fünfjähriger Tätigkeit, wo bisweilen sicher auch Irrwege gegangen sind, hat heute das Bauhaus den Beweis erbracht, daß durch die Art und Weise der Erziehung und durch die wirtschaftliche Auswertung der Resultate sowohl sein ideelles Ziel als auch die Art seiner Durchführung und Verwirklichung richtig ist. Die bedeutende Resonanz, die seine Bestrebungen im In= und Auslande gefunden haben, zeigt, daß aus seiner Arbeit bereits eine allgemeine geistige Bewegung hervorgeht.

Das Bauhaus ist in Weimar ein Opfer von Intrigen geworden, die von Akademieprofessoren ausgegangen ist, die bei Gründung des Bauhauses abgebaut sind. Ihnen gelang es, die Fragen der Kunst in unheilvoller Weise mit der Politik zu vermischen und die Entlassung der Bauhausmeister bei der Staatsregierung durchzusetzen.

Alle Eingaben und Proteste des gesamten geistigen Deutschlands haben es nicht vermocht, das thüringische Staatsministerium zur Zurücknahme seiner Verfügung zu veranlassen. Alle künstlerisch und kulturell führenden Persönlichkeiten haben sich für das Bauhaus ausgesprochen. Von den Namen seien nur genannt: Peter Behrens, Gerhart Hauptmann, Hans Driesch, Albert Einstein, Theodor Fischer usw. Von den großen Organisationen hat sich vor allem die Vertretung der gesamten

ten deutschen Architektenschaft, der Bund deutscher Architekten und dann der Deutsche Werkbund für die Erhaltung des Bauhauses eingesetzt. Es soll auch nicht unerwähnt bleiben, daß auch der mitteldeutsche Industriellenverband die Leistungen des Bauhauses anerkannt hat.

Als die Auflösung bekannt wurde, haben sich verschiedene Großstädte mit dem Bauhaus verhandelt und ihm Arbeitsmöglichkeiten geboten: Mannheim, München, Frankfurt a.M. und Köln. Schwierigkeiten, wie das Fehlen von Werksätten in Mannheim oder die Existenz einer großen, gut geleiteten Kunstgewerbeschulen wie in Frankfurt und München haben die Meister des Bauhauses bewogen, die Übersiedlung nach Dessau zu planen. Vor allem war von Einfluß die Erwägung, daß Dessau eine große wirtschaftliche Entwicklung vor sich hat, das Mitteldeutsche Braunkohlenrevier in unmittelbarer Nähe liegt, und so ein Arbeitsfeld für das Bauhaus von großem Umfange gegeben ist.

Die Einzelmeister wurden in ihrem Entschlusse nicht etwa durch die Sorge um ihre persönliche Zukunft bestimmt, haben sie doch bereits sämtlich einen Ruf an Akademieen und Kunstgewerbeschulen erhalten. Außerdem könnten sie auch als freischaffende Künstler leben, da sie sich in Deutschland und im Auslande einen Namen gemacht haben. Der Glaube aber an die Idee des Bauhauses veranlaßt sie allein, alles zu versuchen, sich ihrer Gemeinschaftarbeit von Walter Gropius zu erhalten.

Was bedeutet die Übersiedlung des Bauhauses für die Stadt Dessau, für das Land Anhalt?

Dessau besitzt eine Kunstgewerbe= und Handwerkerschule. Sie ist ausgestattet mit dem modernen Maschinen und allen technischnen Hilfsmitteln. Überdies hat sie einen Etat, den nur wenige Städte ihren Kunstgewetbeschulen bewilligen können. Mit 150000 Mark übertrifft er den Etat des Staatlichen Bauhauses in Weimar um ein Drittel. Ein großer Apparat von Lehrern ist aufgeboten. Wer aber außerhalb Dessaus weiß etwas von der Existenz unserer Kunstgewerbeschule? Wo sind die Leistungen, die diese großen Aufwendungen rechtfertigten? Welche Austellungserfolge hat sie aufzuweisen? In welchen deutschen Zeitungen und in welchen Zeitschriften ist sie erwähnt? Die Verdienste des gegenwärtigen Dirktors als Organisator und Leiter soll nicht

herabgesetzt werden. Eine künstlerisch führende Persönlichkeit kann er zweifellos nicht genannt werden, und auf die allein kommt es bei einer Kunstgewerbeschule an.
Mit der Berufung des Bauhauses würde Dessau ein Institut erhalten, das den großen Aufwendungen entspricht. Und das ist möglich ohne eine Erhöhung der Zuschüsse, es ist lediglich eine Frage der Versetzung von einigen wenigen festangestellten Lehrern der Kunstgewerbeschule an andere Anstalten. Es liegt also in der Hand der städtischen Körperschaften, ob sie die nie wiederkehrende Gelegenheit zur völligen Reorganisation der Kunstgewerbeschule durch Übernahme der Bauhauslehrerschaft benutzen wollen, die Dessau und das Land Anhalt an die Spitze der künstlerischen Entwicklung Deutschlands stellen würden. Die Blicke des gesamten geistigen Deutschlands würden auf unsere Stadt gelenkt. Dessau würde einen Ruf bekommen ähnlich dem, den es unter der Regierung des Fürsten Franz gehabt hat.
Der Zusammenhang mit der Frequenz des Fremdenverkehrs wird jeder Weitblickendere ohneweiteres ersehen, sodaß an dieser Stelle weitere Ausführungen über diesen Punkt erspart werden können. Die Bauhauswoche hatte 1923 eine große Anzahl von Fremden nach Weimar geführt. Der Aufenthalt von Künstlern wie Feininger, Kandinsky, Muche, Schlemmer, Gropius, deren Namen weithin in der europäischen Kunstwelt bekannt sind, wird ständig Kunstfreunde nach Dessau hinziehen.

Noch wichtiger und von ausschlaggebenderer Bedeutung wird der Einfluß dieser Künstlerpersönlichkeiten auf das kulturelle und geistige Leben sein. Die Bauhausidee lebt sich ja keineswegs in der bildenden Kunst aus, sondern durchdringt alle Lebensgebiete. Anläßlich der Bauhauswoche fanden in Weimar Theateraufführungen statt, die der Bühnenkunst neue Wege zeigten. Neuartige Dekorationen und neuartige Kostüme sind damals geschaffen; auch wurden neue Beleuchtungsarten ausprobiert. Die Bühnenwerkstatt des Bauhauses hat ihre Anerkennung heute gefunden, ihr Leiter, Professor Schlemmer, ist zur Zeit von der Volksbühne in Berlin mit dem Entwurf von Dekorationen beschäftigt. Hier bietet sich also für die künstlerische Entwicklung unseres Friedrichstheaters neue Möglichkeiten.

Das Bauhaus weiß, daß zur künstlerischen Entwicklung praktische Aufgaben gehören, an fingierten Fällen kann der Lehrling niemals einen praktischen Umblick erlerben. Den Schülern wird kein falscher Künstlerehrgeiz anerzogen; sie sind Lehrlinge und müssen nach dreijähriger Lehrzeit ihre Gesellenprüfung vor der Handwerkskammer ablegen. Die Kunstgewerbeschule würde also keineswegs den Charakter einer Handwerkerschule verlieren.

Aus der oben flüchtig umrissenen Idee des Bauhauses wird ohneweiters ersichtlich, welche wertvollen Resultate die wechselseitige Befruchtung von Bauhaus und Industrie hervorbringen kann. Es zieht sich nicht in weltfremder Künstlerüberheblichkeit zurück, sondern sucht im Gegenteil, wo es immer nur kann, mit dem wirtschaftlichen Leben in Berührung zu kommen.

In der Arbeitsmethode des Bauhauses liegt begründet, daß das einheimische Handwerk in ihm auf keinen Fall einen Konkurrenten zu erblicken hat. Es liegt ihm nichts an der Herstellung einzelner Stücke. Es will Modelle und Typen schaffen, die industriell ausgewertet werden können.

Mit Gropius würde der beste deutsche Architkt für industrielle Bauten nach Dessau kommen. Neben Fabrikanlagen müssen Siedlungen und Wohnungen für die Arbeiter und Angestellten geschaffen werden. Bei der schnellen Zunahme der Stadt Dessau können dem Bauhaus Aufgaben erwachsen, die geradezu ideal genannt werden müssen. Für ganz Deutschland vorbildliche Lösungen des Arbeiterhauses können gefunden werden. Der Gedanke des Typenhauses würde zur Ausreifung kommen, bis zur Türklinke und allem Mobiliar kann der Typus der Arbeiterwohnung ausgebildet werden.

Auch das wird in keiner Weise eine Konkurrenz für das hiesige Handwerk bedeuten. Dieses würde bei der Massenherstellung der Bauhausentwürfe in erhöhtem Maße heran gezogen werden. Bei dem werkgerechten Vorgehen des Bauhauses bin ich überzeugt, daß unser Handwerk auch in seiner Arbeitsweise und Technik mannigfache Anregungen erhalten wird.

Es würde im einzelnen zuweit führen, die Industrieen und ihr Arbeits=

beitsgebiet, soweit es das Bauhaus angeht, anzuführen. So würde die Waggonfabrik die Durchformung eines Eisenbahn= oder Straßenbahn=wagens dem Bauhaus mit Nutzen übertragen können. Gropius hat unter anderem eine solche Arbeit bereits für Siemens und Schuckert ausgeführt. Weiter könnte die Fa. Junkers die Gestaltung der Badeöfen, auch von Flugzeugkabinen=Einrichtungen in Auftrag geben. Dann sei daran erinnert, daß Dessau eine sich stark entwickelnde Möbelindustrie und aufblühende Werkstätten für Beleuchtungskörper besitzt.

Es wird Sache einer guten Geschäftlichen Organisation des Bauhauses sein, sich solche und ähnliche Arbeitsgebiete zu erschließen.

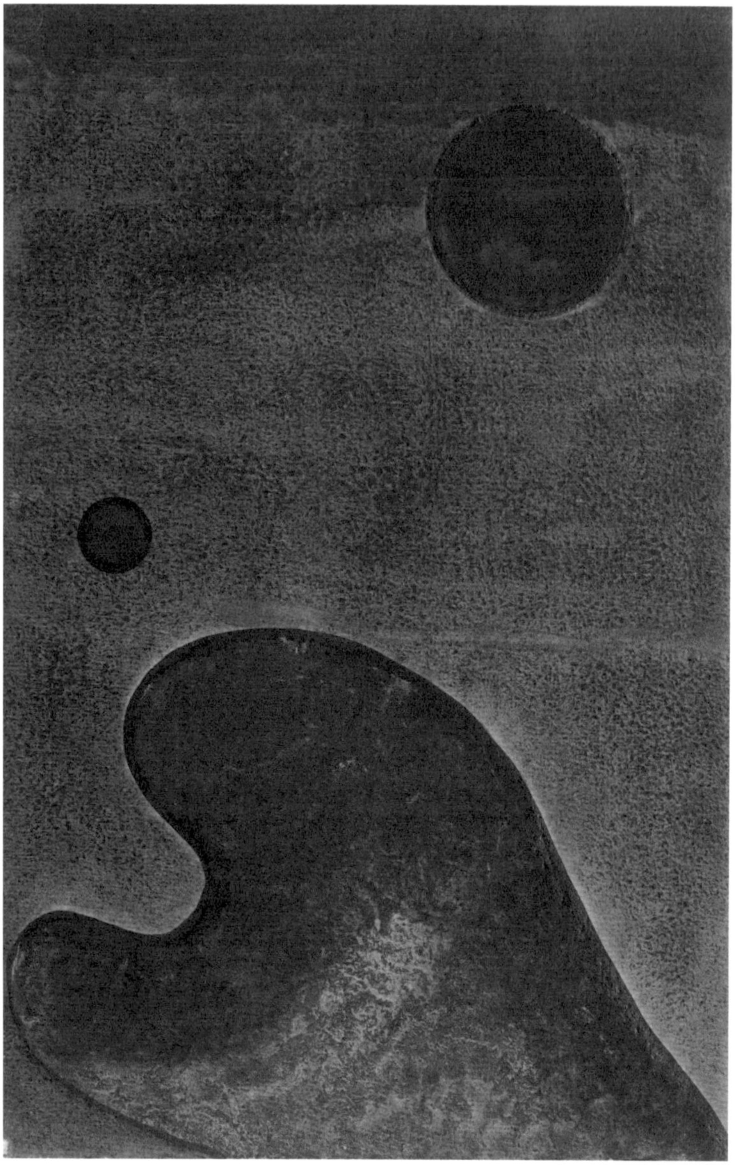

Fig. 1 Wassily Kandinsky, *Schwere Fläche* (Heavy Plane), watercolor, 1925

Ludwig Grote in Dessau: A Modern Gallerist and Museum Director

Nadine Willing-Stritzke

Ludwig Grote was the founding director of the Anhaltische Gemäldegalerie (Anhalt Paintings Gallery) in Dessau; with its collecting focus on German and Dutch painting, it still holds the largest collection of old masters in Saxony-Anhalt. Moreover, as Landeskonservator (State Curator) of what was then the Free State of Anhalt, he helped shape the beginnings of the state historical preservation agency. The title of this essay therefore seems misleading, but on closer inspection it becomes clear that Grote was decidedly operating as a modern museum director in implementing art pedagogical approaches influenced by the reformist movement and at the same time integrating the old masters and their significance from a contemporaneous perspective.

In 1922 that brought Ludwig Grote to Dessau, having just received his doctorate from the Universität Halle with a dissertation on the printmaking of Georg Lemberger. He had been recommended by his dissertation adviser, Paul Frankl, who praised Grote in his letter of recommendation as an art expert who "is already considered a recognized authority in the field of the history of painting."[1] In Dessau, they were searching for just such an expert in order to bring to a successful conclusion efforts to establish an art museum that had already been underway for many years.[2] Large sections of the art holdings of the former house of the Duke of Anhalt, which had been absorbed by the Joachim-Ernst-Stiftung (Joachim Ernst Foundation);[3] the art holdings of the City of Dessau; and the holdings of the Amalienstiftung[4] were supposed to provide the foundation for this museum. In preparing for the founding of the Gemäldegalerie, Grote was hired to produce a catalog of the holdings of paintings of the municipal Amalienstiftung and to inventory the holdings of paintings of the Gotisches Haus in Wörlitz. His committed and competent work was convincing. From then on, Dessau's mayor, Fritz Hesse, had the art historian advise him on all official issues in the field of art.[5] In 1924 Grote was appointed Landeskonservator of the Free State of Anhalt. In connection with that task, he also took over the artistic direction of the Anhaltischer Kunstverein. Until 1932, the Landeskonservator of Anhalt reported directly to the state ministry. The tasks consisted of advising the government of the State of Anhalt on questions of historical preservation and art as well as conserving, studying, and preserving the historically and artistically valuable architectural and art monuments, fostering understanding of the history of art and architecture through lectures and talks, protecting the regional landscape, safeguarding nature reserves and certain natural monuments, and maintaining war graves. In addition, he was supposed to support the Anhaltischer Kunstverein by organizing exhibitions and the like.

In March 1927 Grote presented the board of trustees of the Joachim-Ernst-Stiftung with a list of paintings in the foundation's holdings that would be suitable for the gallery to be founded.[6] The Anhaltische Gemäldegalerie opened on September 17 of that year; Grote was named as its director, in formal terms as an additional office of the Landeskonservator. The intention to create an art museum in Dessau was in keeping with the popular education aim of the museum debates of the early twentieth century.[7] The expectations that the State Ministry of Anhalt had of an art museum are clear from a bill passed in 1924. In addition to its scholarly objectives, the museum to be founded was to operate in the spirit

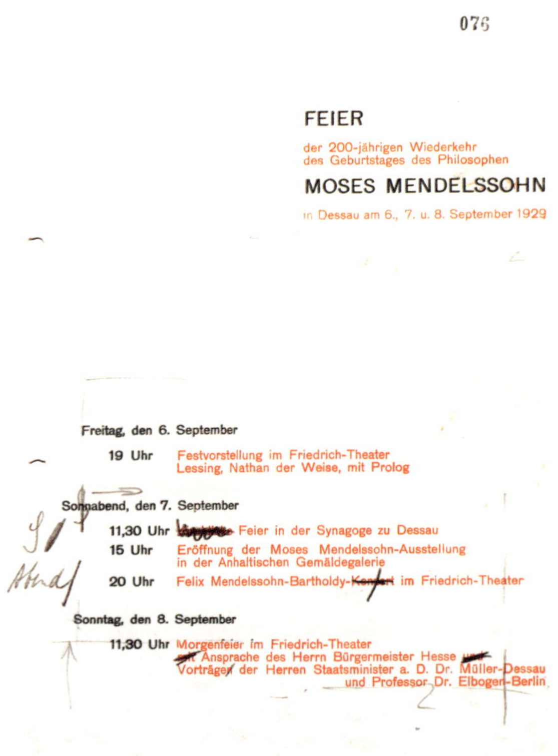

076

FEIER

der 200-jährigen Wiederkehr
des Geburtstages des Philosophen

MOSES MENDELSSOHN

in Dessau am 6., 7. u. 8. September 1929

Freitag, den 6. September

19 Uhr Festvorstellung im Friedrich-Theater
Lessing, Nathan der Weise, mit Prolog

Sonnabend, den 7. September

11,30 Uhr Feier in der Synagoge zu Dessau

15 Uhr Eröffnung der Moses Mendelssohn-Ausstellung
in der Anhaltischen Gemäldegalerie

20 Uhr Felix Mendelssohn-Bartholdy- im Friedrich-Theater

Sonntag, den 8. September

11,30 Uhr Morgenfeier im Friedrich-Theater
Ansprache des Herrn Bürgermeister Hesse
Vorträge der Herren Staatsminister a. D. Dr. Müller-Dessau
und Professor Dr. Elbogen-Berlin

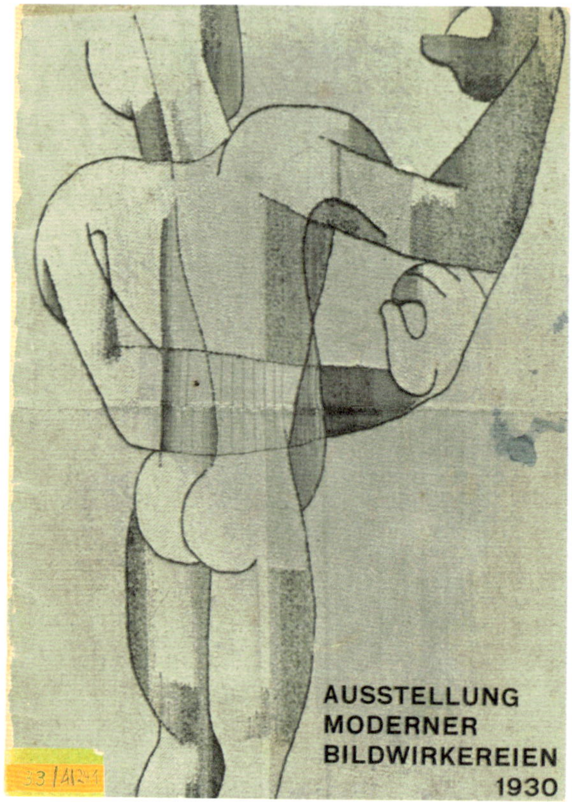

Fig. 2 Draft program for the memorial celebration for Moses Mendelssohn, with Grote's corrections, 1929

Fig. 3 Cover of the *Moderne Bildwirkereien* (Modern Tapestries) catalog, 1929. Cover illustration: Johanna Schütz-Wolff.

of democracy, that is to say, by means of regular tours and lectures, the publication of catalogs and texts of popular scholarship, and the establishment of a reading room for the general public, it should serve as an educational institution. Understanding of and respect for art should be taught by educating the people to see and to develop their taste in the process. An entire program had been prepared to achieve that goal, including evening tours and extended operating hours. In order to reach new groups of visitors, the Volkshochschule (community college), public schools, and the Arbeiterbildungsverein (Association for Workers' Education) would work together with the Anhaltischer Kunstverein to present regional artists. The goal was a cultural center for public education that would build a bridge between scholarship and the life of the people. Grote's hanging in the Gemäldegalerie appears to have been inspired by Ludwig Justi, the director of the Nationalgalerie in Berlin. In Dessau, too, the presentation of paintings was limited to the most valuable pieces, leaving the individual objects enough space to have their effect. The hanging was thus independent of the format of the paintings and was arranged in terms of art historical contexts. As had been done in Berlin, Grote had the walls of the exhibition spaces painted in strong colors. Hinnerk Scheper and the wall painting workshop of the Bauhaus handled this task.[8] The interior of the director's apartment, which was located in the same building as the Gemäldegalerie, was decorated by the Bauhaus furniture workshop.[9]

The move of the Bauhaus to Dessau, which Grote famously helped make happen, was also a lucky stroke for Grote himself. His understanding of modernity was very closely tied to his reception of the Bauhaus idea. His focus was on the painting of the avant-garde school. In 1926 he co-organized with the Kunstverein Wassily Kandinsky's first exhibition in Dessau.[10] A year earlier, surely also at Grote's instigation and with funding from the Free State of Anhalt, Kandinsky's watercolor *Schwere Fläche* (Heavy Plane) had been purchased for 440 reichsmarks and transferred to the collection of the Anhaltische Gemäldegalerie (fig. 1).[11] In addition, in conjunction with the opening of the Anhaltische Gemäldegalerie, the Kunstverein presented in its spaces in the Gemäldegalerie building an exhibition of works by the Bauhaus artists Kandinsky, Lyonel Feininger, Paul Klee, and László Moholy-Nagy, presented together with works by local artists such as Wilhelm Krause, Karl Triebel, Adolf Schweitzer, Bernhard Fiedler, Paul Riess, and Paul Jünemann. The art historian Wilhelm van Kempen was surely summing up Grote's didactic objective when he remarked of this exhibition: "anyone who believes that older, that is, Impressionist art would never be compatible with modern, abstract art would see here how surprisingly exquisitely Riess stands alongside Feininger and Moholy—all the best is found in each and every work."[12]

In 1928 Grote acquired for the City of Dessau Kandinsky's painting *Drei Klänge* (Three Sounds) from the Galerie Neue Kunst Fides in Dresden. Before doing so, he had argued in a letter to Mayor Hesse that the painting should be acquired: "In its quality and stately poise, it meets the demands that must be made of a work to be displayed in a public collection."[13] This clearly expresses Grote's goal of building a collection of contemporary art and presenting it in the Gemäldegalerie's permanent exhibition. Maud Grote also tells of this plan in the biography of her husband that she wrote.[14] She also emphasizes that Grote wanted to create a department specifically dedicated to the Bauhaus masters. This can be confirmed by looking at the list of his acquisitions, which includes not only Kandinsky but also Feininger, Klee, and Oskar Schlemmer. In addition, he acquired all four Bauhaus portfolios,[15] as well as works by the Bauhaus students Alexander Schawinsky and Fritz Winter.[16] This list also includes names such as Alexej von Jawlensky, Alfred Kubin, and Emil Nolde. The circle of artists of the graphic works acquired is larger and more heterogeneous, including, for example, sheets by Oskar Kokoschka, Max Pechstein, Lovis Corinth, and Heinrich Campendonk.[17]

The year 1929 was an especially productive one for Grote. Once again through the Galerie Neue Kunst Fides, he acquired the painting *Gelbe Dorfkirche* (Yellow Village Church) by Lyonel Feininger[18] and the painting *Märchen* (Fairy Tale) by Klee. Both artists exhibited at the Kunstverein that same year.[19] In addition, in 1929 there were also exhibitions by Bernhard Fiedler, Otto Dill, Käthe Kollwitz, and the annual exhibition of Dessau artists.[20] Grote curated for the Anhaltische Gemäldegalerie a special exhibition of cultural history on the occasion of the two hundredth anniversary of the Dessau-born philosopher Moses Mendelssohn, for which he published a small catalog. The exhibition was under the patronage of the Free State of Anhalt, which was organizing a memorial celebration for Mendelssohn. Grote had the invitation cards designed and printed at the Bauhaus as a commission from the State Ministry of Anhalt (fig. 2).[21] That year of exhibitions ended with an especially innovative project conceived as a traveling exhibition: *Moderne Bildwirkereien* (Modern Tapestries). As Grote emphasizes in the catalog's foreword, Gunta Stölzl and Anni Albers made essential contributions to its organization.[22] It showed fifty-nine artists, including Ernst Ludwig Kirchner, Karl Schmidt-Rottluff, Fernand Léger, Jean Arp, Ida Kerkovius, Gunta Stölzl, Emil Hartwig, and Johanna Schütz-Wolff. In an article in the journal *Die Form*, Grote emphasized the autonomy of modern tapestries in contrast to painting. The use of new materials in weaving was said to result in new possibilities of expression. Emil Hartwig, a student in the Bauhaus weaving workshop, was also in the exhibition. Grote emphasized the works of Johanna Schütz-Wolff for their artist quality. Her *Männerakt* (Male Nude) is, in his opinion, her "most mature achievement, which can stand alongside works by Schlemmer and Baumeister."[23] His high esteem for this work is also evident from the fact that Grote had it illustrated on the cover of the catalog (fig. 3). The exhibition subsequently traveled to several German cities, including Essen, Leipzig, Berlin, and Munich. It is remarkable that Grote was so strongly advocating tapestries as an autonomous art form, since they are usually regarded more as craft works, and also presented the achievements of women and men but also of students as equals.

That Grote was prepared to dedicate himself not only to new themes in art but also to new forms for communicating them was also clear from a two-page organization plan for an exhibition at the Anhaltische Gemäldegalerie, which is also dated 1929–30 (figs. 4, 5). This plan offers an overview of several contemporaneous painting styles that can be traced back to the historical model of Rembrandt's

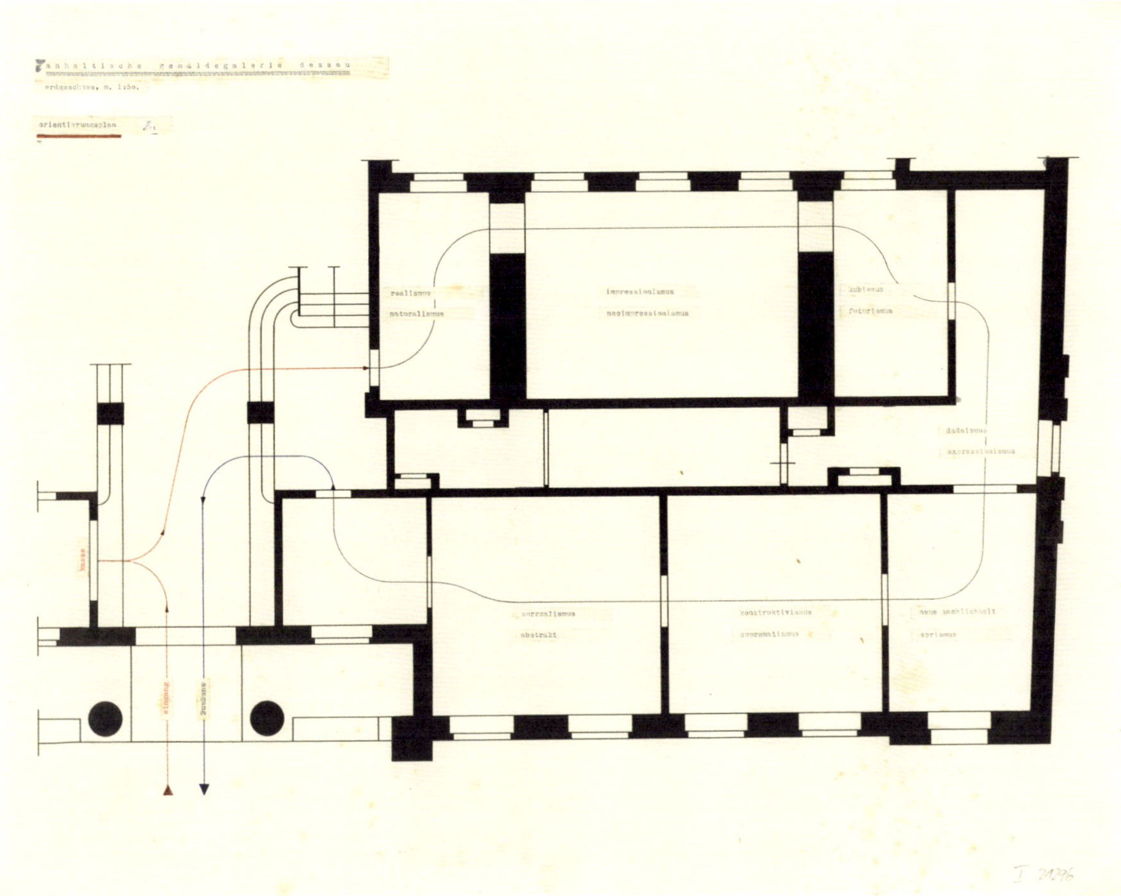

Fig. 4 Eduard Ludwig, “Orientierungsplan” (Orientation Plan) for the Anhaltische Gemäldegalerie, 1929–30

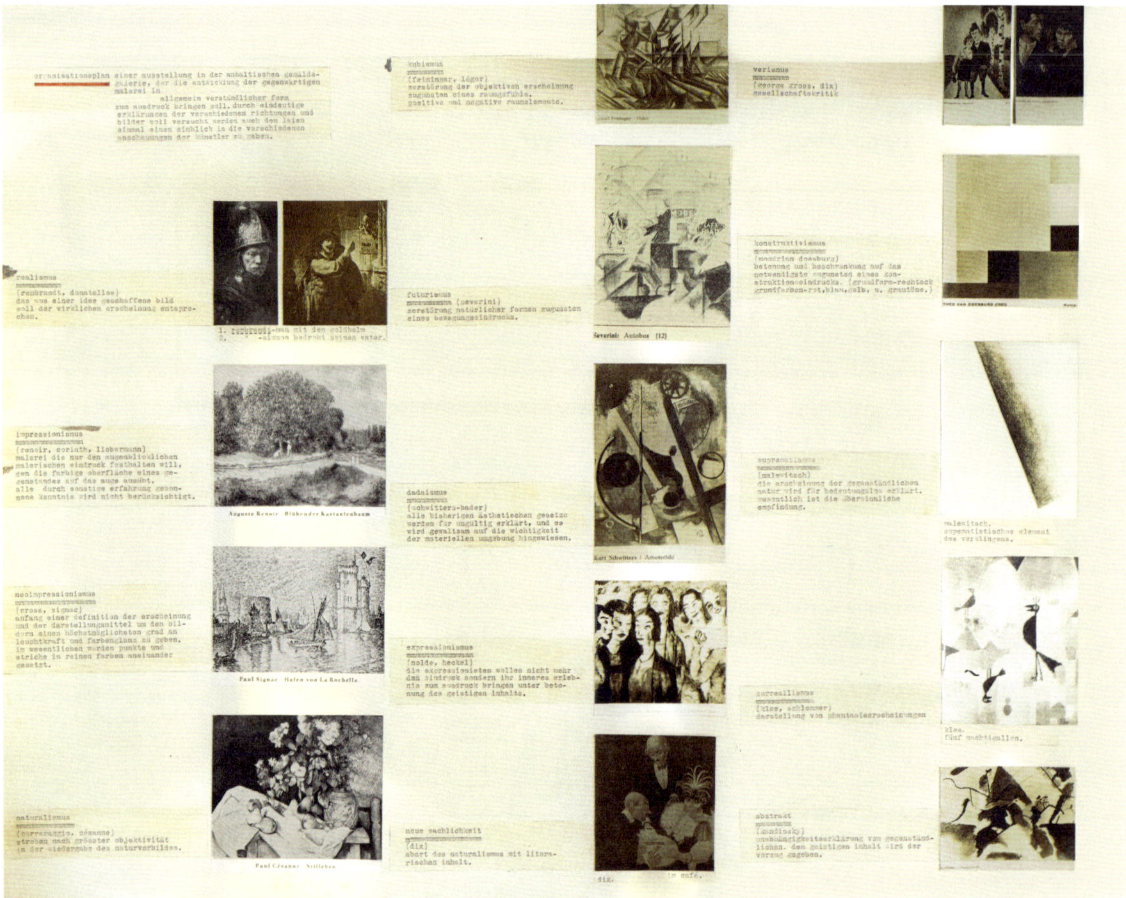

Fig. 5 Eduard Ludwig, "Organisationsplan einer Ausstellung" (Organization Plan of an Exhibition) for the Anhaltische Gemäldegalerie, 1929–30

realistic painting. On the second page is the note: "orientation plan of an exhibition at the anhaltische gemäldegalerie that is intended to express the evolution of contemporary painting in a universally intelligible form. clear explanations of the different directions and paintings are intended to offer even the layperson an overview of artists' differing views." Accordingly, after Rembrandt the subsequent rooms were to exhibit Impressionism, Neoimpressionism, Naturalism, and so on. The three stars of Bauhaus painting were also represented: Feininger stood for Cubism, Klee for Surrealism, and Kandinsky for the "abstract." Two isms were to be shown in each room.[24]

In addition to this energetic exhibition activity, Grote also produced numerous publications in his role as Landeskonservator in 1929, including the first comprehensive cultural history of Anhalt, titled *Das Land Anhalt*. The book ended with the chapter "Die Neuzeit" (The Modern Era), in which Grote addressed industrial architecture and the Bauhaus. He concludes with this assessment: "The tired cultural pessimism of the turn of the century, which diagnosed the inner conflict of modern civilization from the unity of ancient cultures, can be contrasted with the faith in the present and the future. [...] A new style is emerging; despite the oppressive antitheses and battles of the day, the internal connections that form the basis of any style must already be more solid than it seems to us."[25] This optimism was already out the window just three years later: in 1932, the National Socialist Party of Germany achieved majorities in both the Free State of Anhalt and in the Gemeinderat (Municipal Council) of Dessau. That resulted in a radical break with the cultural policy up to that point, with the consequence that the Bauhaus Dessau was closed and, in the following year, that Grote was dismissed as Landeskonservator and director of the Anhaltische Gemäldegalerie.[26] At the beginning of this period of upheaval, Grote was still hoping to take up a role as mediator and to harmonize his view of art with the new, by no means yet statically fixed view of art of the National Socialists. He was not alone in that hope at the time; Ludwig Thormaehlen, a colleague of the director of the Nationalgalerie in Berlin, Ludwig Justi, tried to pave modernity's way into the National Socialist ideology of culture.[27] Grote had begun the exhibition year of 1932 at the Kunstverein with a solo exhibition on Karl Schmidt-Rottluff, which he saw as connected to the earlier exhibitions on Emil Nolde and Erich Heckel.[28] He was, however, already prevented from carrying out his plan to acquire a painting by Schmidt-Rottluff in that context.[29] At the Gemäldegalerie, Grote organized in parallel two successful exhibitions on cultural history: on the occasion of the celebration of the hundred anniversary of the death of Johann Wolfgang von Goethe[30] and at the end of the year an exhibition on Anhalt during the Thirty Years' War for the three hundredth anniversary of the death of King Gustav Adolf of Sweden.

Grote's final exhibition there was a last attempt to present his understanding of art and to offer it to the new system taking shape without abandoning his own positions but at best contributing them. It was a joint exhibition with the Kunsthalle Mannheim and its director, Gustav Friedrich Hartlaub.[31] Grote and Hartlaub had been in closer contact since 1925 at the latest. The exhibition *Neue Sachlichkeit: Deutsche Malerei seit dem Expressionismus* (New Objectivity: German Painting since

Expressionism) that Hartlaub curated was shown at the Kunsthalle Mannheim and then went on tour. In 1926 Hartlaub and Grote discussed the selection of artists in their correspondence. Hartlaub wanted Nolte, Nolde, Heckel, and Feininger to participate so as not to present too one-sidedly the artists who imitated the Romantics in a somewhat old-fashioned way.[32] With regard to the title, Grote argued for the use of the term *Heimat* (homeland) and pointed out that a Romantic touch was inevitable, since it was inherited trait of the Germans to view their landscape romantically. Hartlaub strictly rejected this opinion, because he feared being associated too closely with *Heimatkunst* (homeland art). Only a few days ahead of the opening of the exhibition in Mannheim, the first venue, the directors agreed on the title *Mannheim-Dessauer Wanderausstellung: Deutsche Provinz (erster Teil), Beschauliche Sachlichkeit* (Mannheim-Dessau Traveling Exhibition: German Province, Part One: Contemplative Objectivity). The title triggered protest from the participating artists. On February 2, 1933, Grote wrote Hartlaub: “It is, after all, our duty as museum directors to show all of the available movements to the extent they possess artistic quality. I see with increasing clarity how necessary our enterprise is, and how necessary it is to express our intentions clearly in the catalog so that minds are not confused by it. Above all things, it has to be prevented that the exhibition is seen as conditioned by fashion.”[33] In their catalog, the two curators tried to treat the developments in painting of Neue Sachlichkeit in a politically neutral way and observed “that in addition to the linear-graphic idyllic quality (if one may call it that) coming from so-called Neue Sachlichkeit, the old painter Impressionism has been brought out visibly again today.”[34] The exhibition received overwhelmingly bad reviews, and Hartlaub himself concluded that the level of most of the artists was poor. It was, however, well received in National Socialist circles, as Hartlaub reported. Nevertheless, he was dismissed as director in Mannheim at the end of March 1933. In March and April, the exhibition could be seen in Dessau under an altered title: *Neue Wege zur Heimat* (New Paths to Homeland). For Grote too, however, that exhibition ended with his dismissal from the civil service. The *Anhaltischen Staatsanzeiger* of May 30, 1933, read: “Landeskonservator Dr. Grote has been permanently retired at his request.”[35] The exhibition nevertheless went on its planned tour to several German cities. In the end, it did indeed correspond to the new cultural policy of the National Socialists, however much Grote and Hartlaub struggled against that in their written statements. But it illustrates how broadly Grote had put himself forward in his work as state curator, director of the Anhaltische Gemäldegalerie, and artistic director of the Kunstverein—to the limit of what he could still advocate. In the process, he revealed himself to be a practicing advocate of the museum reform movement who was concerned with broad dissemination and with cultural education as popular education. Debate on contemporaneous positions, especially with that of the Bauhaus in his town, was necessarily part of that. One only does justice to Grote if his exhibitions on modernism are viewed in the context of his overall work. Old masters at the Gemäldegalerie, new masters at the Kunstverein, and both together under the roof of the gallery was a concept that was important to him, so that even after World War II he took it up again in his post as director of the

Germanisches Nationalmuseum in Nuremberg: alongside the gallery, he was also, in accordance with his express wish, director of the Fränkische Galerie, which exhibited contemporary art.

1 Paul Frankl to the chairman of the board of the Joachim-Ernst-Stiftung, 6 November 1922, Stadtarchiv Dessau-Rosslau, Angelegenheiten des Bürgermeisters als Mitglied des Kuratoriums der Joachim-Ernst-Stiftung (Kulturstiftung), fol. 188.
2 See Norbert Michels, ed., *Verrat an der Moderne: Die Gründungsgeschichte und das erste Jahrzehnt der Anhaltischen Gemäldegalerie Dessau, 1927–37*, exh. cat. (Dessau: Anhaltische Gemäldegalerie, 1996); on the connections to the Joachim-Ernst-Stiftung, see also Ingo Pfeiffer, "Die herzoglichen Kunstsammlungen in Dessau nach 1918," *Mitteilungen des Vereins für Anhaltische Landeskunde* 23 (2014): 31–41.
3 The Joachim-Ernst-Stiftung had been founded in anticipation of the "dissolution of the property" of the former house of the Duke of Anhalt in accordance with the constitution of the Weimar Republic; see Fabian Schubert, *100 Jahre Kulturstiftung Dessau-Wörlitz: Eine Chronik*, Kataloge und Schriften der Kulturstiftung Dessau-Wörlitz 41 (Dessau-Rosslau: Kulturstiftung Dessau-Wörlitz, 2019); for more precise details of the founding of the Anhaltische Gemäldegalerie, see Michels, *Verrat an der Moderne* (see note 2).
4 The Amalienstiftung was a testamentary trust of Princess Henriette Amalie von Anhalt-Dessau, who had been dedicated to poverty relief in Dessau. In addition to property holdings, the foundation also had the princess's extensive art collection; see Norbert Michels, ed., *Sammlerin und Stifterin Henriette Amalie von Anhalt-Dessau und ihr Frankfurter Exil* (Frankfurt am Main: Haus Giersch, 2002).
5 See Fritz Hesse, *Von der Residenz zur Bauhausstadt*, vol. 1, *Erinnerungen an Dessau* (Bonn: the author, 1990), 164–65.
6 See Pfeiffer, "Die herzoglichen Kunstsammlungen" (see note 2), 38. The paintings were intended to be transferred to the Gemäldegalerie as permanent loans.
7 See Michels, *Verrat an der Moderne* (see note 2), 32–49; and Helga Heise, "Die ersten Jahre der Anhaltischen Gemäldegalerie," in ibid., 51–79.
8 Scheper was also commissioned to paint the exhibition spaces of the gallery's branch in the Schloss Oranienbaum; see the essay by Elisabeth Kremer in the present volume.
9 See figure 2 in the essay by Elisabeth Kremer in the present volume.
10 See "Anhaltischer Kunstverein: Ausstellung Malklasse Kandinsky," *Volksblatt für Anhalt*, in Ludwig Grote, *Das Land Anhalt* (1929; repr., Halle: Waldersee, 2008). Grote was also able to persuade Kandinsky to join the Kunstverein.
11 See Heise, "Die ersten Jahre der Anhaltischen Gemäldegalerie" (see note 7), 72; the watercolor escaped being confiscated by the National Socialists during the Entartete Kunst (Degenerate Art) action and is still in the collection of the Anhaltische Gemäldegalerie. Grote had an annual acquisitions budget of 18,000 reichsmarks; 10,000 reichsmarks came from the State Ministry of Anhalt and 8,000 reichsmarks from the City of Dessau. The acquisitions budget from the city was used primarily to acquire works of modern painting; the Free State of Anhalt seems to have been more conservative in this respect. Grote used the funds from the Free State of Anhalt primarily to acquire German painting of the nineteenth century; see ibid., 62.
12 Wilhelm van Kempen, "Die Anhaltische Gemäldegalerie," *Dessauer Zeitung*, no. 218 (September 17, 1927): 3–4.
13 Stadtarchiv Dessau-Rosslau, Magistratsakte "Anhaltische Gemäldegalerie" A 1.2-25, fol. 296.
14 See Gertrud Maud Grote, "Lebenserinnerungen und biografische Aufzeichnungen zu Ludwig Grote (ca. 1910–1990)," typescript with handwritten notes, February 23, 1980, and 1990, GNM, DKA, NL Grote, Ludwig, ASS 2.
15 See Hans Maria Wingler, *Die Mappenwerke "Neue Europäische Graphik"* (Berlin: Kupferberg, 1965).
16 The purchases were made in 1928 for the gallery's watercolor collection. *Marin* (Marine) by Alexander Schawinsky was purchased for 200 reichsmarks; and *Das rote Pferd* (The Red Horse) and *Das blonde Mädchen* (The Blonde Girl) by Fritz Winter for 100 reichsmarks each.
17 See Michels, *Verrat an der Moderne* (see note 2), 120–21.
18 The price was 7,000 reichsmarks, from which the artist received only 1,705 reichsmarks after the gallery commission was deducted, because the remainder was collected by the Magistrat (Municipal Administration) of the City of Dessau for outstanding rental payments on his apartment in the Masters' House; see Heise, "Die ersten Jahre der Anhaltischen Gemäldegalerie" (see note 7), 68.
19 See the list in Michels, *Verrat an der Moderne* (see note 2), 118.
20 See ibid.
21 See ibid., 73.
22 See Ludwig Grote, ed., *Moderne Bildwirkereien*, exh. cat. (Dessau: Anhaltische Gemäldegalerie, 1930).
23 See Ludwig Grote, "Moderne Bildwirkereien," *Die Form: Zeitschrift für gestaltende Arbeit* 5, no. 10 (1930): 256–62, esp. 262.
24 Proof has yet to be found that this exhibition ever took place. Eduard Ludwig, a Bauhaus student, was responsible for the graphic design.
25 Grote, *Das Land Anhalt* (see note 10), 226.
26 See the essays by Elisabeth Kremer and Christian Eger in the present volume.
27 The phase of transition to an unambiguously ideologically clear program of National Socialist cultural policy and museum work was still ongoing even in 1934, so that artists such as Ernst Barlach, Erich Heckel, Emil Nolde, and Ludwig Mies van der Rohe signed a "call for fidelity to the Führer" in order to be able to continue working unhindered. See Margit Schermuck-Ziesché, "Die Anhaltische Gemäldegalerie in der Zeit des Nationalsozialismus," in Michels, *Verrat an der Moderne* (see note 2), 91–93.
28 The organization of the exhibition is well documented in surviving archival materials, including the correspondence between Grote and Schmidt-Rottluff, in the archive of the Kulturstiftung Dessau-Wörlitz under the title "Akten des Anhaltischen Landeskonservators zu Dessau betreffend Ausstellungen des Anhaltischen Kunstvereins, Angefangen 1931 / Geschlossen 1932."
29 See Reinhard Melzer, "'Für das rätselhafte Jahr 1932 alles Gute wünschen': Zwei Ausstellungen von Ludwig Grote in der Dessauer Krisenzeit 1931/1933 nach Auffindung zweier Akten," *Mitteilungen des Vereins für Anhaltische Landeskunde* 27 (2018): 57–80, esp. 60.
30 This exhibition had 5,000 visitors, according to the retrospective article "Anhalt im 30 jährigen Kriege," *Die Weltkunst*, no. 46 (November 13, 1932).
31 On Hartlaub, see Ulrike Wendland, *Biographisches Handbuch deutschsprachiger Kunsthistoriker im Exil: Leben und Werk der unter dem Nationalsozialismus verfolgten und vertriebenen Wissenschaftler*, part 1 (A–K) (Munich: Saur, 1999), 261–66. The preparation and realization of the exhibition is documented in the archive of the Kulturstiftung Dessau-Wörlitz.
32 On what follows, see ibid.
33 Quoted in ibid., fols. 74ff.
34 Quoted in ibid., fol. 44.
35 Quoted in Heise, "Die ersten Jahre" (see note 7), 78.

Opening Speech of the Exhibition *Young Bauhaus Painters* (1928)

Ludwig Grote

Transcript of the manuscript "Speech by Ludwig Grote on the Occasion of the Opening of the Young Bauhaus Painters Exhibition in Halle an der Saale,"(1928), GNM, DKA, NL, Grote, 1368.

The central task of modern architecture is *to liberate the forces of life*—only to the extent that it does is it more than a daily whim and fashion. Modern spaces begin to make sense when they are no longer seen as already per se an *interior decoration* designed without relationship to the human being but when one *lives* in them, when a *human being* moves within them.

The integration of human beings does not by any means happen exclusively in the technical, organizational sense: their forms, their *gestalt*, take on a particularly intense sculptural energy. And not just the human being but every *organic* being: flower, fruit, or work of art in the new spaces brings the irrational quality of that which is created from life to its impressive unfolding. Now, when they no longer have to struggle for their *mere validity* in an ornamental-decorative structure, the organisms reveal the particularity of their gestalt, the unity in the diversity of their forms, and hence their essence in general.

Why these words at the opening of an exhibition of young Bauhaus painters? They are intended to counter a one-sided assessment of the work of the Bauhaus based on forms of outward appearance, based on contemporary and propagandistic catchwords, even when they are issued by the Bauhaus itself as the watchword of the day.
Anyone who sees in the Bauhaus only the technical research institute and the workshops for developing standardized equipment sees only the outward—the center of its life rests *in the human being*, to which all work refers: the human being taken as a whole with body, soul and spirit.
Art at the Bauhaus is by no means a phenomenon in reaction to the machine for living in, to functionality in general; it is a driving force; it is the source of all design work.

The paintings by young Bauhaus people that you see before you are thus not daisies that have grown sparsely in the cracks in a concrete post or in a leaky flat roof!

It would go entirely without saying that the first years in Dessau, that had to fulfill and preserve the ideas of Weimar claimed quite exclusively the forces of everyone, so that free artistic creativity receded during that period.

And who would not understand that the *abuse* committed with the words *"Art and soul,"* which were *bashfully avoided*, even mocked, at the Bauhaus.

"The school had best keep quiet about genius; it had best keep a respectful distance. The school had best lock up the secret and guard it well," says Paul Klee. The great X, that which turns *art* into *art*, cannot be the subject of teaching. But it is indeed possible to reveal and study analytically the *elements* of art—and their knowledge may expose the sources of artistic design—*that is* the extraordinary effect of the preliminary course at the Bauhaus with the teaching of Klee, Kandinsky, and Albers.

Free artistic creation, painting especially, is seen at the Bauhaus as the most personal opportunity of a few individuals. Apart from the masters, no one lives *only* from painting. All of the others among those whose paintings are shown here have to be active in a workshop at the same time. This healthy obligation prevents the emergence of "little Kandinskys & Klees," of an artistic proletariat in general. Mistrust of every gesture of genius confronts everyone repeatedly with the question whether what they are painting has an inner justification.

I believe that this constant self-criticism *and* the knowledge of theoretical foundation of art lends all the works a character that is so honest and serious.
Searching for commonalities in this crowd which at first glance seems so diverse, one finds it in the stance toward *purely painterly* problems. It is a shame for youth to be obliged to their teachers and masters—here they *truly grapple* with their role models and do not simply copy their style.

Since Manet and Cézanne, European painting, to the extent it is *painting* and not *representation*, has been working to develop the *new sense of space* and has thus prepared the way for modern architecture. *Renaissance* space, which was national and static, has been smashed. Forms and colors are not tied together on the picture plane into an irrational, mysteriously vibrating, floating, tension-filled dynamic space.

It is well known how each of the four great Bauhaus masters is grappling with this central problem of modern painting, and which pioneering work each of them has achieved in that. Out of the new, boundless, profound sense of space, new tasks are set for painting technique and it is given new meaning.

Paul Klee, especially, has made unheard-of artistic discoveries that lead into the depths of the soul, where the common roots of all art lie. He has developed the tensions and vibrations of previously unused grounds, new forms of surface treatment, into the supreme refinement of pictorial structures. Who before him knew how spatially deep the weave of a canvas can be or how loose and easy and expressive a delicate brushstroke?
We see the young painters basing themselves on his achievements. On the foundation of this grammar, the most diverse emotions find expression—it does not matter at all how much the *representational* is connected to artistic questions.

With casual shades of watercolor and dabs, *Lou Scheper* narrates brief stories, dreams of theatrical plays, and wonderful esoteric adventures.—In *Fritz Winter*, Expressionism, which has already been declared dead, celebrates a kind of resurrection. In darkly glowing shades and enormous figures from primeval times, the world of mines and blast furnaces, which Fritz Winter experienced in the arduous work of his first years of apprenticeship, breaks through. We see how he sets off on voyages of discovery in search of new structural effects, how he grasps color as mass, how he inscribes into it or digs or rubs the forms out of it.

Röseler works more abstractly. The representational still shines through, but it merely provides the elements for the composition. Röseler loves the *cool* shades that he stretches out in large, flawless surfaces, to which he assigns, as charming contrasts, roughed-up opaqueness. From Feininger he adopts the eternally beautiful theme of sailing ships, but he seeks to design it in his own way. The great French Cubists Picasso and Braque are also in the background in his work.

Schawinsky's paintings breathe the air of the theater & circus, white and red against lightning blue, the corporeal, including classicistic architecture, seems—despite the meticulous technique with which the cornices and moldings are drawn—unreal, strange against the deep backgrounds. Searching for analogies, one finds them perhaps in Chirico and Italian Neoclassicism, but Schawinsky is really indebted to *Oscar Schlemmer*, who continues the line of Hans von Marées in German art. In Schawinsky, everything is *skilled*. He is absolutely certain in the master of his means. The new attitude toward spaces makes everything representational *easy*; it shines, rings, peels, dances as if to jazz music. *The stage* is both the result and the subject matter of his paintings.

I want to restrict myself to these four names. With their common origin, they are diverse enough to bear witness to the *un*dogmatic attitude of the Bauhaus. Just how rich in tensions the world of the Bauhaus is, is demonstrated by the Poles Schawinsky and Fritz Winter: the latter most intimately tied to "Romanticism," the former a theater person who aims at effect.
Despite their young age around *twenty*, all of them possess a confident craft ability and at the same time a great talent. Even someone who is not positively inclined to abstract painting has to recognize the conscientiousness and sense of artistic responsibility of which every painting speaks.

For all those who follow the overall artistic situation of our time, the exhibition will be meaningful and revealing at once, because it shows the new dawn of young artists who are not throwing themselves into the arts of the so heavily promoted New Objectivity. The terrain of abstract painting is far from being completely explored, and its discoverers are not isolated as special cases, as the art critics would have us believe. After the ebbing of the Expressionist storm tide, modern painting is not enjoying any particular sympathies at all on the art market and in the journals dependent on it.

This exhibition shows that young people absolutely do not wish to devote themselves to the ethics of the wretchedness of New Objectivity and to philistine magical realism. It is, however, equally far removed from expressionistically revolutionary bohemianism.

This art wants order and law—wants design!

Fig. 1 Hannes Meyer (left) and the Bauhaus student Erich Consemüller, 1928

"It's not working with Hannes Meyer any longer": Ludwig Grote's Role in the Dismissal of the Second Director of the Bauhaus

Peter Bernhard

On May 13, 1930,
Ludwig Grote wrote to Walter Gropius:

"Dear Mr. Gropius,
The enclosed lead article from the *Anhalter Anzeiger* will inform you sufficiently about the long-anticipated crisis at the Bauhaus. The position of Hannes Meyer on these proceedings is confused and unclear. He cannot, in any case, be declared innocent of having encouraged this development out of his inner inclination to the concerns of the Communists and his pedagogical ideal—which, of course, having actively participated in it in any way. What is bad for us is not the fact of radicalization of these young people as such but rather that they have devoted themselves to the bleakest party communism and without intentions of building are seeking purely destructive tendencies. It has even gone so far that that people are following the slogans and confusions of outsiders and not sparing the internal structure of the Bauhaus. In the communist newspaper *Die Tribüne*, an article against Kandinsky and Klee was published that was very offensive and denied them the right to exist at the Bauhaus. The resolutions of the student assembly, which are aimed above all at Albers, are similar. One notices the intention of removing all of the masters who are not unquestioned party communists. Although Hannes Meyer himself has also been attacked, he does not put up any resistance to the students because deep inside he shares their view and would like it most if all the old Bauhaus masters were gone so he can finally build the institute in accordance with his intensions. He admitted and confessed that in a discussion with Hesse and me.

The students are truly dominated by the Communist cell. For 150, around 40 are party members, almost 70% of the others sympathize with them. The preliminary course has very quickly become radicalized; already at the beginning of the class, he wrote resolutions against the class.

I believe I have described the situation reasonably clearly for you here. Hesse is now very much inclined and willing to intervene; he has to do so if only because of public opinion. Yet he doesn't want to do it without your advice and consequently asked me first to inform you and then ask you for a conversation as soon as possible after your return from Paris.

It would be about two questions. First, how should and can one repress this politicization within the Bauhaus without good energies getting lost and while avoiding a general exodus.

But then the question of successorship has to be discussed. It's not working with Hannes Meyer any longer; the resistance to him as a person is growing within the Council of Masters more and more. The inner split of H.M. can no longer be concealed forever."[1]

This letter had been preceded by an ever-escalating development.[2] The previous summer, Grote and Gropius had already met to discuss the crisis of the Bauhaus led by Hannes Meyer (fig. 1). The cause was Oskar Schlemmer's move to the Kunstakademie (Academy of Art) in Breslau. Shortly before his departure was certain, Schlemmer wrote to Otto Meyer:

"Breslau seems to be going from lukewarm to hot. There is now just one more hurdle to pass (the Prussian Ministry of Culture). Given the mood here, I can only say thank God. I have never felt more alienated from the Bauhaus than now, thanks to Meyer's total failure as a director. [...] The 'executor of the estate,' as he calls himself, will prove its executioner yet. At the moment I have it easy at the Bauhaus, furloughed from theater work because the 'youngsters' are doing a play of their own, a Bauhaus revue intended to express the revolutionary program of the new Bauhaus. Something like this: a soviet republic of the Bauhaus, the 'masters' being capitalist kings who must be deposed and stripped of their privileges ('I'm on my way out!')."[3]

A little later, Grote noted in his diary: "O. Schlemmer to Breslau. Fear collapse of the Bauhaus.[4] Consultations, consultations [*sic*] because of Hannes Meyer.[5] Visit to Gropius for that reason. Doubt about strong design abilities of H.M. / Kandinsky, *Klee* for H. Meyer[6] / Calling off of all actions against H.M. From the outset, I called for a self-purge, not an intervention from outside."[7] The calm that then returned lasted until March 1 of the following year, when the carnival celebration at the Bauhaus caused local spirits to run high. The two conservative daily newspapers *Anhalter Anzeiger* and *Anhaltische Rundschau* reported "almost in accord that Bauhaus students 'expressed their heartfelt political wishes in dissolute singing of *Communist-Bolshevist* songs and countered those who rightly refused to tolerate this with *insolences, loutishness*, and even threats.'"[8] Although the actual course of events later turned out to be far less spectacular,[9] the atmosphere that had been stirred up in the public as a result made intervention urgently necessary. The Magistrat (Municipal Administration) of Dessau looked into the case, and the Bauhaus set up a disciplinary committee of three masters. As a consequence, the student Naftali Rubinstein was expelled and the Communist cell that had existed at the Bauhaus until then was banned.[10] The measures taken did not, however, have the desired effect,[11] especially with respect to the activities of the Kostufra (Kommunistische Studentenfraktion [Communist Student Faction]),[12] so that ultimately the responsible school authorities of the State of Anhalt also stepped in to warn the Bauhaus administration to take stricter action.[13] Oil could no longer be poured on troubled waters, however, on the contrary: Just four weeks later—highly symbolically, on May 1—a hectographed newspaper was published under the title "schlicht und freudig" (simple and joyful) that named "the 'banned' communists at the bauhaus" as editors. For the conservative press, it was "a dissolute Communist smear sheet to incite Bauhaus students," which showed "that the Communist cell not only continues to exist but merely concludes from the ban that it should advocate all the more actively for Bolshevism."[14] Faced with this, one could only demand "to tackle this Bolshevist herd with all energy, [...] even if the whole Bauhaus blows up in the process!"[15] Similarly imperious notes came from the Sozialdemokratische Partei Deutschland (SPD; Social Democratic Party of Germany) faction of the Gemeinderat (Municipal Council) of Dessau: it must be noted, according to the SPD Stadtverordnete (City Assemblyman) Ludwig Sinsel, that "a *well-organized Communist cell*" was operating at the design school "with the goal of making the Bauhaus a kind of *Communist stronghold* [...]. And to that, however, we Social Democrats say as well: *that cannot and may not be under any circumstances* [...]. Here curing the symptoms no longer has any point, as the 'organ of the banned Communists at the Bauhaus' proves clearly enough. Here the Platonic explanations of the Magistrat are not satisfying either, just as it does not matter that the director of the Bauhaus gullibly and credulously tolerates the political exercises of the Communist students. Here it is necessary rather to *act and energetically take bold action.*"[16]

Helene Nonné-Schmidt, who was a Bauhaus student at this time and the wife of the young master Joost Schmidt, later told Grote about this: "At the time I went to Kmiec,[17] the head of the KPD [Communist Party of Germany] in Dessau, and asked him to bring Hannes M. to his senses, because he was putting the Bauhaus at risk. Answer: 'Hannes Meyer is a fool.' That made it clear to me that the KPD wanted to unscrupulously exploit the members of the Bauhaus, and then I reported it to Schmidtchen, and we decided to alert you."[18] Confirming this, Grote likewise recalled that "Albers and Schmidtchen visited me in my office and explained that they no longer wanted to go along with the activity at the Bauhaus,"[19] which caused him to prompt Dessau's mayor Fritz "Hesse to the crucial discussion with Hannes Meyer."[20] That led to the conversation on May 5 that Hesse later portrayed as follows:

"That afternoon, we turned up unannounced at Hannes Meyer director's office at the Bauhaus. What Hannes Meyer had to offer when discussing the existing complaints sounded feeble and not very convincing. In response to his repeated reassurances that he was constantly striving to prevent a politicization of the Bauhaus, we pointed to the lack of success of those efforts thus far. The discussion, which seemed to be at risk of fizzling out, suddenly escalated dramatically. Dr. Grote, tired of the back and forth of words, swung into a surprise attack. He interrupted Hannes Meyer in the middle of his explanations, and with powerful inner turmoil yelled at him: 'Hannes Meyer, I believe you want to dupe us.' Hannes Meyer recognized immediately where the attack was going and—leaving aside the caution he had sown in all earlier discussions with me—answered with lightning speed: 'Mr. Grote, you know, of course, that I am a scientific Marxist.' With that declaration, it seemed to me the purpose of the discussion had been achieved. Hannes Meyer had himself handed us the key to decoding the unfortunate events at the Bauhaus. A few more noncommittal words were exchanged. Then we said our goodbyes to Hannes Meyer and left his office. 'Hannes Meyer can no longer remain director of the Bauhaus,' I said to Grote on the way home.[21] As much as I admired Hannes Meyer for abandoning the game of hide-and-seek he had been playing until then and confessed—albeit only after a challenge from Dr. Grote—completely openly to the Communist ideology, there could no longer be any doubt that this confession almost automatically excluded him from the directorship of the Bauhaus. Never—that was as clear as day—would the parties that had been supporting the Bauhaus up to that point show the slightest inclination to approve even a penny for a Bauhaus directed by a Communist."[22]

Grote would later remember Meyer's crucial sentence differently. In a lecture at the Bauhaus-Archiv in Darmstadt in January 1963, he explained: "Mayor Hesse and a representative from the school administration of Anhalt[23] [...] had, together with me, a conversation with Hannes Meyer, and then I very brusquely interrupted his long explanations and asked him outright: 'Stop deceiving us! I no longer believe you. Tell me openly what you are planning with the Bauhaus!' And he said straight out, he declared drily: 'I would like to transfer the Bauhaus as a whole to Moscow!'"[24]

After the lecture, there were intense discussions with former members of the Bauhaus,[25] so Grote, wanting Hesse's reassurance, wrote him:

"It is very important to me to speak to you about several questions concerning the Bauhaus, because recently various false accounts about the departure of Hannes Meyer have been circulated. If I remember correctly, a conversation in which you, a representative of the school administration, and I participated brought the decision. I asked H. Meier [*sic*] the question what he was really planning for the Bauhaus, because we no longer wanted to be deceived by him. His answer was that he intended to transfer the Bauhaus as a unit to Moscow. Based on that, you decided to dismiss him without notice. I would be grateful to you if you could let me know whether this account of the process accords with yours."[26]

Hesse responded: "It is correct that the conversation that I had together with you with H.M. at the Bauhaus led to the decision. During it, when challenged by you, he professed himself for the first time a Marxist (that is, Communist) and thus put in an end to his previous hide-and-seek. Nevertheless, however, he did not speak of Moscow."[27] But even thereafter, Grote stuck to his version.[28] In view of that, the question arises how this memory to which the sixty-seven-year-old clung should be evaluated. It can presumably be ruled out that it was Freudian slip resulting from later regret; it was more likely based on his decided anti-Marxism. Perhaps, though, an annoyed Hannes Meyer had indeed said the sentence in jest, and because it was not meant seriously, and was therefore irrelevant, Hesse had forgotten it, but Grote, who did not see it that way, remembered it. The fate of the second director of the Bauhaus was, in any case, sealed after that conversation. From now on, the task was to find a successor, since the change in director should occur without an interim phase and hence an opportunity for the enemies of the Bauhaus to intervene.[29] Grote was once again given the role he had already played in the move of the Bauhaus to Dessau in 1925, namely, in lieu of Hesse, "because too official,"[30] negotiating with possible candidates for this post.[31] Gropius already had one ready. Just three days after Grote's letter, he replied: "all of that seems quite bad to me; the right moment to dial these things down was missed, for which the masters are to blame. I almost fear that it will no longer be possible to convince häseler [*sic*: Otto Haesler], whom, after much reflection, I consider the best, to take over the directorship, but the attempt should be made in any case."[32] When that attempt had definitively failed, Grote wrote to Hesse: "It must be seriously considered whether a renewed appointment of him [Gropius] was a possibility. We would then with one blow be rid of all worries about the internal situation of the institute."[33] But that variation, too, would fail as a result of the desired candidate's refusal.

In June the situation continued to escalate with the publication of a new issue of the Kostufra journal.[34] The right-wing press observed that the "Bolshevization of the Bauhaus Dessau" was taking its inexorable course.[35] Concerned, Hesse wrote to Grote: "On the Bauhaus matter, I spoke to Kandinsky and Albers yesterday.[36] Things are getting ever worse, and I fear that everything will break up if we don't act quickly. Because on July 10 the Bauhaus vacations begin, so the choice of the new director must have been made by then."[37] At nearly the same time, Grote was informed by Albers that now the teacher responsible for technical fields, Friedrich Engemann, was thinking about resigning, shortly before Klee's departure became public,[38] so that the "danger that the whole institute blows up"[39] did indeed seem real.[40] Grote's negotiations with Haesler dragged out, however,[41] and after the latter's rejection Gropius was not able until mid-July to report to Gropius that Ludwig Mies van der Rohe was "in principle prepared" to take over the direction of the Bauhaus.[42] What followed after he agreed was described by Meyer as follows: "on july 29, in a conversation with mayor hesse, to my great surprise, my immediate resignation from my post was suggested; the reason I was given for this demand was literally 'that it was impossible for a marxist to be director of the bauhaus.'"[43] After Meyer had rejected this demand, he had been "dismissed without notice as director of the bauhaus by letter of august 1, 1930 [...] from the magistrat of the city dessau with reference to sec. 626 of the BGB [Bürgerliches Gesetzbuch, the German Civil Code]."[44] Hesse's plan of a seamless change of Bauhaus director had fallen into place. In a press article about Meyer's departure published that same day, Mies van der Rohe was immediately presented as his successor.[45] Meyer had not, however, accepted his termination. Only when Hesse offered him a resolution by a court of arbitration did he resign from his post on August 3, freeing it up, and only with that resignation did Mies van der Rohe accept the director's position offered to him. Not until November 5 did the court of arbitration conclude with the following settlement:

"The City of Dessau has stated that the termination of the contract between the City of Dessau and Hannes Meyer, to take place prior to the expiration of the official period within which notice must be given, has been decided on by a city administration because of its concern for a situation brought on by the abuse of the intellectually political aims of Mr. Meyer for party-political agitation, which would have endangered the continued existence of the Bauhaus.

The arbitration committee recognizes that the City of Dessau with this move has acted in the interest of retaining the Bauhaus, the transfer and continuation of which has to be appreciated as an act of politico-cultural importance. On the other hand, the arbitration committee equally acknowledges the significance of the intellectually political objectives and particularly the architectural theory of Hannes Meyer. It also commends his initiative in submitting his resignation in the interest of the Bauhaus, in order thereby to enable the immediate appointment of a successor and thus serve the continuation of the Bauhaus."[46]

The Kostufra showed solidarity with Meyer after his dismissal.[47] Still in August, the now third issue of the journal appeared, in which serious accusations about those it identified as being behind the intrigues in this affair, Gropius and Kandinsky, already appeared on the front page. It also dedicated two longer articles to the process. They suggested that anticommunism and the conflict over the teaching of conservative ideas of morality were additional reasons for the dismissal. The libertinage at the Bauhaus, to which there were objections from both inside and outside of the school, was not just tolerated but also practiced by Meyer.[48] When he took over the directorship, he insisted that a room in the student dormitory be stipulated in his contract, and he presumably used it frequently.[49] While he was still married (but separated), his liaison with the student Charlotte (known as Lotte) Beese became public in 1928, which became a political issue, so that she had to end her studies and leave Dessau.[50] Immediately thereafter, Meyer brought Margret Mengel and their illegitimate son to Dessau and placed her in charge of the administrative office of the Bauhaus. Shortly thereafter began his relation with Helene (known as Lena) Bergner, whom he would marry in 1931. In the Kostufra's *Bauhaus* journal, under the headline "Aus Budoiren [*sic*] und Amtszimmern" (Out of Boudoirs and Offices), one could read:

"the petit-bourgeois wife of the great artist cannot smell the petit-bourgeois wife of the other great artist, but if an unfortunate person comes between, who does not participate in the petty, sourly moralizing gossip that smells of unaired beds, then they are all united, then woe betide this poor man. this poor man was hannes meyer; these wives are the ladies nina, feininger, lürs [*sic*], grote, and nonne, the appendages of the ditto husbands, of powerful office, etc., the petty atmosphere, mixed of bread, envy, megalomania, and moralistic stuffiness was the birthplace of this big fuss, at least when measured by dessau's scale."[51]

The "ladies" mentioned were Nina Kandinsky; Mira Lührs, wife of the Dessau city councilman Armin Lührs and managing director of the Kreis der Freunde des Bauhauses (Circle of Friends of the Bauhaus); Grote's wife, Maud; and Helene Nonné-Schmidt, who had been married to Joost Schmidt since 1925 and shortly thereafter (on June 16) earned her Bauhaus diploma. Grote's archive contains a sheet with the following typewritten text:

"dear mrs. grote,
we deeply regret having mentioned your name in our journal *bauhaus 3* in connection with the incidents at the bauhaus. this oversight was based on false information. we hereby apologize and ensure you that we have done everything to correct this misunderstanding.
the editorial staff."[52]

Because the name Grote does not appear anywhere else in that issue, the letter clearly refers to the passage above. Moreover, there is a surviving copy of this issue in which "grote" is blackened out in this passage.[53] The issue survives with two different covers (figs. 2 and 3). Both are imitations of issues of the official journal *Bauhaus*: that of the year 1926–27, designed by László Moholy-Nagy, and that of the year 1929, designed by Joost Schmidt. Because the latter's design was already used for issue 2 of the Kostufra journal,[54] it is reasonable to assume that the third issue initially used that design as well. By changing the cover design, Kostufra was perhaps trying to distance itself from Schmidt after his involvement in Meyer's dismissal became known. The only change to the content in the new production of the cover is that "i.a.h." (internationale arbeiter-hilfe, international workers' aid) has been replaced by "rote hilfe" (red aid). The reason for that is not known. It refers to the fact that Meyer had donated money via the Internationale

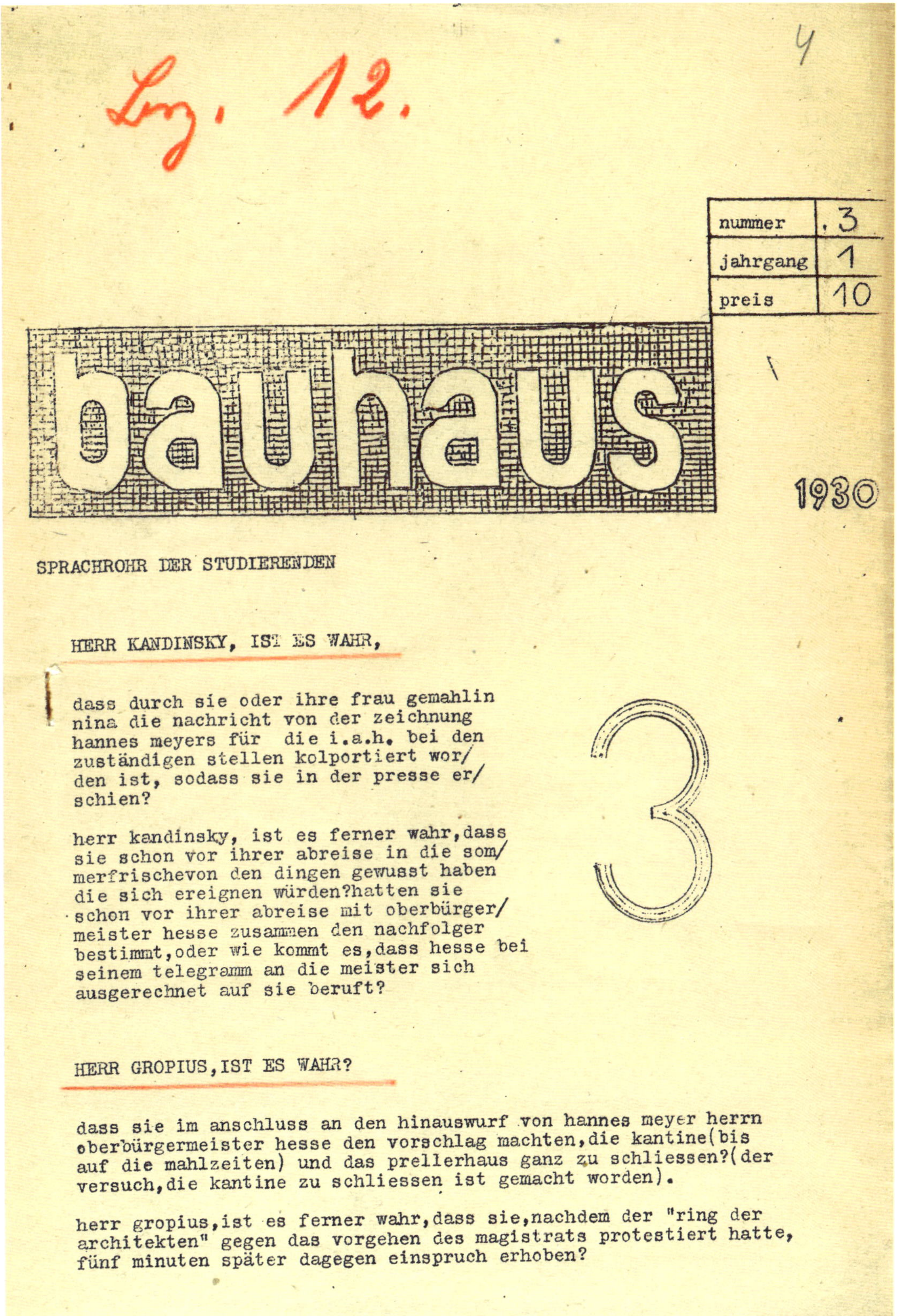

Lrz. 12.

4

nummer	3
jahrgang	1
preis	10

bauhaus

1930

SPRACHROHR DER STUDIERENDEN

HERR KANDINSKY, IST ES WAHR,

dass durch sie oder ihre frau gemahlin
nina die nachricht von der zeichnung
hannes meyers für die i.a.h. bei den
zuständigen stellen kolportiert wor/
den ist, sodass sie in der presse er/
schien?

herr kandinsky, ist es ferner wahr,dass
sie schon vor ihrer abreise in die som/
merfrischevon den dingen gewusst haben
die sich ereignen würden?hatten sie
schon vor ihrer abreise mit oberbürger/
meister hesse zusammen den nachfolger
bestimmt,oder wie kommt es,dass hesse bei
seinem telegramm an die meister sich
ausgerechnet auf sie beruft?

3

HERR GROPIUS,IST ES WAHR?

dass sie im anschluss an den hinauswurf von hannes meyer herrn
oberbürgermeister hesse den vorschlag machten,die kantine(bis
auf die mahlzeiten) und das prellerhaus ganz zu schliessen?(der
versuch,die kantine zu schliessen ist gemacht worden).

herr gropius,ist es ferner wahr,dass sie,nachdem der "ring der
architekten" gegen das vorgehen des magistrats protestiert hatte,
fünf minuten später dagegen einspruch erhoben?

Fig. 2 Front page of issue number 3 of the Kostufra magazine *bauhaus: sprachrohr der studierenden* (mouthpiece of the students), 1930, which is based on Joost Schmidt's design of the cover for the *bauhaus* journal (from 1929). With polemically formulated questions for Kandinsky and Gropius concerning their participation in the "expulsion of Hannes Meyer."

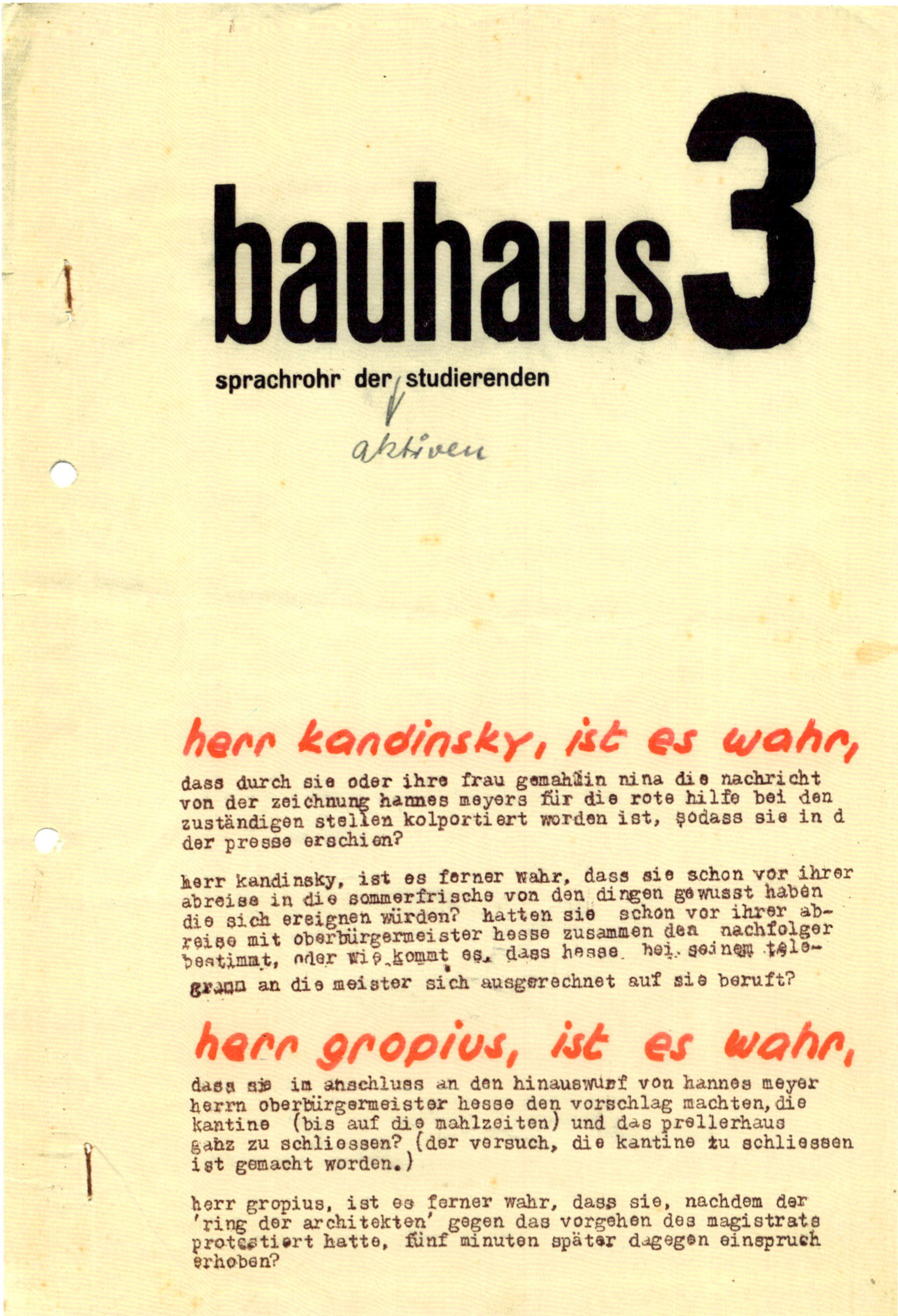

bauhaus 3

sprachrohr der studierenden

aktiven

herr kandinsky, ist es wahr,

dass durch sie oder ihre frau gemahlin nina die nachricht von der zeichnung hannes meyers für die rote hilfe bei den zuständigen stellen kolportiert worden ist, sodass sie in d der presse erschien?

herr kandinsky, ist es ferner wahr, dass sie schon vor ihrer abreise in die sommerfrische von den dingen gewusst haben die sich ereignen würden? hatten sie schon vor ihrer abreise mit oberbürgermeister hesse zusammen den nachfolger bestimmt, oder wie kommt es, dass hesse bei seinem telegramm an die meister sich ausgerechnet auf sie beruft?

herr gropius, ist es wahr,

dass sie im anschluss an den hinauswurf von hannes meyer herrn oberbürgermeister hesse den vorschlag machten, die kantine (bis auf die mahlzeiten) und das prellerhaus ganz zu schliessen? (der versuch, die kantine zu schliessen ist gemacht worden.)

herr gropius, ist es ferner wahr, dass sie, nachdem der 'ring der architekten' gegen das vorgehen des magistrats protestiert hatte, fünf minuten später dagegen einspruch erhoben?

Fig. 3 Front page of issue number 3 of the Kostufra magazine *bauhaus: sprachrohr der studierenden*, 1930, based on László Moholy-Nagy's design of the cover of the bauhaus journal (1926–28). The subtitle "mouthpiece of the students" has been expanded to "mouthpiece of the active students."

Arbeiterhilfe to support the strike at the Mansfeld coal mine organized by the KPD, which not only caused a sensation in the press[55] but was, according to Meyer, the flimsy excuse for his dismissal.[56] Meyer's accusation does not seem very plausible, however. It is, in any case, not mentioned in Hesse's detailed explanation of the firing.[57] It seems more likely, moreover, that the donations of the "Bauhaus Dessau" repeatedly mentioned in the press would have worried Hesse.[58] That is also suggested by a letter from Grote to Hesse after the first donation was revealed, in which he wrote: "In the meanwhile, more stupidities have been committed at the Bauhaus that the [*Anhalter*] *Anzeiger* has, of course, registered. The collection for the Communists in Mansfeld was indeed organized at the Bauhaus. H.M. will say once again: What am I supposed to do to stop it?"[59]

But it was not just Kandinsky and Gropius who became part of the public debate over Meyer's cause; Grote came into its sights as well. One could read in *Berlin am Morgen*, for example: "Naturally, the Landeskonservator of Anhalt, Dr. Grote, was an opponent of Meyer. For what was to become of 'high art' if the students [of the Bauhaus] were assigned the task unworthy of a student to build apartments for the proletariat. It was also this Grote who declared on the occasion of a conflict between Meyer and the loyal but completely floundering [social] democratic mayor Hesse declared: 'Mr. Meyer is duping us. He is a party communist, after all!'"[60] The text was based on an interview with Meyer, but his detailed article about his "being thrown out of the Bauhaus" that was published at almost the same time does not say a word about Grote. Meyer's article was explicitly declared to be an "Open Letter to Lord Mayor Hesse of Dessau," but a few days later a "response from the Kreis der Freunde des Bauhauses was published in the *Volksblatt für Anhalt*—perhaps because Meyer had sent the text to all its members.[61] No author of the response is named, but based on the information it contains it could only be Hesse or Grote, the vice chairman of the association. In view of their close cooperation on this matter, it can be noted in any case that they spoke with one voice here. The response justifies the firing above all from the internal perspective of the school, noting:

"In your open letter in the *Tagebuch*, Mr. Hannes Meyer, you have been open for the first time, you have finally courageously professed your attitude once [...]. Now the masters are finally experiencing your true opinion, how you assess their work at the Bauhaus, now, afterward, you provide the program that has been expected by you for three years. All of the masters, not just the 'individualist sector,' will now recognize that all of the enervating battles and fruitless conflicts within the institution have been [...] a consequence of your 'diplomacy,' your lack of openness. Because all of the masters—not just the 'individualists'—have come to feel the consequences of your system—or, better, your system change."[62]

But he also observes, in a partial concession, albeit with an arrogant undertone: "If we are not to deny your goodwill, we would have to seek the cause of this conflict in your essence."[63] Finally, and, because stated publicly, an especially touchy point—the author takes a position on the political dimension of the proceeding and declares: "And the appointment of Mies van der Rohe also deprives you of the red Bengal light of being the victim of culturally reactionary despotism."[64] When Mies van der Rohe assumed his post, the dismissal of Meyer had indeed come to a good end for Grote; decades later, he would sum it up: Meyer's "successor, Mies van der Rohe, returned art and freedom, which had been suppressed by the dictatorship of Marxist dogmas, to their rights."[65]

1 Ludwig Grote to Walter Gropius, 13 May 1930, draft, GNM, DKA, NL Grote, Ludwig (hereafter NL Grote), 360.
2 For additional details about the dismissal of Hannes Meyer, see Klaus-Jürgen Winkler, *Der Architekt hannes meyer: Anschauungen und Werk* (Berlin [East]: VEB Verlag für Bauwesen, 1989), 124–30; Magdalena Droste, "Unterrichtsstruktur und Werkstattarbeit am Bauhaus unter Hannes Meyer," in Bauhaus-Archiv, Berlin; Deutsches Architekturmuseum, Frankfurt am Main; Institut für Geschichte und Theorie der Architektur an der ETH Zürich, eds., *hannes meyer, 1889–1954: architekt, urbanist, lehrer*, exh. cat. (Berlin: Ernst & Sohn 1989), 134–65, esp. 161–65; and Philipp Oswalt, "Die verschwiegenen Bauhaus-Krisen," in Thomas Flierl and Philipp Oswalt, eds., *Hannes Meyer und das Bauhaus: Im Streit der Deutungen* (Leipzig: Spector, 2018), 247–76, esp. 254–65.
3 Oskar Schlemmer to Otto Meyer, 9 June 1929, in *The Letters and Diaries of Oskar Schlemmer*, ed. Tut Schlemmer (Middletown, CT: Wesleyan University Press, 1972), 244.
4 It is not known precisely how familiar Grote was already at that time about the background details of Schlemmer's departure. In retrospect, in any case, he considered the fact that Hannes Meyer "in association with the [student] activists" was calling for "current, political, contemporary trends" instead of Schlemmer's "stage of types" to be a "rejection of the spirit of the Bauhaus"; Ludwig Grote, "Zum Vortrag 'Von Weimar nach Dessau: Zum Gestaltenwandel des Bauhauses,'" lecture in Darmstadt, January 30, 1963, NL Grote, 998. And it was surely the decree to end the work for the stage that motivated Schlemmer to leave Dessau: "Toward the theater, my special area, he [Meyer] is 'personally' negative; he wants a social and political slant, which rubs me the wrong way," he wrote to Willy Baumeister on April 8, 1929; see *The Letters and Diaries of Oskar Schlemmer* (see note 3), 241–42, esp. 241. In any case, it is not obvious that a progressive Meyer pedagogy would have been too much for Schlemmer, as Oswalt supposes when he writes that Schlemmer reported on it in a "distraught" way; see Philipp Oswalt, "Einleitung," in *Hannes Meyers neue Bauhauslehre: Von Dessau bis Mexiko* (Basel: Birkhäuser, 2019), 9–17, esp. 13, and Oswalt, "Die verschwiegenen Bauhaus-Krisen" (see note 2), 259. If one read the Schlemmer letter he cites in full, it is clear that the artist conveyed it rather with the irony typical of him, paired with some coolness, because at this point he was no longer at the Bauhaus; see Oskar Schlemmer to Otto Meyer, 8 September 1929, in *The Letters and Diaries of Oskar Schlemmer* (see note 3), 247–49; this is already clear in the source cited by Oswalt, which reprinted only part of the letter.
5 The reservations about Meyer that had existed from the beginning were probably not hidden to Grote. Presumably, he was also present when Gropius's departure was announced and Meyer named as his successor, since a colleague, the art historian Sigfried Giedion, gave a guest lecture at the Bauhaus that evening; see Sigfried Giedion, *Walter Gropius* (New York: Dover, 1992), 36–37. The Bauhaus student Fritz Kuhr had then cried out spontaneously: "Hannes Meyer as director of the Bauhaus will be a catastrophe! That is our downfall!"; quoted in Oskar Schlemmer to Tut Schlemmer, February 5, 1928, in *The Letters and Diaries of Oskar Schlemmer* (see note 3), 225; Kuhr's vehement reaction also found its way into Ise Gropius's diary; see Hans M. Wingler, *The Bauhaus, 1919–1933, Weimar, Dessau, Berlin, Chicago*, 2nd ed. (Cambridge, MA: MIT Press, 1981), 136; the Bauhaus student Helene Nonné-Schmidt was also convinced: "Now M.[eyer] is pushing the cart so deep into the muck that no one will be able to pull it out again"; Helene Nonné-Schmidt to Ludwig Grote, 13 April 1965, NL Grote, 811.
6 Klee had probably advocated for Meyer repeatedly. For example, he wrote to Meyer after his dismissal: "at the tempo that you naturally like to adopt, and which further increases the politically risky qualities of your stance, i have seen such an end coming soon for some time now. I was able to contribute to postponing it now and again"; Paul Klee to Hannes Meyer, 8 August 1930, copy, Bundesarchiv Berlin-Lichterfelde, R32/399, fol. 132; Helene Nonné-Schmidt later conjectured about this: "The old gentlemen [Klee and Kandinsky] cared only about the painting class, after all, which had never existed in Gropius's era. H. M. had surely only introduced it—in contradiction to his program—in order to make the old masters well-disposed to him!"; Nonné-Schmidt to Grote, 13 April 1965 (see note 5).
7 Ludwig Grote, "Tagebuchaufzeichnungen," n.d., NL Grote, 31.
8 "Ein Sowjet-Intermezzo am Bauhaus," *Volksblatt für Anhalt*, no. 54 (March 5, 1930); cf. "Das Faschingsfest des Bauhauses," *Anhalter Anzeiger*, no. 52 (March 3, 1930), and [Wilhelm Friedrich] Loeper, "Das Bauhaus-Faschingsfest," *Anhalter Woche*, no. 11 (March 16, 1930).
9 See "Politische Umtriebe am Bauhaus werden nicht geduldet!," *Volksblatt für Anhalt*, no. 73 (March 27, 1930); according to it, a Bauhaus student had cursed just one comrade and, temporally and spatially separate from that, several "Bauhaus members [sang] foreign songs, especially folksongs [...]. The Internationale was sung here as well."
10 See the minutes of the fifth public meeting of the Gemeinderat of Dessau, April 15, 1930, Stadtarchiv Dessau-Rosslau, sign. 3175: V51.
11 The Bauhaus student Annemarie Lange gave a detailed interview on this subject in 1974: Hannes Meyer "was very kindly disposed to the C[ommunist]. P[arty]. Although he had to 'ban' the cell on the orders of the mayor of the city of dessau. That is to say, they just gathered in some apartment for their cell meetings. hannes meyer was one of us"; reprinted in Oswalt, *Hannes Meyers neue Bauhauslehre* (see note 4), 105; and at the end of August 1930 Meyer himself also said "of the banning of the C.P. cell, that it had been done by agreement with its leadership for tactical reasons"; Hannes Meyer to Karel Teige, 29 August 1930, in Bauhaus-Archiv Berlin, *hannes meyer* (see note 2), 178.
12 See Michael Siebenbrodt, "Zur Rolle der Kommunisten und anderer fortschrittlicher Kräfte am Bauhaus," *Wissenschaftliche Zeitschrift der Hochschule für Architektur und Bauwesen Weimar*, no. 23 (1976): 1–11.
13 See senior governmental and school councilor Theodor Blum to Bauhaus director Hannes Meyer, 1 April 1930, NL Grote, 1358. Blum's warnings do not obscure the fact that he was a supporter of the Bauhaus and also of Hannes Meyer, as the latter certainly realized. Meyer thus wanted to call him as an expert before the court of arbitration that was arranged after his dismissal; see Hannes Meyer to the chairman of the court of arbitration, Edwin Redslob, 20 August 1930, in Bauhaus-Archiv, *hannes meyer* (see note 2), 176–78, and after his "departure from dessau" considered it "a special need" to "express gratitude for the great help" he had "as one of the few true friends of the bauhaus" offered him; Hannes Meyer to Theodor Blum, 15 August 1930, NL Konrad Püschel, SBD I 14976 D.
14 Dr. W. A. K., "'schlicht und freudig': Die Wühlarbeit der Kommunisten am Dessauer Bauhaus; Die Monatszeitschrift der 'Verbotenen,'" *Anhalter Anzeiger*, no. 107 (May 7, 1930); this is the lead article mentioned in Grote to Gropius, 13 May 1930 (see note 1).
15 Dr. W. A. K., "'schlicht und freudig' (see note 14).
16 L[udwig] Sinsel, "'Die verbotenen Kommunisten am Bauhaus,'" *Volksblatt für Anhalt*, no. 108 (May 10, 1930). Statements of this kind surely encouraged the view of the Communists that the Social Democrats, led by the president of the Landtag (State Parliament) of Anhalt, Richard Paulick, should be held responsible for Meyer's dismissal; Meyer himself fueled that suspicion; see "Kommunismus 'verboten': Bauhausleiter Hannes Meyer muss gehen," *Die Rote Fahne* (August 3, 1930); "Der Fall Hannes Meyer," *bauhaus: sprachrohr der studierenden* 1, no. 3 (1930): n.p., NL Grote, 1358; Fritz Schiff, "Gespräch mit Hannes Meyer," *Berlin am Morgen*, no. 191 (August 17, 1930): and Hannes Meyer, "Mein Hinauswurf aus dem Bauhaus: Offener Brief an Oberbürgermeister Hesse, Dessau," *Das Tagebuch*, no. 11 (1930): 1307–12, esp. 1309, translated as "My Expulsion from the Bauhaus: An Open Letter to Lord Mayor Hesse of Dessau," in Wingler, *The Bauhaus* (see note 5), 163–65.
17 Paul Kmiec had since 1924 been a Communist member of the Landtag of Anhalt and head of the Dessau subdistrict of the party; see Heinz Eckler, *Paul Kmiec: Leben und Kampf eines Dessauer Kommunisten* (Dessau: n.p., 1986).
18 Nonné-Schmidt to Grote, 13 April 1965 (see note 5); shortly before that, Grote had informed her: "There were a few noisemakers who called themselves Communists without knowing what that meant. In their youthful ignorance, they allowed themselves to be misused by the KPD, which did so very consciously and

unscrupulously. Hannes Meyer was a demagogue"; Helene Nonné-Schmidt to Ludwig Grote, 10 March 1965, NL Grote, 811.

19 Albers was angry at the Bauhaus director in part because of the latter's public criticism of the preliminary course he was teaching. For example, in the catalog of the Bauhaus exhibition in Basel that had been organized by Meyer in 1929 one could read: "the bauhaus student who comes into [the] strictly practical functional workshops [of the bauhaus] can do nothing more urgently than forget the preliminary course in which he was allowed to live for a semester in all innocence and unpunished, so to space, unlimited material and structural fantasies"; the text was written by Ernst Kállai, whom Meyer had brought to the Bauhaus; see the facsimile of the catalog in Flierl and Oswalt, *Hannes Meyer und das Bauhaus* (see note 2), 55–74, esp. 57; on this exhibition, see Dara Kiese, "Hannes Meyers Bauhaus: Die 'Wanderschau,' 1929–30," in *bauhauskommunikation: Innovative Strategien im Umgang mit Medien, interner und externer Öffentlichkeit*, ed. Patrick Rössler (Berlin: Gebr. Mann, 2009), 215–22. Already the previous year, in an essay in the *Bauhaus* journal, Albers had complained that the "sociological parallels" of his course "have not been noted"; Josef Albers, "Teaching form through practice," in *Bauhaus Journal, 1926–1931: Facsimile Edition, with Commentary and English Translation*, ed. Lars Müller, trans. Eva Gaida and Jana Mainel (Zurich: Lars Müller, 2019), 38–39, esp. 38. When Meyer used an excerpt from this text for an advertising prospectus for the Bauhaus, he left this passage out, revealingly, although Albers was speaking in that context of "most important aspect of contemporary interest in forms" (ibid.); cf. the prospectus *junge menschen kommt ans bauhaus!*, facsimile in Flierl and Oswalt, *Hannes Meyer und das Bauhaus* (see note 2), 3–52, esp. 14–15, and Hannes Meyer, "situationsbericht, 1.9.1929," in Bauhaus-Archiv, *hannes meyer* (see note 2), 168–70, esp. 169. So it should not be seen as inconsistent if Kostufra, which had also severely criticized the preliminary course, used a slightly altered quotation from this excerpt to misrepresent Albers's course; see *bauhaus: organ der kommunistischen studierenden am bauhaus: monatsschrift für alle bauhausfragen* 1, no. 2 (June 1930): 6, Stadtarchiv Dessau-Rosslau, Sammlung Bauhaus, SB-98. Oswalt's claim that at the time they sought out Grote, Albers and Schmidt were also afraid their contracts would not be renewed does not correspond to the facts, since their contracts had already been renewed the previous year—very surprisingly, by a bare majority, since two members of the Magistrat had taken the side of the opponents of the Bauhaus, so that from then on Hesse had to keep a close eye on developments at the school; see Oswalt, "Die verschwiegenen Bauhaus-Krisen" (see note 2), 259, and Fritz Hesse, *Erinnerungen an Dessau*, vol. 1, *Von der Residenz zur Bauhausstadt* (Bad Pyrmont: the author, 1963), 242.

20 Ludwig Grote to Helene Nonné-Schmidt, 17 March 1965, NL Grote, 811.

21 Forgács translates incorrectly here and places these words in Grote's mouth (she also gives the wrong date for the talk); see Éva Forgács, "Between the Town and the Gown: On Hannes Meyer's Dismissal from the Bauhaus," *Journal of Design History* 23, no. 3 (2010): 265–74, esp. 265.

22 Hesse, *Erinnerungen* (see note 19), 244.

23 In addition to Hesse and Grote, Blum was present at the conversation.

24 Grote, "Zum Vortrag 'Von Weimar nach Dessau'" (see note 4).

25 See Nonné-Schmidt to Grote, 10 March 1965 (see note 18), and Grote to Nonné-Schmidt, 17 March 1965 (see note 20).

26 Ludwig Grote to Fritz Hesse, 31 October 1963, NL Grote, 351. Shortly thereafter, Hesse sent the first volume of his *Erinnerungen*, which contains the passage cited above, to Grote on 5 December 1962; see Fritz Hesse to Ludwig Grote, 5 December 1963, NL Grote, 351). That same day, Grote described the event with almost identical words in letters to Albers and Nonné-Schmidt as well; see Ludwig Grote to Josef Albers, 31 October 1963, NL Grote, 702, and Ludwig Grote to Helene Nonné-Schmidt, 31 October 1963, NL Grote, 811.

27 Fritz Hesse to Ludwig Grote, 8 November 1963, NL Grote, 351.

28 See Ludwig Grote to Fritz Hesse, 11 January 1964, NL Grote, 351.

29 Hesse was convinced: "the bauhaus without a director, that is an impossible situation, for that would be the end of the institution" (minutes of a discussion between Mayor Fritz Hesse and the student representatives of the Bauhaus, n.d. [early August 1930], Bundesarchiv Berlin-Lichterfelde, R32/399, fols. 135–36, esp. fol. 136; Albers wrote something similar to Grote: Hesse "believes: provisional solution political impossible. So a successor first"; Josef Albers to Ludwig Grote, 17 June 1930, NL Grote, 701. Meyer was also convinced of the necessity of that strategy. So after assuming his post as director, he explained in a talk with the student representatives, who had not been informed in advance: "Before the decision [concerning Gropius's resignation] could be published, a successor had to be chosen. The Bauhaus stood or fell on this point"; Hannes Meyer, "Address to the Student Representatives on the Occasion of His Appointment as Director," in Wingler, *The Bauhaus* (see note 5), 141.

30 Fritz Hesse to Ludwig Grote, 17 June 1930, NL Grote, 351.

31 See, for example, Otto Haesler to Ludwig Grote, 30 June 1930, NL Grote, 775, and Walter Gropius to Ludwig Grote, 17 July 1930, NL Grote, 360; Gropius also recommended Grote for the negotiations with possible candidates for successor; see Albers to Grote, 17 June 1930 (see note 29). On the negotiations for taking over the Bauhaus in 1925, see Peter Bernhard, "The Bauhaus Comes to Dessau," in the present volume.

32 Walter Gropius to Ludwig Grote, 16 May 1930, NL Grote, 360. With regard to the necessity of Meyer's dismissal, to which Grote said there was no alternative, Gropius did not have to be persuaded; he had repeatedly been treated brusquely by his successor from the beginning of the latter's term in office; see Magdalena Droste, "Enterbung des Nachfolgers: Der Konflikt zwischen Hannes Meyer und Walter Gropius," in *Bauhaus Streit, 1919–2009: Kontroversen und Kontrahenten*, ed. Philipp Oswalt (Ostfildern: Hatje Cantz, 2009), 68–84, esp. 77.

33 Ludwig Grote to Fritz Hesse, 10 July 1930, NL Grote, 1358.

34 The journal now appeared at more or less regular intervals; see Wolfgang Paul, "Die politische und ideologische Lage am Bauhaus in den Jahren 1930/31 im Spiegel der kommunistischen Hochschulzeitschrift 'bauhaus,'" *Wissenschaftliche Zeitschrift der Hochschule für Architektur und Bauwesen Weimar* 21, no. 1 (1974): 1–11.

35 See "Die Bolschewisierung des Dessauer Bauhauses," *Anhalter Woche*, no. 26 (June 29, 1930).

36 After Kandinsky had advocated for Meyer a year earlier, according to Grote's diary (see note 7), he had become an enemy of the Bauhaus director by this point. Meyer's support for the students' criticism of Kandinsky's course must surely be seen as one reason; see "Albers +++ Kandinsky +++," *bauhaus: sprachrohr der studierenden* 1, no. 3 (1930): n.p., NL Grote, 1358, and Fritz Hesse to Ludwig Grote, 24 June 1930, NL Grote, 1358. Accordingly, Kandinsky expressed satisfaction after Meyer's dismissal: In March 1931, he wrote to a former student: "In other respects, too, proper work is being done at the House [Bauhaus], and the atmosphere has become healthy again after the forced departure of the former director Hannes Meyer. H. M. wanted to turn the BH into a Marxist school; several students pursued politics so rabidly that the others (by far the majority) could no longer get any work done"; Wassily Kandinsky to Werner Drewes, 15 March 1931, in Kandinsky, *Briefe, Texte, Schriften aus der Zeit am Bauhaus*, ed. Alexander Graeff (Weimar: Weimarer Verlagsgesellschaft, 2016), 42–44, esp. 44.

37 Hesse to Grote, 24 June 1930 (see note 36). Meyer was therefore wrong to assert that his dismissal had been planned "[j]ust when the Bauhaus was closed for the vacation and all my Bauhaus intimates were away"; Meyer, "My Expulsion from the Bauhaus" (see note 16), 165. All but ruling out this supposition, Albers also wrote to Grote in mid-June: "He [Meyer] cannot be permitted to be alone here during the vacation," and cited bad experiences: Edvard Heiberg's "appointment was, it is now clear to us, rigged. Happened during the Easter break. Meisterrat (Council of Masters) presented with faits accomplis"; Anni and Josef Albers to Ludwig Grote, 20 June 1930, in Bauhaus-Archiv, *hannes meyer* (see note 2), 173; Heiberg had been hired to teaching urban planning during the summer semester of 1930.

38 See ibid. Hans Wittwer, the head of the architecture department, had already announced his resignation as of April 1, 1929, "angered by Hannes Meyer's presumptuous behavior in connection

with their joint competition design for the trade union school in in Bernau"; Angela Dolgner, "'Er war für einen Augenblick der kommende Mann,'" *baudenkmal bundesschule bernau: Beiträge zur Bau- und Nutzungsgeschichte*, no. 2 (2003): 10–28, esp. 13; cf. Hans-Jakob Wittwer, *Hans Wittwer* (Zurich: gta, 1985), 16–17. The press had reported in early July on Klee's transfer to the Kunstakademie Düsseldorf; see Paul Klee to Lily Klee, 6 July 1930, in Paul Klee, *Briefe an die Familie 1893–1940*, vol. 2, *1907–1940* (Cologne: DuMont, 1979), 1132. Already in May, the painter had written his wife, Lily: "Hannes Meyer is already oriented. It affects him less than my resignation in the fall will affect the city. [...] In any case, he knows that I am quitting on April 1, 1931"; Paul Klee to Lily Klee, 15 May 1930, ibid., 1120–22, esp. 1121. The negotiations over his appointment were then delayed, so that in the end he did not take up the new position until October 1931. When Grote blamed Klee's departure on Meyer's course, that was therefore justified and not a falsification of the history caused by anti-Meyer resentment, as Oswalt asserts; see Philipp Oswalt, "Verschwiegen, verunglimpft, wiederentdeckt," in Flierl and Oswalt, *Hannes Meyer und das Bauhaus* (see note 2), 507–36, esp. 524. Meyer himself clearly assumed that Klee's departure played a not insignificant role in his own dismissal. For example, in an open letter he had pointed to the discrepancy between his own understanding of the Bauhaus and that of his employer, the City of Dessau, which desires above all "those odd people which the world has come to revere as great artists"; Meyer, "My Expulsion from the Bauhaus" (see note 16), 165. By contrast, Meyer told the Stadtverordneten (state assemblymen) of Dessau to take it to heart: "The clover-field of young Bauhaus painters, cultivated by the most extraordinary painter individualist, will lie fallow in our period of greatest social upheaval and collective need. Moreover, it is a crime to offer young people, who have to be designers in the society of tomorrow, the stale feed of yesterday's art theories as provisions on their way" (ibid.). Meyer had used this amusing dismissive talk of the "clover-field" [*Klee* is German for "clover"—Trans.] publicly previously, in 1929—that is to say, when he was still in office; see Hannes Meyer, "Vorträge in Wien und Basel 1929," in *Bauen und Gesellschaft: Schriften, Briefe, Projekte*, ed. Lena Meyer-Bergner (Dresden: VEB Verlag der Kunst, 1980), 54–62, esp. 55.

39 Ludwig Grote, "Vorträge zum Bauhaus," drafts, single pages, and incomplete typescripts with handwritten notes that cannot be associated with any lecture, n.d., NL Grote, 1467; see Grote, "Von Weimar nach Dessau: Zum Gestaltwandel des Bauhauses," typescript of a lecture at the Bauhaus-Archiv, Darmstadt, January 30, 1963, NL Grote, 998.

40 The mood of alarm was fueled a short time later by a letter from a member of the Bauhaus to Gropius; the former director of the Bauhaus forwarded a copy to Grote without identifying its author. It reads: "with an almost criminal irresponsibility, meyer, who is turning out ever more clearly to be an evil psychopath, is directing the bauhaus to a fall; if we do not make the decisive change soon, [...] then we are finished"; anonymous to Walter Gropius, 15 July 1930, copy, enclosure with Gropius to Grote, 16 July 1930 (see note 31).

41 See Haesler to Grote, 30 June 1930 (see note 31).

42 Gropius to Grote, 16 July 1930 (see note 31).

43 Hannes Meyer to the chairman of the court of arbitration, Edwin Redslob, 11 August 1930, in *hannes meyer* (see note 2), 173–76, esp. 173. Hesse contradicted this account and noted in his explanation of the dismissal: "The declaration that he [Meyer] is a Marxist and in that sense influences the work at the Bauhaus would have very specially obliged him to avoid the risks of politicizing the Bauhaus that result from such a stance, and he would have had to do everything to prevent the students' manifestations of party politics inside and outside of the Bauhaus"; Mayor Fritz Hesse to the chairman of the court of arbitration, Edwin Redslob, 19 August 1930, Bundesarchiv Berlin-Lichterfelde, R32/399, fols. 102–12, esp. fol. 105.

44 Ibid.; see Mayor Fritz Hesse to Bauhaus director Hannes Meyer, 1 August 1930, copy, Bundesarchiv Berlin-Lichterfelde, R32/399, fol. 157, and Hesse, *Erinnerungen* (see note 19), 244–45. Section 626 of the BGB specified at the time (and almost identically today) that a contractual relationship "can be terminated by either party without a period of notice if an important reason exists." The addition that the dismissal can "follow only within two weeks," on which Droste bases her doubt that Hesse's handling of the matter was legal, was not added until 1969; see Droste, "Unterrichtsstruktur und Werkstattarbeit am Bauhaus" (see note 2), 163.

45 See "Wechsel in der Leitung des Bauhauses," *Anhalter Anzeiger*, no. 179 (August 1, 1930). To preserve the right of the Bauhaus masters, most of whom were on vacation, to propose a director, Hesse sent them all a telegram with the following message: "After dismissal of Hannes Meyer, Professor Kandinsky proposes Mies van der Rohe for the director's post. In case of objects, request immediate telegraphic message. Hesse, Oberbürgermeister"; quoted in Droste, "Unterrichtsstruktur und Werkstattarbeit" (see note 2), 134–65, esp. 164. Kostufra alluded to this rigged game on the cover of its *bauhaus*, no. 3 (see figs. 2 and 3).

46 "Recommended Settlement of November 5, 1930," in Wingler, *The Bauhaus* (see note 5), 165.

47 See student representatives of the Bauhaus to the government of Anhalt, department of schools, 4 August 1930, Bundesarchiv Berlin-Lichterfelde, R32/399, fol. 134.

48 Nonné-Schmidt, for example, called Meyer "a 'madman,' who wanted above all to live out his repressed erotic complexes"; Nonné-Schmidt to Grote, 10 March 1965 (see note 18).

49 According to Günter, this was "the famous room 110 in the Bauhaus: Hannes Meyer had it reserved for himself. He generously handed out the key sometimes—as a sign of friendship to students from his group of sympathizers"; Roland Günter, *Hundert Jahre Bauhaus, 1918–2018* [*sic*], http://www.roland-guenter-werke.de/Content.aspx?mID=65&pageID=40, n.p. (accessed November 11, 2020); Meyer's application for director of the Bauhaus is in Bauhaus-Archiv, *hannes meyer* (see note 2), 176–77.

50 Meyer had placed Beese in the architectural office in Berlin that he ran with Hans Wittwer, where she could work on the planning of the realization of the trade union school in Bernau.

51 "Aus Budoiren [*sic*] und Amtszimmern," *bauhaus* (see note 19). These suggestions were reinforced by the report by the Bauhaus student "Hubert Hoffmann (1904–1999), who as a Bauhaus student trusted by Walter Gropius, among others, had extensive detailed knowledge about the affair [Meyer's dismissal]," and in the 1990s reported that Hesse had "left it up to Hannes Meyer to choose the reason for his dismissal: for the 'stories about women' that were being spread by enemies of the Bauhaus? [*sic*] or for supporting the Communists?"; Günter, *Hundert Jahre Bauhaus* (see note 49).

52 NL Grote, 2429.

53 See SBD I 8345/1-10 D.

54 The first issue of the journal is still regarded as lost; its contents can only be guessed from the contemporaneous articles written about it (see notes 14 and 16).

55 See "'schlicht und freudig' haben noch mehr Geld," *Anhalter Anzeiger*, no. 163 (July 14, 1930), and "Kommunismus am Bauhaus," *Anhalter Woche*, no. 29 (July 20, 1930).

56 See Meyer to Redslob, 11 August 1930 (see note 43), 173, and Meyer, "Mein Hinauswurf aus dem Bauhaus" (see note 16), 165.

57 See Hesse to Redslob, 19 August 1930 (see note 43), fol. 102.

58 See the ads "Zur Nachahmung: Sammlung für die Mansfelder Kumpels," *Tribüne: Kommunistische Tageszeitung für den Bereich Magdeburg-Anhalt*, no. 154 (July 5, 1930), and no. 160 (July 12, 1930).

59 Grote to Hesse, 10 July 1930 (see note 33); see "Schlicht und Freudig hat Geld," *Anhalter Anzeiger*, no. 158 (July 8, 1930).

60 Schiff, "Gespräch mit Meyer" (see note 17).

61 See Hannes Meyer to the members of the Kreis der Freunde des Bauhauses, 14 August 1930, Bibliothek der Brandenburgischen Technischen Universität Cottbus-Senftenberg, Ulrich-Conrads-Archiv, Schuber 39 [with sincere gratitude to Magdalena Droste]. By another route and, because they were on vacation, somewhat later, Anni and Josef Albers also received Meyer's article. Immediately thereafter, they asked Grote: "Should someone respond? What is true, what is lies?"; Anni and Josef Albers to Ludwig Grote, 21 August 1930, NL Grote, 701. Ise Gropius did not want to let Meyer's article stand either; she wrote to Maud Grote: "there is no later examination, and there is a true falsification of history to Gropius's disadvantage"; Ise Gropius to Maud Grote, 23 September 1930, NL

Grote, 814. The article did not receive a response until half a year later, written by the former Bauhaus student Alexander (known as Xanti) Schawinsky; "KOPF oder ADLER? zum fall bauhaus," *Berliner Tageblatt und Handels-Zeitung*, no. 17 (January 10, 1931); on the background details of this publication, see Droste, "Enterbung des Nachfolgers" (see note 32), 77.

62 "Ein offener Brief … und eine Antwort," *Volksblatt für Anhalt*, no. 192 (August 19, 1930).

63 Ibid.

64 Ibid. The refutation of Meyer's accusation of culturally reactionary actions by reference to his successor, Mies van der Rohe, is also found in similar wording in Hesse's explanation of the firing; see Meyer to Redslob, 20 August 1930 (see note 13), 175, and Hesse to Redslob, 19 August 1930 (see note 43), fol. 109; inconsistently with this, even Meyer points to the progressivity of his successor; see Meyer, "My Expulsion from the Bauhaus" (see note 16), 165.

65 Ludwig Grote, "Zum Vortrag 'Das Bauhaus—eine Stätte schöpferischer Erziehung,'" lecture at the Deutsches Haus, Paris, NL Grote, 1440.

The Politics of Depoliticization: Ludwig Grote's Dedication to a *German* Bauhaus

Christian Eger

On November 25, 1932, everything was over. With the refusal of the Munich publisher and National Socialist activist Hugo Bruckmann (1863–1941) to continue to support Ludwig Mies van der Rohe (1886–1969), the efforts of Ludwig Grote over more than half a year to advocate into the top levels of the Nationalsozialistische Deutsche Arbeiterpartei (NSDAP; National Socialist German Worker's Party) for a continuation of the design and architecture school in Dessau as a *German* Bauhaus had fizzled out. These forays had been undertaken with Mies van der Rohe's knowledge but ultimately had not been fought by him. The internationally successful architect was not reliant on the Bauhaus,[1] which he had headed since 1930 and dissolved in 1933; in Grote's case, things looked different. With the dissolution of the school, for which he had been active with great personal commitment from 1925 onward, the art historian's future was in question. This fact explains why Grote so tirelessly stuck to a position that in retrospect seems to have been lost from the beginning. With his commitment to the Bauhaus, Grote was struggling for the core of his professional existence.[2] The Dessau years of the Bauhaus were the formative years of his career.[3]

"Always on the Ball": Grote Explains the Bauhaus to the Residents of Dessau

"It was evident," Dessau's liberal mayor Fritz Hesse recalled, that Grote "was all but fascinated by the prospect of transplanting the Bauhaus with Gropius at its head and with artists such as Kandinsky, Klee, and Feininger to Dessau.[4] He presumably felt instinctively that taking over the Bauhaus would also open up new opportunities for him and his work and that he too would grow with the Bauhaus and by means of the Bauhaus."[5] Grote, who in 1924 had been appointed Landeskonservator (state curator) of the Free State of Anhalt and three years later also director of the newly founded Anhaltische Gemäldegalerie, immediately saw the opportunities that relocating the Bauhaus opened up for Anhalt. In March 1925, he was promoting it in the local press: "In the economic and industrial development of Dessau, tasks can accrue to the Bauhaus that must be called almost ideal. In Gropius, a leading architect for industrial architecture will be coming to Dessau. In addition to factories, housing developments, and apartments have to be created for blue- and white-collar workers, and the idea of the standardized house and its rational construction can come to maturity in the process."[6] Grote was not, however, concerned solely with practical impulses. The "effect and influence on the entire cultural and intellectual life from strong artistic personalities like his masters" was for him "a fact that would come easily."[7]

As Hesse's adviser on art policy, Grote was the intermediary between the municipal administration and the school; he was part of the "Bauhaus community," was a crisis manager and propagandist. The Grotes had friendly relationships with Julia and Lyonel Feininger, Nina and Wassily Kandinsky, El and Georg Muche, Lou and Hinnerk Scheper, and Lily and Paul Klee (figs. 1 and 2). With Hesse's support, Grote put together a modern art collection for Anhalt, acquiring works by, among others, Feininger, Kandinsky, and Klee—all artists who were honored with special exhibitions; nevertheless, the establishment of a new department of the gallery dedicated exclusively to the Bauhaus acquisitions remained an unfinished project.[8] Grote was, as Hesse saw it, "always on the ball."[9] It was not just that he was active in the international Kreis der Freunde des Bauhauses (Circle of Friends of the Bauhaus); as a member of the board of the Dessauer Theaterstiftung (Dessau Theater Foundation) he also found time to join the Bund zur Förderung der Farbe im Stadtbild (League to Promote Color in the Cityscape); for the Anhaltischer Kunstverein he directed, he won Kandinsky over to be a member of the board in 1926.[10]

The historian, whose concept of art was influenced by German Romanticism,[11] tried to feed the Bauhaus into the narrative of the regional culture. Grote published art and architectural historical monograph *Das Land Anhalt* with the Deutscher Kunstverlag in 1929.[12] "Shifts in the social structure are coming; the old ties are loosening," he wrote in the final chapter, "Zur Neuzeit" (On the Modern Era). "Young capitalism is creating an unbridled individualism that is destroying the unity of thinking and feeling." The development could be averted through faith "in a modern style based on all the expressions of the era," which combines the arts, the crafts, and life, which Grote saw represented in the work of Gropius and his "community" at the Bauhaus.[13] The book ends with the finding: "A new style is emerging; despite the oppressive antitheses and battles of the day, the internal connections that form the basis of any style must already be more solid than it seems to us."[14] Except that the "internal connections" that were ultimately supposed to have an effect were in social and moral respects different ones than those to which the founders of the Bauhaus had attached themselves.

A "German" School: Grote Seeks Connection to the Right

In October 1931 the right wing gained a majority in Dessau's Gemeinderat (Municipal Council)[15] and in April 1932 in the Landtag (State Parliament) of Anhalt;[16] the closing of the school that had been declared the enemy for years was now just a question of time. In order to save it, Grote undertook the effort in cultural policy for a Bauhaus now interpreted as radically *German*, allegedly in coordination with Mies van der Rohe and Hesse.[17] Like many of his colleagues Grote seems to have regarded the National Socialist movements as an open adventure that could still be controlled politically. So Grote courted the cultural elite from the right. On May 23, 1932, two days after the National Socialist Alfred Freyberg had been elected Minister President of Anhalt, Grote wrote a five-page letter to the renowned Munich art historian, psychiatrist, and Nazi sympathizer Hans Prinzhorn (1886–1933) (fig. 3), who since 1932 had been the assistant of the publisher Bruckmann. Prinzhorn, who was a friend of Mies van der Rohe[18] and an admirer of Mussolini, had given several lectures at the Bauhaus[19] and published a series of articles from a psychological perspective titled "Über den Nationalsozialismus" (On National Socialism) in the conservative weekly newspaper *Der Ring*,[20] which Mies van der Rohe had passed on to Grote. Grote described to Prinzhorn the Bauhaus as a specifically German school. "Again and again, I found that the internal situation of the Bauhaus expressed the German intellectual situation in each case. All of the intellectual struggles of the era, above all the struggles of the artistic youth, are reflected in it. One can probably not assert this of other German art institutes."[21]

Fig. 1 Ludwig Grote with Wassily Kandinsky in the garden of the masters' houses, 1929

Fig. 2 In front of Zerbst castle, near Dessau, June 1931: (*from left*) Rudolf Bach, Paul Klee, Maud Grote (photo: Ludwig Grote)

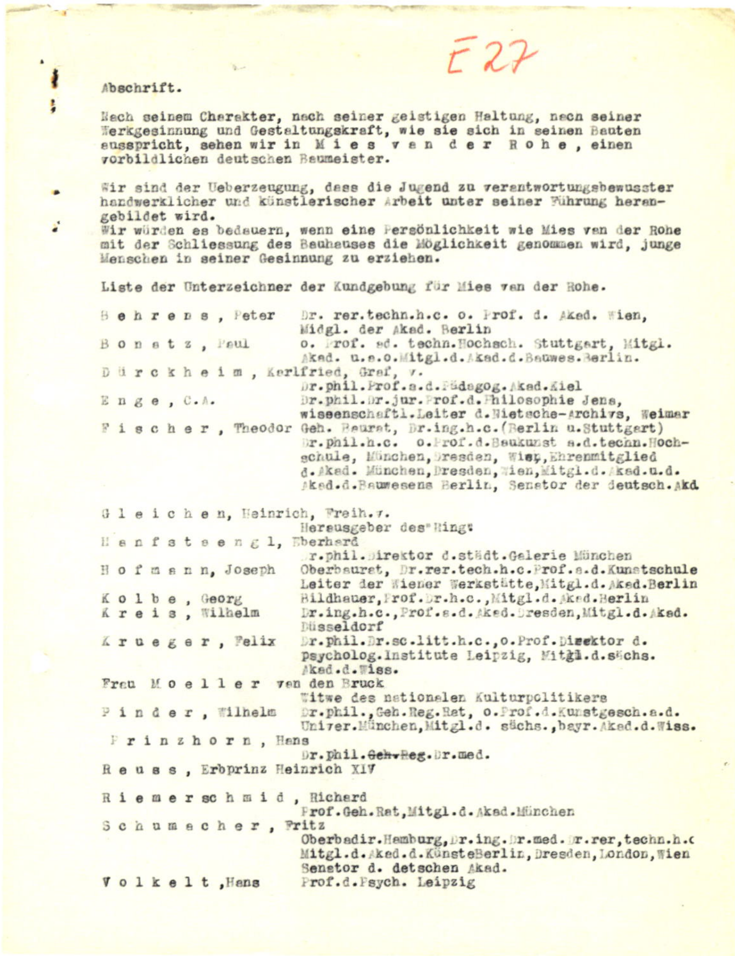

E27

Abschrift.

Nach seinem Charakter, nach seiner geistigen Haltung, nach seiner Werkgesinnung und Gestaltungskraft, wie sie sich in seinen Bauten ausspricht, sehen wir in M i e s v a n d e r R o h e , einen vorbildlichen deutschen Baumeister.

Wir sind der Ueberzeugung, dass die Jugend zu verantwortungsbewusster handwerklicher und künstlerischer Arbeit unter seiner Führung herangebildet wird.
Wir würden es bedauern, wenn eine Persönlichkeit wie Mies van der Rohe mit der Schliessung des Bauhauses die Möglichkeit genommen wird, junge Menschen in seiner Gesinnung zu erziehen.

Liste der Unterzeichner der Kundgebung für Mies van der Rohe.

B e h r e n s , Peter — Dr. rer.techn.h.c. o. Prof. d. Akad. Wien, Midgl. der Akad. Berlin
B o n a t z , Paul — o. Prof. ad. techn.Hochsch. Stuttgart, Mitgl. Akad. u.a.o.Mitgl.d.Akad.d.Bauwes.Berlin.
D ü r c k h e i m , Karlfried, Graf, v. — Dr.phil.Prof.a.d.Pädagog.Akad.Kiel
E n g e , C.A. — Dr.phil.Dr.jur.Prof.d.Philosophie Jena, wissenschaftl.Leiter d.Nietsche-Archivs, Weimar
F i s c h e r , Theodor — Geh. Baurat, Dr.ing.h.c.(Berlin u.Stuttgart) Dr.phil.h.c. o.Prof.d.Baukunst a.d.techn.Hochschule, München, Dresden, Wien, Ehrenmitglied d.Akad. München, Dresden, Wien, Mitgl.d.Akad.u.d. Akad.d.Bauwesens Berlin, Senator der deutsch.Akd

G l e i c h e n, Heinrich, Freih.v. — Herausgeber des "Ring"
H a n f s t a e n g l, Eberhard — Dr.phil.Direktor d.städt.Galerie München
H o f m a n n, Joseph — Oberbaurat, Dr.rer.tech.h.c.Prof.a.d.Kunstschule Leiter der Wiener Werkstätte, Mitgl.d.Akad.Berlin
K o l b e , Georg — Bildhauer, Prof.Dr.h.c., Mitgl.d.Akad.Berlin
K r e i s , Wilhelm — Dr.ing.h.c., Prof.a.d.Akad.Dresden, Mitgl.d.Akad. Düsseldorf
K r u e g e r , Felix — Dr.phil.Dr.sc.litt.h.c., o.Prof.Direktor d. psycholog.Institute Leipzig, Mitgl.d.sächs. Akad.d.Wiss.
Frau M o e l l e r van den Bruck — Witwe des nationalen Kulturpolitikers
P i n d e r , Wilhelm — Dr.phil., Geh.Reg.Rat, o.Prof.d.Kunstgesch.a.d. Univer.München, Mitgl.d. sächs., bayr.Akad.d.Wiss.
P r i n z h o r n , Hans — Dr.phil.~~Geh.~~Reg.Dr.med.
R e u s s , Erbprinz Heinrich XIV

R i e m e r s c h m i d , Richard — Prof.Geh.Rat, Mitgl.d.Akad.München
S c h u m a c h e r , Fritz — Oberbadir.Hamburg, Dr.ing.Dr.med.Dr.rer, techn.h.c Mitgl.d.Akad.d.KünsteBerlin, Dresden, London, Wien Senator d. detschen Akad.
V o l k e l t , Hans — Prof.d.Psych. Leipzig

Fig. 3 Hans Prinzhorn, 1932
Fig. 4 Hans Prinzhorn, announcement in support of Mies van der Rohe, August 1932
Various German architects, artists, and intellectuals assure that they regard Mies van der Rohe as "an exemplary German master builder" based on "his character, his intellectual attitude, his work ethic, and creative power." It would be regrettable if "with the closure of the Bauhaus" such a person would be "deprived of the opportunity to educate young people in their attitudes."

This reading enabled Grote to condemn the Marxist currents at the Bauhaus without turning them against the school. The replacement of Hannes Meyer by Mies van der Rohe, in which Grote declared himself to have been involved, is described by him as a rescue. Mies van der Rohe is for him "the best architect," an antimaterialist man, "who for me is the model type of a German artist, of a German human being." What "German" means for Grote is suggested: beauty *and* function, community before society, idealism instead of materialism, the dominance of a prerational, ingenious, enthusiastic concept of art.[22] "The dominant style of an era is transformed in the process of designing a work of art by the individuality of the artist, the special character of the people and the race, and by the special quality of the landscape and the historical situation," Grote wrote in *Deutsche Stilfibel* of 1936, which continued to be reprinted until 1991. "In Europe, the various styles are developed in each case by the people that takes over cultural leadership."[23]

By driving out the Communists, Mies van der Rohe was supposed to make it possible for the Bauhaus to connect with a future National Socialist cultural policy, which in 1932 was still very much in flux. "For me, the German fate is once again playing out at the Bauhaus thanks to Mies van der Rohe," Grote wrote. "For everyone who grasps Germanness as an obligation and follows this development at the Bauhaus, it must be clear that it would be profoundly regrettable if this process were to be interrupted now by external interventions."[24] He emerged cautiously from his cover: "If the goal of the cultural policy of the National Socialism movement is not stubborn reaction but living growth, it must and can step in for the continued existence of the Bauhaus."[25] Or at least not close it immediately but continue observing it for a year. Grote wagered on a tactical policy of depoliticization. The "influx of Polish and Hungarian elements" had already been stopped; instead, increasingly English and American students were arriving.[26] Grote argued that a modern school could only be promoted by a modern party, which was not to be expected of the "bourgeois parties of the old school." He was aware that the National Socialists would be betraying their voters by doing so and tried to praise maneuverability as clever action: that would, of course, presume the isolation of the prominent Kampfbund member and notorious Bauhaus opponent Paul Schultze-Naumburg (1869–1949), whom Grote considered a reactionary.

Prinzhorn responded quickly. With him, the intellectual spearhead of the National Socialists would be brought into play against the province. On [June?] 3, 1932, Grote declared that he was now officially working "together" with Mies van der Rohe. Grote mentions that "sympathies [for Mies] from certain National Socialist circles in Berlin" had reached as far as Dessau, and he pointed out that Mies van der Rohe had been called a "'stooge' of fascism" by the Communist members of the Bauhaus—a catchword that did indeed have to be used for him. He brought up Schultze-Naumburg, whose activities in Weimar as an expert opinion against the Bauhaus he saw as a "great danger." His book *Kampf um die Kunst* (1932) demonstrates that it would not be possible to come to an agreement with him about "modern design questions as an expression of the German essence."[27] Only in the case that that should prove impossible should Prinzhorn turn to Schultze-Naumburg—as he had offered to do.

Grote asked Prinzhorn to write a text in which he took up the cudgels against Schultze-Naumburg and for a *German* Bauhaus; he proposed the title "Von deutscher Art und Kunst" (On the German Manner and Art), borrowed from a programmatic Sturm und Drang text from 1773.[28]

"Schultze-Naumburg's position is, however, very weak. On the one hand, he assesses modern German art based on inferior achievements and, on the other hand, he portrays Jewish art such as [blank], Italian such as [blank], and Spanish such as Picasso, without pointing out its foreignness. But his struggle for art is made even more fragile by the fact that he cannot cite a single painter or sculptor who makes German art to his liking. The rebuttal would have to be built on that. There is no era of complete artistic impotence, therefore German art must be alive today, as at all times. That Schultze-Naumburg cannot see it is the fault of his own eyes."[29]

That the National Socialist concept of art was by no means set in stone yet is demonstrated by Goebbels's courting of the renowned Expressionist artists.[30] Grote pointed to this fact, even though he did not know whether this attitude was limited to the circle around Goebbels. What he wanted to avoid was a trite National Socialist evaluation of the Bauhaus. "I am convinced that we can gain the time, the Bauhaus can be saved."[31] Prinzhorn argued for the "necessity of a press war," but Grote wanted to keep it out of the daily newspapers. Prinzhorn recommended that Mies van der Rohe seek out contact with the Munich old master of architecture Theodor Fischer, who was skeptical of the Bauhaus but also friendly with it.[32] And he clearly followed Grote's proposal to mobilize the Deutscher Werkbund as well as renowned German architects such as Peter Behrens, Heinrich Tessenow, and Hans Poelzig for the Bauhaus. Prinzhorn organized a "demonstration of trust" for Mies van der Rohe, which Hesse then used in his last speech before the final vote on the National Socialist motion to dissolve the Bauhaus (fig. 4).

In the Lions' Den: Grote Ropes in the Nazi Kampfbund

The journalistic initiative went hand in hand with a political one. Prinzhorn was clearly the one who had paved Grote's way to Munich into the house of his influential employer, Hugo Bruckmann, the NSDAP member of the Reichstag and personal acquaintance of Hitler.[33] Since the turn of the century, the publisher and his wife, Elsa, had been hosting a cultural salon, which the major figures of the Nazi movement had been attending since the mid-1920s.[34] In 1924 Hitler appeared at the salon for the first time; Rudolf Hess and Alfred Rosenberg were regular members of the circle. Bruckmann's relationships to the Nazi elite and, on the one hand, to the Reich administration of the Kampfbund für deutsche Kultur (Militant League for German Culture), headed by Rosenberg, and, on the other hand, his journalistic influence as the editor of the journal *Die Kunst für alle*, which was aimed at the educated bourgeoisie and close to the Nazis but entirely conforming with them, made this networker seem to be the right person to introduce a change in direction in Bauhaus matters. Grote sent a letter of five densely written pages to Bruckmann on August 3, 1932, after he had been invited to converse with him and his wife. What Grote provided is the outline of a Bauhaus memoranda that he did not write himself. He identifies arguments that could make it possible for the NSDAP to say yes to the Bauhaus in order to correct from the top down the position of the Dessau National Socialists around the Paul Hofmann, Gauleiter (regional party leader) and chairman of the Stadtverordnetenversammlung (Assembly of City Councilors). According to Grote, they were "simply not capable" of grasping the matter:

> "The local authorities cannot be expected to be able to judge the significance of the Bauhaus and its present internal situation; and they have rightly recognized that and therefore brought in Schultze-Naumburg as an advisor. But it would have been better to ask in Munich first. In my view, all of the material should be handed over to the Kampfbund for processing, which for its part should have formed a committee. Perhaps that is the path that leads out of the political thicket."[35]

Grote noted why that might succeed. First, he saw modernism as a style that was equal to the great styles of the past and not indebted to politics, which contemporaries of 1932 could no more reject "than a Gothic person the Gothic style."[36] Second, Mies van der Rohe was precisely the right person to lead a new Bauhaus indebted to community to success. "I know few people who are as exemplarily German as he is," Grote wrote, also speaking a great deal of "fate."[37] "It is my profoundest conviction that the question of the Bauhaus will be crucial for the intellectual significance of your movement and for its place in history. That will show whether it is more than a party, whether it is a movement born of the German essence, comparable to German Romanticism."[38] Third, he argued that a new party that wants to be young and modern has to approach artistically activated youth, who are waiting for precisely that signal. Grote enticed and pulled; he built intellectual bridges that could be crossed by the National Socialists. He believed that the Bauhaus could be connected to all sides politically. Using the oft-cited Bauhaus formula of the "cathedral of socialism,"[39] he declared that there was "no debate" over the "necessity" of socialism at the Bauhaus "but rather over the how, over German socialism in the spirit of Strasser or Marxist socialism."[40] For Grote, it was certain: "The new style can be Marxist and community, but it can also be German and classical."[41]

Grote's intervention was not inconsequential. Rosenberg, the chief Nazi ideologue and founder of the Kampfbund, appealed to Freyberg, the head of the NSDAP government in Anhalt, who had long since received a negative report on the Bauhaus from Schultze-Naumburg,[42] for the continued existence of "Mies van der Rohe's school"—albeit without the name "Bauhaus" and without Jewish and foreign teachers; Hofmann, the NSDAP Stadtverordneter for Dessau, was not interested in that. After the motion to close the school had already failed once,[43] National Socialists had a successful motion on August 22, 1932, to dissolve the Bauhaus Dessau in late September 1932. Only the mayor and four Communists voted against it; the Sozialdemokratische Partei Deutschlands (SPD; Social Democratic Party of Germany) abstained, out of fear of losing voters. The matter was thus closed, and not only locally. On November 25,

1932, Bruckmann informed Grote "that all my efforts for Mies van der Rohe personally have failed."[44] The hope to promote the Bauhaus in a Kampfbund cultural journal that was being planned had also been dashed with the rejection of the planned journal project.[45] Bruckmann, who was losing influence with the Kampfbund,[46] withdrew. Bruckmann remarked that Mies van der Rohe had in the meanwhile reestablished the Bauhaus in Berlin-Steglitz and had himself participated in an exhibition in Moscow, which "on the one hand, bolstered the critics who accused him of having a bolshevist inclination but, on the other hand, was reassurance that he will continue on his path even without state support."[47] Grote replied only after a month had passed; there was no time pressure any longer. It pointed out that the architecture show in Moscow in which Mies van der Rohe had participated had been organized by the German Foreign Office and that the Reich Interior Minister had personally asked Mies van der Rohe to get involved. For the people around Bruckmann, that was by now irrelevant: They did not even want to know the details. Nevertheless, Grote did not appear to be resigned yet. That is suggested by the fact that in December 1932 he applied to the Mendelssohn-Stiftung for a subsidy for the closed school. This suggests that Grote's advocacy for the Bauhaus was not primarily ideological but quite pragmatically focused on saving it.[48]

Fighting a Losing Battle: Grote Fails across the Board

It may seem surprising today how open Grote was about actively petitioning the National Socialists on behalf the Bauhaus, as if the only issue that could divide opinions was pro or contra the flat roof and not the fact that the National Socialists were pursuing an openly racist party platform that wanted to remove Jews not just from the school but from society as a whole. But Grote was by no means alone in that respect. The elite of state art educators was entirely "on the ball" in the 1920s; an ideological hodgepodge of idealistic anticapitalism, Romantic pathos of community, and German religiosity of art made the advocates of modernism equally open to connect to the left and the right.[49] Driven by his long-standing personal commitment, Grote viewed the Bauhaus through a soft-focus lens that abstracted everything political and moral. Grote's cult of "beauty," which was nominally remote from politics but also always politically maneuvering, represented a common denominator with Mies van der Rohe. He had made the Augustinian tenet "Beauty is the radiance of truth" the motto of his architectural work.[50] That did not affect his political involvement: he was one of the signers of the "Aufruf der Kulturschaffenden" (Appeal of the Cultural Creators) for Hitler on August 18, 1934.[51] But even if the National Socialists initially looked in various aesthetic directions, they were certain that it must always be possible to instrumentalize art for politics and propaganda. It cannot be held against Grote that it was apparently not clear that his struggle was in vain; with the exception of Thuringia, where an NSDAP minister had been appointed to the cabinet in 1930, no one had any experience with National Socialists in government.

In retrospect, Grote's failure seems inevitable. First, the closing of the Bauhaus in Dessau[52] was unavoidable from the perspective of Dessau: the struggle against the Bauhaus stereotypically scorned as "bolshevist" was one of the hits of National Socialist election campaigns in the region, including the demolition of the building.[53] The front lines had thus been established not objectively but in terms of ethics and ideology, and that had been true since the school's Weimar period. The Bauhaus served as a cheap battle cry to direct social resentment against the hated urban elites of the Weimar Republic; nothing about that could be moderated. Second, Hitler by no means sought an apolitical architecture but rather one that conveyed power and was correspondingly laden with history. Hitler found his ideal of architecture not in Mies van der Rohe or Gropius but in the classicistic heroic architecture of Paul Ludwig Troost (1878–1934), whom Bruckmann introduced to the party leader at his salon in 1930.[54] Third, the National Socialists deliberately organized their power polycratically in order to invigorate business through internal competition; total governing of Dessau from Munich was impossible. Fourth, the question that Grote repeatedly asked, how modern or unmodern Schultze-Naumburg's vineyard-cottage architecture is, played no role for the National Socialists, also because they had long considered Schultze-Naumburg old hat. They took from what was called "Bauhaus" as if from a toolkit, without upholding the Bauhaus brand. Nor did they have any practical objections to it. Nearly all of the former members of the Bauhaus, except those who were Jews or Communists, were able to become members of the Reichskulturkammer after 1933[55]—including Gropius and Mies van der Rohe, who were involved in the design of the Nazi propaganda exhibition *Deutsches Volk—Deutsche Arbeit* (German People—German Work) in 1934.[56] When former students were persecuted, it was because they were Jews or Communists, not because they had studied at the Bauhaus.[57]

Reinterpretation after 1945: Grote Invents the Bauhaus as an Artists' School

"It will perhaps interest you," Grote's last letter to Bruckmann in 1932 ends, "that I am now preparing a large exhibition, which will, I hope, travel through Germany, in which I want to show, under the title 'New Paths to Homeland,' the new, landscape-related German art; all of the German tribes should be represented in it."[58] The show was the last one that Grote would curate in Dessau.[59] His closeness to the Bauhaus and the acquisition policy for the Gemäldegalerie for which he was responsible made him someone who could not be entrusted with governmental tasks.[60] In May 1933 he was pensioned off; his book on Anhalt was removed from distribution.[61] After briefly considering leaving the country with the help of his wife's English family, Grote chose instead the existence of a freelance scholar. The network of colleagues and artists he had set up during the Dessau years continued through the Nazi years and beyond. From the autumn of 1933, the family lived in the villa in Halle of the sculptor Gustav Weidanz; in 1935 they moved to Berlin and four years later to Munich. Apparently prior to June 1934, Grote joined the SA (Sturmabteilung), apparently guided by the idea of "being able to achieve something by disseminating other intellectual elements," as Gertrud Maud Grote noted, an idea that turned out to be "completely superfluous and useless," and Grote himself supposedly soon left it as a passive membership; nevertheless, the fact of membership was relevant enough for him to have suppressed it in 1945.[62] After 1933 Grote was active as a freelance writer on art, which required membership in the Reichsschrifttumskammer (Reich Chamber of Literature), and stonework conservator,[63] before being conscripted into military service in 1941; from 1940 onward, Grote was an employee of the Galerie Zinckgraf in Munich, which also handled commissions for the Führermuseum in Linz.[64]

With the end of the Nazi state, the cultural politician Ludwig Grote had his hour of glory. Through the agency of German Federal President Theodor Heuss (1884–1963),[65] whom he knew personally, Grote became director of the Germanisches Nationalmuseum in Nuremberg in 1951,[66] not without securing the right to organize four exhibitions on contemporary art a year at the Fränkische Galerie in Nuremberg. Grote was back in play. And along with him, his reading of the Bauhaus as an apolitical school. From 1949 to 1951 he organized the first exhibitions at the Haus der Kunst in Munich, including the show *Die Maler am Bauhaus* (The Painters at the Bauhaus) in 1950, which was followed in 1968 by an exhibition for which he was partly responsible: *50 jahre bauhaus* (50 years bauhaus), which opened in Stuttgart and traveled to London, Amsterdam, Paris, Chicago, Toronto, Pasadena, Buenos Aires, and Tokyo.[67] With these two exhibitions began the interpretation of the design and societal legacy of the school by the Bonn Republic. In 1950 Grote's focus on the top-quality works of the avant-garde presented the Bauhaus as a unique artists' school; in the show in 1968, the institute appears as a "cultural representative of a past uncontaminated by National Socialism."[68] This museumization, which was politically desirable and whose subject matter was dominated by the circle of friends around Gropius, went hand in hand with a dehistoricizing of the school; in both cases, the context of its origin and the years of National Socialism are passed over without commentary; the students disappear behind the figures of the prominent teachers.[69] This, too, was a policy of dehistoricizing: The Bauhaus purified of all political and societal ambiguities that Grote still believed in 1932 could connect to the right-wing suddenly seems to be a fundamentally democratic project that was incompatible with the Nazi regime[70]—no longer as a "cathedral of socialism" but as a miniaturized Federal Republic of diligent masters and painters with no origin.

1 When Mies van der Rohe was asked by Grote to contribute to the exhibition *50 jahre bauhaus*, he replied: "I have absolutely nothing to do with the Bauhaus"; quoted in Anke Blümm, "Die Bauhaus-Ausstellungen 1938 und 1968," in *Entwürfe der Moderne: Bauhaus-Ausstellungen, 1923–2019*, ed. Hellmut Seemann and Thorsten Valk, Klassik Stiftung Weimar, Jahrbuch 2019 (Göttingen: Wallstein Verlag, 2019), 197–218, esp. 210.

2 Ludwig Grote to Fritz Hesse, n.d. (presumably spring 1932): "The fate of the Bauhaus and my own future keep going through my head"; quoted in Helga Heise, "Die ersten Jahre der Anhaltischen Gemäldegalerie unter Ludwig Grote," in ed. Norbert Michels, *Verrat an der Moderne: Die Gründungsgeschichte und das erste Jahrzehnt der Anhaltischen Gemäldegalerie Dessau, 1927–1937* (Dessau: Anhaltische Gemäldegalerie, 1996), 51–79, esp. 77.

3 See Christian Eger, "Formwillen unserer Zeit: Ludwig Grote in Anhalt," in Ludwig Grote, *Das Land Anhalt*, Deutsche Lande/Deutsche Kunst, ed. Burkhard Meier (1929; repr. Halle: Waldersee, 2008), 229–49.

4 It was Dessau's director general of music, Franz von Hoesslin (1885–1946), who together with Hesse provided the impetus in January 1925 to bring the Bauhaus, which was being driven out of Weimar, to Dessau. Ludwig Grote, "Erinnerung an Paul Klee" (1959), in *von dürer bis gropius: Aufsätze zur deutschen Kunst*, 2nd ed. (Munich: Prestel 1975), 118.

5 Fritz Hesse, *Erinnerungen an Dessau*, vol. 1, *Von der Residenz zur Bauhausstadt* (Bad Pyrmont: the author, 1963), 197.

6 Ludwig Grote, "Das Weimarer Bauhaus und seine Aufgaben in Dessau," *Anhalter Anzeiger*, no. 58 (March 10, 1925).

7 Ibid.

8 Gertrud Maud Grote, "Lebenslauf von Ludwig Grote," unfinished typescript, early 1980s to 1994, GNM, DKA, NL Grote, Ludwig (hereafter "NL Grote"), 246.

9 Hesse, *Erinnerungen an Dessau* (see note 5), 197.

10 "Bericht zur Mitgliederversammlung des Anhaltischen Kunstvereins," June 18, 1926, fol. 195, Landesarchiv Sachsen-Anhalt, Anhaltischer Landeskonservator DE, Nr. 1.

11 The monograph *Die Brüder Olivier und die deutsche Romantik*, published in 1938 and most recently reissued in 1999, is Grote's art historical magnum opus, for which he prepared with individual studies from the mid-1920s onward; the art historian's life theme was his work on Romantic painting.

12 See Grote, *Das Land Anhalt* (see note 3).

13 Ibid., 155.

14 Ibid., 156.

15 On October 25, 1931, the NSDAP, which was running in elections in Dessau for the first time, won fifteen of thirty-six seats; four additional seats were occupied by other right-wing groups; see Bärbel Reuter and Günter Ziegler, *100 Jahre Stadtverordnete in Dessau: Biographische Skizzen* (Dessau: Museum für Stadtgeschichte, 1998), 9.

16 On April 24, 1932, the right wing received an absolute majority with twenty seats; see Günter Ziegler, *Kommunale Spitzenbeamte Anhalts: Biographische Skizzen, 1832–1933* (Dessau: Stadtverwaltung Dessau, Kulturamt 1995), 53.

17 That was reported by Gertrud Maud Grote. According to her, but not documented by sources, Grote, Hesse, and Mies van der Rohe "agreed after extensive consultations to set another aid action in motion. They wanted to target a group that was not oriented to the 'left' with a materialistic worldview." The names mentioned were Arthur Moeller van den Bruck, Hans Prinzhorn, and Elsa Bruckmann. Gertrud Maud Grote, "Lebenslauf von Ludwig Grote" (see note 8), 50.

18 Mies van der Rohe's wife, Ada, had attended the school in Hellerau along with Prinzhorn's wife; see Magdalena Droste, *Bauhaus, 1919–1933*, trans. Jane Michael (Cologne: Taschen, 2006), 228.

19 Prinzhorn had previously been invited by Gropius and Hannes Meyer to give lecturers. In 1931 he appeared as part of the lecture program drawn up by Mies van der Rohe under the sign of the "Geisteskampf" (intellectual struggle) of that era; see ibid. and Peter Bernhard, "Die Gastvorträge am Bauhaus: Einblicke in den 'zweiten Lehrkörper,'" in *Mythos Bauhaus: Zwischen Selbsterfindung und Enthistorisierung*, ed. Anja Baumhoff and Magdalena Droste (Berlin: Reimer Verlag, 2009) , 90–111, esp. 108–11.

20 See Hans Prinzhorn, "Über den Nationalsozialismus," *Der Ring* 3 (1930): 884–85; Prinzhorn, "Zur Problematik des nationalen Radikalismus: Über den Nationalsozialismus II," *Der Ring* 4 (1931), 573–77; Prinzhorn, "Moralische Verpflichtungen: Über den Nationalsozialismus III," *Der Ring* 5 (1932): 88–90; Prinzhorn, "Psychologisches zum Führertum: Über den Nationalsozialismus IV," ibid: 769–70. Prinzhorn admired about the National Socialists the "true urge to devotion of young people who see meaning and fulfillment for their lives [...] in it; make an effort for a value, a thing, something suprapersonal; and sacrifice themselves when it is necessary." The philosopher Ludwig Klage, whom Prinzhorn admired, rejected this reflection in 1931: "What you [...] say about National Socialism is very correct in itself; but the thing has one terrible catch. The fact that a willing and uncritical youth is enthusiastic about a so-called idea or a person is unfortunately no argument either for the rightness of the idea nor for any leadership qualities of the person"; quoted in Wolfgang Martynkewicz, *Salon Deutschland: Geist und Macht, 1900–1945* (Berlin: Aufbau, 2009), 451–52.

21 Ludwig Grote to Hans Prinzhorn, 23 May 1932, NL Grote, 1361.

22 This concept of art shaped Grote's view of modernism: "I see in modernism a style that has grown organically, whose formation can be traced far back into the nineteenth century. This style stands as an equal alongside the great styles of the past. Because it does not historicize, is not eclectic, but rather necessary, fateful, we can no longer place ourselves outside of it. It forces us under its spell, whether we want it or not; we are influenced and reformed by it." Ludwig Grote to Hugo Bruckmann, 3 August 1932, ibid, 1360.

23 Ludwig Grote, *Deutsche Stilfibel* (Leipzig: L. Staackmann, 1958), 6.

24 Ludwig Grote to Hans Prinzhorn, 23 May 1932, NL Grote, 1361.

25 Ibid.

26 Ibid.

27 Ludwig Grote to Hans Prinzhorn, 3 [June?] 1932, NL Grote, 1361.

28 See Johann Gottfried Herder, *Von deutscher Art und Kunst: Einige fliegende Blätter* (Hamburg, 1773).

29 Grote to Prinzhorn (see note 27).

30 Karl Schmidt-Rottluff, Erich Heckel, Emil Nolde, and Ernst Barlach were invited to the opening of the Reichskulturkammer on November 15, 1933, and respectfully greeted. The ranks of National Socialist supporters of Expressionism were broad. Not until 1937 was the Nazi discourse on art brought in line; the central program for discipline was the journal *Die Kunst im Dritten Reich*—known as *Kunst im Deutschen Reich* from 1939 onward—which strictly followed the party line; see Martynkewicz, *Salon Deutschland* (see note 20), 486–87.

31 Grote to Prinzhorn (see note 27).

32 Although Theodor Fischer (1862–1938) rejected the radicalness of modern architecture, he defended the Bauhaus. Bruckmann's journal *Die Kunst für alle* published Fischer's argument for the Bauhaus in October 1932 under headline "Um das Bauhaus" (About the Bauhaus). It ended: "Once again the German people stands before the opportunity to obtain form. And once again it is the German people itself that is setting about to demolish this opportunity. One desperately tries now and again to study what is truly 'German.' I know only one thing: Fanaticism is not German." Theodor Fischer, "Um das Bauhaus," *Die Kunst für alle* 48, no. 1 (October 1932): 32.

33 See Droste, *Bauhaus, 1919–1933* (see note 18), 230.

34 For a detailed account, see Martynkewicz, *Salon Deutschland* (see note 20).

35 See Grote to Bruckmann (see note 22).

36 Ibid.

37 Ibid.

38 Ibid.

39 Talk of the "cathedral of socialism," which was only later translated by Feininger into the woodcut of a cathedral he produced for the Bauhaus manifesto of 1919, can be traced back to a formulation by Oskar Schlemmer from a withdrawn prospectus for the Bauhaus exhibition in 1923. It reads: "The State Bauhaus, founded after the catastrophe of the war, in the chaos of revolution, and in the era of the heyday of an emotionally charged, explosive art, first became the collecting point for those who believed in the future and wanted to build the cathedral of socialism." Quoted in Sebastian Neurauter, *Das Bauhaus und die Verwertungsrechte: Eine Untersuchung zur Praxis der Rechteverwertung am Bauhaus, 1919–1933* (Tübingen: Mohr Siebeck, 2013), 225. Grote explained this slogan:

"It never meant political socialism but rather one of the Romantic ideas of the ideal image formed from the unity of the people, because as the ideal the Bauhaus had envisioned before its founding was to serve the people and not create for the rich"; Grote to Bruckmann (see note 22).
40 Ibid.
41 Ibid.
42 As an expert consultant for the Nazis, Schultze-Naumburg had taken part, along with Hesse, Freyberg, and Hofmann, in a tour of the Bauhaus guided by Mies van der Rohe; see Hesse, *Erinnerungen an Dessau* (see note 5), 251–52.
43 On January 21, 1932, Hofmann had proposed the motion to close the Bauhaus on April 1 and begin demolition of the building; it was rejected with twenty-five votes against and fifteen in favor.
44 Hugo Bruckmann to Ludwig Grote, 25 November 1932, NL Grote, 1360.
45 The organization had been publishing the *Mitteilungen des Kampfbundes für deutsche Kultur* since 1929, but ceased in 1931. Prinzhorn had been hired by Bruckmann in 1932 to draw up a project of a "free nationalist" newspaper on "renewals of the culture and soul of the German people," which was abandoned at the end of 1932 because of fundamental differences of opinion; see Martynkewicz, *Salon Deutschland* (see note 20), 452–53.
46 Power had wandered away from Munich to Berlin, away from Rosenberg to the leading Nazi functionary for culture, Hans Hinkel, who had excellent contacts to Rosenberg's competitor Goebbels. From 1932 to 1933, Hinkel edited *Deutsche Kultur-Wacht: Blätter des Kampfbundes für deutsche Kultur*; see Martynkewicz, *Salon Deutschland* (see note 20), 454.
47 Bruckmann to Grote, 25 November 1932 (see note 45).
48 The minutes of the meeting of the advisory board of the Bauhaus on December 20, 1932, remark: "visit from dr. grote on December 16. grote tried to get mayor hesse to support the bauhaus with funds from the mendelssohnstiftung in dessau. The committee of this foundation includes, among others, redslob, spranger, gropius, paul kempner" (SBD, I 8383/1-2 D).
49 To cite just two examples from Grote's native city Halle: Max Sauerlandt, from 1908 to 1919 director of the Städtisches Museum für Kunst und Kunstgewerbe Moritzburg, openly showed sympathies to the NSDAP from 1931 onward and promoted Expressionism as a contemporary "German art"; Alois Schardt, director of the Moritzburg from 1926 to 1933, was an NSDAP member and from May 1933 a member of the Nazi Kampfbund für deutsche Kultur.
50 See Winfried Nerdinger, *Das Bauhaus: Werkstatt der Moderne* (Munich: C. H. Beck 2018), 98.
51 See Peter Hahn, "Wege der Bauhäusler in Reich und Exil," in *Bauhaus-Moderne im Nationalsozialismus: Zwischen Anbiederung und Verfolgung*, ed. Winfried Nerdinger (Munich: Prestel, 1993), 202–13, esp. 208.
52 The cities of Magdeburg and Leipzig, which were governed by Social Democrats, made offers to take over the Bauhaus: in the end, Mies van der Rohe took it to Berlin, where it continued to operate from October 1932 to April 1933. It was now Mies van der Rohe who lobbied before Nazi institutions to preserve the school.
53 The call to close the Bauhaus headed the list of the National Socialists' campaign promises in October 1931. A Nazi leaflet from Dessau reads: "We call for: Complete elimination of all expenditures on the Bauhaus. Terminating without notice all foreign teaching staff, because it is incompatible with the responsibility good community leadership has to its citizens that the German people should go hungry while foreigners are paid excessively from the tax monies of starving people. German teachers should be accommodated by communities in Dessau or elsewhere. Accommodations should be found elsewhere for the schools of the crafts at the Bauhaus. The demolition of the Bauhaus must be initiated immediately." This leaflet is illustrated in Droste, *Bauhaus, 1919–1933* (see note 18), 226.
54 Martynkewicz, *Salon Deutschland* (see note 20), 90–91.
55 See Nerdinger, *Das Bauhaus* (see note 49), 114.
56 See Hahn, "Wege der Bauhäusler" (see note 51), 206.
57 For an instructive view of the professional and career paths of former members of the Bauhaus in the National Socialist state, see Winfried Nerdinger, "Bauhaus-Architekten im 'Dritten Reich,'" in Nerdinger, *Bauhaus-Moderne im Nationalsozialismus* (see note 50), 153–78. Among other things, on page 153 it refers to Hinnerk Scheper, who had designed the color schemes for the gallery spaces and Grote's private rooms in the Palais Reina and also decorated Hermann Göring's country house in Carinhall in 1940.
58 Ludwig Grote to Hugo Bruckmann, 22 December 1932, NL Grote, 1360.
59 The title of the exhibition in May 1933: *Der Weg in die Heimat* (The Path to Homeland), organized by the Anhaltischer Kunstverein. See the list of exhibitions organized by Ludwig Grote in the present volume.
60 See Helga Heise, "Die ersten Jahre der Anhaltischen Gemäldegalerie unter Ludwig Grote" (see note 2), 63ff.
61 See Gertrud Maud Grote, "Lebenslauf von Ludwig Grote" (see note 8), 45.
62 Gertrud Maud Grote does not date his joining the SA. She merely points out that "the political opinions" prior to the "embarrassing Röhm Putsch" [June 30 to July 2, 1934] were "still uncertain." Only vague information is offered: With Ludwig Grote's move to Berlin in 1935, the "SA history absolutely receded to the background" and at the end of 1944 was "for us in fact resolved." After the war ended, however, that was clearly not the case, since Maud Grote writes: "Only when taking over the Germanisches Museum in Nuremberg (first director from 1952, then general director until 1962), when his right to a pension was being determined, the membership in the SA that he had not indicated in 1945 was discovered in his personnel files and declared null and void by Federal President Heuss, who knew Grote as a person very well." This states clearly that Ludwig Grote had kept his SA membership hidden to the very end, which ultimately made that fact a matter for the boss; all quotations from Gertrud Maud Grote, "Ludwig Grote, SA betreffend," 1934, NL Grote, 2322.
63 Grote used the material Deckosit to restore, among other things, sculptures on the Chinesisches Pavillon in Sanssouci and Andreas Schlüter's masks of warriors on the Zeughaus in Berlin.
64 See the essay by Birgit Jooss in the present volume.
65 The former Deutsche Demokratische Partei (DDP; German Democratic Party) member of the Reichstag, journalist, and Werkbund managing director Heuss (1921–24, then member of the board until 1933) had met Grote in Berlin in the circle of the art historian Carl Georg Heise (1890–1979); see Theodor Heuss, "Ludwig Grote," *Anzeiger des Germanischen Nationalmuseums* (1963): 7.
66 See Theodor Heuss to Ludwig Grote, 18 August 1951, in *Theodor Heuss: Der Bundespräsident; Briefe, 1949–1954*, ed. Ernst Wolfgang Becker, Martin Vogt, and Wolfram Werner (Berlin: De Gruyter, 2012), 267–68.
67 See Torsten Blume, "From Stuttgart into the World," in the present volume.
68 Regina Bittner, "Experiment Bauhaus: ein Mauersprung?," in Seemann and Valk, *Entwürfe der Moderne* (see note 1), 261–78, esp. 267.
69 This pattern has held since the Bauhaus exhibition in New York in 1938. At the time, the journalist Martha Davidson was struck by the discrepancy. She asked how a school could have trained successfully if it is represented overwhelmingly by its famous teachers; see Blümm, "Die Bauhauausstellungen 1938 und 1968" (see note 1), 204.
70 At the opening of the exhibition in Stuttgart, the representative of the federal government, Lauritz Lauritzen, declared: "The spirit of the Bauhaus was democratic and liberal. […] Without national arrogance, one can say that it represents a German contribution to the culture and civilization of the world in this century, a contribution to the humanization of the technological age"; quoted in ibid., 207–8.

The First Exhibition of "Degenerate Art" in Germany: Ludwig Grote's Role after the Closure of the Bauhaus by the National Socialist Party

Elisabeth Kremer

Ludwig Grote's final years as director of the Anhaltische Gemäldegalerie (Anhalt Paintings Gallery) and as Landeskonservator (State Curator) in Anhalt were marked by the political debates over the Bauhaus. In right-wing nationalist circles, the Bauhaus represented the epitome of everything that they felt threatened the soul of the German people and encouraged the degeneration of German culture: cosmopolitan thinking and internationalism, modern art and industrial mass culture. In 1925 the voices in Dessau being raised against the Bauhaus were still considerably in the minority; indeed, in 1925 it was greeted unanimously from right to left.[1] From the later 1920s onward, however, the Bauhaus was increasingly defamed, regulated, and pilloried by the local press and politicians. This development culminated in 1932 in the resolution of the Gemeinderat (Municipal Council) to close the school and in the first National Socialist *Schandausstellung* (exhibition of shame) in Germany with paintings by Bauhaus artists from the Anhaltische Gemäldegalerie. Grote, as a prominent supporter and collector of the Bauhaus, also found his existence threatened and tried to save it by adapting to the new circumstances.

Alois Schardt, director of the Moritzburg in Halle and a collector of works by Bauhaus painters such as Paul Klee, Lyonel Feininger, and Wassily Kandinsky, tried in 1941 from exile in the United States to analyze the causes of the radical right-wing actions against modern painting. In his view, the defamations and public displays resulted not so much by order of the Nationalsozialistische Deutsche Arbeiterpartei (NSDAP; National Socialist German Workers' Party) and its cultural associations; rather, they could be traced back to initiatives of local party members and citizens.[2] Schardt explained this phenomenon by noting that municipal Social Democratic governments supported above all modern Expressionist and Constructivist painting, which made a large part of Jugendstil artists and artisans feel at a disadvantage and deprived of recognition and reward. "In every city, there was a group of artists who because they believed their were being discriminated against—either open party members or secret supporters—were in any case opponents of the museum directors (and supporters of modern art)."[3] Schardt's arguments can certainly be judged problematic precisely because of his own membership in the NSDAP and his efforts to win the favor of National Socialists, to whom he tried to offer his services in 1933 by reconceiving the Nationalgalerie in Berlin for a *völkisch* (ethno-nationalist) modernism.[4] Even so, when considering the course of events in Dessau, it certainly seems there is something to be gained from this argumentation. The first and strongest opposition in Dessau to the Bauhaus came from the crafts and from the artists at the Kunstgewerbe- und Handwerkerschule (Crafts and Artisans School). With arguments and actions, they prepared the way for the National Socialists, as was revealed in the debate over the future and directorship of the Kunstgewerbeschule in Dessau: the city's takeover of the Bauhaus took the form of annexing the Bauhaus to the local Kunstgewerbeschule. To ensure that Walter Gropius had the directorship and authority over guidelines, the school's director, Richard Kieser, who had been very successful until then, was dismissed and Gropius made the director of both schools, which from then on worked under one roof but for the most part

Fig. 1 Ludwig Grote's official residence, ca. 1927

separately from each other. This gave rise to protest from the local tradespersons and applied artists. In particular, Gropius's credo that the future of the crafts lay in building types and models for industry made him unpopular among tradespersons, who rather saw their existence threatened by industry. Kieser became a founding member of the Bürgerverein (Citizens' Association), which was the gathering place for the enemies of the Bauhaus in Dessau.[5] Another member was the municipal architect Kurt Elster, member of the board of trustees of the Deutscher Werkbund (German Association of Artisans), who provided the Bürgerverein with helpful arguments. Under the headline “Der Kampf gegen ein Bauhaus in dieser Form beginnt” (The Struggle against a Bauhaus in This Form Begins), Elster criticized in the Bürgerverein's advertisement in the *Anhalter Woche* an “education leading to megalomania,” “strident advertisements,” and an art and architecture that have “nothing in common with the German essence.”[6] This critique, published on the occasion of the dedication of the school's building, could do little harm to the Bauhaus, which enjoyed an international response. Nevertheless, in the next election in the autumn of 1927, the Bürgerverein established an “Einheitsliste” (unity list). Its top themes were the squandering of public funds by Mayor Fritz Hesse and “the grotesque Bauhaus.”[7] The Einheitsliste straightaway won eleven seats (of forty) in Dessau's Gemeinderat. Then in 1931, the next election, the National Socialists adopted the polemics of the Bürgerverein and soon followed words with deeds.

Grote, by contrast, was a supporter of the Bauhaus; he organized events and exhibitions at the Kunstverein (Arts Society) in Dessau, for example, on Neue Sachlichkeit (New Objectivity) in February 1926 in order to convey the Bauhaus and its art to a wider audience. As Landeskonservator, he awarded commissions to the school's workshops to renovate and decorate palaces and museums.[8] For example, he contracted Hinnerk Scheper and the wall painting workshop to paint the rooms of the Palais Reina[9] and of Schloss Oranienbaum,[10] which then housed the state archives. For the decoration of the Anhaltische Gemäldegalerie in the Palais Reina, Grote did not leave it at a contract for the facades and walls but also brought in the carpentry and weaving workshops of the Bauhaus to furnish his official residence located there (figs. 1 and 2). Together with the head of the advertising workshop at the Bauhaus, Joost Schmidt, he prepared an illustrated brochure for the City of Dessau for which he provided the texts.[11] As director of the Anhaltische Gemäldegalerie, he acquired several works by Bauhaus painters or proposed their acquisition (fig. 3).[12] As a member of the Kunstverein board, he also planned a separate exhibition with paintings by Bauhaus artists for the opening of the Anhaltische Gemäldegalerie, but this idea was ultimately abandoned and nineteenth- and twentieth-century art from Anhalt was presented instead—probably because it was feared that the local cultural scene would have protested.[13] Nor were the paintings hung in the Anhaltische Gemäldegalerie but rather in Grote's official residence there. Hesse and Grote did not believe the public was ready yet for that sort of painting.[14]

After the Bauhaus Dessau was closed in September 1932, by order of the right-wing nationalist majority in the Gemeinderat, and after Hitler's seizure of power, Hesse was forced to step down on March 8, 1933, and placed in protective custody. On the initiative of the NSDAP district councilman Richard Harms, a committee was formed to investigate him. At the instigation of Harms and the district attorney of Dessau, the Bauhaus Berlin was sealed to secure evidence against Hesse. It was never reopened. Harms wrote another letter to the Gestapo in Berlin in which he expressly warned against the reopening of the Bauhaus in Berlin in light of the results of the investigating committee in Dessau.[15]

Hesse was accused of wasting public funds by taking over the Bauhaus and of tolerating the "Bolshevist" activities among the students at the Bauhaus. The final item of the accusation was subsidizing the Anhaltische Gemäldegalerie with 30,000 marks to acquire paintings by Bauhaus artists. The paintings were said to be "Jewish Bolshevist" dross that poisoned the German soul. The Anhaltische Gemäldegalerie was also searched as part of the investigations into Hesse, and in Grote's official residence they struck gold. A Dessau newspaper wrote on March 15, 1933: "six paintings were found, for which Mr. Hesse paid Messrs. Feininger, Kandinsky, Nolde, Möller, according to the statements of the finders, the unusually high sum of 30,000 marks. Apparently, the mayor himself was ashamed to present these daubs to the public, because the paintings were found in a storeroom of the Gemäldegalerie and in an unused kitchen in the Messelhaus.[16] As reported, they are now being made accessible to the public."[17] The paintings confiscated must have been *Gelbe Dorfkirche* (Yellow Village Church) and *Marine* (Marine) by Lyonel Feininger, *Paukenorgel* (Kettledrum Organ) and *Märchen* (Fairy Tale) by Paul Klee, *Drei Klänge* (Three Sounds) by Wassily Kandinsky, *Renaissancekopf* (Renaissance Head) by Alexej von Jawlensky,[18] and *Zwei Frauen am Tisch* (Two Women at a Table) by Oskar Schlemmer.[19] Shortly before May 22, 1933, the painting *Duo* by Emil Nolde was also confiscated, as Grote wrote in a letter to an acquaintance.[20]

In a documentary by Massimo Salsi and Helmut Dotterweich filmed in 1960, Grote mocked this action by Dessau's Gemeinderat in retrospect:

"With us in Dessau, what happened was that one day a committee of Stadtverordnete [city councilors] showed up, led by a flour merchant, along with a number of other especially artistically talented people, and demanded that I hand the modern paintings over to them. Because they had been purchased with funds from the city, I could not stop them, and so they took them and went to the office, to the editorial staff, of the Nazi newspaper of Dessau, in order to exhibit the paintings there and write about them: this is how public funds are squandered. [...] Now I have the satisfaction that all my paintings are now found in prominent places, for example, in the Museum of Modern Art in New York or at the Guggenheim Foundation in New York."[21]

Grote was therefore still in his post when the paintings by Bauhaus masters were taken from the Anhaltische Gemäldegalerie, so the "exhibition of shame" in Dessau took place before he was forced into early retirement in May 1933.[22] Until now, it has been a matter of contention in the literature when this exhibition was held; eyewitness reports also contradict one another. A letter from Julia Feininger to Schardt, however, makes it possible to date it more

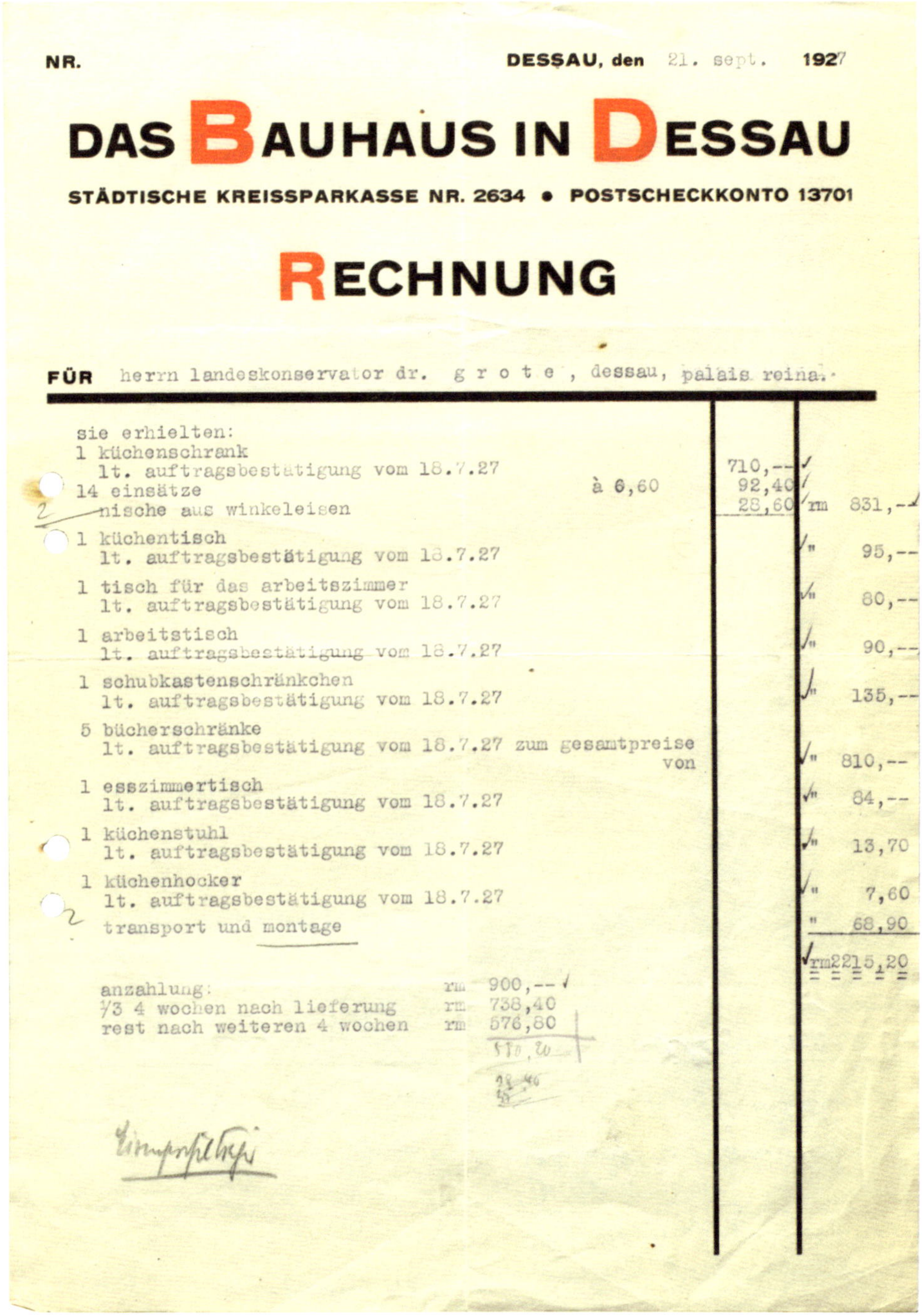

NR. DESSAU, den 21. sept. 1927

DAS BAUHAUS IN DESSAU

STÄDTISCHE KREISSPARKASSE NR. 2634 • POSTSCHECKKONTO 13701

RECHNUNG

FÜR herrn landeskonservator dr. g r o t e , dessau, palais reina.

sie erhielten:
1 küchenschrank
lt. auftragsbestätigung vom 18.7.27 710,--
14 einsätze à 6,60 92,40
nische aus winkeleisen 28,60 rm 831,--
1 küchentisch
lt. auftragsbestätigung vom 18.7.27 " 95,--
1 tisch für das arbeitszimmer
lt. auftragsbestätigung vom 18.7.27 " 80,--
1 arbeitstisch
lt. auftragsbestätigung vom 18.7.27 " 90,--
1 schubkastenschränkchen
lt. auftragsbestätigung vom 18.7.27 " 135,--
5 bücherschränke
lt. auftragsbestätigung vom 18.7.27 zum gesamtpreise von " 810,--
1 esszimmertisch
lt. auftragsbestätigung vom 18.7.27 " 84,--
1 küchenstuhl
lt. auftragsbestätigung vom 18.7.27 " 13,70
1 küchenhocker
lt. auftragsbestätigung vom 18.7.27 " 7,60
transport und montage " 68,90
rm 2215,20

anzahlung: rm 900,--
1/3 4 wochen nach lieferung rm 738,40
rest nach weiteren 4 wochen rm 576,80

Fig. 2 Furniture invoice from the Bauhaus to the state curator Ludwig Grote dated September 21, 1927. It lists: “1 kitchen cabinet […], 1 kitchen table […], 1 table for the study […], 1 work table […], 1 drawer cabinet […], 5 bookcases […], 1 dining room table […], 1 kitchen chair […], 1 kitchen stool […]” as well as “transport and assembly.”

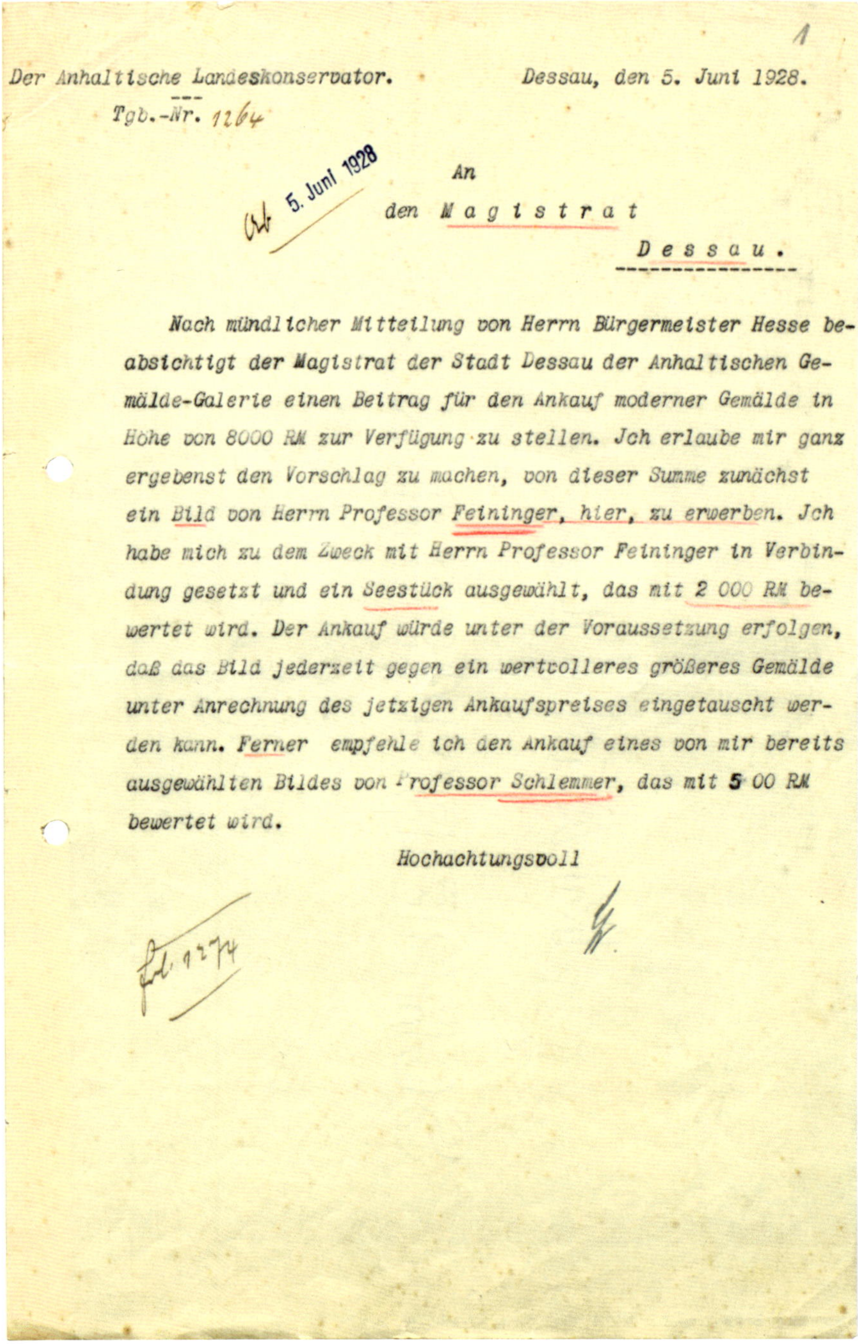
Der Anhaltische Landeskonservator. Dessau, den 5. Juni 1928.

Tgb.-Nr. 1264

5. Juni 1928

An

den M a g i s t r a t

D e s s a u .

Nach mündlicher Mitteilung von Herrn Bürgermeister Hesse beabsichtigt der Magistrat der Stadt Dessau der Anhaltischen Gemälde-Galerie einen Beitrag für den Ankauf moderner Gemälde in Höhe von 8000 RM zur Verfügung zu stellen. Jch erlaube mir ganz ergebenst den Vorschlag zu machen, von dieser Summe zunächst ein Bild von Herrn Professor Feininger, hier, zu erwerben. Jch habe mich zu dem Zweck mit Herrn Professor Feininger in Verbindung gesetzt und ein Seestück ausgewählt, das mit 2 000 RM bewertet wird. Der Ankauf würde unter der Voraussetzung erfolgen, daß das Bild jederzeit gegen ein wertvolleres größeres Gemälde unter Anrechnung des jetzigen Ankaufspreises eingetauscht werden kann. Ferner empfehle ich den Ankauf eines von mir bereits ausgewählten Bildes von Professor Schlemmer, das mit 5 00 RM bewertet wird.

Hochachtungsvoll

Fig. 3 Letter from the Anhalt state curator to the Magistrat (Municipal Administration) of Dessau, June 5, 1928, concerning the “purchase of modern paintings” by Lyonel Feininger and Oskar Schlemmer

precisely and also localize it. In her letter of March 18, 1933, she writes: “the paintings by contemporary painters that were acquired by the city and by the state over the course of the years and have not yet been shown publicly have been exhibited by the new government in the store windows of the most radical national socialist newspaper and a ‘review’ was published that day in the same newspaper. it simply isn’t possible for me to relate this review. […] the consequence of that was that yesterday our house was searched. […] my greatest worry, more than before, is the paintings.”[23] The “exhibition of shame” probably began between March 15 and 17, 1933, and was thus the first exhibition of “degenerate art” in Germany. The next “exhibition of shame” followed at the Städtische Kunsthalle in Mannheim, whose director, Gustav Hartlaub, was a prominent supporter of Neue Sachlichkeit.

Both the Feiningers’ home and that of their neighbors, the Klees, were searched on March 17, 1933: “led by a police officer […] SA [Sturmabteilung] men, with the Klees absent, forced their way into their house and searched the house, probably on order from the Magistrat [Municipal Administration] of Dessau. They confiscated three laundry baskets full of files: The files included documents from Swiss banks, correspondence with people of other political beliefs [Social Democrats and Communists] who had already fled Germany and several texts that clearly expressed his aversion to the new regime.”[24] Klee immediately returned to Dessau with his wife, Lily; they pressed charges for theft; thereafter, Paul Klee traveled to Switzerland, fearing arrest. His wife, Lily, remained in town and saw to it, with the aid of an attorney, that the confiscated goods were returned.[25]

The building in whose display windows the paintings were exhibited had originally been the office of the editorial staff and printers of the organ of the Social Democratic Party, *Das Volksblatt: Zeitung für Anhalt*. On March 13, 1933, the SA forced its way into the building, devastating and occupying it. The large letters of the neon sign of the *Volksblatt* were bent in such a way that only the letters S and A could be seen on the roof of the building from afar (fig. 4). The building now became the office of the NSDAP party organ, *Der Mitteldeutsche*.

Disciplinary proceedings were initiated against Grote as well in May 1933, “because he can be considered the driving force behind bringing the Bauhaus to Dessau and […] acquired for the City of Dessau Dadaist paintings of little value at extraordinarily high prices.”[26] He was also blamed for his vain attempt to prevent the closure of the Bauhaus Dessau by appealing via the Munich section of the Kampfbund für deutsche Kultur (Militant League for German Culture) to its chairman, Alfred Rosenberg.[27] His written explanation of this is not a glorious chapter in his biography. It reads:

“I must begin this statement with the explanation that I am informed only in general about the complex of the Bauhaus. The Bauhaus belonged to the department of Mayor Hesse. I was not called in by him to deal with it; my knowledge is therefore based essentially on the statements made in sessions of the Gemeinderat or of its committees […]. I was never called into the negotiations between Mayor Hesse and the directors of the Bauhaus or representatives of its teaching staff. The first knowledge I had of a possible takeover of the Bauhaus by Dessau was from a session of the

Magistrat. The mayor provided only general information about it [...].[28] From its first director, Mr. Gropius, I got the impression from his activity here that administrative work was 'not his thing' [...], so that the municipal offices always had to be careful that the documents required for orderly administration existed. For that reason, I did not consider it a disadvantage when I heard that Mr. Gropius wanted to resign as director. [...] [In the case of] the successor proposed by Gropius, Hannes Meyer [...], however, the effects of a Marxist ideology were evident, especially in the behavior of the students. [...] I communicated to the mayor in each case my impressions, especially with regard to pedagogical effects, and believe that this contributed significantly to his being dismissed of the contractual relationship without notice. The director who was appointed then, Mies van der Rohe, undertook a complete change of course with lasting energy."[29]

In May 1933 Grote was "at his request granted permanent retirement with immediate effect by the Reichsstatthalter (Reich Governor) in Anhalt."[30] This was the official announcement that the new powers that be had conceded to Grote since they could have dismissed him anyway under the Gesetz zur Wiederherstellung des Berufsbeamtentums (Law for the Restoration of the Professional Civil Service). In a letter, Grote ensured Wilhelm Pinder, the chairman of the Deutscher Kunstverein and a proponent of *völkisch* art history under National Socialism, that he wanted to avoid the impression of a dishonorable dismissal and for that reason asked Pinder to refrain from intervening with the ministry on his behalf. In this letter Grote attributed responsibility for his dismissal not to local politicians in Dessau, who in their "revolutionary zeal" had been fooled by a misunderstanding, but rather to a "gentleman from the staff administration of the NSDAP."[31] The NSDAP had in this same period dismissed from service more than twenty museum directors and employees who had advocated modernism.[32]

For Grote, this dismissal meant the temporary end of his career. Nevertheless, he continued to hold out hope: "my efforts will be taken up by the national revolution [...]. I hope that the nature of my departure will not make my plans impossible [...], [namely,] the organization of a central German Heimatakademie [Homeland Academy],"[33] Grote wrote in a letter to the businessman Wilhelm Fahrenholtz. Grote was now searching for a job. Lily Klee informed him in early August 1933 about a position in Krefeld that had opened up, not without adding: "In my opinion, in order to get by again, you will have to join the NSDAP in the foreseeable future. Otherwise, there is no prospect at all. By the way, positions here at the museum in Krefeld are probably filled by the city. If Dr. Sch[ardt]. were not in the party, then he probably would not have come to the Nationalg[alerie] either."[34]

Around June 1934, Grote did indeed join the Sturmabteilung (SA, Storm Detachment) before submitting an application to the Deutsche Forschungsgemeinschaft (German Research Society) for a grant for travel and printing costs for his work on the Olivier brothers. The report by the Deutscher Verein für Kunstwissenschaft (German Association for Art Scholarship) remarked favorably: "Dr. Grote, former museum director and inventory cataloguer in Dessau—who left his position on his own, for reasons of local circumstances, and is, by the way, an SA man, so he is not po-

Fig. 4 The *Volksblatt für Anhalt* building after it was searched by the police and the Sturmabteilung, March 13, 1933

litically discredited."[35] The publication was not subsidized by the DFG but rather by the Moses-Mendelssohn-Stiftung and the Deutscher Verein für Kunstwissenschaft. For this support of Grote and other dismissed museum civil servants, state funding in the amount of 15,000 marks was withheld from the Verein in 1937.[36]

The events and their course in Dessau show that the initiatives to defame the Bauhaus certainly began with local actors and that a sense of being disadvantaged was not inessential to that. Nevertheless, the crucial role was played by the staff headquarters of the NSDAP, as Grote reported. The local actors were not all uneducated people, as Grote and Schardt presented it: the chairman of the investigating committee, Richard Harms, for example, had a doctorate in law. Certainly, too, it was not the responsibility of the Sozialdemokratische Partei Deutschlands (SPD, Social Democratic Party of Germany), whose acquisitions and exhibitions of modern art allegedly asked too much of an uneducated populace. Grote's arguments and even more so Schardt's are striking for a certain blindness to the role of art scholars and their own contributions to this uncivilized crudeness.[37] Not only was Schardt chairman of the Kampfbund für deutsche Kultur in Halle, but already in the early 1920s he believed that an essential function of art in a given country was the formation of a "community of *völkisch* feeling"[38]—and in that view he was not alone among art scholars.[39] Grote was probably a convinced nationalist but not a National Socialist. Like so many other civil servants and academics at the time, he was trying to save his existence by adapting to the new regime. Especially in the phase of the seizure of power from March to May 1933, there were massive, disproportionally high admissions of civil servants and teachers to the NSDAP and its party organizations, with motives similar to those of Ludwig Grote: securing commissions, positions, and prestige.

Adolf Hitler thus also spoke of "Konjunkturritter" (opportunists) and of the imminent risk of the party becoming bourgeois, which would threaten its self-image as a militant organization. For that reason, on April 19, 1933, the party leadership imposed a ban on new members that went into effect on May 15. Nevertheless, in the phase of the seizure of power the NSDAP did indeed become "bourgeois" as feared: "It was as if the sluice gates had been opened: Whereas prior to the 'seizure of power' around 44,000 civil servants and 13,000 teachers had been organized in the party, their numbers increased in 1933 to 179,000 and 71,000, respectively, according to official 'party statistics.' Just how much civil servants and especially teachers pushed their way into the party is also demonstrated by the following comparison of figures: 7.3% of all professionals but 20% of all civil servants and 30% of all teachers were already members of the NSDAP in 1933–34."[40] The *Konjunkturritter* especially, with their eagerness to adapt and opportunism, provided the NSDAP with its broad social foundation and established it as a sole ruling party.[41]

1 See Fritz Hesse, *Erinnerungen an Dessau*, vol. 1, *Von der Residenz zur Bauhausstadt* (Bad Pyrmont: the author, 1963), 217.
2 See Alois Schardt, "Kurze Übersicht über die künstlerische Lage und Entwicklung zwischen 1900 und 1940," in *Alois J. Schardt: Ein Kunsthistoriker zwischen Weimarer Republik, "Drittem Reich" und Exil in Amerika*, ed. Ruth Heftrig, Olaf Peters, and Ulrich Rehm (Berlin: Akademie, 2013), 247–61.
3 Ibid., 261.
4 See Ruth Heftrig, Olaf Peters, and Ulrich Rehm, "Vorwort," in Heftrig, Peters, and Rehm, *Alois J. Schardt* (see note 2), xiv.
5 See "Einladung zur öffentlichen Bürgerversammlung," October 29, 1925, Stadtarchiv Dessau-Rosslau, Zellersche Sammlung, SB-86, fol. 32.
6 Bürgerverein Dessau, "Zur Bauhaus-Einweihung," *Anhaltische Rundschau*, n.d. [1926], Stadtarchiv Dessau-Rosslau, SB-86.
7 Bürgerverein Dessau, "Wählt die Einheitsliste!," leaflet, Stadtarchiv Dessau-Rosslau, Sammlung Bauhaus, S3-227.
8 When Germany became a republic in 1919, considerable holdings of collections, parks, and buildings were transferred from the house of the princes of Anhalt to the possession of the City of Dessau and the State of Anhalt. As a result, museums had to be found for the collection to make them accessible to the public. The palaces of the princes of Anhalt were also converted to public use, for example, the Palais Hilda became the headquarters of the municipal building department and the Kunsthalle the natural history museum to show the former princely collection of minerals. The Bauhaus received commissions from the City of Dessau and the State of Anhalt for facade design, graphic corporate design, and in some cases also the furnishing of the accommodations, which enabled it to compensate for the commissions from industry that it sought but failed to obtain in its early years.
9 See Ludwig Grote, Redemanuskript zur Eröffnung der Anhaltischen Gemäldegalerie, 17.9.1927, GNM, DKA, NL Grote, Ludwig (hereafter "NL Grote"), 1081.
10 The color schemes the wall painting workshop selected for the rooms of the Palais Reina and Schloss Oranienbaum can still be seen today.
11 See Ute Brüning, *Das A und O des Bauhauses: Bauhauswerbung: Schriftbilder, Drucksachen, Ausstellungsdesign* (Leizpig: Edition Leipzig 1995), 175, and Gemeinnütziger Verein Dessau e.V., Abt. Verkehrsbüro, ed., *Dessau—auf dem Boden alter Kultur, lebendiges Schaffen der Gegenwart*, Dessau 1931, SBD I 1022 D.
12 See Anhaltischer Landeskonservator to Magistrat of the City of Dessau, 5 June 1928, NL Grote, 1081.
13 For example, the *Heimat* painter Paul Riess of Dessau repeatedly reminded Dessau's mayor, Fritz Hesse, of his existence and lamented the preference for Bauhaus artists, which was also echoed in the local press; see Helga Heise, "Die ersten Jahre der Anhaltischen Gemäldegalerie unter Ludwig Grote," in *Verrat an der Moderne: Die Gründungsgeschichte und das erste Jahrzehnt der Anhaltischen Gemäldegalerie Dessau, 1927–37*, ed. Norbert Michels (Dessau: Anhaltische Gemäldegalerie, 1996), 51–79, esp. 69.
14 Both Hesse and Schardt mention as one of the reasons for the agitation against and outrage over modern painting in so-called *Schandausstellungen* was that they were the work of people who "had never set foot in the exhibition"; Hesse, *Erinnerungen an Dessau* (see note 2), vol. 2, *Aus den Jahren 1925 bis 1950* (Dessau: Anhaltische Verlagsanstalt, 1995), 51–52, or, who saw a "thoughtless" public exhibition of modern paintings by Social Democratic representatives of the government.
15 See Sebastian Neurauter, *Das Bauhaus und die Verwertungsrechte* (Tübingen: Mohr Siebeck, 2013), 459–60.
16 The Palais Cohn-Oppenheim, designed by the architect Alfred Messel, was the official residence of the mayor of Dessau after World War I.
17 "Herrn Hesses wunder Punkt," newspaper clipping, March 15, 1933, Stadtarchiv Dessau-Rosslau, SB-39, Handakte OB Fritz Hesse 1926–33, fol. 62.
18 "In 1938 I had an experience I would like to relate. [...] L. Gr. met the art historian Dr. [Rolf] Hetsch on the street in Berlin by chance. They immediately discussed the paintings confiscated by the Nazis; it was known that they were being collected in Berlin; and this Dr. H. was supposed to supervise and direct their storage in Schloss Belvedere (?). Gr. asked him whether he knew the location of the paintings he had acquired in Dessau for the gallery and city. He was particularly interested in the interesting Roman head by Jawlensky. [...] The Jawlensky head, yes, he had it in his hands yesterday; it was going to Lucerne. Quite naively, Gr. asked: 'Does it have to go to Lucerne?' 'If you have foreign currency, you too can buy it.' That was 1938, when he was already living in the Engadine. 'I do, how much should it be?' 'You are free to choose; it simply has to indicate a sum in a foreign currency.' In jest, Gr. said: 'Well, then, ten Swiss francs.' 'Deal,' said Hetsch. 'You can have the picture and transfer the money.' That is what happened, and today one must struggle to understand that this game did not continue, which of course 'cleverer' people did. With the weight that Gr. had taken upon himself and his general state of conscience, he could no longer buy things." Gertrud Maud Grote, "Lebenserinnerungen und biografische Aufzeichnungen zu Ludwig Grote" (ca. 1910–1990) typescript with handwritten notes, February 23, 1980, and 1990, NL Grote, ASS 2. The painting is now in the Kunstmuseum Winterthur in Switzerland.
19 Ibid., The newspaper clipping mentions a painter named Möller, but probably the Galerie Möller is intended, from which the paintings had been acquired and as it is also noted in the files of the investigating committee; see the appendix in, *Verrat an der Moderne* ed. Norbert Michels (see note 13) ; Stadtarchiv Dessau-Rosslau, Handakte Harms, Verfügungen, fol. 57; see also Ludwig Grote, "Bericht über meine Entlassung für Geh[eimrat] Prof. Dr. [Wilhelm] Pinder," NL Grote, 2357.
20 Ludwig Grote to Wilhelm Adolf Fahrenholtz, 22 May 1933, ibid. , 2357.
21 Massimo Salsi and Helmut Dotterweich, *Bildersturm im Dritten Reich* (1962), broadcast on Bayerischer Rundfunk, February 15, 1988, quoted in Susanne Neubauer, "Ludwig Grote und die Moderne, 1933–1959: Paradigma einer Internationalisierung," *RIHA Journal 0180* (October 10, 2017), n. 105.
22 The exhibition cannot therefore have been held as late as July 1933, as Susanne Neubauer suspects (ibid.), citing Margit Ziesche, "Die Anhaltische

Gemäldegalerie in der Zeit des Nationalsozialismus," in Michels, *Verrat an der Moderne* (see note 13), 104.
23 Julia Feininger to Alois Schardt, 18 March 1933, Moeller Fine Art Projects | The Lyonel Feininger Project, New York and Berlin.
24 Stefan Frey and Andreas Hüneke, "Paul Klee: Kunst und Politik in Deutschland 1933; Eine Chronologie," in *Paul Klee 1933*, ed. Städtische Galerie im Lenbachhaus, exh. cat. Städtische Galerie im Lenbachhaus, Munich (Cologne: Verlag der Buchhandlung Walther König, 2003), 268–306, esp. 282.
25 See ibid.
26 Magistrat file concerning the committee investigating Mayor Hesse and the proceeding against Dr. Grote, 1933. Stadtarchiv Dessau-Rosslau, SB-34.
27 See the essay by Christian Eger in the present volume.
28 Thirty years later, Grote wrote to Hesse of all people, after the latter had described in his memoirs the Bauhaus being taken over by Dessau and how pleased he was that his services were finally being appreciated; see Fritz Hesse, *Erinnerungen an Dessau* (see note 1), 195–207, and Ludwig Grote to Fritz Hesse, 31 October 1963, NL Grote, 351.
29 Ludwig Grote, "Stellungnahme zum Umzug des Bauhauses von Weimar sowie zu seinen Leitern," 1933, ibid., 1469. Grote's distancing himself is also expressed in a letter from Josef Albers to Maud and him of March 26, 1933. He writes: "shame that I didn't see Mrs. Grote again. And Grote was also in Berlin once without getting in touch. And my birthday card reads: Mr. Albers [...]. But the abstract artists don't have much to hope for" (ibid., 702); the relationship would, however, quickly normalize again; see the subject correspondence, ibid.
30 "Personalien," *Amtsblatt für Anhalt* 170, no. 43 (1933): 183.
31 Ludwig Grote to Wilhelm Pinder, 21 June 1933, NL Grote, 2357.
32 See Heise, *Die ersten Jahre der Anhaltischen Gemäldegalerie* (see note 13), esp. 78.
33 Ludwig Grote to Wilhelm Adolf Fahrenholtz, 22 May 1933, NL Grote, 2357.
34 Lily Klee to Ludwig Grote, 1 August 1933, Zentrum Paul Klee, Bern, Schenkung Nachlass Familie Grote.
35 Deutscher Verein für Kunstwissenschaft, "Grote: Die Brüder Olivier u. ihr Gang durch die deutsche Romantik, Deutsche Forschungsgemeinschaft," application of June 4, 1934, Bundesarchiv 1532, Standort 51, Haus 901/KG8 (with thanks to Ulrich Lange for its use).
36 See Heinrich Dilly, *Deutsche Kunsthistoriker, 1933–1945* (Munich: Deutscher Kunstverlag, 1988), 41.
37 For example, Schardt, as the recently appointed director of the Nationalgalerie, in a letter dated July 8, 1933, asked Klee for an Aryan certificate in preemptive obedience, supposedly to protect him and his works; see Heftrig, Peters, and Rehm, *Alois J. Schardt* (see note 2), xi n. 4. Klee considered this request an imposition and wrote his wife, Lily, in outrage: "even if it were true that i am a jew [...], that would not change one iota about my person and my achievement. this is my personal standpoint: anyone who believes that a jew and a foreigner are not worth less than a german and native can be relied on, in my view. i would certainly accept hardship than represent the tragicomical figure of someone currying favor from those in power"; Paul Klee, *Briefe an die Familie*, vol. 2: *1907–1940*, ed. Felix Klee (Cologne: DuMont, 1979), 1233–34.
38 See Alois Schardt, "Verstandeskultur—Kunstbetrachtung—Gefühlskultur," in Heftrig, Peters, and Rehm, *Alois J. Schardt* (see note 2), 33–44, esp. 44.
39 Heinrich Wölfflin developed the method of a "psychology of national forms" in his lecture course and publication *Kunstgeschichtliche Grundbegriffe* during World War I; translated by Jonathan Blower as *Principles of Art History: The Problem of the Development of Style in Early Modern Art*, ed. Evonne Levy and Tristan Weddigen (Los Angeles, CA: Getty Research Institute, 2015), 89. Using this method, he explained form "as the expression of the essence, of the temperament of an artist, of the general temperament of a race"; cf. Hans Körner, "'Grundbegriffe der Kunstgeschichte': Heinrich Wölfflins Münchner Vorlesung im Wintersemester 1914/15," *kritische berichte* 16, no. 4 (1988) 65–73, esp. 68. Wölfflin was, moreover, a registered supporter of the Kampfbund für deutsche Kultur. Wilhelm Pinder, who was influential in his field and in politics, also tried as early as 1926 to provide a biological and *völkisch* foundation for art history in his treatise *Das Problem der Generation in der Kunstgeschichte Europas*; see Dilly, *Deutsche Kunsthistoriker* (see note 36), 13.
40 Jürgen W. Falter, "Die Märzgefallenen: Neue Forschungsergebnisse zum sozialen Wandel innerhalb der NSDAP-Mitgliedschaft während der Machtergreifungsphase," *Historical Social Research*, Supplement 25 (1998): 280–302, esp. 300, https://nbn-resolving.org/urn:nbn:de:0168-ssoar-379908 (accessed November 17, 2020).
41 Ibid., 302. I am grateful to Peter Bernhard, Torsten Blume, and Ulrich Lange for their valuable suggestions.

Ludwig Grote and the Galerie Zinckgraf (formerly Heinemann) in the Years 1940–1946

Birgit Jooss

Ludwig Grote has thus far been regarded as one of Germany's art historians who had been crucial advocates of modernism both before and after World War II and had to withdraw into so-called inner emigration during the period of National Socialism.[1] For example, it had been Grote who saw to it that the Bauhaus moved from Weimar to Dessau, and it was he who organized pioneering exhibitions, initiated by Eberhard Hanfstaengl (1886–1973), at the Haus der Kunst after the war, with which they were able to show the modernism of "defamed" and "degenerate" artists in a proper light and thereby rehabilitate it.[2] Following his early retirement as Landeskonservator (State Curator) in Anhalt in May 1933, he remained, according to his biographer, "faithful" in the sense that he was active as a writer on art and, as one learns from only a few biographies, worked in the art trade in Munich. As with so many of his generation, the period under National Socialism is abridged in the common biographies. If one reads Gert von der Osten's (1910–1983) detailed, seven-page obituary for Grote in *Kunstchronik*, one finds that he mentions the period between 1933 and 1945 in one brief sentence: "For a time, however, in the meagerness of the era he had to make do with something like the art trade,"[3] in order to emphasize his services to modernity. What remains unmentioned: What art trade? Where? Under what conditions? In what role? In his commemorative address, Stephan Waetzoldt (1920–2008) did not speak of this period either, summarily vouching for Grote's "blameless past": "Then came the war. The officer from World War I was conscripted again, was sent to the Eastern front, but had the fortune and fate to experience the end of the war in Munich. There, aided by his blameless past and old international connections and friendships, Grote conceived and organized the exhibitions from 1949 onward that became world-famous success and have now made history again: Blauer Reiter [Blue Rider], Beckmann memorial, Kokoschka retrospective, painters at the Bauhaus, graphic works by Toulouse-Lautrec."[4] The "fortune and fate to experience the end of the war in Munich," that is, not on the Eastern front, presumably spared Grote bad experiences. Nevertheless, it remains to be explained what is hiding behind this formulation.

In Grote's papers in the Deutsches Kunstarchiv in the Germanisches Nationalmuseum in Nuremberg, biographies of varied length and varied detail are preserved. It is unclear who wrote them, since—because sometimes his death is already mentioned—he cannot have written them himself. Whereas some of them merely mention "1942 military service," one of these curricula vitae states "from 1939 active in the art trade in Munich. 1942 military service."[5] Another set of documents contains Grote's autobiographies, as is clear in some cases from his handwriting. Whereas some versions leave out his Munich period entirely—in these cases it says only "1933 dismissal by the National Socialists. Until 1951 active as a freelance writer on art"—there is one curriculum vitae with a handwritten note by him: "1940–51 in Munich. From 1940 to 1946 in the art trade there. 1941–44 army."[6] In all these documents, it remains unclear in what art trade. A name is never mentioned. This is not surprising, because the art dealer in question is not just any old one but a formerly Jewish-owned one that in its day was considered one of the most renowned, not just in Munich but Germany-wide, if not even worldwide: the

Galerie Heinemann, founded in 1872, which had been "Aryanized" in 1939 by Friedrich Heinrich Zinckgraf (1878–1954) and renamed the Galerie am Lenbachplatz in 1941 (fig. 1). Working in a formerly Jewish-owned art gallery with a rich tradition that had been transferred to "Aryan hands" at the instigation of the National Socialists clearly no longer made a good impression in a curriculum vitae after 1945.[7]

Grote's Hiring by the Galerie Zinckgraf

Grote's friend the art historian Eberhard Hanfstaengl had arranged this job for him (fig. 2). His dismissal in Dessau in 1933 must have come as a shock to the thirty-nine-year-old father of two children. The writing on art to which Grote referred in his curricula vitae cannot have brought in much. At the same time, he was trying to gain a foothold in the area of historical preservation in Berlin. The offer from Munich must therefore have seemed like a sheet anchor. That is evident from a speech in which he expresses his thanks for the kind wishes on his eightieth birthday in 1973. It begins not with his activity in Dessau but with his appointment in Munich: "Honored and dear friends, I truly do not know how I can thank you for so much kindness and honor! My thoughts return to the year 1939 when my unforgotten friend Eberhard Hanfstaengl invited me to follow him from Berlin to Munich. He had been offered a position in an art dealership in Munich, which he passed on to me. My subsequent involvement with Munich art from before and around 1900 was a rather strange experience after several years of freelance activity and the years of the Bauhaus, but it considerably expanded my knowledge and quickly made me feel at home in Munich."[8] In this speech, too, Grote fails to mention the art dealership in question. Only its profile is made clear: it dealt with Munich art of the nineteenth century and of the turn of the century.

Eberhard Hanfstaengl, an officer's son, was an art historian and a cousin of Ernst Hanfstaengl (1887–1975), who was initially a close political fellow traveler of Adolf Hitler (1889–1945), who had aided him in his rise in Munich society. In 1933 Eberhard Hanfstaengl had succeeded Ludwig Justi (1876–1957) as director of the Nationalgalerie in Berlin, but was removed from that post in 1937.

From the documents in Grote's papers that concern his hiring by the Galerie Zinckgraf, one learns about the conditions. Only two letters and two replies in carbon copies have survived that provide insight into the business connection between Grote and Friedrich Heinrich Zinckgraf. The latter confirmed on the stationery of the Galerie am Lenbachplatz, formerly Galerie Heinemann, on January 17, 1940, an oral employment agreement. From February 1, 1940, he employed Grote in a permanent position with a rather lavish monthly salary of 750 reichsmarks (fig. 3). Just three days later, on January 20, 1940, Grote confirmed his service. Because he wished to retain both his place of residence in Berlin and his membership in the Reichsschrifttumskammer (Reich Chamber of Literature), he emphasized that he would be available as a freelance worker: "It seems to me appropriate for reasons of professional organization and taxes that my relationship to your firm be that of a freelance scholarly associate. As an employee, I would presumably have difficulties keeping my official place of residence in Berlin and

Fig. 1 Galerie Heinemann, on Lenbachplatz, ca. 1910
Fig. 2 Eberhard Hanfstaengl and Ludwig Grote, 1951

membership in the Reichsschrifttumskammer, to which I attach importance."[9] In 1953, however, Grote asked Zinckgraf for proof of his employee insurance for the period of his employment, from which it can be inferred that he ultimately switched to an employee relationship.[10]

The Galerie Zinckgraf under National Socialism

So who was this Friedrich Heinrich Zinckgraf (fig. 4)? He had begun training at the Galerie Heinemann already in 1900 and had worked for the company ever since. In January 1938, as a long-standing non-Jewish employee, a member of the Reichskulturkammer der bildenden Künste (Reich Cultural Chamber of the Fine Arts), and expert in the painting of the Munich school, he became a partner in the gallery, which at the time was being run by Franziska Heinemann (1882–1940), the daughter-in-law of the gallery's founder (fig. 5). Her son Fritz (1905–1983) had emigrated to Switzerland, and his twenty-five-percent share had been taken over by Zinckgraf. Zinckgraf had not only the necessary expertise but also sales experience, personal customer contacts, and presumably at first the trust of Franziska Heinemann as well. His involvement seemed to ensure that her interests would continue to be preserved. She remained chief executive officer, and the gallery continued to be categorized as a "Jewish company."[11]

"The situation grew worse after the Pogrom Night in November 1938, however. Now commerce was no longer possible for her; the end of the gallery's operation can be dated to November 10, 1938.[12] Soon thereafter, on December 16, 1938, Franziska Heinemann was arrested and brought to Stadelheim prison. She was charged with fraudulent foreign currency exchange."[13]

Zinckgraf immediately negotiated with her over the value of the business, the dividing up of the holdings of paintings, and the sale as well as with the Industrie- und Handelskammer (Chamber of Industry and Commerce) and the Gauleitung (district administration) over the "Aryanization" of the art gallery. He had no capital of his own, however, with which to purchase the gallery. For that, he contacted one of the most influential financial experts of the time, the president of the Reichsbank, Hjalmar Schacht (1877–1970), who, after extended negotiations, granted him a loan in exchange for silent partnership (fig. 6). Zinckgraf had commissioned Eberhard Hanfstaengl to assess the holdings of goods; an architect estimated the value of the real estate. The "Aryanization contract" was signed on February 17, 1939, by Zinckgraf and Franziska Heinemann, after she was released from pretrial detention. He acquired the company for far less than its value: For a sum of 500,000 reichsmarks, he took over not only the buildings and the holdings of paintings but also the assets of the business. The liabilities of the company were not transferred to him, so that Franziska Heinemann's outstanding debts had to be paid. On February 23, 1939, she left the country and emigrated via Lucerne, Switzerland, to New York, where she died on November 18, 1940. Not until December 1, 1939, did Zinckgraf receive the necessary approval for the sale from the Reichswirtschaftsministerium (Reich Ministry of the Economy) and thus finally became the owner of the Galerie Heinemann. Shortly thereafter, on November 14, he had taken out the corresponding loan from Hjalmar Schacht.

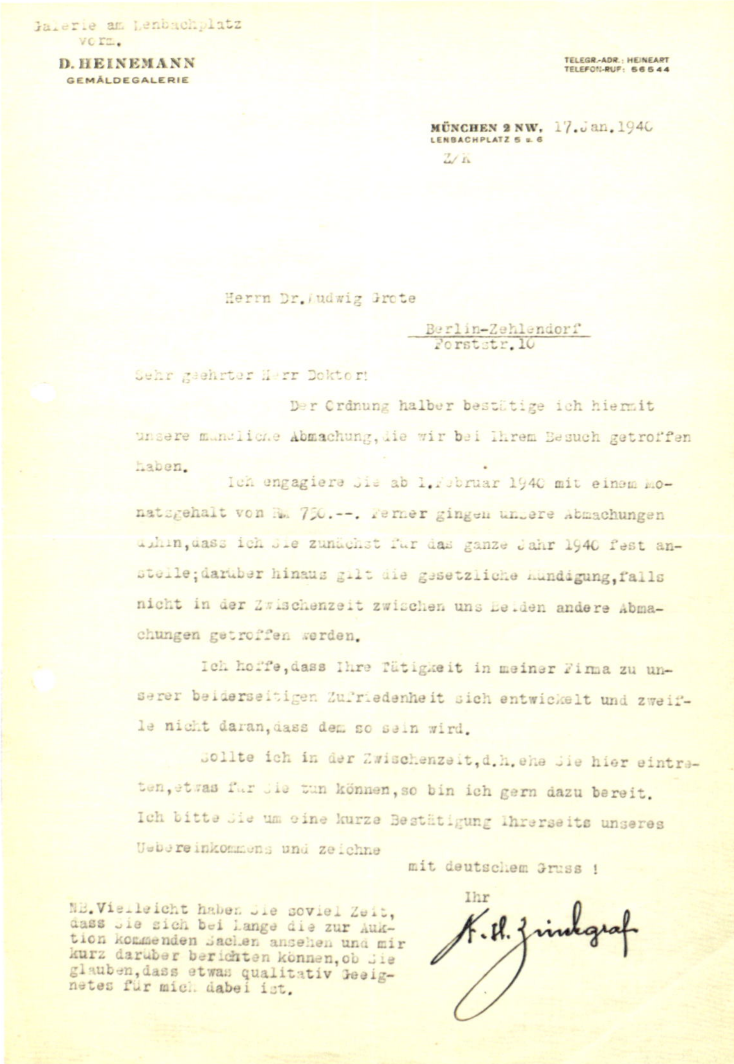

Galerie am Lenbachplatz
vorm.
D. HEINEMANN
GEMÄLDEGALERIE

TELEGR.-ADR.: HEINEART
TELEFON-RUF: 56544

MÜNCHEN 2 NW. 17.Jan.1940
LENBACHPLATZ 5 u. 6

Z/K

Herrn Dr.Ludwig Grote

Berlin-Zehlendorf
Forststr.10

Sehr geehrter Herr Doktor!

Der Ordnung halber bestätige ich hiermit unsere mündliche Abmachung, die wir bei Ihrem Besuch getroffen haben.

Ich engagiere Sie ab 1.Februar 1940 mit einem Monatsgehalt von RM 750.--. Ferner gingen unsere Abmachungen dahin,dass ich Sie zunächst für das ganze Jahr 1940 fest anstelle;darüber hinaus gilt die gesetzliche Kündigung,falls nicht in der Zwischenzeit zwischen uns Beiden andere Abmachungen getroffen werden.

Ich hoffe,dass Ihre Tätigkeit in meiner Firma zu unserer beiderseitigen Zufriedenheit sich entwickelt und zweifle nicht daran,dass dem so sein wird.

Sollte ich in der Zwischenzeit,d.h.ehe Sie hier eintreten,etwas für Sie tun können,so bin ich gern dazu bereit. Ich bitte Sie um eine kurze Bestätigung Ihrerseits unseres Uebereinkommens und zeichne

mit deutschem Gruss !

Ihr

F.H. Zinckgraf

NB.Vielleicht haben Sie soviel Zeit, dass Sie sich bei Lange die zur Auktion kommenden Sachen ansehen und mir kurz darüber berichten können,ob Sie glauben,dass etwas qualitativ Geeignetes für mich dabei ist.

Fig. 3 Letter from Friedrich Heinrich Zinckgraf to Ludwig Grote regarding his position beginning February 1, 1940

Fig. 4 Friedrich Heinrich Zinckgraf, ca. 1953

After settling "Aryanization," Zinckgraf was able to mark large profits. Sales of paintings are documented until March 1944 and show constant turnover. The high profits did not, however, result from artificial deductions of works of art, because he set the book values of works very low and thus relied on the hidden reserves he had formed by taking over the storeroom cheaply. In May 1941, finally, he gave the Galerie Heinemann the new name *Galerie am Lenbachplatz*, under which it operated until Zinckgraf's death in 1954. Thus the name of the extremely successful, Jewish dynasty of the art market disappeared from Munich's cityscape and fell into oblivion. Restitution proceedings against Friedrich Zinckgraf brought by Franziska's sons, Fritz and Paul Heinemann (1909–1965), in 1949 ended in a settlement. Like Hjalmar Schacht, both brothers had a share in profits of twenty-five percent each until the gallery was closed down. On October 8, 1954, after Zinckgraf's death, everything was auctioned off, not just the paintings but the entire inventory. It was all over for one of Munich's most important galleries. Only the building remained, but there is no reference today to remind us of its history.[14]

The Fate of the Jewish-Owned Galerie Heinemann

In its day, the Galerie Heinemann was considered one of the most influential art dealers in the world. Since 1883 it had had its headquarters in Munich; in addition, it had numerous branches, including in Nice and New York, and served an international clientele from Tokyo to Seattle.

One high point in the history of the gallery was no doubt the completion of the stately family home and gallery building at Maximiliansplatz 3/4 (later Lenbachplatz 5/6) in 1904, which the founder of the company, David Heinemann (1819–1902), did not live to see. The renowned architect Emanuel von Seidl (1856–1919) had been commissioned to design and build it. Heinemann thus created, in terms not only of its dimensions but also of its functional decoration, one of the most important locations for art that Munich ever had.[15] Its retrospective self-assessment reads: "the expansive exhibition spaces, whose size alone made them the greatest exhibition opportunity not just in Germany but on the whole continent and yet also deserve to be called absolutely functional, since they were built by Professor v. Seidl, as noted in the outset, specifically for the purposes of the art trade and for exhibitions of paintings."[16] It had what was at the time one of the largest private halls with skylights in the city—comparable only to museum buildings. A total of "twelve well-adapted halls and galleries"[17] allowed for a diverse program and several exhibitions side by side at the same time (fig.7). In addition to solo presentations, there were large retrospective thematic exhibitions with the goal of educating the public in Munich. The gallery thus functioned not only as a place for the art trade but also had a programmatic ambition, which included presenting exhibitions put together according to art historical perspectives, which were not determined by the contingencies of the market, as was common in the art trade at the time. Without a doubt, the Galerie Heinemann was one of the most important exhibition venues in the art city of Munich, which was mentioned in the same breath as its museums, the

Fig. 5 Franziska and Theobald Heinemann, 1904

Kunstverein (Arts Society), the Glaspalast (Crystal Palace), and the Secession.

In terms of subject matter, it had a striking focus, which essentially did not correlate with Grote's interests: It had specialized in the Munich school. Grote's wife, Gertrud Maud (1906–1996), later recalled: "Above all, however, it was the sort of art sold there, which did not suit him at all. Almost exclusively Munich school [...] up to the modern era. [...] Plush carpets, damask walls, enormous halls, and stately exhibitions are conceived for the sentimental, Bavarian, and for the rich average buyer. [...] But soon the Munich collectors arrived: 'You are here'—the best connoisseur of the Romantics, author of an Olivier book, etc.—'what good fortune for us here in Munich.'"[18]

A look at the heyday of the Galerie Heinemann quickly makes it clear that both the traded works and those sold on consignment were dominated—more than seventy-two percent—by works by artists from Germany, Austria, or Switzerland. An important share came from the circle of the Akademie der Bildenden Künste (Academy of the Fine Arts) in Munich, which especially in the second half of the nineteenth century was one of the leading German schools of painters.[19] Its proponents, such as Franz von Defregger (1835–1921), Eduard von Grützner (1846–1925), Franz von Lenbach (1836–1904), Hermann (1846–1909) and Friedrich August von Kaulbach (1850–1920), Carl Spitzweg (1808–1885), Josef Wenglein (1845–1919), Heinrich von Zügel (1850–1941), and Ludwig von Zumbusch (1861–1927), numbered among the artists most frequently sold by the Galerie Heinemann. Customers abroad were the primary target audience, above all Americans. That explains why Heinemann made such an effort with its branches to attract international attention and connect to a corresponding clientele. Whereas community documents record 72 sales to the Neue Pinakothek in Munich, 529 works were sold to customers in New York during the same period.[20]

Following the death of Theobald Heinemann (1860–1929), one of David Heinemann's sons, on May 18, 1929, his widow, Franziska, continued to run the gallery self-confidently and energetically until November 1938. Even after the National Socialists seized power and after the "boycott of Jews" was announced in 1933, she continued to trade in art; and that despite restrictions that made it increasingly difficult to run the business after the Bund der Deutschen Kunst- und Antiquitätenhändler (Association of German Art and Antiques Dealers) was restructured and affiliated with the Reichskammer der Bildenden Künste and actions for a "new uniform regulations for the German art trade" in the summer of 1935.[21] Although Jewish art dealers and other sellers of cultural goods had been excluded from the Reichskulturkammer already since 1935, most Jewish-owned art dealerships had been closed down, and in 1937 "the 'Aryanization' of the Jewish-owned art trade in Germany [had been] largely completed,"[22] the Galerie Heinemann was able to conduct its business with relatively minimal restriction until Pogrom Night.[23]

The continued existence of the gallery was beneficial to the National Socialist regime above all because its extensive export business brought important foreign currency to the Reich. Franziska Heinemann continued to conduct international art trade, especially with the United States and Switzerland. As late as

Fig. 6 Hjalmar Schacht, 1931
Fig. 7 Galerie Heinemann, ca. 1910

January 1937, the Industrie- und Handelskammer certified that the Heinemann company continued to have brisk business abroad that was of great importance to the German economy.[24] Moreover, the art trade was certainly also of significance for the important figures in National Socialist cultural policy, who acquired their works of art here. For example, people such as the gallerist Maria Almas-Dietrich (1892–1971), who was active for the Führermuseum in Linz on behalf of Adolf Hitler, bought there on a large scale. The racial ideology and economic interests of the National Socialist regime did not always coincide, and that was presumably the reason why the Galerie Heinemann was allowed to conduct its business for so long. The questions that have yet to be answered is whether the gallery was being protected and if so by whom.

Because the Zinckgraf archive has not survived, it remains uncertain whether the profile of the Galerie Heinemann was adopted and continued or rather altered. The few files that were continued in the Heinemann system point to the portfolio's being maintained. Grote himself spoke of "Munich art prior to and around 1900."[25]

Grote's Conduct under National Socialism

Grote was aware of the fate of the Jewish-owned Galerie Heinemann, which, after all, still retained its original name when he began to work there. It is difficult to imagine that this fate left him cold; nevertheless, he clearly did not see that as a reason to turn down the lucrative offer to work there. The need to earn money will have been powerful for the father of two children, despite a pension from Dessau of an unknown amount. Moreover, even around half a year after he was hired, his letters to his wife do not express enthusiasm about his position at Zinckgraf. He wrote that although he was still close to art and was making an adequate living, his position as "employee" did not seem to please him. His area of responsibility remained "scholarly," because, he wrote, Zinckgraf did not involve him in "sales and other things."[26] His wife, Gertrud Maud, later recalled: "At first, he felt very bad, because his boss, the authorized signatory of the former Jewish company of this house (Heinemann right next to Bernheimer), does not know how to handle him—he is too subaltern in some respects, L. already too old and too far along to accept much of subordinate role, etc."[27]

In October 1941 Grote was conscripted into the army and in May 1942 promoted to "first lieutenant of the available reserve." Although deployed in Germany at first, in January 1943 he was sent to the Eastern front. When on leave, he continued to work in the gallery,[28] so that he experienced the first night of bombing in Munich of September 19–20, 1942, during which the gallery building was hit, which took days to clean up.[29] He was discharged on June 6, 1944, because of a myocardial insufficiency, but the intervention of the gallery was apparently decisive, if his wife's report is to be believed: "I forgot to say that Ludwig has since returned from Russia (May 15), because his business had required him and something is wrong with his heart, both of which, underscored whether the necessary red pencil, led to him being discharged from the army!"[30]

For his civil deployment, Grote applied in November 1944 to wear his uniform "in particular when serving in the Volkssturm."[31] When he was indeed called up for the

Volkssturm in February 1945, he applied to be discharged for pneumonia. As justification, he cited, among other things, his deployment for the heavily damaged Zinckgraf art gallery in Munich and referred to special relationships to the special envoy of the Führer (whom he does not name): "On January 7, the Galerie Zinckgraf, the largest art dealer in Munich and in all of Germany was completely damaged. The extraordinarily valuable cultural asset of more than 1,200 paintings was threatened by rain and meltwater and absolutely had to be protected. Since that attack, I have been negotiating with an aide-de-camp to the Reichsführer SS (Reich leader of the SS) and the Gaustabsamt (Office of the Regional Staff). Both authorities are very interested, for reasons of cultural policy, in our continued existence, as is the Führer's special envoy for the museum in Linz."[32] Grote did not hesitate to point out the gallery's significance for the National Socialists in order to underscore his own importance. He spoke of "world dominance" and a "glorious victory."[33] As far as we know today, however, Grote never joined the National Socialist Party and because he had "not listed" the "embarrassing affair" of his SA membership on his de-Nazification form,[34] he was quickly officially categorized as "exonerated" on December 7, 1946.[35]

Continuities after the War's End

Even after the war ended, Grote was working in the gallery, where he continued to receive a high salary: "Now L. is working in the office for three hours every morn.—it is being run in the corridor of the entrance, but it is gradually being repaired. Now the question is what will happen, will the art trade hold out? If Mr. Zinckgraf remains in the business—he did not do anything to the Jews, everything is in order in their relationship—he can continue to pay L. 1000 marks a month even with the current low sales—if the Amer. allow the business to continue at all, etc." And the next passage makes it clear how much Grote had profited from the gallery's business under National Socialism. She continues: "L. could, of course, now return to the civil service, he would have been given a very interesting position in Bavaria, but after the free life and financial boom of the last eight years we can no longer go back to the low level of life in the civil service,—[*sic*] but we don't know whether that thinking is correct. Strictly speaking, we have become more flexible, and because the pension from Dessau has not been coming in since January, we don't believe in so-called security anymore, because the Russians will surely not think of paying 'victims of the Nazis,' which is what L. is, remunerations and pensions."[36] With his pension and salary, Grote had a considerable income over the years; it was high enough to make a position in the civil service unattractive to him. At least in a financial sense, then, one can scarcely speak of a "meagerness of the era."[37] To speak in this context of "victims of the Nazis" sounds highly insidious in the face of the immeasurable suffering inflicted on Jews and others.

Like many of his fellow art historians, after 1945 Grote dedicated himself intently to High Modernism, and thus to "defamed" and "degenerate" artists, especially the Expressionists but also the Bauhaus artists, even though, as a specialist in Romanticism, he was no expert in that field. A look at his publishing activity confirms this: prior to 1933, he published first and foremost on art historical themes of the Middle Ages, the Renaissance, Romanticism, and on Wörlitzer Park. From 1933 to 1945, publications on Romanticism and German architecture of the Middle Ages dominate, and there is no scholarly work at all on the Munich school of the nineteenth century. After 1946, he published titles on High Modernism strikingly often, beginning with a two-page exhibition catalog on Kandinsky for the Galerie Stangl in Munich to the more substantial catalogs for the Haus der Kunst on, for example, Blauer Reiter and the Bauhaus.[38] Working on High Modernism was no doubt the best opportunity to avoid any suspicions of working with the Nazi system, since "It seems to have been assumed there was an inner connection between modern art and a democratic conviction."[39]

Grote did ultimately return to the civil service. After his exhibition activity for Hanfstaengl at the Haus der Kunst, he was appointed director of the Germanisches Nationalmuseum in 1951, and he remained in that post until 1962. There, too, he worked to cover up his time under National Socialism and arranged for a largely expurgated biography.

1 See Ulrike Wendland, "Ludwig Grote," in *Biographisches Handbuch deutschsprachiger Kunsthistoriker im Exil: Leben und Werk der unter dem Nationalsozialismus verfolgten und vertriebenen Wissenschaftler*, part 1 (A–K) (Munich: Saur, 1999), 251–55. "Inner emigration" has to be seen as a topos for relieving guilt in the art world; see Beate Marks-Hanssen, *Innere Emigration? "Verfemte" Künstlerinnen und Künstler in der Zeit des Nationalsozialismus* (Berlin: dissertation.de, 2006). I am sincerely grateful to Christian Fuhrmeister for advice and suggestions.

2 See Andrea Bambi, "Eberhard Hanfstaengl und seine Amtszeit bei den Bayerischen Staatsgemäldesammlungen von 1945 bis 1953," in *"So fing man einfach an, ohne viele Worte": Ausstellungswesen und Sammlungspolitik in den ersten Jahren nach dem Zweiten Weltkrieg*, ed. Julia Friedrich and Andreas Prinzing (Berlin: De Gruyter, 2013), 157–65, esp. 158.

3 Gert von Osten, obituary for Ludwig Grote, *Kunstchronik: Monatsschrift für Kunstwissenschaft, Museumswesen und Denkmalpflege* 27, no. 7 (1974): 231–37, esp. 234. The obituaries in various other newspapers do not mention the wartime period either; see GNM, DKA, NL Grote, Ludwig (hereafter "NL Grote"), 2.

4 Stephan Waetzoldt, "Gedenkrede in Nürnberg," Germanisches Nationalmuseum, July 5, 1974, p. 4., NL Grote, 995.

5 Curricula vitae of Ludwig Grote, NL Grote, 246.

6 Autobiographies of Ludwig Grote, NL Grote, 1128.

7 See Birgit Jooss, "Galerie Heinemann: Die wechselvolle Geschichte einer jüdischen Kunsthandlung zwischen 1872 und 1938," *Anzeiger des Germanischen Nationalmuseums* (2012): 69–84; idem, "Die Geschäftsunterlagen der Galerie Heinemann: Eine bedeutende Grundlage für die weiterführende Provenienzforschung," in *Provenienzforschung in deutschen Sammlungen: Einblicke in zehn Jahre Projektförderung*, ed. Deutsches Zentrum Kulturgutverluste (Berlin: De Gruyter, 2019), 265–72; and Anja Heuss, "Friedrich Heinrich Zinckgraf und die 'Arisierung' der Galerie Heinemann in München," *Anzeiger des Germanischen Nationalmuseums* (2012): 85–94.

8 Ludwig Grote, "Dankesrede" (1973), NL Grote, 960.

9 Ludwig Grote to Friedrich Heinrich Zinckgraf, 20 January 1940, NL Grote, 1085.

10 See Ludwig Grote to Friedrich Heinrich Zinckgraf, 14 September 1953, NL Grote, 1085.

11 The Gewerbeamt (Trade Office) complained that the partnership was illegal under the law to protect retail trade and demanded that Zinckgraf leave the company; see Wolfram Selig, *"Arisierung" in München: Die Vernichtung jüdischer Existenz, 1937–1939* (Berlin: Metropol, 2004), 627–28.

12 See Stadtarchiv München, Gewerbeamt Arisierungsakten Abg. 7/12a, no. 62, Galerie Heinemann.

13 See Beate Schreiber and Frank Drauschke, "Heinemann online: Eine Datenbank für die Provenienzforschung," *Archiv und Wirtschaft: Zeitschrift für das Archivwesen der Wirtschaft* 43 (2010): 177–84, esp. 179.

14 See Heuss, "Friedrich Heinrich Zinckgraf" (see note 7). Her research is based to a great extent on information from a file among Hjalmar Schacht's papers in the military archive in Moscow.

15 See Meike Hopp, "Art Trade Palaces: Galleries of Art Dealers as Architectural Task and Their Reception in Munich around 1900," *Journal for Art Market Studies* 2, no. 1 (2018): 1–16, https://fokum-jams.org/index.php/jams/article/view/35.

16 Anonymous letter of 9 September 1935 on the stationery of "D. Heinemann. Gemäldegalerie," 5 pages. GNM, DKA, NL Heinemann, Galerie, I,B-1.

17 Handwritten note by Hyazinth Holland. Bayerische Staatsbibliothek, Handschriftenabteilung, Hollandiana, Personal.

18 Report by Gertrud Maud Grote from July 1942 to August 1945, p. XIV, addendum of August 12, 1945, NL Grote, 133.

19 See Nikolaus Gerhart, Walter Grasskamp, and Florian Matzner, eds., *200 Jahre Akademie der Bildenden Künste München: "… kein bestimmter Lehrplan, kein gleichförmiger Mechanismus"* (Munich: Hirmer 2008).

20 This can be verified in the online database of the Galerie Heinemann: http://heinemann.gnm.de.

21 Bayerisches Wirtschaftsarchiv, Munich, BWA, K1, X, 78a, IHK Munich, Organisation des Kunst- und Antiquitätenhandels 1935. In August 1935 more than forty Jewish-owned art and antiques dealers in Munich were ordered in an open letter to "regroup" or "close down" their businesses within four weeks. Only economically significant businesses were granted an extension.

22 Michael Anton, *Illegaler Kulturgüterverkehr: Rechtshandbuch Kulturgüterschutz und Kunstrestitutionsrecht* (Berlin: De Gruyter, 2010), 414.

23 From 1935 onward, there was, however, a lien of 250,000 reichsmarks on the gallery's property for Reichsfluchtsteuer (tax on fleeing the Reich); see Schreiber and Drauschke, "Heinemann online" (see note 13), 179.

24 See letter from the Industrie- und Handelskammer, 15 January 1937, Staatsarchiv München, Polizeidirektion München, 13682.

25 Grote, "Dankesrede" (see note 8). The source material on this subject is sparse in general; see Christian Fuhrmeister and Meike Hopp, "Der Handel mit Kunst des 19. Jahrhunderts in München, 1937–1945: Überlegungen zu einem Forschungsfeld," in *Kunsthändler, Sammler, Stifter: Günther Franke als Vermittler moderner Kunst in München, 1923–1976*, ed. Felix Billeter (Berlin: De Gruyter, 2017), 163–186.

26 Ludwig Grote to Gertrud Maud Grote, 15 June 1940, NL Grote, 61.

27 Report by Gertrud Maud Grote from July 1942 to August 1945 (see note 18).

28 Ibid.

29 Ibid.

30 Ibid.

31 Ludwig Grote to the Wehrbezirkskommand (Regional Command of the Army), Munich I/IIa, 4 November 1944, NL Grote, 992.

32 Ludwig Grote to Second Company of the Volkssturm, Rathaus Rottach, Oberach, 21 February 1945, NL Grote, 992.

33 See Ludwig Grote to Gertrud Maud Grote, letters from 15 to 30 June 1940, NL Grote, 61. Cf. Susanne Neubauer, "Ludwig Grote und die Moderne, 1933–1959: Paradigma einer Internationalisierung," *RIHA Journal* 0180 (October 10, 2017), http://www.riha-journal.org/articles/2017/0180-neubauer, sec. 25 and 26.

34 Gertrud Maud Grote, "Lebenserinnerungen und biografische Aufzeichnungen zu Ludwig Grote" (ca. 1910–1990), NL Grote, ASS 2.

35 See Neubauer, "Ludwig Grote und die Moderne" (see note 33), sec. 22. Neubauer writes: "No de-Nazification file for Ludwig Grote exists, in part because files were created in the proceedings only for those who had belonged to the National Socialist Party or one of its divisions. There are no currently known indications that he was a member of the National Socialist Party. Robert Bierschneider of the Staatsarchiv München to the author July 5, 2016." See also the essay by Christian Eger in the present volume.

36 Report by Gertrud Maud Grote from July 1942 to August 1945, p. XIV, addendum of August 12, 1945 (see note 18).

37 Von der Osten, obituary for Ludwig Grote (see note 3), 234.

38 See the bibliography in the present volume.

39 Friedrich and Prinzing, "Einleitung," in *"So fing man einfach an, ohne viele Worte"* (see note 2), 8–15, esp. 9.

Fig. 1 *Ausstellung Brasilianischer Künstler* (Exhibition of Brazilian Artists), Haus der Kunst, Munich, 1959

Fig. 2 Exhibition *Bauhaus*, fourth Bienal de São Paulo, 1957

Ludwig Grote and Brazil's Interest in the Bauhaus: International Entanglements and Adaptations in Cultural Policy

Susanne Neubauer

In June 1959, when the *Ausstellung brasilianischer Künstler* (Exhibition of Brazilian Artists) opened at the Haus der Kunst in Munich, the German-Brazilian cultural exchange that had been reestablished after the caesura of World War II came to a temporary culmination for a time. In the foreword to the catalog, Ludwig Grote, who was then director general of the Germanisches Nationalmuseum, summed up his ideas of Brazil, which he had been able to form for himself as commissioner of the German participations in the Bienal de São Paulo, which had been founded in 1951. The ambitious project of the Bienal de São Paulo, modeled on the Venice Biennale and initiated by the Italian-Brazilian industrialist Francisco Matarazzo Sobrinho, also fell in that fruitful period of the founding of the Museu de Arte de São Paulo (MASP) (1947), the Museu de Arte Moderna de São Paulo (MAM-SP) (1948) and the Museu de Arte Moderna do Rio de Janeiro (MAM-RJ) (1949). All three of these museums founded by private parties are testimony to the rapid capitalization and expansion of Brazilian metropolises at the time. The two educational institutions for industrial design formed in the same period—the Instituto de Arte Contemporânea (IAC) at the MASP (1951) and the Escola Superior de Desenho Industrial (ESDI) in Rio de Janeiro (1962)—in particular testify to a will to design of tropical and global caliber that was adapted to local needs. Despite European visits by important architects, artists, and critics such as Lúcio Costa, Roberto Burle Marx, and Mário Pedrosa and Brazil's strong connection to the old world as a consequence of colonialism, the influence of the Bauhaus before World War II was surprisingly limited. An "expressive, Brutalist" prewar modernism influenced by Le Corbusier dominated.[1] Pietro Maria Bardi, the Italian founder of the MASP, spoke of the "very Teutonic severity of Gropius's Bauhaus," which he said could be recognized, for example, in the furniture designs of the Ukrainian-Brazilian architect Gregori Ilych Warchavchik.[2] Only after Max Bill showed up in Brazil did interest turn to the recently founded Hochschule für Gestaltung (HfG) in Ulm and consequently indirectly to the Bauhaus again. Bill was a crucial influence on Brazilian modernism, especially in the field of painting, as a result of his prominent solo exhibition at the MASP which showed all aspects of his work and his winning the first international prize for sculpture at the first Bienal.[3] As director of the HfG, he would later bring the Brazilians Alexandre Wollner, Almir Mavignier, and Mary Vieira to study in that small town in southern Germany. The controversial discussion in Brazil of Bill's functionalism, of the "decorative" Brazilian architecture criticized by Bill, and the tropical architectural style seen as a "new sensuality"[4] did not keep the new art museums in particular from conceiving progressive higher education schools based on the pedagogical ideas of the Bauhaus and its successor initiatives. Pietro Maria Bardi and his wife, the architect Lina Bo Bardi, had initiated a curriculum at the IAC in São Paulo as early as 1951 that leaned heavily on the Bauhaus and the American School of Design.[5] The institute, whose brief included training young designers in the applied arts for industry, offered programs such as material studies, composition, cultural history, psychology and sociology, ceramics, art glass, typography, photography, and film as well as communication and industrial design. Teachers became such famous figures as the architect Jacob Ruchti, the painter Lasar Segall, and the landscape designer

Roberto Burle Marx. In Rio de Janeiro in the mid-1950s, after the museum director Niomar Moniz Sodré Bittencourt was already in contact with Max Bill and Tomás Maldonado,[6] the first design courses were offered at the MAM-RJ, influenced by the HfG. The first teachers came from Ulm, such as Tomás Maldonado and the designers Otl Aicher and Alexandre Wollner.[7] In addition to these career-related training programs, Bittencourt also introduced numerous courses from painting to dance for a general audience and for children and teenagers. Founded in 1962, the ESDI was institutionally and personally closely connected to the MAM-RJ; the German Karl Heinz Bergmiller, who emigrated to Brazil in the 1950s and had been a student and colleague of Bill at the HfG, and Alexandre Wollner were members of the founding committee.[8] This educational institution referred even more strongly to the social relevance propagated in Ulm, the pedagogical structure of the college, and the concept of "good form"; it also adopted the focus on combining theory and science and thus crucially influenced the Brazilian discourse on design in the 1960s.[9]

In the context of these rapid developments in Brazil, the *Ausstellung brasilianischer Künstler* in Munich (fig. 1) not only should be understood as part of cultural policy but also can be indirectly integrated into the history of the reception of the Bauhaus as an export product of cultural policy. Ludwig Grote, whose exhibitions particularly influenced the West German reception of the Bauhaus after World War II, played a role in Brazil that was only marginal to an assessment today of this historical period immediately after the war but nevertheless pointed the way forward. The preface to the Munich exhibition catalog that Grote wrote initially led back to the first Bienal de São Paulo, which began to play a big instigating role for the exchange with Latin America that was now forming under global portents.[10] The direct contact person for Germany's national participations in Brazil was the cultural attaché of the Foreign Office, which funded and organized such prestigious, international occasions and appointed the commissioner in each instance. In this case, the choice was Grote, who had made a name with sensational and also well-attended exhibitions of prewar modern art such as *Der blaue Reiter, 1908–1914* (1949) and *Die Maler am Bauhaus* (1950) at the Haus der Kunst in Munich. Shortly before the opening of the Bienal, the exhibition department of the Haus der Kunst in Munich had asked about the possibility of sending German artists to the Bienal.[11] At the same time, the Haus der Kunst announced its interest in having an exhibition of "South American artists," since "the organization of artists' groups abroad" was also part of its program.[12] The interest in such an exhibition reciprocated by the artistic director of the Bienal, Lourival Gomes Machado, met with no response, however. It took an initiative from the Brazilian consul in Munich, Franck Teixeira de Mesquita, proposing a Brazilian-German exchange project with the Haus der Kunst and finding a suitable partner for it in the director of the MAM-RJ, Niomar Moniz Sodré Bittencourt. At the beginning of their negotiations, Mesquita spoke of exhibitions that would range "from 1905 to our era."[13] For the exhibition of German art in Brazil, Bittencourt was hoping for a larger number of works by the best artists. "The names Kandinsky and Klee, although the former is Russian and the latter Swiss, would be seen with interest, and we believe that these

a arte do **bauhaus**

exposição oficial da alemanha
na IV bienal do museu de arte moderna de são paulo

ITINERÁRIO DAS ARTES PLÁSTICAS

JAYME MAURÍCIO

O professor Grote nas obras do Museu

Em visita às obras do Museu de Arte Moderna do Rio, estiveram há dias o professor Ludwig Grote, delegado da Alemanha à IV Bienal de São Paulo, acompanhado do adido cultural da Embaixada alemã, sr. von Bayme. Presente ainda o representante do "New York Times", que lá se achava para entrevistar a diretora da instituição. Recebido por Niomar Moniz Sodré e Affonso E. Reidy, o professor Grote percorreu detidamente as obras, examinou com atenção o projeto de Reidy, e manifestou o seu entusiasmo pela obra que ali se concretizava. O fato do Museu tentar repetir no Brasil, em condições bem mais desenvolvidas, os objetivos e princípios da Bauhaus e da Escola Superior de Desenho de Ulm, era particularmente grato aos alemães. Louvou o equilíbrio, sobriedade e acêrto do projeto de Reidy, o cuidado da construção e do material empregado. Previu para o Museu um futuro fecundo e um desenvolvimento radioso, paralelo ao próprio desenvolvimento do Brasil.

No clichê, um flagrante dessa importante visita.

Coquetel à delegação alemã da IV Bienal

Realizou-se ontem, nos salões do Clube Transatlantico, um coquetel em homenagem ao chefe da delegação alemã à IV Bienal, presidente do juri internacional, dr. Grote. As fotografias focalizam dois aspectos da recepção, mostrando a primeira o homenageado, cercado pelo dr. Heyligers, delegado da Holanda, e do sr. von Nostitz, consul-geral da Alemanha, além dos consules Schlegl e Wolfram e do sr. Heuberger, diretor da Pro-Arte. Na outra, os srs. dr. Turelli, diretor do Colegio Visconde de Porto Seguro, sr. Ahrens, sr. Troppmair, diretor das "Noticias Alemãs", e outras personalidades da colonia alemã, radicada entre nó

Fig. 3 Leaflet for the *Bauhaus* exhibition at the fourth Bienal de São Paulo, 1957

Fig. 4 Newspaper clipping from *A Gazeta São Paulo*, September 18, 1957

Fig. 5 Newspaper clipping from *Correio da Manhã* (Rio de Janeiro), September 10, 1957

masters can be included among the German artists. Nay, Werner, Winter, and Hartung should also be generously represented. [...] The director of the museum asks us to propose to you that the whole group of the earlier 'BAUHAUS' be represented, namely, Albers, Moholy-Nagy, and Vonderberghe [*sic*]."[14]

The Bienal de São Paulo was held five times in all from 1951 to 1959, four of which were organized by Grote.[15] Grote traveled to Brazil himself for the first time for the fourth Bienal in 1957. He had organized a special show on Paul Klee for the second Bienal and now, encouraged by Walter Gropius (who in turn was approached by the Bienal management), was asked to organize an exhibition on the Bauhaus (fig. 2).[16] The director of the MAM-RJ's desire to show another Bauhaus focus as part of the institutional exchange with Munich two years after the ultimately unsatisfactory Bauhaus exhibition can be first explained in the context of the founding of design colleges at that time and the increasing need for industrial designers in Brazil and, second, tied to the original idea of establishing the temporal horizon for the exchange exhibitions "from 1905" onward. "In principle," Bittencourt asked, presumably "the whole group of the old Bauhaus [was] supposed to participate? [...] It is very important that this time Germany be exhibited very well."[17]

Restricting the Bauhaus exhibition at the fourth Bienal to its painters and their students was not only Grote's concept but also the desire of the secretary general of the Bienal, Arturo Profili,[18] even if this meant not making a "purely German" selection.[19] Grote's fears that the exhibition could be too international were not justified, both from the Foreign Office side and that of the Bienal.[20] The president of the Bienal, Matarazzo Sobrinho, confirmed that the construction of a "Bauhaus hall" alongside the sections for architecture and theater would make the German contribution highly attractive, both as far as the Bauhaus masters were concerned and their students as well. Grote's personal participation in the jury would lead to "even more brilliance from the German contribution."[21]

The hopes for a representative exhibition of Germany were great, thus the presentation of the Federal Republic of Germany was that much more disappointing: late deliveries of works and too few illustrations in the architecture and theater sections, inadequately representative works by the Bauhaus painters, and an overly rigid exhibition concept. The Bauhaus exhibition received fewer reviews than was generally hoped for, and because of its retrospective character was not competing with any of the other countries. It was already clear during the run-up that the German contribution would go without a jury prize—a decision initiated by Grote himself.[22] Grote's report on the Bienal for the Foreign Office reads:

"At the request of the Museu de Arte Moderna, Germany put together a collection of the Bauhaus painters. It united not only the heroes, not only those called young masters at the time, but also a selection of painters who completed their studies at the Bauhaus. As a result, Fritz Winter, Schawinsky, Max Bill, Arndt, Herbert Bayer, and Joost Schmidt were hanging next to Kandinsky, Klee, Itten, Feininger, Moholy, Muche, Schlemmer, and Albers. Although it was not limited to the Bauhaus period, the German section had a retrospective character and could not be seen as a national presentation either. The Bauhaus has in Brazil, as it does in the whole world, a legendary aura, and everyone sees in it the idea of creative collaborative work and education."[23]

A positive summary of his exhibition refers to the leaflet that caused a sensation with its "modern typographic design"—the leaflet was designed in the lowercase style of the Bauhaus (fig. 3). Later, within the diplomatic mission in Brazil, Grote was ultimately blamed for failing to live up to his concept. The impression was left in Brazil that the Bauhaus, according to the consulate general, existed only as an "art historically important direction."[24] It was said to have scarcely lived up to expectations in terms of subject matter. "For the modern Brazilian, who thinks predominantly from architecture, the Bauhaus as a place in which the design of our time received from fine art to industrial production crucial impulses, is an entirely different nimbus." It lacked an account of the creation as a whole, of the "influence and succession of the Bauhaus."[25] It was much more disastrous that the works shown by internationally known Bauhaus painters were of rather poor quality.[26] Grote's text in the leaflet for the exhibition described the Bauhaus as a pioneer for many successor institutions, especially in the United States, and as a place of international contact. The exhibition would show that each of the graduates of the Bauhaus would go his or her own way, with personal independence, specific talents, and a "feeling of responsibility."[27] Grote declined, however, to mention the model function of the Bauhaus for the intellectual resistance and democratization of Germany after World War II.

That the German contributions were indeed in the Brazilian press was thanks to Grote's presence in São Paulo and Rio de Janeiro. As president of the jury, he attended numerous events and regarded his presence as conveying a diplomatic act as well (fig. 4).[28] It is reasonable to suspect that Grote, who had not traveled to Brazil until 1957, was first able to understand for himself thanks to that visit the diverse connections of Brazilian art and architecture to the Bauhaus (and ultimately also to the Hochschule für Gestaltung in Ulm). These were precisely the references he was able to recognize on visiting the MAM-RJ, designed by Affonso Reidy and still under construction in 1957. The *Correio da Manhã*, which was very important in Rio and in which the art critics Ferreira Gullar and Mário Pedrosa regularly published, reported Grote's enthusiasm on seeing the construction project (fig. 5). The objectives and principles of the Bauhaus and of the Hochschule für Gestaltung in Ulm were not to be repeated "under highly adapted conditions," wrote critic Jayme Maurício, a fact for which one would be very grateful to the Germans. According to the article, Grote had predicted that both the museum and Brazil would have a "fruitful future and a radiant evolution."[29]

Even though Grote's Bauhaus exhibition at the fourth Bienal did not completely do justice to the contemporaneous conditions of the Brazilian art centers São Paulo and Rio de Janeiro, his visit at least left its mark on his preface in the catalog of the *Ausstellung brasilianischer Künstler* in Munich. Grote emphasizes the special importance of architecture in Brazil, which revived the arts as well with its modern spirit. He wrote that it was obvious that "lively" and "fresh" modernism in Brazil had become part of a "genuine style of international scale," that would prepare the way that the "European avant-garde had set out on at the beginning of our century."[30] Maurício Nabuco, president of the new museum in Rio de Janeiro, made these statements more precise in his welcome. Using the example of the new Museu de Arte Moderna, one could recognize the fulfillment of a "comprehensive program," which not only included art exhibitions, courses, lectures, theater, film, and ballet but also housed a "technical school for creation." Young artists were to be educated there on the university level with the goal of realizing "the special plan of 'industrial design' in Brazilian life."[31]

1 See Adrián Gorelik, *Das vanguardas a Brasília: Cultura urbana e arquitetura na América Latina* (Belo Horizonte: Editora UFMG, 2005), 164. A brief survey of the reception of the Bauhaus is provided by Katerina Rüedi Ray, *Bauhaus Dream-House: Modernity and Globalization* (London: Routledge, 2010); see also Mário Pedrosa, "Modern Architecture in Brazil," in *Mário Pedrosa: Primary Documents*, ed. Mário Pedrosa, Glória Ferreira, and Paulo Herkenhoff (New York: Museum of Modern Art, 2015), 339–46.

2 Pietro Maria Bardi, *New Brazilian Art* (New York: Praeger, 1970), 84.

3 Bill, however, harshly criticized Brazilian architecture (and indirectly Le Corbusier as well); see Angela Lammert, "Der 'Schweizer Uhrmacher' und der 'Urwald im Bauwesen': Max Bill und die Moderne in Brasilien; oder, Was ist moderne Kunst?," in *Das Verlangen nach Form: Neoconcretismo und zeitgenössische Kunst aus Brasilien*, ed. Robert Kudielka (Berlin: Akademie der Künste, 2010), 56–68.

4 On the reception of Brazilian modernist architecture and its negative criticism by Max Bill, Bruno Zevi, and Nikolaus Pevsner, see Hugo Segawa, *Architecture of Brazil, 1900–1990* (New York: Springer, 2013), 118–23.

5 The reference to the Bauhaus, its collective spirit, and its modern production techniques is cited in numerous magazine reports on the opening of the institute; see, for example, "Debatidos o programa e finalidades do Instituto de Arte Contemporânea," *Diário de São Paulo*, March 22, 1950, and Jacob Ruchti, "Instituto de Arte Contemporânea," *Habitat*, no. 3 (1951): 62.

6 In 1956 the MAM-RJ organized an exhibition with photographs and texts about the HfG in Ulm in order to present it as a successor to the Bauhauses. The reception of the works of its relevant employees such as Hans Gugelot, Tomás Maldonado, Gui Bonsiepe, and Max Bense in Brazil is largely yet to be addressed. See Mari Carmen Ramírez, *Hélio Oiticica: The Body of Color*, exh. cat. (London: Tate 2007), 352.

7 See Pedro Luiz Pereira de Souza and Karl Heinz Bergmiller, "Uma contribuição para o design moderno brasileiro," in *Martius-Staden-Jahrbuch*, no. 59 (São Paulo: Instituto Martius-Staden, 2012), 77–103, esp. 91. The head of education was Flexa Ribeiro, who also wrote the introduction to the catalog of the *Ausstellung brasilianischer Künstler* in Munich.

8 See ibid.

9 The Bauhaus idea of the integrative designer and architect who has an education not only in construction, administration, photography, and other fields but also in politics and who understands his or her work as a missionary activity for the benefit of society also flowed into Vilanova Artigas's curriculum for the Faculdade de Arquitetura e Urbanismo (FAU-USP). Its foundation was based on the idea of the "project," on which the seminars were built, and on the construction of "studios" as accommodations for instruction; see Segawa, *Architecture of Brazil* (see note 4), 170–71.

10 On the prehistory of the biennial in Brazil, see: Mário Pedrosa, "The Bienal from Here to There," in Pedrosa, Ferreira, and Herkenhoff, *Mário Pedrosa* (see note 1), 153–57; and Martina Merklinger, *Die Biennale São Paulo: Kulturaustausch zwischen Brasilien und der jungen Bundesrepublik Deutschland, 1949–1954* (Bielefeld: transcript 2013).

11 The inquiry came too late: not only had the Bienal already established official contact with the Federal Republic of Germany, but it was shortly before the opening date, October 20, 1951. See Wolf Röhricht, head of exhibitions, Haus der Kunst, to the Museu de Arte Moderna de São Paulo, 20 August 1951, Archiv Ausstellungsleitung der Künstler im Haus der Kunst München, and Martina Merklinger, "Arena of Modernism: The Founding Years of the São Paulo Biennial and the Foreign Cultural Policy of the Young Federal Republic of Germany," in *German Art in São Paulo / Deutsche Kunst auf der Biennale, 1951–2012*, ed. Ulrike Groos, Sebastian Preuss, and Andrea Scrima (Ostfildern: Hatje Cantz, 2013), 33–41.

12 Wolf Röhricht to the Museu de Arte Moderna São Paulo, 20 August 1951, Archiv Ausstellungsleitung e.V. Haus der Kunst, München.

13 "A Arte Alemã. Desde 1905 até os nossos dias" (German art: From 1905 to the present day) and "Exposição Brasileira na Haus der Kunst. Arte Moderna Brasileira, Desde 1900 até os nossos dias" (Brazilian exhibition at the Haus der Kunst: Modern Brazilian art, from 1900 to the present day): Frank Teixeira de Mesquita to Niomar Sodré Bittencourt, 17 April 1958 and 16 June 1958, archive, MAM-RJ.

14 Teixeira de Mesquita to Peter A. Ade, 28 March 1958, Archiv Ausstellungsleitung e.V. Haus der Kunst, München. Teixeira de Mesquita took this list almost word for word from a letter by Niomar Sodré Bittencourt to Teixeira de Mesquita, 19 March 1958, archive, MAM-RJ.

15 The third Bienal in 1955 was the responsibility of Walter Passarge, then director of the Kunsthalle Mannheim.

16 Ludwig Grote to Gabriele Münter, 3 April 1956, Kulturabteilung Auswärtiges Amt Bonn, Archiv Auswärtiges Amt B95, no. 599A.

17 In her letter, Bittencourt refers to a difficulty with the exhibition *Arte Alemã contemporânea* (Contemporary German Art), which was held in 1956 in collaboration with a Frankfurt gallery: "É muito importante que a Alemanha esteja bem representada desta vez, pois há dois anos fizemos, no Museu, uma exposição por intermédio de uma Galerie da Frankfurt, e foi dificientíssima" (It is very important that Germany is well represented this time, because two years ago we held an exhibition at the museum through a Frankfurt gallery, and it was extremely difficult); Niomar Sodré Bittencourt to Teixeira de Mesquita, 19 March 1958, archive, MAM-RJ.

18 Ludwig Grote, report to the Foreign Office, October 19, 1957 (see note 16).

19 Noting that "our section [is] not national, however, as far as the passports of the painters is concerned. In that configuration, the Bauhaus painters would not yet have been shown. We will cause a sensation with this." Grote included Feininger, Kandinsky, Klee, Moholy-Nagy, Muche, and Schlemmer, whereby he saw only Klee, Muche, and Schlemmer "as Germans." "If the next generation is supposed to be taken into account, as would be necessary, then the ratio of foreigners to Germans becomes even more precarious. Albers (born German but now USA), Bayer (born German but now USA), Max Bill (Swiss, now in Ulm), Fritz Winter (German). [...] I don't know whether we should simply include foreigners here. Feininger had, when he was still alive, rejected his inclusion in an exhibition of German art." Grote to Münter (see note 16).

20 This reference to the participation of artists who are not or are no longer seen as German is a seismographic reference to the still complex state of the nation. This is also revealed by a letter from the Norddeutscher Künstlerbund (Northern German Artists' League) from Berlin-Wilmersdorf of May 7, 1957, signed by the former Bauhaus student Albert Hennig, in which he criticizes the exhibition of "foreigners in the *German* section." Albert Hennig to the Culture Section of the Foreign Office, Bonn, 7 May 1957 (see note 16).

21 Francisco Matarazzo Sobrinho to the culture department of the Foreign Office, Bonn, 26 October 1956, ibid.

22 German Consulate General in São Paulo to the Foreign Office, 8 October 1957, ibid. Grote personally was also president of the jury for the Bienal art prize. Trützschler of the Foreign Office to Ludwig Grote, 15 November 1957, ibid.

23 Consulate General in São Paulo to the Foreign Office, 11 March 1958, ibid.

24 Ibid.

25 Brazilian reviews in the present author's archive confirm this picture. The Bauhaus exhibition was described as the largest educational exhibition of the Bienal. In longer articles, Grote was always mentioned with details of his biography or quotations from his leaflet text.

26 Consulate General in São Paulo to the Foreign Office, 8 October 1957, ibid.

27 Ludwig Grote, "Bauhaus," leaflet, Bienal de São Paulo, 1957, ibid.

28 Ludwig Grote, report to the Foreign Office, October 19, 1957, ibid.

29 Jayme Maurício, "O professor Grote nas obras do Museu," *Correio da Manhã* (Rio de Janeiro), September 10, 1957, DKA, NL, Grote, Ludwig, 1802.

30 Ludwig Grote, "Vorwort," in *Ausstellung Brasilianischer Künstler*, exh. cat. (Munich: Haus der Kunst, 1959), xiii.

31 Maurício Nabuco, "Grusswort," in ibid., ix.

Fig. 1 Herbert Bayer (design), poster for the exhibition *50 jahre bauhaus* (50 years bauhaus), Württembergischer Kunstverein, Stuttgart, 1968

From Stuttgart into the World: The Bauhaus as Romantic and Representing the State

Torsten Blume

On May 4, 1968, when the exhibition *50 jahre bauhaus* (50 years bauhaus) opened in the spaces of the Württembergischer Kunstverein, it was not just the first large presentation in Germany in which the Bauhaus as a whole had been presented since its dissolution in 1933. It was also the last show marked by Walter Gropius and decidedly dedicated to him, in which he could himself help shape the account of the Bauhaus as *his* idea. Not least for that reason, the exhibition was oriented around Gropius's interpretation of the Bauhaus as an ideal program defined by him.[1] For example, the former Bauhaus director could observe as a guest at the opening that the undertaking had succeeded as an "illustration of the idea of the Bauhaus,"[2] even though his descriptions of the Bauhaus idea, especially since the 1950s, became increasingly vague. Accordingly, in his speech at the opening of the exhibition, too, he described the Bauhaus as an idea with a great potential for "interpretability."[3] He said that the Bauhaus was not about a new style but about an attitude, which went hand in hand with an overcoming of specialization in order ultimately "to incorporate everything, to exclude nothing that belongs to the whole of life, or, as Kandinsky said, to say 'and' rather than 'either/or.'"[4] Ludwig Grote was able to take up this reference to Wassily Kandinsky in particular; for him, the Bauhaus show he directed would be the most comprehensive and most successful but also the final project of the work he had begun in Dessau in 1925 as a mediator, propagandist, and interpreter of the design school. Gropius's reference to the special "Bauhaus education," which he said was based on a "kind of impersonal science of seeing," gave Grote the opportunity to manifest once more, in the context of a large exhibition, his interpretation of the Bauhaus as an education for designers that was essentially borne by Romantically inspired artists. Kandinsky's model of a synthesis of all the arts based on abstract painting played a major role for Grote. This model was visually emphasized by the use of the triad of the basic forms of circle, square, and triangle that Kandinsky had introduced at the Bauhaus in 1922 as a leitmotif on all of the printed matter for the exhibition. That many people today regard the combination of blue circle, red square, and yellow triangle as a trademark of the Bauhaus can be traced back not least to this function as a leitmotif and the prominence that the exhibition *50 jahre bauhaus* had lent it thanks to Grote. Because after its premiere in Stuttgart, from May 5 to June 28, 1968—that is, one year before the fiftieth anniversary of the founding—it was shown internationally and thus reached a mass audience. As a large, state-sponsored project, it represented the culmination of the appropriation of the Bauhaus for cultural policy, as a kind of calling card for a de-Nazified, free, democratic West Germany. Its brief was to present the Bauhaus as a symbol of a better Germany, in which the democratic culture of the Weimar Republic had been preserved. To that end, this most extensive Bauhaus show thus far ultimately went on an international tour lasting fourteen years. The exhibition, whose patron was West German President Heinrich Lübke (1894–1972), was largely financed and organized by the Institut für Auslandsbeziehungen (ifa; Institute for Foreign Relations), which is placed under the Auswärtiges Amt (Foreign Office) of the Federal Republic of Germany.[5] The goal was to use the Bauhaus "to restore the German nation's discredited reputation in the world."[6]

Its first, two-month presentation in Stuttgart already had 97,000 visitors, roughly 1,300 a day.[7] The exhibition then traveled to London and Amsterdam; in 1969, to Paris and Chicago; in 1970, to Pasadena and Toronto; and in 1971, to Buenos Aires and Tokyo; it was seen by more than 500,000 people in all.[8] From late 1973, a condensed version of the exhibition with many reproductions was also realized and coordinated by the ifa in Stuttgart. It was shown in Brazil, Australia, Venezuela, Chile, Spain, Manchester, Rotterdam, Israel, Yugoslavia, Italy, and Greece, among other places.[9] The catalog was also reproduced in compressed form, but with its contents unchanged, and translated into Serbo-Croatian and Portuguese as well.[10] *50 jahre bauhaus* ultimately reached millions of people and was thus more popular and influential than any Bauhaus project before or after. In the end, this traveling exhibition essentially realized on its own the international dissemination of the Bauhaus that Grote observed in his introductory essay in the catalog: "literature on the bauhaus in all languages grows more plentiful from day to day. it has become an international concept, its name is no longer translated."[11] Never before and only again as part of the hundredth jubilee of the Bauhaus in 2019 has the Bauhaus been marketed as an article of cultural export so intensely and with so much financial support from the government. Whereas the dissemination of the reputation of the Bauhaus in the 1920s and 1930s more or less via networks of artistic and design avant-gardes and the institutions that supported them—including above all the Deutscher Werkbund exhibition in Paris in 1930 and the Museum of Modern Art (MoMA) in 1939—was limited, the exhibition *50 jahre bauhaus* reached a broad, worldwide audience with its tour. The exhibitions and their supporting programs and publications produced a narrative with a lasting effect and legends of the Bauhaus as an almost ideal, exemplary school for design. Although there have since been numerous studies of the complex history of the Bauhaus, with its many upheavals and contradictions, and of its reception, the grand narrative generated by the exhibition of *one* Bauhaus that seems to be suited to being regarded as a landmark, synonym, and trademark for artistic modernism of the twentieth century is still influential today.

Grote, who headed the committee responsible for the *50 jahre bauhaus* exhibition from 1966 onward, shaped its basic concept, but he could not define it alone. The team included Dieter Honisch (1932–2004), the director of the Kunstverein; Hans Maria Wingler (1920–2004), the director of the Bauhaus-Archiv, which had opened in Darmstadt in 1962; and the young art historian Wulf Herzogenrath, whose primary task was inventorying the exhibition objects and managing the editing of the catalog. Herbert Bayer played a special role; he was not only responsible for the design of the exhibition and of the catalog but also crucially shaped its structure and the orientation of its subject matter. As an early member of the Bauhaus, Bayer had stood out like few others as an international mediator for the Bauhaus from 1923 onward—with presentations of the Bauhaus under Gropius's directorship as well as with Marcel Breuer and Xanti (Alexander) Schawinsky.[12] Wingler was an indispensable team member, because as head of the Bauhaus-Archiv he was able to contribute important loans.[13] In 1962, Wingler had edited the first documentation of the Bauhaus in Germany that covered the entire period of the Bauhaus from 1919 to 1933 but also, for the first time, presented in its second edition (1968) the New Bauhaus founded by László Moholy-Nagy in Chicago in 1937.[14] Much to Grote's annoyance, Wingler was therefore often regarded as the most important Bauhaus expert.[15] Wingler's book *Das Bauhaus, 1919–1933: Weimar, Dessau, Berlin und die Nachfolge in Chicago seit 1937* has since its publication been considered to some degree a standard work of Bauhaus scholarship.[16] When the book was reissued in expanded form in 1968 on the occasion of the *50 jahre bauhaus*, it also served as a kind of second exhibition catalog. For Grote, who after 1945 made numerous attempts to take up the thread of his experiences in Dessau as a promoter of the Bauhaus in order to recommend himself as a trustee of its legacy, it was surely not easy to have to acknowledge that his Bauhaus efforts were now seen as overshadowed by the younger Bauhaus expert.[17] By 1948, Grote had already written Josef Albers to say he had been asked by several early Bauhaus people[18] to take over "the editing of a German book on the Bauhaus" and that he would like to do so; he wanted "to insure that the line of the intellectual movement that the Bauhaus represents, after all, comes out clearly"[19] and in that process above all "to emphasize that the Bauhaus developed new, objective principles of artistic education."[20] The first results of these efforts were the exhibitions he curated at the Haus der Kunst in Munich in 1949 and 1950, respectively: *Blauer Reiter*[21] and *Die Maler am Bauhaus* (fig. 1).[22]

In the very first sentence of his essay in the catalog of his exhibition on the Blauer Reiter, Grote placed Kandinsky in the center as an essential Bauhaus master by emphasizing: "The Blauer Reiter received its spiritual form from Wassily Kandinsky."[23] Because Kandinsky then later taught for more than ten years at the Bauhaus, Grote argued, his ideas had "pointed the way" in the "education of the future generations of artists" and ultimately for the "Bauhaus production."[24] Grote enthused that "the Blauer Reiter wanted [like the Romantics] to know that their art was integrated into the spiritual activity of the world."[25] Above all, however, it was the model put forward by Kandinsky of an artistic synthesis led by painting that provided Grote with the foundation for interpreting the Bauhaus as a school of artists without contradicting all too much in that process Gropius's model of architectonic synthesis. Kandinsky's concept of synthesis,[26] which he had already developed in its outlines in Munich around 1912 and then built on in Russia thereafter, aimed at a reunification of all the arts through a shared "spiritual" quality that was experienced by inspired fine artists as an "inner sound" and could be conveyed as "compositions" in visual works. He imagined a kind of musicalizing of the arts, which would ultimately be able to found a new architecture as well but first and foremost would be "abstract synthesis on the stage."[27] But only once, in Dessau in 1928, did Kandinsky have the opportunity to at least sketch how he pictured his synthesis of forms, colors, sounds, and space: with a staged presentation of Modest Mussorgsky's piano cycle *Pictures at an Exhibition* at the Friedrich-Theater in Dessau. Grote, who supported this project as a representative of the city,[28] wrote of it: "With abstraction, dispensing with representation, and returning it to its most inherent means, Kandinsky achieved from painting the level of music, the purest, absolute art and hence demanded the ability to express sounds with color"; as a result it was now possible to imagine a "proxy of the arts between one another" that "the Romantics were the first to feel."[29]

Grote considered it one of Gropius's greatest achievements that when the Bauhaus was founded he had appointed as teachers essentially only painters "who were striving away from the subjective toward a new objective order."[30] For Grote believed that Gropius had recognized "that since the beginning of the century painting had taken the lead among the arts and had created a new aesthetic which should govern the structuralism principles of the architecture of the future if humanity was to be joined henceforth in a comprehensive cultural unity."[31] Grote considered the two decades from 1905 to 1925 in particular to be "the age of great discoveries in the sphere of artistic design," which he also called a "heroic age"—in the decades thereafter had really been "merely building on what had already been achieved."[32] Grote saw Kandinsky above all as a special "creative genius," because by 1913 he had already formulated "pictorial ideas for an entire epoch"[33] and revealed in his art how "a more deeply grounded unity, a new spiritual order of the world"[34] could be initiated (fig. 2). According to Grote, only abstract painters such as Kandinsky had made it possible for a holistic, cosmological, synthetic thinking to become the foundation of the Bauhaus, which he believed had preserved a cold, functional architecture and all-too-technical design. He also interpreted in this spirit Gropius's dictum of 1923—"Art and technology, a new unity"—when he wrote that Gropius had "emphasized over and over [...] that the realization of a new spatial idea means more than mere structural economy and functional perfection."[35] For Gropius, therefore, function had been "in the end only the means to realizing the new aesthetic," which had first been discovered in abstract painting. Just as, according to Grote, "abstract painting consists of immaterial planes of color, so 'Neues Bauen' (New Building) has stripped material of its weight; the walls are abstract planes. Like abstract pictorial compositions, the buildings float, liberated from the earth, and no longer grow with the ground."[36] Although "the new statics, dematerialization, the view of the wall as a spanned plane, the elimination of support, load, and weight" had long since already been prefigured in industrial architecture, it was only "through the filter of modern art" that it had become "a new, uniform design of the human environment and all of human life."[37] As a "perfect example" that could show how abstract painting could inspire a new functional aesthetic, he cited "Breuer's steel chair," in which "the minimal dimensions of the tubes, the shine of the nickel, the flatness of the belts make the chair light and transparent"[38] and thus immaterial, similar to the way abstract painters have created pictorial spaces that float in the imagination (fig. 3).

Grote was thinking in terms of large-scale models of art theory that could show how modern art and design evolved according to their own, internal laws—transported, as it were, by historical, social, and political changes. In this view, art could first achieve formal self-determination in abstract painting and then produce new conceptions of space and thus inspire design and architecture to new strategies. In this way, students at the Bauhaus had been able to develop a practice-oriented "functionalism" on the basis of the spiritual, painterly

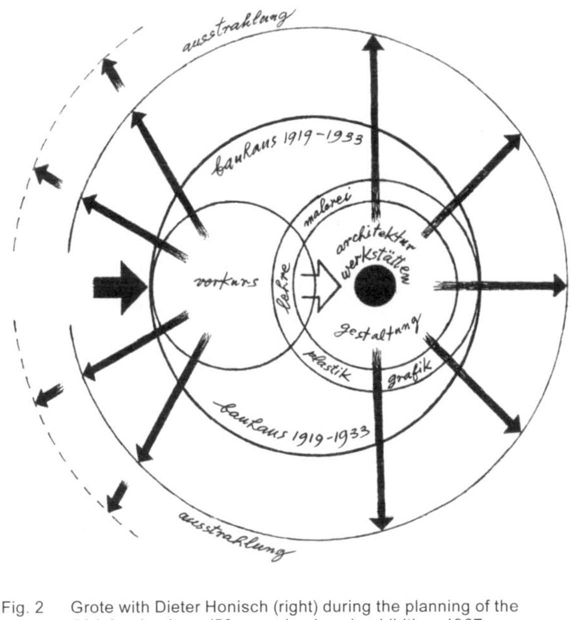

Fig. 2 Grote with Dieter Honisch (right) during the planning of the *50 jahre bauhaus* (50 years bauhaus) exhibition, 1967

Fig. 3 Herbert Bayer, concept for the exhibition *50 jahre bauhaus* (50 years bauhaus), Stuttgart, 1968

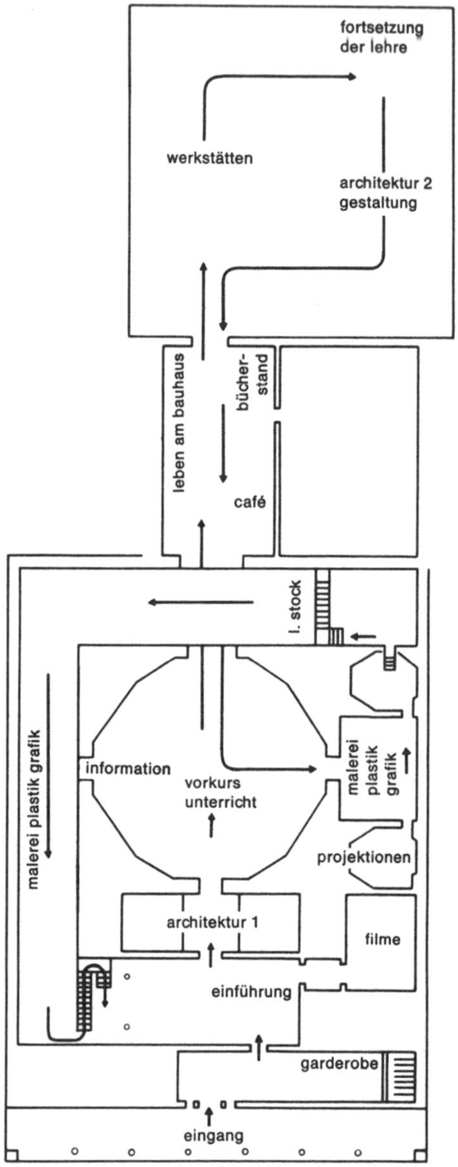

Fig. 4 Ludwig Grote with sphere, cube, tetrahedron, 1968
Fig. 5 Herbert Bayer, floor plan for the exhibition *50 jahre bauhaus* (50 years bauhaus), Stuttgart, 1968

Constructivism of the painters, which then, as the Modern Movement, conquered the world as the "style of our era." This "style" was, however, by no means connected with "manner, stylization, stencil, rigidity, rejection of life and its changing demands."[39] Rather, it was said to describe a design strategy with which the Bauhaus had managed to develop prototypes for industrial or series production on the basis of the holistic, abstract concepts of synthesis first developed in art in the workshops (fig. 4). The basis for this strategy had been developed by abstract painters such as Kandinsky but also Paul Klee and Oskar Schlemmer when the discovered geometric pictorial constructions that liberated their art from the "coincidences of subjectivism"[40] could also be conveyed as an objective "foundation of artistic design."[41] As the first and the most resolute of them,[42] Kandinsky is said to have introduced the circle, triangle, and square into his teaching. Bayer, who had been one of Kandinsky's students in the workshop for mural painting in Weimar, then employed these basic forms for promotional purposes already for the first Bauhaus exhibition in Weimar in 1923. He used these forms, which according to Kandinsky correspond to the primary colors blue, yellow, and red, for a painted design of the stairwell that was the entrance to the central exhibition spaces in Stuttgart. In 1968 Grote wrote that the blue circle, the yellow triangle, and the red square had been introduced as "leitmotifs" at the Bauhaus, but that their "spiritual significance" was then retained for much longer. Although they had repeatedly been called into question—in particular the affinity of the basic forms to the primary colors that Kandinsky asserted—"it should not be forgotten," Grote wrote," that it was the three basic forms that led to the most strict discipline and exactness in design work"; Gropius is said to have celebrated them as well as "pictorial building blocks" and even "seen them as symbols of an eternal order established by the human spirit."[43] That is why they were chosen as motifs for the exhibition poster and the cover of the catalog. And ultimately their three-dimensional derivations as sphere, cone, and cube, which Bayer staged sculpturally in the introductory room of the exhibition, almost as a monument to Kandinsky, were essential to the character of the exhibition (fig. 5).

The backdrop for this installation was a wall-sized reproduction of Schlemmer's print *Figur und Raumlineatur* (Figure and Space Delineation) of 1924. This arrangement thus honored not only Kandinsky but also the Stuttgart-born Bauhaus master Schlemmer, who would also have turned eighty in 1968. That was also the reason that Schlemmer was represented by especially many works in the exhibition, of which his painting *Bauhaustreppe* (Bauhaus Stairway) was doubtless the most important. According to Grote, with this painting he had not only "expressed the humanity of the Bauhaus" but also the "elevated the idea of the Bauhaus [...] to a symbol"; it shows "young people [...] inspired by a spirit and given wing by the unique, wide-ranging task of designing the environment in which Gropius led them."[44] Also in that spirit was the performance of recreated *Bauhaustänze* (Bauhaus Dances) initiated by Grote for the exhibition opening as a special demonstration of the "humanity of the Bauhaus" represented by Schlemmer. After he had been appointed by the copyright holder, Tut Schlemmer,[45] Grote had commissioned Georg Verden and the choreographer Margarete Hasting in 1967 to do so.[46] On May 4, 1968, not only were their interpretations of Schlemmer's *Raumtanz* (Spatial Dance), *Gestentanz* (Gestural Dance), *Stäbetanz* (Rod Dance), and *Reifentanz* (Hoop Dance) performed, but on the basis of that performance the Bavaria film studio in Munich produced a color film, funded by Inter Nationes,[47] for which additional *Bauhaustänze* were also filmed: *Metalltanz* (Metal Dance), *Formentanz* (Form Dance), *Kulissentanz* (Backdrop Dance), *Baukastenspiel* (Construction Kit Game), and *Maskenchor* (Mask Choir). Under the title *Mensch und Kunstfigur: Oskar Schlemmer und die Bauhausbühne* (Human Being and Art Figure: Oskar Schlemmer and the Bauhaus Stage), the film traveled to all of the exhibition's international venues and was also broadcast on television.[48] As soon as it was completed, Grote began arranging for the recreation and filming of Schlemmer's *Triadisches Ballett* (Triadic Ballet),[49] so that the film *Das Triadische Ballett: Ein Film in drei Teilen nach den Tänzen von Oskar Schlemmer* (The Triadic Ballet: A Film in Three Parts after Dances by Oskar Schlemmer) then also became part of the international exhibition program (fig. 6). Both productions were not purely documentary projects—although Tut Schlemmer had initially requested that. Verden had written about that in the exposé he developed for Grote that he wanted to update Schlemmer's approach to dance. He argued that the latter's idea of addressing on stage the interaction of art and technology was more topical than ever. Schlemmer's work "fulfills the basic requirement to be expected of an industrial art that works with highly advanced and elaborate technology"; for that reason "its renewed interpretation by contemporary forces is urgently necessary."[50] In the end, in the filmed version of the *Triadisches Ballett*, Schlemmer's sculptural characters in plastic costumes look like weightless figures, almost like representatives of the age of space travel.[51]

With such contributions to the popular modern aesthetic of the 1960s, the film version of the *Triadisches Ballett* was well suited to this Bauhaus show, which was visually attractive and by all means designed to be entertaining for a broad audience. It centered on an account of teaching the preliminary course that was overwhelmingly formal and experimental in its orientation. In addition, around a hundred works from the preliminary course and the workshops were exhibited in two centrally located main rooms. In the smaller adjoining rooms, these exemplary testimonies were connected to the influence and magnetism of their teaching on architectural projects and contemporaneous education programs in design and art.[52] Because many of the historical works from the preliminary course were no longer extant, several were reproduced, some in enlarged form, and, in order to make them more easily transportable, executed in sheet metal rather than paper, like the originals. As a result, many of the students' original ephemeral studies and experiments in form looked like sculptural works of art. Added in front of these complexes of rooms were the introductory room with the three basic forms and Schlemmer's spatial graphics and a room in which both architecture and the three Bauhaus directors—Gropius, Meyer, and Ludwig Mies van der Rohe—as architects were presented for the first time, albeit works by Gropius clearly predominated in quantity and presence. Of the roughly 2,000 exhibits, the catalog presented 867 works by 31 Bauhaus teachers and

Fig. 6 Margarete Hasting and Georg Verden (concept), film still from *Das Triadische Ballett: Ein Film in drei Teilen nach den Tänzen von Oskar Schlemmer* (The Triadic Ballet: A Film in Three Parts after the Dances of Oskar Schlemmer), 1970 (consultant: Ludwig Grote)

Fig. 7 Cover of the catalog *Bauhaus: Eine Veröffentlichung des Instituts für Auslandsbeziehungen* (Stuttgart: Institut für Auslandsbeziehungen, 1982).

Ausstellungsstruktur entworfen von Herbert Bayer, gezeichnet von Peter Wehr

Auspacken der 5 Container, die zur See verschickt wurden (Tokyo)

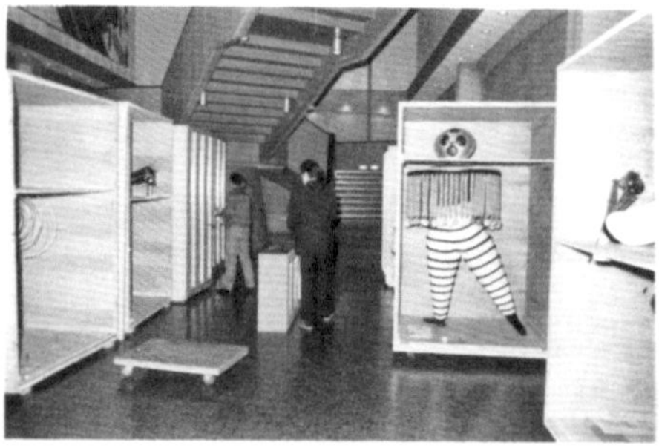

Öffnen der Kisten mit den Figurinen (Tokyo)

Eröffnungspublikum und protestierende Studenten der Hochschule für Gestaltung in Ulm, die zur gleichen Zeit geschlossen wurde (Stuttgart)

Das Kunstgebäude am Schloßplatz während der Eröffnung

Walter Gropius und Bundesminister Lauritz Lauritzen während der Eröffnung in Stuttgart

Walter Gropius beim Signieren des Kataloges

Der Louvre mit dem Bauhaus-Plakat (Paris)

Abb. 8 From the documentation *Bauhaus: Eine Ausstellung der Bundesrepublik Deutschland* (Stuttgart: ifa, 1971–72)

867 works by 167 students. Hence the Bauhaus, to which around 1,250 people in total had belonged as teachers and students was represented by just under 200 former members of the Bauhaus: by the works of its teachers and most talented students. The most prominently represented were Schlemmer, with more than 120 works, and Bayer, with around 100. The exhibition was by no means limited to the historical years of the Bauhaus from 1919 to 1933: Much as had been the case with the Bauhaus exhibition at MoMA in 1938, the exhibition organizers had set store—in keeping with the desire of the former members of the Bauhaus who were involved—on showing as many more recent and even current works as possible. "Younger masters and students" were shown "primarily with more recent works."[53] Bayer and Schawinsky were represented above all by later works; the new filmed Schlemmer dances were well suited to this as a mise-en-scène of modernist atmospheres in a new medium. The idea was to present the Bauhaus "as a concept open to the present,"[54] whereby teaching at the Bauhaus continued to be depicted as exemplary for a modern training of designers, and examples were shown to document a "continuation of its theory."[55]

Richard Biedrzynski, who reviewed the exhibition in Stuttgart, described it as "the most entertaining, loosest, most colorful show the theme ever produced."[56] Very much in the spirit of Grote's intentions, the reviewer also characterized it as an "exhibition of the century," in which the Bauhaus was grasped as the greatest event in the German history of ideas and culture. By contrast, he rather only briefly summed up Grote's interpretation of the Bauhaus as a school shaped by abstract painters, writing: Gropius "sought painters who had an inner affinity to his idea of the construction kit. He could find them only among the Cubists and Constructivists."[57] Like this reviewer, a broad audience was ultimately fascinated by the exhibition, which conveyed the image of a creative living and working community that had started out from the simplest geometric and stereometric basic forms and had clearly created a complex visual vocabulary with which functional architecture could be produced as well as clearly designed furniture, other interior design objects, and overall impressive atmospheres of a modern and comfortable life. The exhibition emphasized in its focus on artistic research in teaching the idea and fascination of creative learning, experimentation, and design in art. By dispensing with a chronological account of the historical Bauhaus, the specific political, social, and economic contexts of the Weimar Republic in which the school had operated were left out as well as the Bauhaus program of Hannes Meyer, which expanded to include the sciences, and the fact that several members of the Bauhaus continued to work in National Socialist Germany. And although the exhibition was connected with the ambition to demonstrate the topicality of the Bauhaus idea, it addressed neither then current artistic developments, such as Fluxus, Situationism, the happening, and performance art, nor the political unrest of 1968. After all, many former members of the Bauhaus were still active as artists, designers, or teachers, making it possible to present their biographies as evidence of fifty years of continuity and the enduring relevance of the Bauhaus. The picture of the Bauhaus it produced was idealizing but also fascinatingly rich, making it seem like a place of the revival of the Romantic idea that all of life or rather the existence of modern human beings could be spiritually elevated and improved by means of art. In that context, the tubular-steel chairs and Bauhaus lamps with which a new urban middle class was stylized as progressive already in the 1920s[58] could become, in harmony with modern abstract works of art and design studies, iconic objects that were now offered to show off the lifestyle of a democratic Federal Republic of Germany purged of the Nazi regime. For Grote, the *50 jahre bauhaus* exhibition was above all the final culmination of his work as a messenger for the Bauhaus and a successful manifestation of his interpretation of Bauhaus as the idea of an art school for design that could still offer inspiration to all who were open to it. But because Grote had helped put the Bauhaus in the service of the Cold War cultural policy of the "free west" versus "dictatorships of the east,"[59] it is not easy to evaluate his idea of the Bauhaus as a school of neo-Romantic artists independently of that because it would require leaving out the ideological context in which Grote finally once again laid out his interpretation of the Bauhaus.

Bauhaus-Kisten vor dem Pasadena Art Museum

Bauhaus-Kisten vor dem Panorama von Pasadena

Besucher der Ausstellung vor dem Museo de Bellas Artes (Buenos Aires)

Das Museum of Modern Art (Tokyo)

Werbung für die Ausstellung (Tokyo)

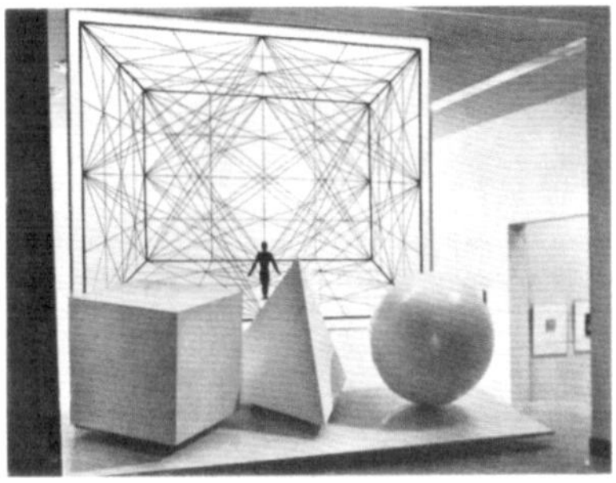

Die drei Grundformen und eine Vergrößerung von Schlemmers Zeichnung »Mensch im Raum« bildeten den Anfang der Ausstellung: Die Grundformen in bezug zum Menschen in seiner Umwelt (Buenos Aires)

Abteilung »Vorkurs und Unterricht« (Stuttgart)

Abb. 9 From the documentation *Bauhaus: Eine Ausstellung der Bundesrepublik Deutschland* (Stuttgart: ifa, 1971–72)

»Architektur und Design« Bauhaus-Gebäude und Bauten von Mies van der Rohe (Toronto)

»Tischlerei« mit erstem Stahlrohrstuhl von Marcel Breuer, 1925 (Tokyo)

Beispiele aus dem Unterricht von Wassily Kandinsky (Toronto)

Design von Wilhelm Wagenfeld und Bilder von Herbert Bayer (Tokyo)

»Fortsetzung der Lehre« mit Beispielen von Johannes Ittens Farblehre (Tokyo)

Raum mit Werken von Paul Klee aus dem Besitz der Kunstsammlung NRW, Düsseldorf (Tokyo)

Michiko und Iwao Yamawaki – zwei Bauhäusler in der Ausstellung (Tokyo)

Eröffnung der Ausstellung (Buenos Aires)

Abb. 10 From the documentation *Bauhaus: Eine Ausstellung der Bundesrepublik Deutschland* (Stuttgart: ifa, 1971–72)

1 See Claudia Heitmann, "Etablierung des Mythos Bauhaus: Die Rezeption in den 60er Jahren; Zwischen Erneuerung und Aktualität," in *Bauhaus-Ideen, 1919–1994: Bibliografie und Beiträge zur Rezeption des Bauhausgedankens*, ed. Andreas Haus and Anke Steinhauer (Berlin: Reimer, 1994), 51–65.
2 Walter Gropius, "Ansprache zur Eröffnung der Ausstellung '50 Jahre Bauhaus,'" in *50 Jahre Bauhaus: Ansprachen zur Eröffnung der Ausstellung am 4. Mai 1968 im Kleinen Haus der Württembergischen Staatstheater*, ed. Württembergischer Kunstverein (Stuttgart: Cantz, 1968), 27–31, esp. 30.
3 Ibid., 27.
4 Ibid.
5 The ifa has since 1949 been the successor institution of the Deutsches Ausland-Institut (DAI), which was founded in Stuttgart in 1917, promoted racial policy in the National Socialist era, and supported the "Germanizing" of foreign territories, sometimes working with the SS. Because the Allied forces had after 1945 classified the DAI as exonerated, it was not closed. It did not begin to address its own position under National Socialism until the 1960s. Especially from the 1970s onward, the ifa dedicated itself to promulgating German art abroad. The exhibition *50 jahre bauhaus* marked the beginning of this. The exhibition Boris Friedewald curated for the ifa in 2019–20, *Die ganze Welt ein Bauhaus* (The Whole World a Bauhaus), took up this thread but its theme was not the worldwide influence by a Bauhaus idea but rather the connections of the historical Bauhaus in international avant-garde networks; see Katja Gesche, *Kultur als Instrument der Aussenpolitik totalitärer Staaten: Das Deutsche Ausland-Institut, 1933–1945* (Cologne: Böhlau, 2006), and the ifa website, www.ifa.de (accessed June 15, 2020).
6 Lausitz Lauritzen, "Ansprache zur Eröffnung der Ausstellung 50 Jahre Bauhaus," in Württembergischer Kunstverein, *50 Jahre Bauhaus* (see note 2), 7–10, esp. 9. In the international editions of the catalog, the exhibition was also emphatically designated a "german exhibition."
7 The enormous success with the public is also evident from the first printing of 25,000 copies of the German edition of the exhibition catalog, which was already sold out after a year.
8 See Wulf Herzogenrath, "'50 Jahre Bauhaus': Bericht über die Tournee einer Ausstellung," *Kunstjahrbuch* 2 (1972): 119–21. The detail of the venues were: in 1968, the Royal Academy of Art, London, and the Stedelijk Museum Amsterdam; in 1969, the Musée d'Art Moderne de la Ville de Paris, the Musée National d'art moderne, Paris, and the Illinois Institute of Technology, Chicago; in 1970, the Pasadena Art Museum, Pasadena, California; the Art Gallery of Ontario, Toronto; and the Museo Nacional de Bellas Artes, Buenos Aires; and, in 1971, the National Museum of Modern Art, Tokyo.
9 The presenters were primarily offices of the Goethe-Institut, which almost always organized supplementary programs; see Wulf Herzogenrath, *Das bauhaus gibt es nicht* (Berlin: Alexander, 2019), 20.
10 See Karl-Georg Bitterberg, ed., *Bauhaus: Eine Veröffentlichung des Instituts für Auslandsbeziehungen* (Stuttgart: Institut für Auslandsbeziehungen, 1982).
11 Ludwig Grote, "walter gropius and the bauhaus," in *50 Years Bauhaus: German Exhibition*, exh. cat. (London: Royal Academy of Arts, 1968), 9–11, esp. 9.
12 For example, Bayer was a member of Gropius's exhibition team for the exhibition of the Deutscher Werkbund in Paris in 1930 (the "Section allemande" of the Parisian salon of the Société des Artistes Décorateurs). Above all, however, he had not only designed but also planned with Walter and Ise Gropius the exhibition *Bauhaus, 1919–1928*, at the Museum of Modern Art in New York in 1938, the first general account of the school after its closure. He was also responsible for the design of the catalog published for the first Bauhaus exhibition in 1923, which was oriented around the design of the exhibition itself, for which Bayer was also responsible.
13 Gropius had met Wingler in 1955 at the opening of the new building for the Hochschule für Gestaltung in Ulm and later authorized him to be the executor of his estate and introduced him to his network of former members of the Bauhaus. Much to Grote's disappointment, Gropius trusted that the younger Wingler, who was not yet tied to any institution, would be in a position to assemble and disseminate the legacy of the Bauhaus in keeping with his instructions and guidelines. After the association Bauhaus-Archiv e. V. was founded on May 5, 1960, the Bauhaus-Archiv, with Wingler as its director, was opened as an institute and museum on April 8, 1961, in the Ernst-Ludwig-Haus on the Mathildenhöhe in Darmstadt. Gropius had donated large parts of his own archive to its initial holdings; see Enrico Santifaller, "Wie Walter Gropius sein Erbe sicherte," *Bauwelt: Zeitschrift für Architektur* 110, no. 10 (2019): 8.
14 Wingler had also organized at the Bauhaus-Archiv several exhibitions of earlier members of the Bauhaus and in 1965 founded the Neue Bauhausbücher (New Bauhaus Books) series.
15 Especially in letters to earlier advocates of the Bauhaus but also to Gropius, Grote had repeatedly made it clear that he considered Wingler entirely unsuited to represent the Bauhaus, because he had neither been at the Bauhaus himself nor could point to any other experiences with the subject; see Ludwig Grote to Walter Gropius, March 21, 1950, quoted in Claudia Heitmann, "Die Bauhaus-Rezeption in der Bundesrepublik Deutschland von 1949 bis 1968: Etappen und Institutionen," PhD diss., Berlin, Hochschule der Künste, 2001, 49.
16 See Hans Maria Wingler, *Das Bauhaus, 1919–1933: Weimar, Dessau, Berlin und die Nachfolge in Chicago seit 1937* (Cologne: DuMont; Bramsche: Rasch, 1962; exp. ed. 1968; 3rd ed. 1975); English ed.: *The Bauhaus: Weimar, Dessau, Berlin, Chicago* (Cambridge, MA: MIT Press, 1969, 1975, and 1978); Japanese ed.: (Tokyo, 1969); Italian ed.: (Milan, 1971); Spanish ed.: (Barcelona, 1975).
17 Grote had already lamented in this connection in a letter to Josef Albers on February 22, 1947, that he "had not left" during the Nazi period and immigrated to the United States, saying that was perhaps why he had been forgotten as an ally of the Bauhaus; and that it was probably also a mistake to have little "spoken of his services to the Bauhaus" which "would not have come to Dessau" without him; GNM, DKA, NL Grote, Ludwig (hereafter "NL Grote"), 702; in the typescript of this letter, the following sentence has been crossed out: "I have, after all, truly done more for the Bauhaus than [Alois] Schardt or [Alexander] Dorner or other museum directors, who at most purchased a few pictures from the painters."
18 Grote mentions Joost Schmidt, Helene Nonné-Schmidt, Gustav Hassenpflug, and Hinnerk and Lou Scheper.
19 Ludwig Grote to Josef Albers, 1 May 1948, NL Grote, 702.
20 Ibid.
21 Ludwig Grote, "Der Weg zum Blauen Reiter," *Der Blaue Reiter: München und die Kunst des 20. Jahrhunderts, 1908–1914*, exh. cat. Haus der Kunst, Munich, September–October 1949 (Munich: Filser, 1949), 14–17. At the opening of the exhibition *Der Blaue Reiter, 1908–1914* in 1949, Staatssekretär (Secretary of State) Dieter Sattler spoke of the former Haus der deutschen Kunst as now having been successfully de-Nazified; see Sabine Brantl, *Haus der Kunst, Munich: A Locality and Its History in National Socialism* (Munich: Allitera, 2007), 115.
22 These exhibitions were made possible for Grote thanks to Eberhard Hanfstaengl, who from 1949 to 1951 was director general of the Bayerische Staatsgemäldesammlungen at the Haus der Kunst (the former Haus der Deutschen Kunst), but also thanks to the American cultural authorities, which regarded exhibitions on modern art as a manifestation of a new cultural beginning. Grote was also supported by Stefan Munsing (1915–1994), the director of Munich's Amerika-Haus and of the American Central Collecting Point for art plundered by the National Socialists. Munsing also designed the poster and catalog for the exhibition *Die Maler am Bauhaus*. Other exhibitions included: *Oskar Kokoschka, aus seinem Schaffen 1907–1950* and *Max Beckmann zum Gedächtnis,1884–1950*, both in 1950, and *Toulouse Lautrec: Das graphische Werk* in 1951.
23 Grote, "Der Weg zum Blauen Reiter" (see note 21), 16.
24 Ibid.
25 Ibid.
26 For Kandinsky: "strictly speaking, the purely abstract form of the theater is the total of the abstract sounds: 1. of painting—color / 2. of music—sound / 3. of dance—movement / within the general sound of architectonic form"; Wassily Kandinsky, "Abstract Synthesis on the Stage" (1923), in Kandinsky, *Complete Writings on Art*, ed. Kenneth C. Lindsay and Peter Vergo (New York: Da Capo, 1994), 504–7, esp. 506–7.
27 At the Bauhaus in Dessau, Kandinsky continued to implement the ideas about abstract compositions for the stage he had developed between

1912 and 1914; to that end, in the 1920s he revived the concept for his stage work *Violett*, written in 1914, and published an excerpt from the work in 1927; see Wassily Kandinsky, "violett," *bauhaus* 1, no. 3 (1927): 6.
28 Grote was a member of the board of trustees of the Dessauer Friedrich-Theater.
29 Ludwig Grote, "Bühnenkompositionen von Kandinsky," *Internationale Revue i 10* 2, no. 13 (1928): 4–5, esp. 4.
30 Ludwig Grote, "Lyonel Feininger zum 60. Geburtstag," in Ludwig Justi, ed., *Museum der Gegenwart*, no. 2 (1931): 41–49, esp. 49.
31 Ludwig Grote, "walter gropius and the bauhaus" (see note 11), 9.
32 Ludwig Grote, *Deutsche Kunst im zwanzigsten Jahrhundert* (Munich: Prestel, 1953), 5.
33 Ibid., 34.
34 Ludwig Grote, "Einleitung," in *Wassily Kandinsky, Rückblick, 1901–1913* (Baden-Baden: Woldemar Klein, 1955), 5–7, esp. 6.
35 Ludwig Grote, "Funktionalismus und Stil," in *Historismus und bildende Kunst*, ed. Ludwig Grote, Studien zur Kunst des 19. Jahrhunderts 1 (Munich: Prestel, 1965), 67–72, esp. 70.
36 Ibid., 69.
37 Ibid.
38 Grote, "Feininger zum 60. Geburtstag" (see note 30), 49.
39 Ibid.
40 Ludwig Grote, "basic form and functionalism," in *50 years bauhaus* (see note 11), 18–21, esp. 19.
41 Ludwig Grote, "Zum Gestaltwandel des Bauhauses," in *Eberhard Hanfstaengl zum 75. Geburtstag*, ed. Eberhard Ruhmer (Munich: F. Bruckmann, 1961), 178–90, esp. 182.
42 That Kandinsky had been an important figure and functionary in the development of a revolutionary pedagogy on art in Russia between 1918 and 1921 went unmentioned for the most part by Grote. In his teaching at the Bauhaus from 1922 onward, Kandinsky had certainly followed on the teaching programs he had developed previously in Moscow for the Free State Art Studios (SVOMAS), the Higher Art and Technical Studios (VKhUTEMAS), and especially for the Institute of Artistic Culture (INKhUK), which includes his concept of the three basic forms; see Valeria Kuzema, "Ein Russland-Import? Kandinskys Lehre am Bauhaus," in *100 Jahre Bauhaus: Vielfalt, Konflikt und Wirkung*, ed. Bernd Hüttner and Georg Leidenberger (Berlin: Metropol, 2019), 206–18.
43 Ludwig Grote, "Zum Vortrag 'Von Weimar nach Dessau: Zum Gestaltwandel des Bauhauses,'" January 30, 1963, Darmstadt, typescript, NL Grote, 998.
44 Ludwig Grote, "Ansprache zur Eröffnung der Ausstellung 50 Jahre Bauhaus," in Württembergischer Kunstverein, *50 Jahre Bauhaus* (see note 2), 16–26, esp. 26.
45 See Tut Schlemmer to Ludwig Grote, 7 February 1968, NL Grote, 414.
46 Georg Verden was the proprietor of an eponymous dance school in Munich; Margarete Hasting was a dancer, choreographer, and dance teacher who worked with him there and who had trained at the Mary-Wigman-Schule in the 1930s.
47 Inter Nationes is a media agency founded as an association in 1951, which was commissioned by the Bundesrepublik Deutschland to impart German culture abroad in cooperation with the Goethe-Institut and the WDR (Westdeutscher Rundfunk, Western German Broadcasting); since 2000, it has been part of the Goethe-Institut and since 2003 under the name Goethe-Institut Inter Nationes.
48 On October 2, 1968, Grote was able to report to Dietrich Mahlow, a curator colleague in Nuremberg, that more than 120 copies of this film had already been sold. In the same letter he also emphasized how important it had been for him to produce this film as part of the exhibition: "I wanted in any event to introduce [the filming of the *Bauhaustänze*] into the exhibition, which I had emphasized Schlemmer's eminent importance by his placement. Schlemmer's ballets are among the most powerful theatrical experiences I have had, which is why I worked so hard to see them realized." Ludwig Grote to Dietrich Mahlow, 2 October 1968, NL Grote, 1928.
49 Grote had already tried in the 1950s to initiate a reconstruction of Schlemmer's *Triadisches Ballett*. He wrote to Schawinsky on November 4, 1957: "Would it be possible for you to revive the *Triadisches Ballett*?"; NL Grote, 1812.
50 Georg Verden, "Exposé," undated typescript (presumably late 1967), NL Grote, 1928.
51 It is therefore fitting that the costume designer, Margit Bárdy, also designed the costumes and props for the science-fiction series *Raumpatrouille: Die phantastischen Abenteuer des Raumschiffes Orion* (Space Patrol: The Fantastic Adventure of the Orion Spaceship) from 1966 to 1975.
52 See Herbert Bayer, diagram for the *50 jahre bauhaus* exhibition and floor plan of the exhibition in *50 years bauhaus* (see note 11), 30, half title page, and jacket flap.
53 Dieter Honisch, "zur ausstellung," in Württembergischer Kunstverein, *50 jahre bauhaus* (see note 11), 31.
54 Ibid.
55 The examples included the New Bauhaus founded by Moholy-Nagy in Chicago in 1937, Hin Bredendieck's teaching at the Georgia Institute of Technology in Atlanta (from 1952), results from the course Fritz Christof Hüffner taught at the Werkkunstschule Darmstadt from 1960 onward, and works by the students in courses by Kurt Kranz (at the Hochschule für bildende Künste in Hamburg), Hannes Neuner (at the Akademie der Bildenden Künste in Stuttgart), and Iwao Yamawaki (at the College of Art at Nihon University, Tokyo).
56 Richard Biedrzynski, "Die Grammatik des Bauhauses: Zur grossen Stuttgarter Ausstellung im Kunstverein," *Stuttgarter Zeitung*, May 4, 1968.
57 Ibid.
58 See Regina Bittner, "The Bauhaus on the Market: On the Difficult Relationship between the Bauhaus and Consumer Culture," in *Bauhaus: A Conceptual Model* (Ostfildern: Hatje Cantz, 2009), 331–36, esp. 336.
59 Grote, "gropius and the bauhaus" (see note 11), 9.

50 Years after *50 Years Bauhaus* in 1968: Hans Christ and Iris Dressler in Conversation with Torsten Blume

TB: From May 5 to September 23, 2018, in an exhibition titled *50 Jahre nach 50 Jahre Bauhaus 1968* (50 Years after 50 Years Bauhaus 1968), the Württembergischer Kunstverein in Stuttgart engaged with a project that was considered pioneering and is still formative for the Bauhaus reception in West Germany. In the same building in which the exhibition *50 jahre bauhaus* (50 years bauhaus), cocurated by Ludwig Grote with Hans Maria Wingler and director of the Kunstverein at the time, Dieter Honisch, and designed by Herbert Bayer, had been shown fifty years earlier, you showed a very different Bauhaus exhibition fifty years later. In the introduction to your project, you wrote:

Fifty years after the opening of *50 jahre bauhaus*, the Württembergischer Kunstverein is critically rereading that exhibition. It begins with the sociopolitical upheavals of the 1960s and examines the Bauhaus, its historical context, and the (hi)stories of its reception from today's perspective. The idea of the Bauhaus as a self-contained, homogeneous system was to be questioned along with the narratives that the Bauhaus and modernism acted uninterruptedly as synonyms for progress, freedom, and democracy. Instead, it was about the ambiguities that are rather inscribed in both, for example, with respect to totalitarianism and colonialism.[1]

How did you approach this project?

ID: The exhibition in 2018 was at first not based at all on the then imminent Bauhaus centenary celebration but rather on our interest in coming to terms with the history of the Kunstverein. The *50 jahre bauhaus* exhibition of 1968 had already been literally landing in our laps repeatedly for years when opening filing cabinets, photo archives, and press and other document files. It seemed to us—also from the perspective of the 1960s—like a different time. Framed by the existing architectonic situation here, which has not changed, at the same time it closely resembled the present in photographs and models. As we looked at the documents more closely, we were struck that the Foreign Office had largely financed this exhibition and in particular its international tour. *50 jahre bauhaus* was, as we will see, a project largely supported by the government of the then still young democracy with a strangely conservative aura.

HC: One photo from our holdings seems particularly revealing in this context: it shows Heinrich Lübke,[2] the Federal President of Germany at the time, attending the exhibition with a special appointment as its patron. Behind him, you can see the Schlossplatz, entirely surrounded by dark limousines and barricaded off. It is obvious that a state occasion is taking place here (fig. 1). At the same time, this federal president was the object of massive criticism at that time because under National Socialism he had worked as a site manager for the architecture and engineering firm, not only for the armaments program headed by Albert Speer—and hence in a power center of the Nazi state—but also for construction projects such as, among others, the grounds for the Luftwaffe testing grounds in Peenemünde, where forced laborers and concentration camp inmates had been employed. Lübke, like other technocrats, engineers, and managerial experts, had become part of the Nazi system as a result of his work without himself having been a convinced Nazi. He had belonged to the elite of Nazi functionaries and yet, like many other civil servants of his generation, was able to pursue a career in the young

Federal Republic. In the 1960s, however, resistance arose to this tolerance of and blindness to former Nazi functionaries.[3]

ID: The student movement in particular, which famously culminated in 1968, had an important part in that, because, especially in Germany, it demanded an open, self-critical, and unsparing coming to terms with National Socialism. In addition, this movement was concerned with a critique of existing circumstances, traditions, values, and rules that had been handed down, and a radical transformation of the society of the time. Art, too, was to operate politically and provoke again. The Bauhaus exhibition of 1968 seems to have remained strangely unaffected by this movement and its subversive ideas as well as by the critique of modernism by the postwar avant-gardes. Its presentation and discourses corresponded to a conservative, rather backward-looking understanding of art and life, toadied to Walter Gropius's perspective, and—supporting the official ideologies of the Cold War—distanced themselves from the leftist aspects of the Bauhaus.

On the photographs of Dieter Honisch, then director of the Kunstverein, guiding Lübke and his retinue through the exhibition, one sees above all elderly ladies and gentlemen who look like the keepers of the Grail of a conservative bourgeoisie. They stiffly view the Bauhaus objects spread out before their eyes as if they were relics of a long-ago culture, which at the same time lends them dignity. There seems to be no connection between the objects and their viewers apart from an unspoken agreement that it is something important, otherwise they would not be here, after all.

We definitely wanted to show these photographs in the exhibition, but not unrefracted. So we asked two artists to translate them into large-format paintings and placed them side by side. Their paintings amplify the authoritarian sedateness and self-satisfaction that can already be sensed in the photographs of these members of a generation who, despite their complicity, had recovered well after the Nazi era and now set about polishing its own image, despite the dark shadows, with the aid of modern art.

HC: The exhibition *50 jahre bauhaus* took place in the rooms of the Württembergischer Kunstverein, and Dieter Honisch was one of the cocurators and organizers, but it nevertheless had a national and international import that went far beyond the role of the Kunstverein.

ID: It was about correcting the image of German culture which after World War II was quite shattered abroad. As Magdalena Droste pointed out already in the 1990s, the Bauhaus was presented after 1945 as a cultural achievement of the Weimar Republic whose thread could be seamlessly taken up again: as a kind of reimport from the United States, where the Bauhaus had been allowed to mature in peace.[4] The Stuttgart exhibition of 1968 and its successor project had a crucial influence on this discourse. They stylized the Bauhaus into an enduring German-American brand that was supposed to stand for freedom, democracy, and resistance to the Nazi system.

After the Bauhaus was closed by the National Socialists in 1933, no small number of former Bauhaus members who remained in Germany worked together with the Nazis in the areas of exhibition and graphic design and industrial and residential architecture and in some cases professed their ideology. These

Fig. 1 Federal President Heinrich Lübke arriving at the exhibition *50 jahre bauhaus* (50 years bauhaus) at the Württembergischer Kunstverein, Stuttgart, May 1968

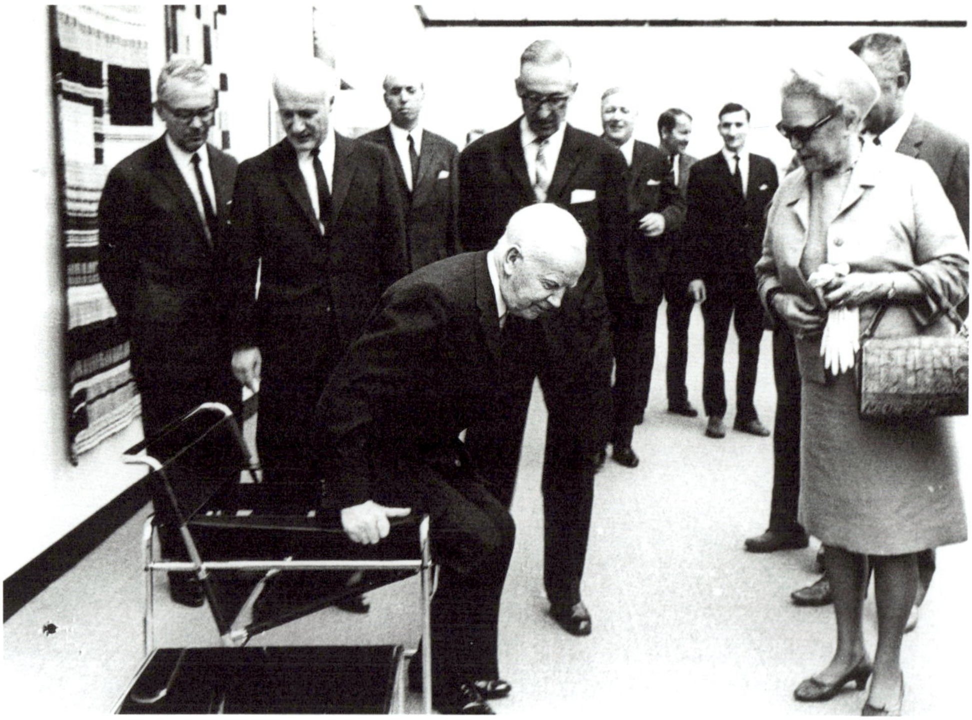

Fig. 2 View of the exhibition *50 Jahre nach 50 Jahre Bauhaus 1968* (50 years after 50 years bauhaus 1968) at the Württembergischen Kunstverein Stuttgart, 2018

Fig. 3 Federal President Heinrich Lübke in the exhibition *50 jahre bauhaus* (50 years bauhaus) at the Württembergischer Kunstverein, Stuttgart, May 1968

aspects were completely ignored in the exhibition in 1968. Fifty years later, our goal was not to judge the moral stance of individual members of the Bauhaus but to reflect, using the influence of the Bauhaus as an example, on the extent to which totalitarianism was itself part of the project we call modernity (figs. 2 and 3).

HC: It could also have become a very different exhibition—without a doubt. After all, neither the history of the modern nor that of the Bauhaus is a narrative that can be concluded with clearly outlined temporal or territorial boundaries. Rather, the Bauhaus and its significance can nevertheless be seen as a historical construction of the postwar years that was controlled, manipulated, and oriented by Walter Gropius in particular right up to the 1968 exhibition in Stuttgart. On the one hand, that school was founded in 1919 and closed again already in 1933. On the other hand, the title of this first comprehensive postwar exhibition that manifested the Bauhaus as a brand suggests an unbroken continuity and influence of the Bauhaus and modernism beyond the historical caesuras. The period between 1933 and 1945 could therefore be leapt over as something very different that ran completely counter to the processes of modernism, as if modernism had simply been paused in Germany during this time span. As a supposedly atypical symptom, the Nazi system, which is commonly depicted as an "irrational apocalypse" that was de facto a system of the administrative, industrial, and rationalist mass murder of Jewish people, opponents of the regime, homosexuals, the mentally and physically handicapped, and Sinti and Roma, was excluded from the narrative of the modern era. Our rather ungainly exhibition title, *50 Jahre nach 50 Jahre Bauhaus 1968*, is therefore also indebted to interrupting the "play-pause-play" temporal construct that made it so easy to establish a seamless, homogeneous narrative of the Bauhaus.

ID: Because the exhibition of 1968 was intended to hand Bauhaus out as a calling card for a better Germany, the former members of the Bauhaus were presented above all as adversaries of or persecuted by the Third Reich, which in many cases was justified. At least since the 1990s,[5] however, it has been known that not a few prominent members of the Bauhaus worked for the National Socialists after the school closed in 1933, including Herbert Bayer in the field of graphic design for campaigns of the Deutsche Arbeitsfront (German Labor Front) and the large propaganda exhibitions *Die Kamera* (1934), *Deutsches Volk—Deutsche Arbeit* (German Nation—German Work) (1934), *Wunder des Lebens* (Miracle of Life) (1935), and *Deutschland* (1936).[6] The Nazi regime was very interested in being considered modern and cosmopolitan in some circles and contexts. They were supported in this by the most innovative designs of the time, not only Bayer but also Ludwig Mies van der Rohe and Lilly Reich,[7] Walter Gropius and Joost Schmidt,[8] the Neuner brothers and Kurt Kranz,[9] and Egon Eiermann[10]—the last of those named here is the only one who was not from the Bauhaus. They all helped to lend a modern face to the inhuman, racist, and anti-Semitic ideologies of the National Socialists. Strange hybrids between simplistic Nazi aesthetics and easy modern forms also emerged. In addition to exhibitions, this is also true of journals such as the fashion magazine *die neue linie*,[11] in whose design a series of former members of the Bauhaus participated.

HC: Our exhibition in 2018 could have been very different if Herbert Bayer of all people—who until 1937 was one of the most prominent suppliers to National Socialist propaganda activities—had not been the scenographer of the *50 jahre bauhaus* exhibition. It would not, perhaps, been relevant to treat his career again if that exhibition had not opened on May 4, 1968, that is, one day after the occupation and immediate clearing of the Université de Sorbonne in Paris.[12] For the events in Paris, which have entered history as "May '68," were linked to the international youth movement, which in Germany was crucially related to the question of the participation of the generation of their fathers and mothers in the horrors of the Third Reich. That the coming to terms with the past vehemently demanded at the time is far from over is painfully evident from the continued existence of violent right-wing populism in Germany and worldwide.

TB: In his speech at the opening of the *50 jahre bauhaus* exhibition and in its catalog, Ludwig Grote addressed "the question of co-determination by the students which is so hotly contested today."[13] He was surely thinking in part of the virulent student protests internationally but above all of the students protesting on May 4, 1968, the threatened closure of the Hochschule für Gestaltung (College of Design) in Ulm. On their posters stood, for example, in lowercase Helvetica: "lament the bauhaus and preserve the hfg," "May 68 / words for the bauhaus are good. actions for the hfg are better," and "resurrection of the bauhaus / ascension of the hfg." But rather than go into more detail, he represented the Bauhaus as an almost exemplary place for student codetermination.

HC: Shortly after the students in Ulm had protested during the opening of the exhibition *50 jahre bauhaus*, numerous projects from the school threatened with closure were to be shown at the fourteenth Triennale di Milano for applied art.[14] In the exhibition in Stuttgart, this school played hardly any role at all, beyond the protests you mention. That was probably in part because those from Ulm themselves did not want to agree to presentation under threat of being shut down. No one less than Walter Gropius explained to the protestors through a megaphone that they should dedicate themselves less to political actions but rather devote themselves more to their tasks as designers. He did say "I hope that the HfG can continue to work" but also "My God, just be careful; don't get involved in politics, because I toed the line at the Bauhaus; namely if we at Bauhaus had decided this or that, we would surely have gone under in the first year, which is why I always saw to it that nothing political entered the institution itself."[15] The recording documenting this address was, of course, part of our exhibition. That codetermination at the Bauhaus, especially under Gropius and Mies van der Rohe, was limited has been pointed out by authors such as Philipp Oswalt (figs. 4 and 5).

TB: For Grote and the other exhibition curators, moreover, the school in Ulm was no longer in 1968 necessarily considered an undertaking that fit with their idea of the Bauhaus.

HC: For our exhibition, from a historical distance yet another, seemingly tangential argument suggested itself that can be seen concretely in the conflict over the HfG Ulm and its significance. The at times fierce to even crude conflict Max Bill and Asger Jorn carried out in correspondence in 1953 and 1954 over the concept of the HfG Ulm as a continuation of the Bauhaus idea reveals the uneasiness over and protest against a historical and contemporaneous positivism that set about tying prewar modernism seamlessly to postwar modernism. Jorn would prove right with his warning that if "the Bauhaus is not the name of an inspiration," it would become the "name of a doctrine" that "without inspiration is dead."[16] This uneasiness, from which in no small measure emerged the artistic movements of the Lettrists, the Bauhaus imaginiste, and the Situationist International, among whose protagonists numbered not only Guy Debord but also and above all Asger Jorn, interested us a great deal.

TB: That the HfG Ulm barely came up in the exhibition *50 jahre bauhaus* was probably also in part because in Ulm since the late 1950s but especially in the 1960s increasing efforts to establish a scientific foundation for training in design had influenced the school's profile. In addition, Ulm also oriented itself more around the program of the second director of the Bauhaus, Hannes Meyer. And famously the latter's idea did not correspond to that of Gropius and Grote. For Grote, Meyer was above all someone who had worked at the Bauhaus against its "artistic idea."[17] But for Grote this "artistic idea" was at the center of his idea of the Bauhaus as a school of artists.

HC: In our view, Ludwig Grote, Hans Maria Wingler, and Dieter Honisch—shoulder to shoulder with Herbert Bayer and Walter Gropius—treated the Bauhaus in the 1968 exhibition as above all an aesthetic educational institution that served as a purely artistic consecration. The question of affirmation, opportunity, or distance with respect to the diverse political systems in which the players at the Bauhaus had operated in the 1920s and thereafter was never thematized. In our exhibition, by contrast, we wanted to stimulate a debate over the relationships between political stances and cultural production that also points beyond the temporal framework of modernism between the wars.

ID: As we said, it was not about making more judgments about one person or another but rather revealing contradictions and antagonisms within the aesthetics of modernism. Bayer's innovations in the field of exhibition and graphic design in particular were a central point of departure for that. They were based on, among other things, the possibilities offered to him by photography—especially photomontage and photographic enlargement techniques—as well as typography and an expanded concept of space. Our exhibition tried to show how Bayer in particular put his aesthetic experiments in the service of very different ideological regimes: from the unions by way of the German fascists to the American war propagandists of the 1940s.

HC: The second strand of the exhibition focused on the Bauhaus and its milieu in relation to radical art movements from the late 1940s to the 1970s. In particular, it was about alternative artistic models to rationalization, standardization, and the functional city. One central figure of the rationalization of housing construction was the former Bauhaus member Ernst Neufert, who worked for the National Socialists, shared their ideologies, and rose to join the staff of Albert Speer.[18] The focus of the third strand was interconnections between the modern avant-garde and the military-industrial complex: between aerial photography and aerial war, housing construction and armaments industry. At the same time, this strand was dedicated to the positions opposing mechanization, militarization, and control of public space and life.

ID: Finally, we understood the fourth strand to be a look forward at the possible narratives of a multiple modernity. At least since 1989 and the globalization that followed, in our view, the image of a modernity dominated by the West is no longer tenable. Instead, it is necessary to reevaluate constantly the relationships between tradition and progress, applied and fine arts, popular and elite arts, and the world of the colonized and that of the colonizers. The theme of our exhibition was not just the Bauhaus. We have looked at it from the perspectives of diverse contexts and discourses of the 1960s—the time when *50 jahre bauhaus* opened—and from today's standpoint.

TB: In the introduction to the catalog of 1968, Grote writes: "the bauhaus was never the same, even though its basic character remained unchanged."[19] He continued: a "unique event in cultural history and is surrounded by a legendary aura."[20] Even though this legendary aura was essentially produced only by mythos and propaganda, it is still influential today. Many still consider the Bauhaus almost synonymous with the art and design avant-gardes of the twentieth century. Were you able to loosen up that consolidation?

HC: The more we distance ourselves from the past, the more we condense it clearly along certain individual phenomena that are then no longer contextualized in detail. With that in mind, we asked ourselves why the history of artistic modernism has concentrated so much in the narrative of the Bauhaus myth. For us, it was and is still astonishing how much the potentials, concepts, and ideas of other modern projects from Dada to Vkhutemas, from the Latin American to Asian schools and movements, which sometimes responded to realities more critically and more complexly than at the Bauhaus are ignored when there is talk of the Bauhaus as *the* one important school of modernism.

ID: Yet it remains a dilemma that if we want to break up the Bauhaus myth, we run the risk of reproducing its narrative in a new way. We won't escape the myth that way. That's why we have tried to contextualize the Bauhaus and its reception differently, above all by asking how we can read the twentieth century in new, complex, and contrary ways.

1 Württembergischer Kunstverein Stuttgart, *50 Jahre nach 50 Jahre Bauhaus 1968*, May 5–September 23, 2018, press information, www.wkv-stuttgart.de (accessed July 5, 2020).
2 Heinrich Lübke (1894–1972) was the second Federal President of the Federal Republic of Germany, from 1959 to 1969.
3 See Edgar Wolfrum, "Die Anfänge der Bundesrepublik, die Aufarbeitung der NS-Vergangenheit und die Fernwirkungen bis heute," in *Solidargemeinschaft und Erinnerungskultur im 20. Jahrhundert*, ed. Ursula Bitzgeio, Anja Kruke, and Meik Woyke (Bonn: Dietz, 2009), 363–77, esp. 369, and Jens-Christian Wagner, "Der Fall Lübke," *Die Zeit*, no. 30 (July 19, 2007).
4 See Magdalena Droste, "Bauhaus-Designer zwischen Handwerk und Moderne," in *Bauhaus-Moderne im Nationalsozialismus: Zwischen Anbiederung und Verfolgung*, ed. Winfried Nerdinger (Munich: Prestel, 1993), 85–102, esp. 100.
5 See Nerdinger, *Bauhaus-Moderne im Nationalsozialismus* (see note 4).
6 As part of an exhibition originally planned by the Deutscher Werkbund, *Die Kamera: Ausstellung für Fotografie, Druck und Reproduktion*, November 4–19, 1933, whose patron was Joseph Goebbels, Herbert Bayer designed a catalog for National Socialist clients for the first time. The exhibition *Deutsches Volk—Deutsche Arbeit* (April 21–June 3, 1934) was the first exhibition designed by Bayer whose concept was based from the beginning on National Socialist propaganda. It was immediately followed by commissions to design the exhibition *Das Wunder des Lebens* (The Miracle of Life, March 23–May 5, 1935) and, on the occasion of the Summer Olympics, *Deutschland* (July 18–August 16, 1936).
7 In 1934 Reich and Mies van der Rohe were involved in the design of various sections of the exhibition *Deutsches Volk—Deutsche Arbeit* in Berlin. In 1937 they designed together the (unrealized) Reich exhibition of the Deutsche Textil- und Bekleidungswirtschaft (German Textile and Clothing Industry) in Berlin, which was ultimately shown in the German pavilion at the World's Fair in Paris in 1937.
8 In 1934 Joost Schmidt and Walter Gropius designed the section "Nichteisenmetalle" (Nonferrous Metals) for the exhibition *Deutsches Volk—Deutsche Arbeit*.
9 They worked for, among others, *die neue linie* from 1933.
10 Egon Eiermann played a crucial role in the design of the monumental photo displays for the exhibition *Gebt mir vier Jahre Zeit* (Give Me Four Years) in Berlin in 1937, which celebrated Hitler's four-year plan.
11 *die neue linie* was the first German lifestyle magazine, published by the Verlag Otto Beyer in Leipzig from 1929 to 1943. After 1933 it was initially allowed to continue to publish in largely unchanged form as a liberal shingle for the Nazi regime but was then increasingly integrated into National Socialist cultural policy. Patrick Rössler described it as "the only publication that more broadly implemented the typographical ideas of the Bauhaus and tapped their potential for the mass market." At the same time, he considered it an example of a "domesticated avant-garde"; Patrick Rössler, *The Bauhaus at the Newsstand / Das Bauhaus am Kiosk: Die Neue Linie, 1929–1943*, exh. cat. Bauhaus-Museum, Weimar (Bielefeld: Kerber, 2009), 7.
12 In 1967–68 there were numerous political protests by students in Germany, the United States, Italy, Czechoslovakia, Poland, Japan, Mexico, Switzerland, and other countries. The central concerns were, in addition to improving the conditions of studies, criticism of the consumer society, capitalism, and police violence as well as opposing the Vietnam War and supporting democratic socialism. Nowhere else, however, were the protests on the scale of those in France. On May 3, 1968, leftist students at the Sorbonne occupied rooms in the university after an assembly at the university had been banned. After the police arrested around 500 students and the Sorbonne was closed on May 4, protests continued expanding into a nationwide general strike.
13 Ludwig Grote, "walter gropius and the bauhaus," in *50 Years Bauhaus: German Exhibition*, exh. cat. (London: Royal Academy of Arts, 1968), 9–11, esp. 9.
14 This Triennale never opened, however, because it was demolished during violent protests by students who were rightly defending themselves against the cooptation and marketing of their own movement; see "Sturm auf Vitrinen," *Der Spiegel*, no. 24 (June 10, 1968).
15 The sound recording was made by Chup Friemert, who participated in the demonstration against the closing of the school on the opening day of the exhibition *50 jahre bauhaus*; a transcription is in the archives of the Württembergischer Kunstverein Stuttgart; see Christiane Wachsmann, *Vom Bauhaus beflügelt: Menschen und Ideen an der Hochschule für Gestaltung* (Ulm: avedition, 2018). That book was published on the occasion of the exhibition *Wir demonstrieren* (We Are Demonstrating) at the HfG-Archiv, Ulm, July 14–November 4, 2018.
16 Asger Jorn to Max Bill, 12 February 1954, quoted in Roberto Ohrt, *Phantom Avantgarde: Eine Geschichte der Situationistischen Internationale und der modernen Kunst* (Hamburg: Nautilus, 1990), 140.
17 Ludwig Grote, "basic form and functionalism," in *50 Years Bauhaus* (see note 13), 18–20, esp. 20.
18 In 1938 Ernst Neufert (1900–1986; a student at the Bauhaus from 1919 to 1920, who then worked in Gropius's architectural firm until 1926) was appointed Reichsbeauftragter für Baunormung (Reich Representative for Building Standards) by Speer. In that position, he produced his *Bauordnungslehre* (Building Code Theory), which was first published as a handbook in 1943 and which took up the thread of his *Bauentwurfslehre* (1936; Architectural Design Theory; published in 1970 as *Architects' Data*). In 1944 Neufert became an employee of Speer's Arbeitsstab für den Wiederaufbau bombenzerstörter Städte (Working Staff for the Rebuilding of Cities Destroyed by Bombing); in 1944, in the final phase of World War II, Adolf Hitler included him in the "Gottbegnadeten-Liste" (List of the Divinely Gifted) of the most important architects, which also protected Neufert from being deployed in the war.
19 Ludwig Grote, "walter gropius and the bauhaus" (see note 13), 9.
20 Ibid.

Fig. 4 Students protesting at the opening of the exhibition *50 jahre bauhaus* (50 years bauhaus), May 4, 1968, to save the Hochschule für Gestaltung, Ulm

Fig. 5 Walter Gropius speaking at the opening of the exhibition *50 jahre bauhaus* (50 years bauhaus), May 4, 1968, to the students protesting to save the Hochschule für Gestaltung, Ulm

Fig. 1 Ludwig Grote, ca. 1925

Biography

1893 Born on August 8 in Halle an der Saale, the son of the master Freemason Otto Grote and the pianist Margarethe Grote (née Dan), baptized Hans Wilhelm Karl Ludwig Grote.

1908 Joins the newly founded Wandervogel (Migratory Bird) association of Halle an der Saale.

1912 Graduates secondary school and in the summer semester begins studying archaeology in Jena. Connects with the Serakreis (Sera Circle) student circle around the publisher Eugen Diederichs; in October, transfers to Braunschweig to study architecture.

1914 Volunteers for World War I, stationed in signal corps in Flanders and France.

1917 Promoted to rank of lieutenant in the reserve.

1918 Discharged from military service in November.

1919 In February, completes basic study in architecture at the Technische Universität in Braunschweig; from October, studies art history in Halle-Wittenberg.

1920 Transfers to Universität München, studies with Heinrich Wölfflin, among others.

1922 Receives doctorate from the Universität Halle with the dissertation "Georg Lemberger: Ein Beitrag zur Geschichte des sächsischen Holzschnitts" (Georg Lemberger: A Contribution to the History of the Saxon Woodcut); from November, research assistant at the Joachim-Ernst-Stiftung in Dessau (until March 1924).

1923 Hired by the City of Dessau as a museum assistant to catalog the Amalienstiftung collection of paintings.

1924 From October, Landeskonservator (State Curator) of Anhalt, responsible for the care of art and monuments in general and for the former ducal castles and gardens of the state; chairman of the board of the Anhaltischer Kunstverein.

1925 In February/March, plays a crucial role in the transfer of the Bauhaus from Weimar to Dessau.

1926 Second managing director of the Kreis der Freunde des Bauhauses (Circle of Friends of the Bauhaus).

1927 From September, part-time director of the newly founded Anhaltische Gemäldegalerie; marries the concert pianist Gertrud Maud Schmitt (1906–1996).

1929 Birth of their son Andreas.

1930 May to July, negotiates with Otto Haesler and Ludwig Mies van der Rohe to take over the directorship of the Bauhaus in the run-up to the planned dismissal of Hannes Meyer.

1931 Birth of their son Christian.

1933 In May, his application for early retirement, to forestall his dismissal, is granted; moves to Berlin; publishes essays and lectures in the social circles of Carl Georg Heise, Theodor Heuss, and Leopold Reidemeister; freelance consultant for Deckosit, an artificial stone binding material, for two stone restoration companies in Potsdam and Berlin.

1934 Joins the SA (Sturmabteilung).

1940 Moves to Munich; from February, works for the art dealer Friedrich Heinrich Zinckgraf at the "Aryanized" formerly Jewish-owned Galerie Heinemann, now Galerie Zinckgraf.

1941 In October, drafted into military service.

1942 Promoted to first lieutenant in the reserve on call.

1943 Promoted to captain in the reserve.

1944 In September, discharged from military service because of myocardial insufficiency. Resumes activity at Zinckgraf (until 1946).

1945 In February, joins the Volkssturm.

1946 After failing to mention his SA membership in the de-Nazification process, categorized as "exonerated" in December.

1949 Organizes the exhibition *Der Blaue Reiter* (The Blue Rider), which opens at the Haus der Kunst in Munich in September.

1950 Organizes additional exhibitions at the Haus der Kunst in Munich: *Die Maler am Bauhaus* (The Painters at the Bauhaus), May to June; *Max Beckmann zum Gedächtnis*, 1884–1950 (Max Beckmann in Memorial), June to July; *Oskar Kokoschka*, 1907–1950 (September); rejects Max Bill's offer to move to Ulm to head the cultural department and serve as museum director.

1951 From February, works in the cultural department of the Federal Ministry of the Interior evaluating exhibitions and working on a cultural policy initiative to prevent valuable national cultural assets from going abroad; from November, "first director" of the Germanisches Nationalmuseum in Nuremberg (from August 1958, his title is Director General); member of the committee for exhibitions abroad of the Foreign

Office and commission of the German exhibitions for the newly founded Bienal de São Paulo.

1952 Organizes the centennial celebration of the Germanisches Nationalmuseum; organizes and directs exhibitions on modern art at the Fränkische Galerie in Nuremberg, including *Pablo Picasso, Radierungen und Lithographien* (Etchings and Lithographs) *Ernst Ludwig Kirchner, Sammlung Dr. F. Bauer/Davos*; *Wassily Kandinsky: Arbeiten, 1912–1942* (1954); in December, sets off on a ninety-day trip to the United States, where he visits a large number of former members of the Bauhaus.

1953 Organizes the reconstruction of the Germanisches Nationalmuseum, together with the architect Sep Ruf.

1956 Honorary professor of museum studies at the Universität Erlangen.

1959 Awarded the Grosses Verdienstkreuzes (Great Cross with Star) of the Verdienstordens der Bundesrepublik Deutschland (Order of Merit of the Federal Republic of Germany) and the Bayerischer Verdienstorden (Bavarian Order of Merit).

1962 Honorary member of the Akademie der Bildenden Künste in Nuremberg; retires at the end of October; until 1974, editor of the Studien zur Kunst des 19. Jahrhunderts (Studies on Nineteenth-Century Art) book series of the Fritz-Thyssen-Stiftung and its Arbeitskreis Kulturgeschichte des 19. Jahrhunderts (Working Circle on the Cultural History of the Nineteenth Century).

1968 Head of the committee preparing for the exhibition *50 jahre bauhaus* (50 years bauhaus), which opens in Stuttgart in May and then travels internationally (until 1971) for the Institut für Auslandsbeziehungen and until 1982 in cooperation with the Goethe-Institut.

1974 Dies on March 3 in Gauting, near Munich.

Fig. 2 Wearing Wandervogel gear, Braunschweig, 1913
Fig. 3 During World War I (*third from left*)
Fig. 4 Mid-1920s

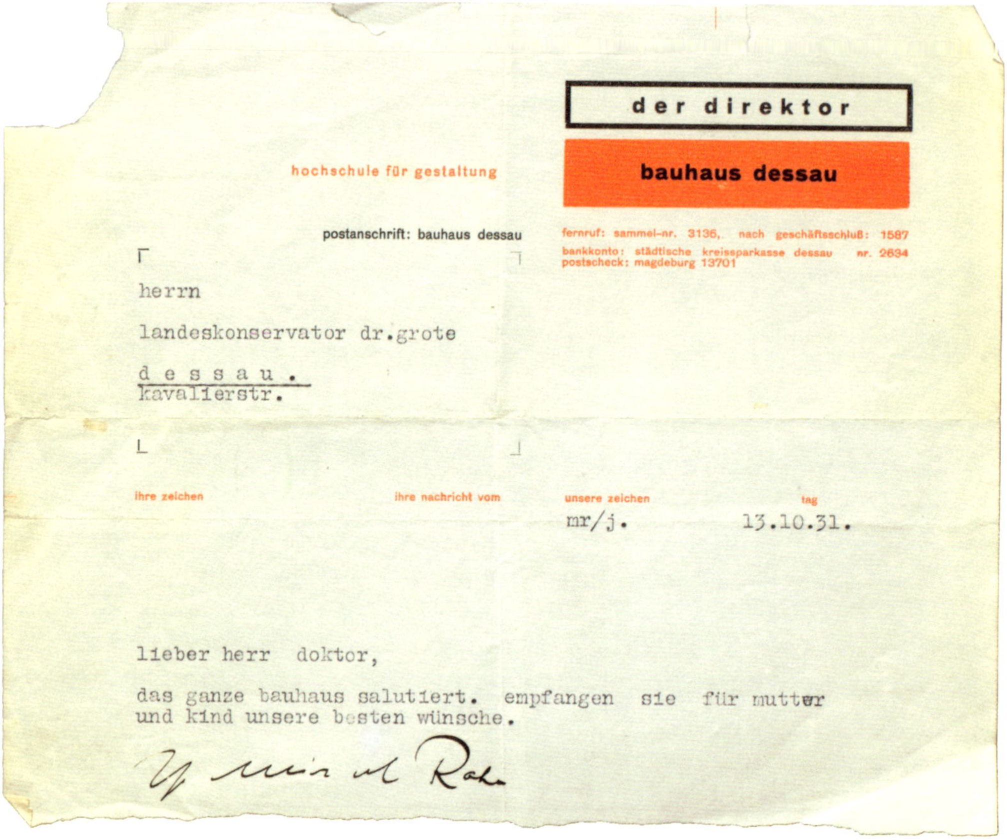

der direktor

hochschule für gestaltung

bauhaus dessau

postanschrift: bauhaus dessau

fernruf: sammel-nr. 3136, nach geschäftsschluß: 1587
bankkonto: städtische kreissparkasse dessau nr. 2634
postscheck: magdeburg 13701

herrn

landeskonservator dr.grote

d e s s a u .
kavalierstr.

ihre zeichen	ihre nachricht vom	unsere zeichen	tag
		mr/j.	13.10.31.

lieber herr doktor,

das ganze bauhaus salutiert. empfangen sie für mutter und kind unsere besten wünsche.

Mies v. d. Rohe

Fig. 5. Congratulatory letter from the Bauhaus to Grote on the birth of his son Christian: “The whole bauhaus salutes. accept our best wishes for mother and child.”

Fig. 6. Mid-1920s

Fig. 7 In Berchtesgaden, late 1930s
Fig. 8 In the army, 1943

Figs. 9, 10 With his wife, Maud Grote, 1950

Fig. 11 In his office at the Germanisches Nationalmuseum, mid-1950s

Fig. 12 Ludwig Grote (1893–1974), ca. 1969

Bibliography

A first bibliography of Grote, compiled by Wulf Schadendorf and supplemented by Maud Grote, was published in 1962 in the *Anzeiger des Germanischen Nationalmuseums*. For the list that follows, it was resystematized, corrected, and completed as necessary.

Monographs

Das Land Anhalt: Aufgenommen von der Staatlichen Bildstelle, beschrieben von Ludwig Grote. Berlin: Deutscher Kunstverlag, 1929; repr. Halle/Saale: Waldersee-Verlag, 2008.

Kardinal Albrecht und die Renaissance in Halle. Der rote Turm 8/9, edited by Kurt Gerstenberg. Halle/Saale: Gebauer-Schwetschke, [1930]; repr. Halle/Saale: Waldersee-Verlag, 2006; repr. Halle/Saale: Mitteldeutschen Verlag, 2016.

Die Stiftskirche in Gernrode. Deutsche Bauten 19. Burg bei Magdeburg: August Hopfer, 1932.

Georg Lemberger. Leipzig: H. Haessel, 1933.

Deutsche Stilfibel. Leipzig: Verlag L. Staackmann, 1936; repr. 1937, 1939, 1940, 1942, 1944, 1946; repr. Bamberg: Carl Baessler Verlag, 1950, 1952, 1953, 1956, 1958, 1960, 1967; repr. Munich: Prestel, 1991.

Die Brüder Olivier und die deutsche Romantik. Berlin: Rembrandt-Verlag, 1938.

Der Park zu Wörlitz. Berlin: Deutscher Kunstverlag, 1944.

Das Antlitz eines Jugendbundes: Zeichnungen von Carl Philipp Fohr. Berlin: Gebr. Mann, 1944.

Die Erasmus-Mauritius-Tafel von Matthias Grünewald. Berlin: Gebr. Mann, 1944, repr. 1947, new ed. Stuttgart: Reclam, 1957.

Die Neapler Fresken von Hans von Marées. Berlin: Gebr. Mann, 1947. New ed. titled *Hans von Marées, Die Fresken in Neapel*. Stuttgart: Reclam, 1958.

Deutsche Kunst im zwanzigsten Jahrhundert. Munich: Prestel, 1953; 2nd ed., 1954.

"Hier bin ich ein Herr": Dürer in Venedig. Munich: Prestel, 1956.

Europäische Malerei in deutschen Galerien, 3 vols. Munich: Prestel, [1960–65]: vol. 1, *Alte Meister* [1960]; vol. 2, *Meister des 19. Jahrhunderts* [1965]; vol. 3, *Meister des 20. Jahrhunderts* [1964].

European Paintings in German Art Galleries, 3 vols. Munich: Prestel, [1960–65]: vol. 1, *Old Masters* [1960]; vol. 2, *Masters of the 19th Century* [1965]; vol. 3, *Masters of the Twentieth Century*, translated by Walter Moss [1965].

Die Tucher: Bildnis einer Patrizierfamilie. Munich: Prestel, 1961.

Dürer: Biographisch-kritische Studie. Geneva: Skira, 1965, repr. Tübingen: Wasmuth, 1990.

Dürer: Biographical and Critical Study, translated by Helga Harrison. Geneva: Skira, 1965.

Gauguin: Biographisch-kritische Studie. Geneva: Skira, 1965.

Die romantische Entdeckung Nürnbergs. Munich: Prestel, 1967.

Joseph Sutter und der nazarenische Gedanke. Munich: Prestel, 1972.

Essays

"Zwei Frühwerke der Gebrüder Olivier in der Kirche zu Wörlitz." *Anhaltische Geschichtsblätter* 1 (1925): 142–47.

"Das Weimarer Bauhaus und seine Aufgaben in Dessau." *Anhalter Anzeiger*, March 10, 1925; and *Anhaltische Rundschau*, March 11, 1925.

"Johann Heinrich Ferdinand Olivier." *Mitteldeutsche Lebensbilder* 1 (1926): 78–91.

"Die beiden Hauptwerke von Joseph Wintergerst." *Zeitschrift für bildende Kunst* 61 (1927/28): 383–85.

"Junge Bauhausmaler." *bauhaus: zeitschrift für gestaltung* 2, nos. 2/3 (1928): 31.

"Die romanischen Kirchen im anhaltischen Harzgebiet (1). Die Stiftskirche in Gernrode." *Heimat-Kalender für die Alt-Bernburger Lande* 3 (1928): 104–11.

"Bühnenkomposition von Kandinsky." *Internationale Revue i10* 2, no. 13 (August 1928): 4–5.

"Der Fürst Franz." *Montagsblatt – das Heimatblatt Mitteldeutschlands: Wissenschaftliche Beilage der Magdeburgischen Zeitung* 70 (1928): 410–12.

"Friedrich Wilhelm von Erdmannsdorf(f)." *Mitteldeutsche Lebensbilder* 4 (1929): 151–70.

"Die romanischen Kirchen im anhaltischen Harzgebiet (2): Die Kirche St. Georgii des Benediktinernonnenklosters zu Hecklingen." *Heimat-Kalender für die Alt-Bernburger Lande* 4 (1929): 96–100.

"Andreas Günther, der Baumeister des Wolfgangbaues des Schlosses zu Bernburg." *Montagsblatt – das Heimatblatt Mitteldeutschlands: Wissenschaftliche Beilage der Magdeburgischen Zeitung* 71 (1929): 377.

"Näheres über den anhaltischen Baumeister Andreas Günther." *Montagsblatt – das Heimatblatt Mitteldeutschlands: Wissenschaftliche Beilage der Magdeburgischen Zeitung* 72 (1930): 167.

"Moderne Bildwirkereien." *Die Form: Zeitschrift für gestaltende Arbeit* 4 (1929): 256–62.

"Das Land Anhalt und seine tausendjährige Kultur." *Serimunt: Mitteilungen aus Vergangenheit und Gegenwart der Heimat: Blätter des Vereins Heimatmuseum für Stadt und Kreis Köthen (Anhalt)* 4, no. 20 (1929): n.p.

"Eine romanische Skulptur um 1150." *Zeitschrift für bildende Kunst* 63 (1929/30): 76–77.

"Die Entdeckung der deutschen Landschaft in der Romantik." *Naturschutz* 11, no. 1 (1929/30): 1–9.

"Das Stiftsschloß zu Mosigkau, ein Werk Knobelsdorffs." *Kunst und Künstler* 28 (1930): 409–15.

"Zurück zur Natur." *Naturschutz* 12 (1930/31): 126–68, 200–203.

"Fundberichte aus Anhalt 1930/31." *Anhaltische Geschichtsblätter* 8/9 (1932/33): 134–45.

"An Paul Klee: Dessau verliert Paul Klee." *bauhaus: zeitschrift für gestaltung* 4, no. 3 (1931): n.p.

"Die Ausgrabungen in der Schlosskirche zu Nienburg im Jahre 1926." *Jahrbuch der Denkmalpflege in der Provinz Sachsen und in Anhalt* (1931): 11–17.

"Lyonel Feininger zum 60. Geburtstage." *Museum der Gegenwart* 2, no. 2 (1931): 41–49.

"Ferdinand Olivier, Friedrich Olivier, Heinrich Olivier." *Allgemeines Lexikon der bildenden Künstler von der Antike bis zur Gegenwart*, edited by Ulrich Thieme und Felix Becker, vol. 26. Leipzig: Seemann, 1932, 1–5.

"Das Problem der Kirchenbeleuchtung, dargestellt in zwei verschiedenen Lösungen." *Die Denkmalpflege* 34 (1932): 167–70.

"Goethe in Dessau und Wörlitz." *Montagsblatt – das Heimatblatt Mitteldeutschlands: Wissenschaftliche Beilage der Magdeburgischen Zeitung* 74 (1932): 89–92.

"Der Chor von St. Marien in Bernburg." *Heimat-Kalender für die Alt-Bernburger Lande* 7 (1932): 102–4.

"Romanische Portale im Bernburger und Ballenstedter Kreis." *Heimat-Kalender für die Alt-Bernburger Lande* 8 (1933): 82–85.

"Das Leben Georg Lembergers." *Montagsblatt – das Heimatblatt Mitteldeutschlands: Wissenschaftliche Beilage der Magdeburgischen Zeitung* 75 (1933): 285–87.

"Unbekannte Bilder Georg Lembergers." *Jahrbuch der Denkmalpflege in der Provinz Sachsen und in Anhalt* (1933/34): 76–93.

"Dokumente romantischer Zeichenkunst: Ferdinand Oliviers Salzburger Landschaften." *Pantheon* 13 (1934): 10–15.

"Die Tafelbilder Georg Lembergers." *Pantheon* 14 (1934): 198–203.

"Georg Lemberger und seine graphische Kunst." *Kunst- und Antiquitätenrundschau* 42, no. 9 (1934): 340–43.

"Wiederherstellungsarbeiten im Naumburger Stifterchor." *Deutsche Kunst und Denkmalpflege* 1 (1934): 198–99.

"Johann Christoph Schütze: Ein mitteldeutscher Barockbaumeister." *Montagsblatt – das Heimatblatt Mitteldeutschlands: Wissenschaftliche Beilage der Magdeburgischen Zeitung* 76 (1934): 369–73.

"Eine Landschaft von J. A. Koch in der Anhaltischen Gemäldegalerie Dessau." *Zeitschrift für Kunstgeschichte* 3 (1934): 144.

"Beiträge zur Frage: Knobelsdorff und das friderizianische Rokoko." *Zeitschrift für Kunstgeschichte* 4 (1935): 51–55.

"Aus den Briefen von Josef Sutter an Overbeck und die Lukasbrüder in den Jahren 1810–15." *Zeitschrift für Kunstgeschichte* 4 (1935): 127–40.

"Hadmersleben." *Deutsche Kunst und Denkmalpflege* 2 (1935): 154.

"Huysburg." *Deutsche Kunst und Denkmalpflege* 2 (1935): 154–55.

"Caspar David Friedrich: Stubbenkammer auf Rügen." In *Deutsche Kunst: Meisterwerke der Baukunst, Malerei, Bildhauerkunst, Graphik und des Kunsthandwerks*, edited by Ludwig Roselius, vol. 1, edition 12, 144. Bremen/Berlin: Angelsachsen-Verlag, 1935.

"Chodowieckis Reise nach Dessau im Jahre 1773." *Montagsblatt – das Heimatblatt Mitteldeutschlands: Wissenschaftliche Beilage der Magdeburgischen Zeitung* 77 (1935): 413–15.

"Der norwegische Maler Dahl und die deutsche Kunst. Zum Johann-Christian-Dahl-Tag in Dresden." *Der Norden: Monatsschrift der Nordischen Gesellschaft* 12 (1935) 343–48.

"Salzburg als romantisches Ideal." *Die Kunst* 71 (1935): 375–78; and *Die Kunst für alle* 50 (1935): 299–302.

"Carl Wilhelm Kolbe, 1758–1835: Ein Beitrag zum Sturm und Drang in der Malerei." *Zeitschrift des Deutschen Vereins für Kunstwissenschaft* 3 (1936): 369–89.

"Johann Heinrich Ferdinand Olivier: Berchtesgadener Landschaft, 1817." In *Deutsche Kunst: Meisterwerke der Baukunst, Malerei, Bildhauerkunst, Graphik und des Kunsthandwerks*, edited by Ludwig Roselius, vol. 2, edition 1, n.p. Bremen/Berlin: Angelsachsen-Verlag, 1936.

"Neue romantische Bilder in der Nationalgalerie." *Die Kunst* 73 (1936): 373–76; and *Die Kunst für alle* 51 (1936): 299–302.

"Dieskau, ein vergessener Garten der Goethezeit." *Der Salzkorb: Heimatjahrbuch für Halle und den Saalekreis* 1 (1936): 94–96.

"Woldemar Friedrich Olivier: Ideallandschaft." In *Deutsche Kunst: Meisterwerke der Baukunst, Malerei, Bildhauerkunst, Graphik und des Kunsthandwerks*, edited by Ludwig Roselius, vol. 3, edition 5, 60. Bremen/Berlin: Angelsachsen-Verlag, 1937.

"Joseph Anton Koch: Die Jungfrau von Unterseen aus, 1813." In *Deutsche Kunst: Meisterwerke der Baukunst, Malerei, Bildhauerkunst, Graphik und des Kunsthandwerks*, edited by Ludwig Roselius, vol. 3, edition 6, 61. Bremen/Berlin: Angelsachsen-Verlag, 1937.

"'Auf der Insel der seligen Phäaken': Zum Gedächtnis der Reise Goethes nach Sizilien vor 150 Jahren." *Atlantis* 9 (1937): 445–48.

"Johann Michael Hoppenhaupt, der Schöpfer des Porzellankabinetts im Deutschen Museum." *Jahrbuch der Preußischen Kunstsammlungen* 59 (1938): 250–57.

"Blick aus dem Fenster." *Die neue Linie* 11, no. 10 (1940): 28, 29, and 37.

"Ein romantisches Nibelungenlied." *Zeitschrift des Deutschen Vereins für Kunstwissenschaft* 8 (1941): 99–112.

"Julius Schnorr von Carolsfeld, 'Kraft ins Herz der Nation': Die Nibelungenfresken im Königsbau der Residenz." *Münchner Mosaik* 4, no. 6 (1941): 122–26.

"Zwei Briefe von Julius Schnorr von Carolsfeld an Karl Friedrich von Rumohr." *Wallraf-Richartz-Jahrbuch* 12/13 (1943): 299–311.

"Die Naumburger Stifterfiguren als Almanachschmuck." *Zeitschrift für Kunstwissenschaft* 2 (1948): 63–66.

"Die Schule des Neuen Bauens." *Die Kunst und das Schöne Heim* 47, no. 5 (1949): 185–87.

"Der Blaue Reiter: Zur Ausstellung in München." *Die Kunst und das schöne Heim* 48, no. 1 (1949): 4–7.

"Zum Plan einer deutschen Ausstellung in London." *Kunstchronik* 3 (1950): 161–63.

"Nürnberg! Du vormals weltberühmte Stadt! Xeller und Kirchner, ihre romantischen Entdecker." In *Eine Gabe der Freunde für Carl Georg Heise zum 28.VI.1950*, edited by Erich Meyer, 194–202. Berlin: Gebr. Mann, 1950.

"Der Wanderer über dem Nebelmeer: Ein Beitrag zu Caspar David Friedrichs Bildgestaltung." *Die Kunst und das Schöne Heim* 48 (1950): 401–4.

"Oskar Kokoschkas Salzburger Landschaft." *Hochland* 43 (1950/51): 627–28.

"Du 'Blaue Reiter' au 'Bauhaus.'" *Documents: Revue mensuelle des questions allemandes* 7 (1951): 27–37.

"Wohnmaschinen von einst und das Bauhaus von heute." *Die Neue Zeitung* (Freiburg i. Br.), no. 38, February 14, 1951.

"Nürnberg und die Romantik: Festrede auf der Hauptversammlung des Bayerischen Verleger- und Buchhändlerverbandes, 2.–4. Mai 1952 in Nürnberg." *Mitteilungen des Bayerischen Verleger- und Buchhändlerverbandes Rundschreiben* 29 (May 27, 1952): 21–29.

"Nürnberg und die Romantik." *Die Besinnung* 7, no. 4/5 (1952): 265–73.

"From the 'Blaue Reiter' to the 'Bauhaus.'" In *German Contemporary Art*, a special issue of *Documents: Revue mensuelle des questions allemandes*, published by the Gesellschaft für übernationale Zusammenarbeit, 27–39. Offenburg in Baden: Dokumente-Verlag, 1952.

"Les Blaue Reiter et le Bauhaus." *Art d'aujourd'hui* 4, no. 6 (1953): 1.

"Les peintres du 'Blaue Reiter.'" *Art d'aujourd'hui* 4, no. 6 (1953): 2–3.

"Les peintres du Bauhaus." *Art d'aujourd'hui* 4, no. 6 (1953): 4–5.

"Begegnungen mit Theodor Heuss." In *Begegnungen mit Theodor Heuss*, edited by Hermann Leins and Hans Bott, 354–57. Tübingen: Wunderlich, 1954.

"Dürer, einmal anders gesehen: Seine Einnahmen und seine wirtschaftlichen Verhältnisse: Vortragsbericht." *77. Jahresbericht des Vereins für Geschichte der Stadt Nürnberg* (1954): 9–11.

"Germanisches National-Museum, Nürnberg." *Museum* 7, no. 1 (1954): 72.

"Die 'Vorder-Stube' des Sebald Schreyer: Ein Beitrag zur Rezeption der Renaissance in Nürnberg." *Anzeiger des Germanischen Nationalmuseums* (1954–59): 43–67.

Introduction to Wassily Kandinsky, *Rückblick*. Baden-Baden: Woldemar Klein Verlag, 1955, 5–7.

"Emil Nolde, gest. 13. April 1956." *Jahresring* 56/57 (1956): 304–6.

"Moritz von Schwind, 1804–1871." In *Die großen Deutschen*, edited by Theodor Heuss et al., vol. 5, 309–17. Berlin: Propyläen-Verlag, 1957.

"Hinnerk Scheper †. Nachruf." *Deutsche Kunst und Denkmalpflege* 15 (1957): 60–61.

"Der Stil unserer Zeit." In Mensch und Technik: Sechs Vorträge, gehalten im Sommer 1958 im Stammhaus der Siemens-Schuckertwerke AG, edited by Heinz Goeschel and Wolfgang Schadewaldt, 42–63. Erlangen: Siemens-Schuckertwerke AG, 1958.

"Nürnberg – die Stadt Albrecht Dürers." *Die Stimme Frankens* 24, no. 3 (1958): 48–52.

"Anton Kress als Mäzen." In *Studies in the History of Art: Dedicated to William E. Suida on His Eightieth Birthday*, 154–70. London: Phaidon Press, 1959.

"The Romantic Movement in Germany." In *The Romantic Movement, Fifth Exhibition to Celebrate the Tenth Anniversary of the Council of Europe*, edited by The Tate Gallery and the Arts Council Gallery London, 33–37. London: Arts Council of Great Britain, 1959.

"Die museale Aufgabe des neuen Baues: Anläßlich der Eröffnung des Theodor-Heuss-Baues am Germanischen Nationalmuseum." *Baukunst und Werkform* 12 (1959): 66–67.

"Expressionismus und Volkskunst." *Zeitschrift für Volkskunde* 55 (1959): 24–31.

"Betrachtungen zu einer Ausstellung (Europarat-Ausstellung 'The romantic movement,' London 1959)." In *Weltbewohner und Weimaraner: Ernst Beutler zugedacht*, edited by Benno Reifenberg and Emil Staiger, 53–71. Zurich: Artemis-Verlag, 1960.

"Die deutschen Museen auf dem Wege zum internationalen Niveau." *Jahresring* 60/61 (1960): 366–68.

"Dürer-Werkstatt und Dürer-Schule." In *Meister um Albrecht Dürer, Ausstellung im Germanischen Nationalmuseum vom 4. Juli bis 17. September 1961*, edited by Peter Strieder and Eugen Sporer, 11–16. Nuremberg: Germanisches Nationalmuseum, 1961.

"Zum Gestaltwandel des Bauhauses." In *Eberhard Hanfstaengl zum 75. Geburtstag*, edited by Eberhard Ruhmer, 178–85. Munich: F. Bruckmann, 1961.

Foreword and "Joachim Sandrart und Nürnberg." *Anzeiger des Germanischen Nationalmuseums* (1962): 5–7, 10–21.

"Joachim von Sandrart und Nürnberg: Festvortrag." In *Dreihundert Jahre Akademie der bildenden Künste in Nürnberg*, edited by Franz Winzinger, 32–43. Nuremberg: Akademie der Bildenden Künste in Nürnberg, 1962.

"Veit Stoß: Der Englische Gruß." In *Kunstwerke der Welt aus dem öffentlichen Bayerischen Kunstbesitz*, edited by Remigius Netzer, vol. 2, n.p. Munich: L. Müller, 1962.

"Ansprache anlässlich der Verleihung der Würde eines Ehrensenators an Prof. Dr. Ing. e. h. Walter Gropius."

Schriftenreihe der Hochschule für bildende Künste Berlin 7 (1963): n.p.
"Conrad Witz: Die Verkündigung an Maria." In *Kunstwerke der Welt aus dem öffentlichen Bayerischen Kunstbesitz*, edited by Remigius Netzer, vol. 3, n.p. Munich: L. Müller, 1963.
"Museum und Geschichte." *Jahrbuch Altonaer Museum in Hamburg* 2 (1964): 7–32.
"Vom Handwerker zum Künstler: Das gesellschaftliche Ansehen Albrecht Dürers." In *Festschrift für Hans Liermann zum 70. Geburtstag*, edited by Klaus Obermayer and Hans-Rudolf Hagemann, 26–47. Erlangen: Universitätsbibliothek, 1964.
"Nachruf auf Georg Schmidt, Basel, 17. März 1896–26. Mai 1965." *Museumskunde* 34 (1965):190–93.
"Das Bauhaus: Eine Stätte schöpferischer Erziehung." *Mitteldeutsche Vorträge* 1 (1965): 7–13.
"Dürer-Studien. 1. Christus als Schmerzensmann in der Staatlichen Kunsthalle Karlsruhe. 2. Eryngium und Eule im Werke Albrecht Dürers." *Zeitschrift des Deutschen Vereins für Kunstwissenschaft* 19 (1965): 151–69.
"Tätigkeitsbericht des Arbeitskreises Kunstgeschichte." In *Historismus und bildende Kunst: Vorträge und Diskussion im Oktober 1963 in München und Schloß Anif*, edited by Ludwig Grote, 9–11. Munich: Prestel, 1965.
"Das Bauhaus und der Funktionalismus." In *Bauhaus, Idee, Form, Zweck, Zeit: Dokumente und Äußerungen*, edited by Eckhard Neumann, 123. Frankfurt am Main: Göppinger Galerie, 1964. Reprinted in *Bauhaus und Bauhäusler: Erinnerungen und Bekenntnisse*, edited by Eckhard Neumann. Bern/Stuttgart: Hallweg, 1971. New ed., Cologne: DuMont, 1985, 280–83. Published in English as "The Bauhaus and Functionalism." In *Bauhaus and Bauhaus People: Personal Opinions and Recollections of Former Bauhaus Members and Their Contemporaries*, edited by Eckhard Neumann, translated by Eva Richter and Alba Lorman, 215–17. New York: Van Nostrand Reinhold, 1993.
"Funktionalismus und Stil." In *Historismus und bildende Kunst: Vorträge und Diskussion im Oktober 1963 in München und Schloss Anif*, edited by Ludwig Grote, 59–72. Munich: Prestel, 1965.
"Arthur Stoll als Kunstsammler: Erinnerung an Corseaux." In *Festschrift für Professor Dr. Dr. h. c. Arthur Stoll zum 80. Geburtstag am 8. Januar 1967*, edited by Sandoz AG, 21–27. [Basel, 1967].
"Arbeiten des Nürnberger Goldschmieds Martin Krafft für das Hallesche Heiltum." *Anzeiger des Germanischen Nationalmuseums* (1967): 30–35.
"walter gropius und das bauhaus." In *50 jahre bauhaus*, edited by Württembergischer Kunstverein, 9–11. Stuttgart: Württembergischer Kunstverein, 1968. Published in English as "walter gropius and the bauhaus." In *50 years bauhaus*, edited by Württembergischer Kunstverein, 9–11. Stuttgart: Württembergischer Kunstverein; and London: Royal Academy of Arts, 1968. Reprinted in *bauhaus* (abridged edition of the exhibition catalog *50 jahre bauhaus*), edited by Institut für Auslandsbeziehungen, Stuttgart, 9–11. Stuttgart: Dr. Cantz'sche Druckerei, 1974, repr. 1982.
"grundformen und funktionalismus." In *50 jahre bauhaus*, edited by Württembergischer Kunstverein, 18–20. Stuttgart: Württembergischer Kunstverein, 1968. Published in English as "basic forms and functionalism." In *50 years bauhaus*, edited by Württembergischer Kunstverein, 18–21. Stuttgart: Württembergischer Kunstverein; and London: Royal Academy of Arts, 1968. Reprinted in *bauhaus* (abridged edition of the exhibition catalog *50 jahre bauhaus*), edited by Institut für Auslandsbeziehungen, Stuttgart, 18–21. Stuttgart: Dr. Cantz'sche Druckerei, 1974, repr. 1982.
"Albrecht Dürers 'Anna Selbdritt': Ein Auftrag von Linhart Tucher." *Anzeiger des Germanischen Nationalmuseums* (1969): 75–88.
"Walter Gropius und das Bauhaus: Nachruf auf Walter Gropius." *Jahresring* 70/71 (1970): 319–23.
"Die vierundzwanzig Alten." *Wallraf-Richartz-Jahrbuch* 33 (1971): 85–98.
"Das Männerbildnis Albrecht Dürers in Boston." *Zeitschrift des Deutschen Vereins für Kunstwissenschaft* 25 (1971): 115–22.
"Der Dessauer Christophorus und der junge Dürer." In *Festschrift für Klaus Lankheit; zum 20. Mai 1973*, edited by Wolfgang Hartmann, 139–50. Cologne: DuMont Schauberg, 1973.
"Eine 'Genoveva' von Joseph Sutter (nach hinterlassenen Unterlagen bearbeitet von Andreas Grote)." *Kunstjahrbuch der Stadt Linz* (1974/75): 61–62 [published posthumously].
Von Dürer bis Gropius: Aufsätze zur deutschen Kunst. Munich: Prestel, 1975 [a collection of his essays, published posthumously].
"Kaiser Maximilian in der Schedelschen Weltchronik." *Mitteilungen des Vereins für Geschichte der Stadt Nürnberg* 62 (1975): 60–83 [published posthumously].

Forewords / Introductions / Accompanying Texts in the Following Exhibition Catalogs

Kandinsky: Jubiläumsausstellung zum 60. Geburtstage, exhibition at the Galerie Arnold. Dresden: C. Rich, 1926.
[with Paul Wahl]. Guide to the *Moses-Mendelssohn-Gedächtnis-Ausstellung*, September 6–October 5, 1929. Dessau: Anhaltische Landesbücherei, 1929.
Olivier-Gedächtnis-Ausstellung, Anhaltischer Kunstverein. Dessau: Zichäus, 1930.
Moderne Bildwirkereien, Anhaltischer Kunstverein, January 1930. Dessau, 1929.
Anhalt im Dreißigjährigen Krieg, exhibition at the Gemäldegalerie zu Dessau on the occassion of the 300th anniversary of the death of Gustav Adolf of Sweden, Autumn 1932. Dessau: C. Dünnhaupt, 1932.
"Die Goethe-Ausstellung in Dessau 1932: Eine Einführung," *Anhalter Anzeiger*, March 24, 1932, suppl. 2: *Anhaltische Gemäldegalerie.* Dessau: Hofbuchdruckerei von Dünnhaupt, 1932.
Caspar David Friedrich: Skizzenbuch aus den Jahren 1806 und 1818. Berlin: Gebr. Mann, 1942, 2. Repr. 1994.
Kandinsky, exhibition at the Galerie Otto Stangl, Munich. [Munich, 1946].
Der Blaue Reiter: München und die Kunst des 20. Jahrhunderts, 1908–1914, exhibition at the Haus der Kunst München, September–October 1949. Munich: Filser-Verlag, 1949.
Große Münchner Kunstausstellung 1949, September 9–November 19. Munich: F. Bruckmann, 1949.
Der Blaue Reiter 1908–1914: Wegbereiter und Zeitgenossen, exhibition at the Kunsthalle Basel, 1950.
Die Maler am Bauhaus, exhibition at the Haus der Kunst München, May–June 1950. Munich: Prestel, 1950.
Oskar Kokoschka: aus seinem Schaffen 1907–1950, exhibition at the Haus der Kunst München, September 1950. Munich: Prestel, 1950.
Fritz Winter, exhibition at the Galerie Otto Stangl, Munich. Diessen vor Munich: Graphische Kunst- & Verlagsanstalt Jos. C. Huber, 1950.
Fritz Winter: 9 Original Handdrucke, edited by the Galerie "Der Spiegel." Cologne, 1950.
Max Beckmann zum Gedächtnis, 1884–1950, exhibition at the Haus der Kunst München, June–July 1951. Munich: Prestel, 1951.
H. de Toulouse-Lautrec 1864–1901: Das grafische Werk: Sammlung Ludwig Charell, exhibition at the Haus der Kunst München. Munich: Prestel, 1951.
Ernst Ludwig Kirchner: Gemälde und Graphik der Sammlung Dr. F. Bauer, Davos. Nuremberg: Verlag Nürnberger Presse, 1952.
Aufgang der Neuzeit: Deutsche Kunst und Kultur von Dürers Tod bis zum Dreißigjährigen Kriege, 1530–1650, exhibition at the Germanischen Nationalmuseum Nürnberg, July 15–October 15, 1952. Bielefeld: Paul Herzogenrath Verlag, 1952.
Deutsche Kunst und Kultur im Germanischen Nationalmuseum. Nuremberg: K. Ulrich & Co. 1952; 2nd ed., 1960.
Walter Gropius: A Path to the Unity of Artistic Design, exhibition at the Institute of Contemporary Art, Boston, and the Smithsonian Institution, Washington. Frankfurt am Main: Müller-Blase, 1952.
Pablo Picasso: Radierungen und Lithographien, 1905 bis 1952, exhibition in Nuremberg, Basel, and others. Munich: Prestel, 1952.
Deutsche Kunst: Meisterwerke des 20. Jahrhunderts, exhibition at the Kunstmuseum Luzern, July 4–October 2, 1953. Munich: Prestel, 1953.

Paul Klee, 1879–1940, Bienal de São Paulo. Munich: Prestel, 1953.

Wassily Kandinsky: Arbeiten aus den Jahren 1912–1942, Galerie Ferdinand Möller, Cologne, November 21, 1953, to January 16, 1954. *Blätter der Galerie Ferdinand Möller*, n.s. no. 12 (1953).

Paul Klee, Haus der Kunst München, April 16–May 16, 1954. Munich: Haus der Kunst, 1954.

Keramik 1895–1954: Gobelins 1950–1954, Fränkische Galerie, Nuremberg. Nuremberg: Germanisches Nationalmuseum, 1954.

Wassily Kandinsky: Arbeiten aus den Jahren 1912–1942, Fränkische Galerie, Nuremberg, February 1954. Nuremberg: Germanisches Nationalmuseum, 1954.

Mit Drehscheibe und Malhorn; volkstümliche Töpferarbeiten aus drei Jahrhunderten, Germanisches Nationalmuseum, Nuremberg, July 2–October 15, 1954. Nuremberg: Germanisches Nationalmuseum, 1954.

Kunst und Kultur in Böhmen, Mähren und Schlesien, Germanisches Nationalmuseum, Nuremberg, May 22 to September 1955. Nuremberg: Germanisches Nationalmuseum, 1955.

Martin Behaim und die Nürnberger Kosmographen im Germanischen Nationalmuseum, Nürnberg, July–September 1957. Nuremberg: Germanisches Nationalmuseum, 1957.

A arte do bauhaus, Exposição oficial da alemanha na IV bienal do museu de arte moderna de são paulo. São Paulo: Museu de arte moderna, 1957.

Aus dem Danziger Pergamentschatz und dem Schatz der Schwarzhäupter zu Riga, Germanisches Nationalmuseum, exhibition on the opening of the Theodor-Heuss-Baues, 1958. Nuremberg: Germanisches Nationalmuseum, 1958.

Junge Maler aus Deutschland und Frankreich, Kunstmuseum Luzern, July 5–September 30, 1958. Luzern: Kunstmuseum Luzern, 1958.

Sammlung Gröppel mit Werken expressionistischer Künstler aus dem Museumsbesitz. Dortmund: Museum am Ostwall, [1958].

Aus der Frühzeit der evangelischen Kirche, exhibition at the Deutschen Evangelischen Kirchentag, Munich, 1959. Nuremberg: Germanisches Nationalmuseum, 1959.

Exposição alemanha, V Bienal do Museu de Arte Moderna a contribuição alema, São Paulo, 1959. Nuremberg: Druckhaus, 1959.

Brasilianische Kunst der Gegenwart, Städtisches Museum Leverkusen Schloss Morsbroich, November 27, 1959–January 10, 1960. Leverkusen: Städtisches Museum Leverkusen Schloss Morsbroich, 1959.

Deutsche Zeichnung heute, exhibition, Fränkische Galerie der Stadt Nürnberg, March–April 1959. Nuremberg: Fränkische Galerie, 1959.

Der deutsche Holzschnitt, 1420–1570: 100 Einblattholzschnitte aus dem Besitz des Germanischen Nationalmuseums in Nürnberg, February 1959. Tübingen, 1959.

Kaiser Maximilian I. (1459–1519) und die Reichsstadt Nürnberg, Germanisches Nationalmuseum, Nuremberg, in conjunction with the Staatsarchiv Nuremberg. Nuremberg: Germanisches Nationalmuseum, 1959.

Willi Baumeister, 1889–1955, exhibition at the Fränkischen Galerie, Nuremberg, January–February 1960. Nuremberg: Fränkische Galerie, 1960.

Handel und Wandel mit aller Welt: Aus Nürnbergs großer Zeit, Germanisches Nationalmuseum, Nuremberg. Munich: Prestel, 1960.

Barock in Nürnberg 1600–1750: Aus Anlaß der Dreihundertjahrfeier der Akademie der bildenden Künste, exhibition in the Germanischen Nationalmuseum, June 20–September 16, 1962. Nuremberg: Germanisches Nationalmuseum, 1962.

Hans Hofmann, Fränkische Galerie, Nuremberg. Nuremberg: Druckhaus, 1962.

Forschung und Technik in der Kunst, Kunstverein Ludwigshafen am Rhein e.V., April 1–May 31, 1965. Mannheim-Neckarau: Vereinigte Offsetdruckerei, 1965.

Klassizismus und Romantik in Deutschland: Gemälde und Zeichnungen aus der Sammlung Georg Schäfer, Schweinfurt, Germanisches Nationalmuseum, Nuremberg, July 1–October 2, 1966. Nuremberg: Germanisches Nationalmuseum, 1966.

Herbert Bayer. London: Marlborough Fine Art, 1968.

Johanna Schütz-Wolff, 1896–1965, zum Gedächtnis, Kunstverein München, January 16–February 23, 1969. Munich: Wolf, 1969.

Reviews

"'Der Blaue Reiter': Bericht über den 2. Deutschen Kunsthistorikerkongreß, München, Schloß Nymphenburg, 5.–9. September 1949." *Kunstchronik* 2 (1949): 224–26.

"Walther Scheidig: Die Weimarer Malerschule des 19. Jahrhunderts. Erfurt 1950." *Kunstchronik* 4 (1951): 195–97.

"Bernhard Degenhart: Marées Zeichnungen. Berlin 1953." *Kunstchronik* 8 (1955): 214–15.

Editorial Work

Waldemar Lessing. *Wilhelm von Kobell.* Munich: Bruckmann, 1923; 2nd ed., 1966.

August Rode. *Beschreibung des Fürstlichen Anhalt-Dessauischen Landhauses und Englischen Gartens zu Wörlitz*. Dessau: C. Dünnhaupt, 1928.

Albrecht Friedrich Heine. *Die Chalkographische Gesellschaft in Dessau 1795–1803*. Dessau: Verlag Walther Schwalbe, 1930.

(coeditor) *Gesamt-Bildnis-Katalog für Ostfalen*, vol. 1, *Gemälde*. Braunschweig: Selbstverlag der Ostfälischen Kommission, 1932–34: book 1: *Die Städte Braunschweig und Wolfenbüttel: Öffentlicher Besitz* (1932); book 2: *Dessau-Köthen: Öffentlicher Besitz* (1933); book 3: *Bildnisse in Braunschweiger Privatbesitz* (1934), book 4: *Bildnisse in Wernigerode* (1934).

(coeditor, with Max Schefold and Alfred Kamphausen) *Zeitschrift des Deutschen Vereins für Kunstwissenschaft* 3, no. 6 (1935).

(coeditor) *Jahrbuch der Denkmalpflege in der Provinz Sachsen und in Anhalt*, 1931 and 1932.

Das Freiburger Münster. Berlin: H. E. Günther, 1940, 2nd ed., 1948.

Das Straßburger Münster. Berlin: H. E. Günther, 1940.

Deutsche Gärten des 18. Jahrhunderts. Stuttgart: H. E. Günther, 1942; 2nd ed., 1946.

Anzeiger des Germanischen Nationalmuseums. Nürnberg: Germanisches Nationalmuseum, 1954–62.

Bilder aus deutscher Vergangenheit: Bibliothek des Germanischen Nationalmuseums Nürnberg zur deutschen Kunst- und Kulturgeschichte, 34 vols. Munich: Prestel, 1956–69:

1. Heinz Stafski. *Aus alten Apotheken* (1956).

2/3. Ludwig Grote. *"Hier bin ich ein Herr": Dürer in Venedig* (1956).

4. Günther Schiedlausky. *Essen und Trinken* (1956).

5. Leonie von Wilckens. *Tageslauf im Puppenhaus* (1956).

6. Werner Doede. *Schön schreiben, eine Kunst* (1957).

7. Paul Grotemeyer. *"Da ich het die Gestalt"* (1957).

8. Johannes Graf Waldburg-Wolfegg. *Das mittelalterliche Hausbuch* (1957).

9. Hans Liermann. *Richter, Schreiber, Advokaten* (1957).

10. Ernst Königer. *Aus der Geschichte der Heilkunst* (1958).

11. Wulf Schadendorf. *Zu Pferde, im Wagen, zu Fuß* (1959).

12. Gustav Friedrich Hartlaub. *Der Stein der Weisen* (1959).

13. Andreas Grote. *Der vollkommen Architectus: Baumeister und Baubetrieb bis zum Anfang der Neuzeit* (1959).

14. Ludwig Veit. *Handel und Wandel mit aller Welt* (1960).

15/16. Ludwig Grote. *Die Tucher: Bildnis einer Patrizierfamilie* (1961).

17. Günther Schiedlausky. *Tee, Kaffee, Schokolade* (1961).

18/19. Alfons Ott. *Tausend Jahre Musikleben* (1961).

20/21. Günter Schöne. *Tausend Jahre deutsches Theater* (1962).

22. Egon Verheyen. *Das Goldene Evangelienbuch von Echternach* (1963).

23. Alexander Freiherr von Reitzenstein. *Der Waffenschmied* (1964).

24. Wulf Schadendorf. *Das Jahrhundert der Eisenbahn* (1965).

25/26. Irmgard Wirth. *Mit Adolph Menzel in Berlin* (1965).

27. Erich Steingräber. *Der Goldschmied* (1966).

28. Ludwig Grote. *Die romantische Entdeckung Nürnbergs* (1967).
29. Klaus Maurice. *Von Uhren und Automaten* (1968).
30. Ludwig Veit. *Das liebe Geld* (1969).
31. Bernward Deneke. *Hochzeit* (1970).
32. Alexander Freiherr von Reitzenstein. *Rittertum und Ritterschaft* (1972).
33. Elisabeth Rücker. *Die Schedelsche Weltchronik* (1973).
34. Irmgard Wirth. *Mit Menzel in Bayern und Österreich* (1974).

Tätigkeitsberichte des Germanischen Nationalmuseums für 1959, 1960 und 1961. Nuremberg: Germanisches Nationalmuseum, 1960–62.
Erinnerungen an Paul Klee. Munich: Prestel, 1959.
Kunst und Kultur der Freien Reichsstadt Nürnberg. Nuremberg: Nürnberger Presse, 1963.
Historismus und bildende Kunst: Vorträge und Diskussion im Oktober 1963 in München und Schloss Anif. Munich: Prestel, 1965.
Albrecht Dürer: Die Apokalypse [facsimile of the original German edition from 1498]. Munich: Prestel, 1970. / *Albrecht Dürer: The Apocalypse*. Munich: Prestel, 1999.
Beiträge zur Motivkunde des 19. Jahrhunderts. Munich: Prestel, 1970.
Die deutsche Stadt im 19. Jahrhundert: Stadtplanung und Baugestaltung im industriellen Zeitalter. Munich: Prestel, 1974.

Miscellanea

"Georg Lemberger: Ein Beitrag zur Geschichte des sächsischen Holzschnitts," [typescript], diss., Vereinigte Friedrichs-Universität Halle/Wittenberg, December 11, 1922.
Führer durch den Wörlitzer Park: Amtliche Ausgabe der Joachim-Ernst-Stiftung. Dessau: C. Dünnhaupt, 1927; 2nd ed., 1933.
Führer durch Dessau. Dessau: C. Dünnhaupt, 1928.
Führer durch die Anhaltische Gemäldegalerie. Dessau: Zichäus, 1927; 2nd ed., 1929.
Foreword to *Vom Nachleben Dürers: Beiträge zur Kunst der Epoche von 1530 bis 1650*. Anzeiger des Germanischen Nationalmuseums 1940 bis 1953. Berlin: Gebr. Mann, 1954.
Preface to Erich Meyer-Heisig, *Deutsche Volkskunst*. Munich: Prestel, 1954, 7–8.
Jahresring. Ein Querschnitt durch die deutsche Literatur und Kunst der Gegenwart. Jahrbuch für Kunst und Literatur, edited by the Kulturkreis im Bundesverband der Deutschen Industrie, with contributions by Ludwig Grote et al., 1955–1961.
Foreword to Peter Metz, *Das Goldene Evangelienbuch von Echternach im Germanischen Nationalmuseum zu Nürnberg*. Munich: Prestel, 1956.
"Lieber Georg Schmidt!" Werk. *Schweizer Monatsschrift für Architektur, Kunst und künstlerisches Gewerbe* 43, no. 6 (1956): 197.
Preface to Erich Meyer-Heisig, *Weberei – Nadelwerk – Zeugdruck: Zur deutschen volkstümlichen Textilkunst*. Munich: Prestel, 1956, n.p.
Preface to Erich Meyer-Heisig, *Der Nürnberger Glasschnitt des 17. Jahrhunderts*. Nuremberg: Nürnberger Presse, 1963, n.p.
"Vorbemerkung." In Ludwig Grote, ed., *Beiträge zur Motivkunde des 19. Jahrhunderts*. Studien zur Kunst des 19. Jahrhunderts 6. Munich: Prestel, 1970, 7.
Explanatory notes for Bundesministerium für das Post- und Fernmeldewesen, ed., *Albrecht Dürer-Gedenkmarke*. Bonn: BPM, 1971.
"Widmung an Sir Nikolaus Pevsner." In Ludwig Grote, ed., *Die deutsche Stadt im 19. Jahrhundert. Stadtplanung und Baugestaltung im industriellen Zeitalter*. Munich: Prestel, 1974, 5–8.

Exhibitions

Arranged by Ludwig Grote

This list of exhibitions and its structure is based on a list compiled by Ludwig Grote's wife, Maud, in 1986 with the title "Exhibitions Organized by Ludwig Grote."[1] In addition, essays by Margit Ziesché and Helga Heise on exhibitions in Dessau were taken into account.[2] Other added information resulted from research in Grote's archive at the Deutsches Kunstarchiv.[3] The title selected by Maud Grote indicates that the projects included were inspired by and usually also organized by Grote, but he can rarely be considered the only person responsible, because not all of the exhibitions listed were curated by him or conceived by him alone. In several cases, the projects were developed elsewhere, in part inspired by Grote, and then taken over by him. Moreover, Grote's exhibitions were, as a rule, initiated in the context of functions and institutions in which he worked together on and with various teams. These include international projects in which he was involved from 1951 onward as a member of the committee for exhibitions abroad of the Foreign Office of the Federal Republic of Germany and as commissioner of the German exhibitions for the Bienal de São Paulo, which was founded in 1951. In 1954 and 1956, Grote was vice commissioner of German exhibitions at the Venice Biennale.

ABBREVIATIONS:
AGG: Anhaltische Gemäldegalerie in Dessau
AKV: Anhaltischer Kunstverein in Dessau
HdK: Haus der Kunst in Munich
FGN: Fränkische Galerie in Nuremberg
GNM: Germanisches Nationalmuseum in Nuremberg

Dessau, 1925–1933[4]

1925

Alfred Mahlhaus-Lübeck (from May 12), AKV
Leipziger Künstlerbund (Leipzig Artists' League) (from May 24), AKV
Lovis Corinth (from November 7), AKV
Bund bildender Künstler, Anhalt-Dessau (League of Fine Artists), first annual exhibition (from November 21), AKV

1926

Kurt Hentschel (from January 10), AKV
Bund bildender Künstler, Anhalt-Dessau, second annual exhibition (April), AKV
Neue Sachlichkeit: Deutsche Malerei seit dem Expressionismus (New Objectivity: German Painting since Expressionism) (from April 2), AKV[5]
Wassily Kandinsky: Gemälde und Aquarelle; Jubiläums-Ausstellung zum 60. Geburtstag (Wassily Kandinsky: Paintings and Watercolors; Anniversary Exhibition for His Sixtieth Birthday) (from December 19), AKV[6]

1927

Arbeiten vom Bühnenbildner Dr. Löffler für das Dessauer Friedrich-Theater (Works by the Set Designer Dr. Löffler for the Friedrich-Theater in Dessau) (n.d.), AKV
Moderne deutsche Porzellankunst (Modern German Porcelain Art) (n.d.), AGG
Paul Riess, on the occasion of the Dessau painter's seventieth birthday (from March 15), AKV
Bund bildender Künstler, Anhalt-Dessau, third annual exhibition (April), AKV
Prof. Oskar Moll—Breslau (from November 14), AKV

1928

Deutscher Künstlerbund Florenz (German Artists' League of Florence) (January), AKV
Neuer Kirchenbau in Dessau: Ausstellung des Ortswettbewerbs (New Church Building in Dessau: Exhibition of the Local Competition) (January), AGG
Honoré Daumier: Lithographien (from January 25), AKV
Albrecht Dürer, graphic works by Dürer from collections in Anhalt (April), AKV
Olaf Gulbransson (May), AKV
Kandinskys Malschule (Kandinsky's Painting School), works from Wassily Kandinsky's Freie Malklasse[7] (Free Painting Class) at the Bauhaus (May 3–27),[8] AKV
Radierungen deutsch-römischer Maler (Etchings by German-Roman Painters) (from July 15), AGG
Bund bildender Künstler, Anhalt-Dessau, fourth annual exhibition (August), AKV
Neuerwerbungen und Zugänge der Anhaltischen Gemäldegalerie (New Acquisitions and Arrivals at the Anhaltische Gemäldegalerie) (from September 23), AGG
Photographische Aufnahmen von Albert Renger-Patzsch (Photographs by Albert Renger-Patzsch) (from October 21), AKV
Albrecht Leistner—Leipzig: Skulpturen, Gemälde, Zeichnungen (Albrecht Leistner—Leipzig: Sculptures, Paintings, Drawings) (from November 18), AKV
Junge Bauhausmaler (Young Bauhaus Painters) (December),[9] Hallescher Kunstverein
Karl Hentschel: Ölgemälde, Aquarelle, Zeichnungen (Karl Hentschel: Oil Paintings, Watercolors, Drawings) (from December 12), AKV

1929

Bernhard Fiedler, 1816–1904, memorial exhibition (from January 19), AGG
Bund bildender Künstler, Anhalt-Dessau, fifth annual exhibition (from February 5), AKV
Lyonel Feininger: Gemälde, Aquarelle und Zeichnungen (Paintings, Watercolors, and Drawings) (from March 9), AKV
Otto Dill: Gemälde und Graphik des 19. Jahrhunderts (Otto Dill: Paintings and Graphic Works from the Nineteenth Century) (from April 14), AKV
Käthe Kollwitz (from May 23), AKV
Moses-Mendelssohn-Gedächtnis-Ausstellung (September 6–October 6), AGG
Paul Klee (from October 15), AKV

1930

Bauten deutscher Technik (Buildings of German Technology) (January), AGG[10]
Max Slevogt: Der Zeichner und Illustrator (Max Slevogt: The Draftsman and Illustrator) (January), AKV
Moderne Bildwirkereien (Modern Tapestries) (January), AGG[11]
Bund bildender Künstler, Anhalt-Dessau, sixth annual exhibition (February), AKV
Düsseldorfer Kunstakademie (Düsseldorf Academy of Art) (March), AKV
Theo von Brockhusen, 1882–1919: Maler und Grafiker (Theo von Brockhusen, 1882–1919: Painter and Graphic Artist) (March), AGG
Die Welt des Kindes (The Child's World) (from April 17), AKV
Oskar Moll, Maler und Grafiker, 1875–1947 (Oskar Moll, Painter and Graphic Artist, 1875–1947) (June–July), AKV
Neuerwerbungen (New Acquisitions) (August), AGG
Das Land Anhalt in der Kunst (The State of Anhalt in Art) (September), AKV

Die Brüder Olivier[12] (The Olivier Brothers) (October–November), AKV
Modernes Porzellan der Staatlichen Porzellan-Manufaktur Berlin (Modern Porcelain from the State Porcelain Manufacturer in Berlin) (from December 14), AKV

1931

Emil Nolde (from January 11), AKV
Bund bildender Künstler, Anhalt-Dessau, seventh annual exhibition (from February 15), AKV
Friedrich Matthisson,1761–1831, in parallel with Paul Wahl (March), Anhaltische Landesbücherei
Otto Strützel, Maler und Grafiker, 1855–1930 (Otto Strützel, Painter and Graphic Artist, 1855–1930), memorial exhibition (from April 5), AKV
Erich Heckel (from May 10), AKV
Lyonel Feininger (June), AKV
Heinz Schmidt, Rom, Dessau—Paul Jünemann, Zerbst—Paul Frost, Köthen—und Max Baumann, Dessau: Vier anhaltische Maler (Heinz Schmidt, Rome, Dessau—Paul Jünemann, Zerbst—Paul Frost, Köthen—and Max Baumann, Dessau: Four Painters from Anhalt) (August), AGG
Lichtbild-Ausstellung (Photography Exhibition) (from October 4), AGG
Bund bildender Künstler, Anhalt-Dessau, eighth annual exhibition (from November 8), AKV
Stille Landschaft: Theo Champion, Franz Lenk, Georg Scholz, Georg Schrimpf (Quiet Landscape: Theo Champion, Franz Lenk, Georg Scholz, Georg Schrimpf) (from December 13), AKV

1932

Karl Schmidt-Rottluff (January), AKV
Paul Riess (Dessau): Gedächtnis-Ausstellung zum 70. Geburtstag (Paul Riess [Dessau]: Memorial Exhibition on His Seventieth Birthday) (February–March), AKV
Erinnerungsausstellung anlässlich der Feier der hundertsten Wiederkehr von Goethes Todestag (Memorial Exhibition on the Occasion of the Celebration of the Hundredth Anniversary of Goethe's Death) (March 20–May 17), AKV
Max Liebermann—Berlin (April 17–May 17), AKV
Berliner Zeichenkunst—Franz Krüger, 1797–1857 (The Art of the Drawing in Berlin—Franz Krüger, 1797–1857) (May 29–August 14), AGG
Kleine Goethe-Gedächtnisausstellung (Small Goethe Memorial Exhibition) (June 5–July 31), AGG[13]
Max Korn, Maler und Grafiker (Max Korn, Painter and Graphic Artist) (July), AGG
Form und Farbe (Form and Color), works from the art classes of various institutions (August 21–September 14), AKV
Karl Wilhelm Kolbe, Maler und Grafiker, 1758–1835 (Karl Wilhelm Kolbe, Painter and Graphic Artist, 1758–1835) (from September 17), AGG
Ewald Vetter, Aschau—Alfred Scotland, Gotha, painting and graphic works (September 18–October 11), AKV
Anhalt im Dreissigjährigen Krieg—Aus Anlass der 300: Wiederkehr des Todesjahres Gustav Adolfs von Schweden (Anhalt in the Thirty Years' War: On the Occasion of the 300th Anniversary of the Death of Gustav Adolf of Sweden) (September 25–January 1, 1933), AKV
Bund bildender Künstler, Anhalt-Dessau, ninth annual exhibition (October 15–November 13), AKV
Kult und Form (Cult and Form), ecclesiastical art by the Freier Künstlerbund (Free German Artists' League) (December 4, 1932–January 29, 1933), AKV

1933

Alexander Kanoldt, graphic art (February 5–March 5), AKV
Neues von Gestern: Abbild und Spottbild der Vorkriegsepoche (1848–1914) in deutschen illustrierten Blättern (Something New from Yesterday: Likeness and Caricature of the Prewar Era [1848–1914] in German Illustrated Magazines) (March 12–April 9), AKV
Neue Wege zur Heimat (New Paths to Homeland) (from April 16), AKV[14]

Munich, 1948–1951

1948

Wassily Kandinsky (n.d.), Galerie Otto Stangl, Munich[15]

1949

Der Blaue Reiter: München und die Kunst des 20. Jahrhunderts; Der Weg von 1908–1914 (The Blue Rider: Munich and the Art of the Twentieth Century; The Path from 1908 to 1914), first *Internationale Kunstausstellung* (September–October), HdK

1950

Die Maler am Bauhaus (The Painters at the Bauhaus), second *Internationale Kunstausstellung* (May–June), HdK[16]
Oskar Kokoschka, 1907–1950, third *Internationale Kunstausstellung* (August), HdK

1951

Max Beckmann zum Gedächtnis, 1884–1950 (Max Beckmann in Memorial, 1884–1950) fourth *Internationale Kunstausstellung* (June–July), HdK
Toulouse-Lautrec, das graphische Werk: Sammlung Ludwig Charell (Toulouse-Lautrec, the Graphic Oeuvre: The Ludwig Charell Collection), fifth *Internationale Kunstausstellung* (October 2–20), HdK

Nuremberg, 1951–1962

1951

Willi Baumeister, Werner Gilles, HAP Grieshaber, Karl Hartung, Gerhard Marcks, Ewald Mataré, Ernst Wilhelm Nay, Karl Schmidt-Rottluff, Johanna Schütz-Wolff, Hans Uhlmann, Fritz Winter, and other contemporary artists from Germany (September), first Bienal de São Paulo[17]
Ewige Märchenwelt (Eternal Fairy-Tale World), Christmas exhibition (December 1, 1951–January 31, 1952), GNM

1952

Farbige Graphik der Gegenwart I (Contemporary Graphic Works in Color I) (January 13–February 10), FGN[18]
Das deutsche Bildnis: Ausstellung des Kupferstichkabinetts (The German Portrait: Exhibition from the Prints and Drawings Collection) (February 1–March 31), GNM
Pablo Picasso: Radierungen, 1905–1951 (Pablo Picasso: Etchings, 1905–1951) traveling exhibition (March 30–April 27), FGN
Aufgang der Neuzeit: Deutsche Kunst und Kultur von Dürers Tod bis zum Dreissigjährigen Kriege, 1530–1650 (Rise of the Modern Era: German Art and Culture from Dürer's Death to the Thirty Years' War, 1530–1650), for the hundredth anniversary of the GNM (July 15–October 15), GNM
Ernst Ludwig Kirchner: Gemälde und Graphik aus der Sammlung Dr. Bauer, Davos (August 3–September 7), FGN
Bilderschmuck der Frühdrucke (Ornament of Early Prints), exhibition from the library (November 30, 1952–April 30, 1953), GNM
Walter Gropius—ein Weg zur Einheit künstlerischer Gestaltung (Walter Gropius—A Path to the Unity of Artistic Design) (October 19–November 9), FGN
Kulturdokumente der Bodenseegebiete aus dem Germanischen Nationalmuseum (Cultural Documents of the Lake Constance Region from the Germanic National Museum), from the prints and drawings collection, the archives, and coin collection (November 30, 1952–April 10, 1953), GNM
Weihnachten im alten Kartäuserkloster (Christmas in the Old Carthusian Monastery) (December 7, 1952–January 11, 1953), GNM

1953

Dankspende des deutschen Volkes (Thank-you Donation from the German People) (March 29–April 12), FGN
Fritz Winter (May 10–June 7), FNG
Kulturdokumente aus Oberpfalz und Niederbayern (Cultural Documents from the Upper Palatinate and Lower Bavaria), an exhibition from the prints and drawings collection, the archives, and coin collection (May 10–September 4), GNM
Schlesien-Ausstellung (Silesia Exhibition), second Central Franconian Silesian Meeting in Nuremberg (May 28–29), GNM
Meisterwerke deutscher Kunst des 20. Jahrhunderts (Masterpieces of German Art of the Twentieth Century) (June 3–9), GNM[19]

Oberschlesien-Ausstellung (Silesia Exhibition), for the federal meeting of the Upper Silesian State Teams (June 26–28), GNM

Paul Klee with other contemporaneous artists from Germany (September), second Bienal de São Paulo[20]

Werke von Paul Klee (Works by Paul Klee) (September 11–20), GNM[21]

Farbige Graphik II (Contemporary Graphic Works in Color II) (September 13–October 4), FGN

Der Goldfund von Enzelsdorf (The Discovery of Gold in Enzelsdorf) (October 25, 1953–April 30, 1955), GNM

Kulturdokumente Frankens (Cultural Documents from Franconia), an exhibition from the prints and drawings collection, the archives, and coin collection (October 25, 1953–March 14, 1954), GNM

Advent, Advent…, Christmas exhibition (November 29, 1953–January 31, 1954), GNM

1954

Gerhard Marcks: Skulpturen, Zeichnungen und Holzschnitte (Gerhard Marcks: Sculptures, Drawings, and Woodcuts), in parallel with the traveling exhibition *Museumsspende 1953 des Kulturkreises im Bundesverband der Deutschen Industrie* (Museum Donation in 1953 from the Cultural Circle in the Federal League of German Industry) (January 6–31), FGN[22]

Wassily Kandinsky: 30 Gemälde aus seinem Lebenswerk (Wassily Kandinsky: Thirty Paintings from His Lifework) (February 7–March 7), FGN

Flüsse, Seen und Brunnen in der Graphik (Rivers, Lakes, and Springs in Graphic Works), exhibition from the prints and drawings collection (April 17–August 30), GNM

Mit Drehscheibe und Malhorn: Volkstümliche Töpferarbeiten aus drei Jahrhunderten. (With Potter's Wheel and Slip Cup: Folk Pottery from Three Centuries) (June 2–October 15), GNM

Keramik, 1895–1954 (Ceramics, 1895–1954), in parallel with *Arbeiten der Nürnberger Gobelinmanufaktur, 1950–1954* (Works from the Nuremberg Tapestry Manufacturer) (July 11–August 22), FGN

Aus der Frühzeit der Germanistik: Quellen und Forschungen (From the Early Period of German Studies: Sources and Research), for the conference of German Germanists in Nuremberg, an exhibition from the library (September 26–December 12), GNM

Zeugnisse alter Fechtkunst (Documents of the Old Art of Fencing), for the German championship of team fencing in Nuremberg (October 21–24), GNM

Karl Schmidt-Rottluff zum 70. Geburtstag (Karl Schmidt-Rottluff for His Seventieth Birthday) (October 24–November 14), FGN

Das Weihnachtszimmer (The Christmas Room) (December 3, 1954–January 6, 1955), GNM

L'Europe humaniste, first exhibition of the Council of Europe (December 15, 1954–February 28, 1955), Palais des Beaux-Arts, Brussels[23]

Kulturdokumente aus Bayrisch-Schwaben (Cultural Documents from Bavarian Swabia), an exhibition from the prints and drawings collection, the archives, and coin collection (December 18, 1954–April 30, 1955), GNM

1955

70 Jahre Plakat, 1860–1930 (Seventy Years of the Poster, 1860–1930) (January 9–February 6), FGN

Johanna Schütz-Wolff: Bildwirkereien, Gemälde, Holzschnitte (Johanna Schütz-Wolff: Tapestries, Paintings, Woodcuts) in parallel with *Hans Wimmer: Plastik und Zeichnungen* (February 20–March 20), FGN

Wertvolle Drucke: Die Entwicklung des Buchdrucks und der graphischen Techniken (Valuable Prints: The Evolution of Book Printing and Graphic Techniques), for the ninth regular main meeting of the Verband der graphischen Betriebe in Bayern e.V. (Association of Graphic Businesses in Bavaria) (May 6–July 15), GNM

Kunst und Kultur in Böhmen, Mähren und Schlesien (Art and Culture in Bohemia, Moravia, and Silesia), for the Sudeten-German conference in Nuremberg in collaboration with the Adalbert-Stifter-Verein (May 22–November 3), GNM

Mittelalterliche Glasmalerei aus dem Ostchor der Sebalduskirche zu Nürnberg (Medieval Stained Glass from the Eastern Chancel of Saint Sebald's Church in Nuremberg) (from June 6), GNM

50 Jahre belgische Kunst 1890–1940 (Fifty Years of Belgian Art) (June 8–July 10), FGN

Hochkultur der Bronzezeit: Schatzfunde aus Mitteleuropa, 1400 bis 800 v. Chr. (High Culture of the Bronze Age: Treasures from Central Europe, 1400 to 800 BC) (June 16–October 31), GNM

Le triomphe du Maniérisme européen, second exhibition of the Council of Europe (July 1–October 16), Rijksmuseum, Amsterdam[24]

Farbige Graphik III (Graphic Works in Color III) (September 4–October 10), FGN

Kulturdokumente aus Oberbayern und Tirol (Cultural Documents from Upper Bavaria and Tyrol), exhibition from the prints and drawings collection, the archives, and the coin collection (November 12, 1955–May 22, 1956), GNM

Aus alten Weihnachtstagen (From Old Christmas Days), December 4, 1955–January 8, 1956), GNM

1956

Moderne Kunst alt und neu (Modern Art, Old and New) (January 6–February 5), FGN

Aquarelle und Zeichnungen von Vincent van Gogh (Watercolors and Drawings by Vincent van Gogh) (February 12–March 11), FGN

Gemälde, Aquarelle und Graphik von Emil Nolde: Auswahl für die Biennale in Venedig 1956 (Painting, Watercolors, and Graphic Works by Emil Nolde: Selection for the Venice Biennale in 1956) (April 24–May 3), FGN

Alte Musik und ihre Instrumente (Early Music and Its Instruments), for the fifth Internationale Orgelwoche in Nürnberg (International Organ Week) in Nuremberg (June 16–November 28), GNM

Weberei, Nadelwerk und Zeugdruck: Deutsche textile Volkskunst (Weaving, Needlework, Fabric Printing: German Textile Folk Art) (July 2–October 30), GNM

Deutsche Spielkarten und magische Literatur vom 15. bis 19. Jahrhundert (German Playing Cards and Literature on Magic from the Fifteenth to the Nineteenth Centuries), for the Internationaler Kongress des Magischen Zirkels (International Conference of the Magic Circle) (August 30–September 15), GNM

Herbert Bayer: 33 Jahre freie und angewandte Kunst (Herbert Bayer: Thirty-three Years of Free and Applied Art) (September 9–October 7), FGN

Schuhwerk und Orthopädie vergangener Tage: Aus der Geschichte der Medizin (Footwear and Orthopedics of the Past: From the History of Medicine) for the forty-fourth annual conference of the Deutsche Orthopädische Gesellschaft (September 19–October 21), GNM

Il seicento europeo: Realismo, classicismo, barocco (The Seventeenth Century In Europe: Realism, Classicism, Baroque), third exhibition of the Council of Europe (December 1956–January 1957), Palazzo delle Esposizioni, Rome[25]

Deutsche Zeichnungen, 1400–1900 (German Drawings, 1400–1900) (December 2, 1956–January 31, 1957), GNM[26]

Weihnachtsbaum und Schlittenfahrt (Christmas Tree and Sleigh Ride) (December 2, 1956–January 6, 1957), GNM

1957

Heinz Trökes, Hann Trier, Joseph Fassbender: 3 rheinische Maler (Heinz Trökes, Hann Trier, Joseph Fassbender: Three Rhenish Painters) (January 9–February 3), FGN

Kulturdokumente der Oberrhein- und Neckargebiete (Cultural Documents from Upper Rhine and Neckar Regions) (January 23–March 17), GNM[27]

Bernard Buffet—Paris, with the collaboration of the Galerie Beyeler, Basel (February 10–March 13), FGN

Die Künstler der Sammlung Domnick, Stuttgart: Abstrakte Malerei Europas (The Artists of the Domnick Collection, Stuttgart: Abstract Painting from Europe) (March 17–April 14), FGN

Kulturdokumente Norddeutschlands (Cultural Documents from Northern Germany), exhibition from the prints and drawings collection, the archives, and the coin collection (March 31–September 27), GNM[28]

Dokumente der Musica Sacra in

Nürnberg (Documents of Musica Sacra in Nuremberg), for the sixth Internationale Orgelwoche in Nuremberg (June 29–July 14), GNM
Junge Maler aus Deutschland und Frankreich (Young Painters from Germany and France) (July 5–September 30), Kunstmuseum Luzern
Martin Behaim und die Nürnberger Kosmographen (Martin Behaim and the Nuremberg Cosmographs), for the 450th anniversary of the death of Martin Behaim (July 13–September 30), GNM
Das malerische Werk der Bauhausschule (The Painted Oeuvre of the Bauhaus School) (September), fourth Bienal de São Paulo[29]
Farbige Graphik 1957 (Graphic Works in Color 1957) (September 8–29), FGN
Hans Hartung—Paris (October 6–27), FGN[30]
Dürer und das Buch (Dürer and the Book), for the Tagung Fränkischer Bibliophiler (Conference of Franconian Bibliophiles) (October 12–December 31), GNM
Kulturdokumente Österreichs (Cultural Documents from Austria) (October 26, 1957–February 2, 1958), GNM[31]
Die Nürnberger Patrizierfamilie von Imhoff: Geschichte und Kunst (The Nuremberg Patrician Family von Imhoff: History and Art), for the Imhoff'schen Familientag (Imhoff Family Day) (October 31–November 22), GNM
Deutsche Bibeldrucke aus sechs Jahrhunderten, Ausstellung der Bibliothek (German Printed Bibles from Six Centuries), exhibition of the library for the Evangelische Bibelwoche (Protestant Bible Week) (November 17, 1957–January 15, 1958), GNM
Weihnachtsausstellung (Christmas Exhibition) (December 1, 1957–January 5, 1958), GNM

1958

Alfred Kubin: 250 Zeichnungen aus öffentlichem und privatem Besitz (Alfred Kubin: 250 Drawings from Public and Private Collections) (February 9–March 9), FGN
10 junge deutsche Maler: Manfred Bluth, Winfred Gaul, Harry Kögler, Rudolf Kügler, Dietmar Lemcke, Hans Platschek, Armin Sandig, K. R. H. Sonderborg, Ernst Weil, Gerhard Wind (Ten Young German Painters) (March 16–April 13), FGN
Kulturdokumente aus Hessen, Thüringen und Sachsen (Cultural Documents from Hesse, Thuringia, and Saxony), exhibition from the prints and drawings collection, the archives, and the coin collection (March 29–July 6), GNM
Die Orgel und die Orgelmusik (The Organ and Organ Music), for the seventh Internationale Orgelwoche in Nuremberg (May 31–June 30), GNM
Europäisches Rokoko, fourth exhibition of the Council of Europe (June 15–September 15), Residenz, Munich[32]
Malerei des jungen Italien (Painting of Young Italy) (June 29–July 27), FGN
Aus dem Danziger Paramentenschatz (From the Danzig Parament Treasure) (September 7, 1958–March 30, 1959), GNM
Der Schatz der Schwarzhäupter zu Riga (The Treasure of the Blackheads in Riga) (September 7–October 30), GNM
Weihnachtsausstellung (Christmas Exhibition) (from November 30), GNM

1959

Xaver Fuhr—sechzigjährig (Xaver Fuhr—Sixty-Years-Old) (January 7–February 1), FGN
Alexej von Jawlensky (1864–1941) und Marianne von Werefkin (1860–1938): Zwei Maler aus dem Umkreis des Blauen Reiters (Two Painters from the Blue Rider Circle) (February 5–March 8), FGN
Deutsche Zeichnung heute (German Drawing Today) (March 13–April 15), FGN
Kaiser Maximilian I. (1459–1519) und die Reichsstadt Nürnberg (Emperor Maximilian I [1459–1519] and the Imperial Free City of Nuremberg) for the 500th birthday of Maximilian, in cooperation with the Staatsarchiv Nürnberg (April 8–May 31), GNM
Bayerische Denkmalpflege (Bavarian Monument Preservation) traveling exhibition of the Bayerischen Landesamtes für Denkmalpflege (Bavarian State Office for Monument Preservation) (April 10–May 3), GNM
Deutsche Zeichenkunst der Goethe-Zeit: Sammlung Dr. Winterstein, München (German Art of the Drawing from the Age of Goethe: The Collection of Dr. Winterstein) (June 6–July 29), GNM[33]
The Romantic Movement, fifth exhibition of the Council of Europe (June 8–September 27), Tate Gallery, London[34]
Altdeutsche Zeichnungen aus der Kunsthalle Karlsruhe (Early German Drawings from the Kunsthalle Karlsruhe) (June 12–September 15), GNM
Liturgisches Gerät der Gegenwart (Contemporary Liturgical Implements) for the eighth Internationale Orgelwoche in Nuremberg; organized by the Bayerische Landesgewerbeanstalt (Bavarian State Commerce Institute) (June 20–28), GNM
Aus der Frühzeit der evangelischen Kirche (From the Early Period of the Protestant Church), for the Deutscher Evangelischer Kirchentag (German Protestant Church Day) in Munich and Nuremberg (September), GNM
Bayreuth in heutiger Sicht (Bayreuth from Today's Perspective) (September), fifth Bienal de São Paulo
Farbige Graphik V (Graphic Works in Color V) (September 10–30), FGN
Der deutsche Expressionismus (German Expressionism), Brücke artists from the Haubrich Collection in Cologne (September 21–December 31, 1959), fifth Bienal de São Paulo[35]
Der deutsche Holzschnitt, 1420–1570: 100 Einzelblattholzschnitte aus dem Besitz des Germanischen National-Museums in Nürnberg (The German Woodcut, 1420–1570: 100 Single-Leaf Woodcuts from the Collection of the Germanic National Museum in Nuremberg) (October 24, 1959–February 21, 1960), GNM[36]
Joachim Utech, Steinbildwerke und Fotografien von Plastiken (Joachim Utech, Stone Sculptures and Photographs of Sculptures), for the sixth Ostdeutsche Kulturtagen des ostdeutschen Kulturrats (Eastern German Culture Days of the East German Cultural Council), Bonn, with the collaboration of the Künstlergilde Esslingen (November 6–29), GNM
In Bethlehems Stall: Krippenausstellung (In Bethlehem's Stable: Exhibition of Nativity Scenes) (November 29, 1959–January 31, 1960), GNM

1960

Die Entdeckung des Pegnitztales (The Discovery of the Pegnitz Valley) an exhibition from the prints and drawing collection (January 9–17), GNM
Gedächtnis-Ausstellung Lasar Segall, 1891–1957 (Memorial Exhibition for Lasar Segall, 1891–1957) (February 28–March 27), FGN
Handel und Wandel mit aller Welt: Aus Nürnbergs grosser Zeit (Trade and Change with the Whole World: From Nuremberg's Great Era), for the 400th anniversary of the Nürnberger Industrie- und Handelskammer (Nuremberg Chamber of Industry and Trade) (April 11–May 31), GNM
Junge holländische Malerei (Recent Dutch Painting) (June 8–July 3), FGN[37]
Das Musikinstrumentarium des 14. bis frühen 16. Jahrhunderts in Kunstwerken des Mittelalters (The Musical Instruments of the Fourteenth to the Early Sixteenth Century in Medieval Works of Art), photography exhibition for the ninth Internationale Orgelwoche in Nuremberg (June 25–July 3), GNM
Bruno Pulga, Bologna—Carlo Ramous, Mailand—Guido Strazza, Mailand (Bruno Pulga, Bologna—Carlo Ramous, Milan—Guido Strazza, Milan) (September 2–October 2), FGN
Deutsche Druckgraphik der ersten Hälfte des 19. Jahrhunderts (German Prints from the First Half of the Nineteenth Century) (September 7–October 31), GNM
Barockmaler in Böhmen (Baroque Painters in Bohemia), exhibition of the Adalbert Stifter Verein (October 10–November 26), GNM[38]
Altes Spielzeug (Old Toys) (December 3, 1960–February 5, 1961), GNM

1961

Ernst Wilhelm Nay: Gemälde, Aquarelle, Zeichnungen und Graphik, 1935–1960 (Ernst Wilhelm Nay: Paintings, Watercolors, Drawings, and Graphic

Works, 1935–1960) (January 10–February 5), FGN
Elf Münchner Bildhauer (Eleven Munich Sculptors) (March 23–April 23), FGN
Kulturdokumente Frankens aus dem Germanischen Nationalmuseum (Cultural Documents of Franconia from the Germanic National Museum) (April 8–June 18) at the Neue Residenz in Bamberg
Städelschule, Staatliche Schule für bildende Künste in Frankfurt/Main (Städel School, State School of the Fine Arts in Frankfurt am Main) (May 5–June 4), FGN
Meister um Albrecht Dürer (Masters around Albrecht Dürer) (July 4–September 17), GNM
Der Brief im Wandel von fünf Jahrhunderten (The Letter in Transformation over Five Centuries), for the conference of the Bund Deutscher Philatelisten (League of German Philatelists), on September 2 and the sixty-second Philatelisten-Tag (Philatelists' Day) on September 3 (August 31–September 5), GNM
Vier Jahrhunderte Kinderbuch (Four Centuries of Children's Books) (December 10, 1961–May 3, 1962), GNM

1962

Fritz Winter: Neue Werke, 1959–1961 (Fritz Winter: New Works, 1959–1961) (March 2–April 1), FGN
Hans Hofmann (April 8–May 6), FGN
Theodor Werner: Aus dem 50-jährigen Schaffen des Malers (Theodor Werner: From Fifty Years of the Artist's Creative Work) (May 18–June 11), FGN
Barock in Nürnberg, 1600–1750, for the celebration of the tricentennial of the Akademie der bildenden Künste in Nuremberg (June 20–September 16), GNM
Sammlung B (Ida Bienert) (September 30–October 28), FGN

Munich, 1962–1972

1962

Europäische Kunst um 1400 (European Art around 1500), eighth exhibition of the Council of Europe (May 7–July 31), Kunsthistorisches Museum, Vienna[39]

1968

50 jahre bauhaus (50 years bauhaus), traveling exhibition of the Institut für Auslandsbeziehungen (May 5–July 28) Kunstgebäude am Schlossplatz, Stuttgart[40]

1969

Johanna Schütz-Wolff, 1896–1965: Bildwirkereien und Graphik; Gedächtnisausstellung (Tapestries and Graphic Works: Memorial Exhibition) (January 16–February 23), Kunstverein München

1971

1471 Albrecht Dürer 1971, anniversary exhibition (May 21–August 1, 1971), GMN[41]

1972

Hans Freiherr von und zu Aufsess und die Anfänge des Germanischen Nationalmuseums (Hans Freiherr von und zu Aufsess and the Beginnings of the Germanic National Museum) (July 1–October 1), GMN[42]

1 See "Ausstellungen veranstaltet von Ludwig Grote," typescript, in "Zur Bibliografie von Ludwig Grote, zusammengestellt von Gertrud Maud Grote," 1986, GNM, DKA, NL Grote, Ludwig (hereafter "NL Grote"), 1053.
2 See Margit Ziesché, "Ausstellungen der Anhaltischen Gemäldegalerie Dessau, 1927–1937," in Norbert Michels, ed., *Verrat an der Moderne: Die Gründungsgeschichte und das erste Jahrzehnt der Anhaltischen Gemäldegalerie Dessau 1927–37* (Dessau: Anhaltische Gemäldegalerie, 1996), 118–20, and Helga Heise, "Die ersten Jahre der Anhaltischen Gemäldegalerie unter Ludwig Grote," NL Grote, 51–79.
3 See "Verzeichnis der von Ludwig Grote veranstalteten Ausstellungen (1926–1933)," n.d., NL Grote, 1539, and "Auflistung der Ausstellungen in der Anhaltischen Gemäldegalerie, 1926–1933," compiled posthumously by Gertrud Maud Grote, ca. 1984, NL Grote, 1049.
4 Grote was chairman of the board of the Anhaltischer Kunstverein from October 1924 and director of the Anhaltische Gemäldegalerie from September 1927. From 1927 onward, the exhibitions of the Anhaltischer Kunstverein were usually held in the Anhaltische Gemäldegalerie after it opened in the Palais Reina on Kavalierstrasse in Dessau.
5 Traveling exhibition that had been organized in 1925 by Gustav Friedrich Hartlaub for the Kunsthalle Mannheim, where it was shown from June 14 to September 18, 1925; then from October 18 to November 22, 1925, at the Sächsischer Kunstverein in Dresden; around the turn of the year 1925–26 at the Städtisches Museum Kunsthütte in Chemnitz; and in February 1926 at the Erfurter Kunstverein; Dessau was its final venue.
6 Traveling exhibition organized by Otto Ralfs, shown first at the Gesellschaft der Freunde junger Kunst in Braunschweig, then at the Galerie Ernst Arnold in Dresden (October 16–November 10, 1926), and at the Galerie Neumann & Nierendorf in Berlin (November 14–December 15, 1926); see "Anhaltischer Kunstverein: Jubiläums-Ausstellung Wassili Kandinsky," *Volksblatt für Anhalt* (December 27, 1926).
7 Wassily Kandinsky taught a Freie Werkstatt Malerei (Free Painting Workshop) at the Bauhaus from 1927, which was also called the "Freie Malklasse" (Free Painting Class).
8 See "Anhaltischer Kunstverein: Ausstellung Malklasse Kandinsky," *Volksblatt für Anhalt* (June 5, 1928).
9 See *bauhaus: vierteljahr-zeitschrift für gestaltung* 3, no. 1 (1929): 24.
10 Traveling exhibition from the Deutscher Werkbund and Museum-Folkwang Essen.
11 Traveling exhibition shown thereafter in, among other places, Essen, Leipzig, Berlin, and Munich; see *bauhaus: vierteljahr-zeitschrift für gestaltung* 3, no. 2 (1929): 25.
12 Exhibition on the brothers Ferdinand, Friedrich, and Heinrich Olivier, German painters of Classicism and Romanticism.
13 Identified by Maud Grote (see note 1) as "'Kleine' Goethe-Gedächtnisausstellung" ("Small" Goethe Memorial Exhibition).
14 This exhibition was a cooperation with Gustav Friedrich Hartlaub and the Kunsthalle Mannheim, where it had been shown previously as the Mannheim-Dessau traveling exhibition *Deutsche Provinz (erster Teil), Beschauliche Sachlichkeit* (German Province, Part 1: Contemplative Objectivity); see the essay by Nadine Willing-Stritzke in the present volume.
15 Grote served as consultant and gave the opening speech.
16 In the spring of 1949, shown under the title *Der Blaue Reiter, 1908–1914: Wegbereiter und Zeitgenossen* (The Blue Rider, 1908–1914: Pioneers and Contemporaries) at the Kunsthalle Basel.
17 Grote was commissioner of the German contribution to the exhibition.
18 Traveling exhibition from the Kestner Gesellschaft in Hanover based on a concept by Alfred Hentzen: Fine artists in the Federal Republic of Germany were invited to submit color prints in editions from 20 to 50, from which a selection by around fifty artists would be exhibited in various museums and also offered for sale. After the first exhibition in 1951, the project, whose goal had been to popularize contemporary art, was repeated every other year until 1959.
19 A selection from the exhibition Grote curated for the Kunstmuseum Luzern (July 4–October 2, 1953).
20 Grote was commissioner of the German contribution to the exhibition.
21 Paintings from the Klee-Stiftung and the artist's estate in Bern that had been intended for the German section of the second Bienal de São Paulo.
22 The Kulturkreis der Deutschen Industrie purchased more than fifty works by contemporary artists, exhibited them, and then donated them to various German museums.
23 Grote was a member of the committee of experts.
24 Grote was a member of the committee of experts.
25 Grote was a member of the committee of experts.
26 Traveled later to Munich, Berlin, and Hamburg as well as to six cities in the United States.
27 Objects from the GNM prints and drawings collection, archives, and coin collection, shown previously at the Stadtmuseum Ludwigshafen (September 15–October 14, 1956).
28 Traveled to the Karl-Ernst-Osthaus-Museum in Hagen (October 13–November 24, 1957).
29 Grote was commissioner of the German contribution to the exhibition.
30 Venue of a traveling exhibition in cooperation with the Kestner Gesellschaft in Hannover, the Württembergische Staatsgalerie in Stuttgart, the Haus am Waldsee in Berlin, the Kunsthalle Hamburg, and the Kölnischer Kunstverein.
31 Traveled to the Wessenberg Galerie in Konstanz (April 26–June 8, 1958) and the Kunstmuseum Linz (August 30–September 28, 1958).
32 Grote was a member of the committee of experts.
33 Shown before and after at the Staatliche Graphischen Sammlung in Munich, at the Kunsthalle Hamburg, and at the Kurpfälzisches Museum, Heidelberg.
34 Grote was a member of the committee of experts and head of the German section.
35 Grote was commissioner of the German contribution to the exhibition.
36 Shown previously at the Kunsthalle Tübingen (February 13–March 15, 1959) and at the Kunstmuseum Ravensburg (April 4–May 2, 1959).
37 Traveled to the Stedelijk Museum Amsterdam.
38 Previously shown at the Wallraf-Richartz-Museum in Cologne and subsequently at the Prinz-Carl-Palais in Munich (May to November 1961).
39 Grote was a member of the committee of experts.
40 Grote was director of the exhibition committee; after its first venue in Stuttgart, the show was seen in London, Amsterdam, Paris, Chicago, Toronto, Pasadena, Buenos Aires, and Tokyo until 1971; thereafter, it was shown in abridged form by the Goethe-Institut in other countries until 1982.
41 Grote was involved as an employee.
42 Grote was involved as an employee.

Image credits and abbreviations

Peter Bernhard, Torsten Blume:
Ludwig Grote: A Conservative Friend of the Bauhaus

Fig. 1 Photo: Erich Consemüller, © Bauhaus Dessau Foundation, I 46176/1-2, © (Erich Consemüller) Stephan Consemüller
Fig. 2 Photo: unknown, © Stadtarchiv München Kunstverein, FS-Erg-H-0665, © VG Bild-Kunst, Bonn 2021
Fig. 3 Photo: unknown, excerpt from the illustrated report on the exhibition *Die Maler am Bauhaus* at the Haus der Kunst in Munich from the illustrated supplement to the *Neue Zeitung*, May 20–21, 1950, © Bauhaus Dessau Foundation, I 17258 D
Fig. 4 © Württembergischer Kunstverein, Stuttgart

Peter Bernhard:
Grote's Bauhaus Idea

Fig. 1 © (Walter Gropius) VG Bild-Kunst, Bonn 2020
Fig. 2 © Bauhaus Dessau Foundation, I I 2849/1-2 D, ©(Lyonel Feininger; Walter Gropius) VG Bild-Kunst, Bonn 2020
Fig. 3 © Bauhaus Dessau Foundation, I 17258 D

Torsten Blume:
On the Bauhaus Idea as "Open Form"

Fig. 1 © Bauhaus Dessau Foundation, I 746 L
Fig. 2 Design: Stefan P. Munsing, © Bauhaus Dessau Foundation, Bibliothek, 2.4.8 Maler/31960, © (Walter Gropius) VG Bild-Kunst, Bonn 2020
Fig. 3 Photo: unknown, © Württembergischer Kunstverein, Stuttgart, © (Herbert Bayer) VG Bild-Kunst, Bonn 2020
Fig. 4 © Bauhaus Dessau Foundation, Bibliothek, 2.2 Gropius/20510, ©(Walter Gropius) VG Bild-Kunst, Bonn 2020
Fig. 5 © (Herbert Bayer) VG Bild-Kunst, Bonn 2020

Peter Bernhard:
The Bauhaus Comes to Dessau: A Chronology

Fig. 1 Photo: unknown, © Stadtarchiv Dessau-Rosslau
Fig. 2 Nuremberg, Germanisches Nationalmuseum, Deutsches Kunstarchiv, NL Grote, Ludwig 1354
Fig. 3 Nuremberg, Germanisches Nationalmuseum, Deutsches Kunstarchiv, NL Grote, Ludwig, 1354_11a + 14
Fig. 4 Nuremberg, Germanisches Nationalmuseum, Deutsches Kunstarchiv, NL Grote, Ludwig, 1355-3a
Fig. 5 © Bauhaus Dessau Foundation, I 915 Z
Fig. 6 Nuremberg, Germanisches Nationalmuseum, Deutsches Kunstarchiv, NL Grote, Ludwig, 1470, © (Josef Albers) The Josef and Anni Albers Foundation, ©(Josef Albers; Herbert Bayer; Adelgunde Stadler-Stölzl (Gunta); Walter Gropius; Lyonel Feininger) VG Bild-Kunst, Bonn 2020, ©(Georg Muche) Bauhaus-Archiv / Museum für Gestaltung, Berlin; ©(Fritz Kuhr) Hermann Famulla, ©(Hans Volger) Alexander Volger, ©(Hinnerk Scheper) Bauhaus Dessau Foundation

Ludwig Grote:
Das Weimarer Bauhaus
(The Bauhaus Weimar) (1925)

Facsimiles, pp. 56–61 Typescript of Ludwig Grotes' article "Das Weimarer Bauhaus und seine Aufgaben in Dessau," Nuremberg, Germanisches Nationalmuseum, Deutsches Kunstarchiv, NL Grote, Ludwig, 1355

Nadine Willing-Stritzke:
Ludwig Grote in Dessau: A Modern Gallerist and Museum Director

Fig. 1 Anhaltische Gemäldegalerie, Grafische Sammlung, inv.-no. Z 1023
Fig. 2 Design: Joost Schmidt (probably), Landesarchiv Sachsen-Anhalt, Abteilung Dessau, Z 109 Staatsministerium Dessau 3, Nr. 2460, fol. 76
Fig. 3 © (Johanna Schütz-Wolff), Christiane Haslacher
Fig. 4 © Bauhaus Dessau Foundation, I 21297 G
Fig. 5 © Bauhaus Dessau Foundation, I 21296 G

Peter Bernhard:
"It's not working with Hannes Meyer any longer": Grote's Role in the Dismissal of the Second Director of the Bauhaus

Fig. 1 Photo: Hermann Bunzel (probably), © Bauhaus Dessau Foundation, I 44787
Fig. 2 © Bundesarchiv, M4870
Fig. 3 © Bauhaus Dessau Foundation, I 8658 D

Christian Eger:
The Politics of Depoliticization: Ludwig Grote's Dedication to a German Bauhaus

Fig. 1 Photo: unknown, 1929, ©Bibliothèque Kandinsky, MNAM/CCI, Centre Pompidou–Dist. RMN-Grand Palais
Fig. 2 Photo: Ludwig Grote, Zentrum Paul Klee, Obj.Id 31880 [private collection, Germany]
Fig. 3 Photo: Walthari Dietz, Sammlung Prinzhorn, Heidelberg
Fig. 4 © Bauhaus Dessau Foundation, I 10804/6-43 D

Elisabeth Kremer:
The First Exhibition of "Degenerate Art" in Germany: Ludwig Grote's Role after the Closure of the Bauhaus by the National Socialist Party

Fig. 1 Photo: Erich Consemüller, © Bauhaus Dessau Foundation, I 46176/1-2, © (Erich Consemüller) Stephan Consemüller
Fig. 2 Nuremberg, Germanisches Nationalmuseum, Deutsches Kunstarchiv, NL Grote, Ludwig, 5, © Bauhaus Dessau Foundation
Fig. 3 Nuremberg, Germanisches Nationalmuseum, Deutsches Kunstarchiv, NL Grote, Ludwig, 1081
Fig. 4 Photo: unknown, © Stadtarchiv Dessau-Rosslau

Birgit Jooss:
Ludwig Grote and the Galerie Zinckgraf (formerly Heinemann) in the Years 1940–1946

Fig. 1 Photo: unknown, reproduction by Galerie Heinemann, stock catalog, 1910/11, p. II, Zentralinstitut für Kunstgeschichte, Munich
Fig. 2 Photo: Felicitas Timpe, Nuremberg, Germanisches Nationalmuseum, Deutsches Kunstarchiv, NL Grote, Ludwig, AMK 9, no. 42
Fig. 3 Nuremberg, Germanisches Nationalmuseum, Deutsches Kunstarchiv, NL Grote, Ludwig, 1085
Fig. 4 Photo: unknown, reproduction from *Weltkunst*, 23, 20, 1953: 5
Fig. 5 Photo: unknown, Stadtarchiv Munich, Judaica (Fotos 0001/Hei)
Fig. 6 Photo: Georg Pahl, © Bundesarchiv, Bild 102-2733
Fig. 7 Photo: unknown, reproduction from Galerie Heinemann, stock catalog, 1910/11, p. III, Zentralinstitut für Kunstgeschichte, Munich

Susanne Neubauer:
Ludwig Grote and Brazil's Interest in the Bauhaus: International Entanglements and Adaptations in Cultural Policy

Fig. 1 Photo: unknown, Archiv der Ausstellungsleitung am Haus der Kunst, Munich
Fig. 2 Photo: unknown, Fundação Bienal de São Paulo / Arquivo Histórico Wanda Svevo

Fig. 3 Nuremberg, Germanisches Nationalmuseum, Deutsches Kunstarchiv, NL Grote, Ludwig, 1816
Fig. 4 Nuremberg, Germanisches Nationalmuseum, Deutsches Kunstarchiv, NL Grote, Ludwig, 1817
Fig. 5 Nuremberg, Germanisches Nationalmuseum, Deutsches Kunstarchiv, NL Grote, Ludwig, 1817

Torsten Blume: From Stuttgart into the World: The Bauhaus as Romantic and Representing the State

Fig. 1 © Bauhaus Dessau Foundation, I 17257 G, © (Herbert Bayer) VG Bild-Kunst, Bonn 2020
Fig. 2 © Württembergischer Kunstverein, Stuttgart
Fig. 3 reproduction from: ed. Württembergischer Kunstverein, *50 jahre bauhaus*, Stuttgart: Württembergischer Kunstverein 1968, © (Herbert Bayer) VG Bild-Kunst, Bonn 2020
Fig. 4 Photo: unknown, © Württembergischer Kunstverein, Stuttgart
Fig. 5 reproduction from: ed. Württembergischer Kunstverein, *50 jahre bauhaus*, Stuttgart: Württembergischer Kunstverein 1968, © (Herbert Bayer) VG Bild-Kunst, Bonn 2020
Fig. 6 © Bauhaus Dessau Foundation, © (Inter Nationes) Goethe-Institut, © Bavaria Atelier GmbH
Fig. 7 Front cover from *Bauhaus. Eine Veröffentlichung des Instituts für Auslandsbeziehungen*, Stuttgart: Institut für Auslandsbeziehungen 1982, © (Bayer, Herbert) VG Bild-Kunst, Bonn 2020
Figs. 8, 9, 10 From the documentation *50 jahre bauhaus. Eine Ausstellung der Bundesrepublik Deutschland*, ifa Stuttgart [1971/72], Nuremberg, Germanisches Nationalmuseum, Deutsches Kunstarchiv, NL Grote, Ludwig, 2505

50 Years after *50 Years of the Bauhaus 1968*: Hans Christ and Iris Dressler in Conversation with Torsten Blume

Figs. 1–5 © Württembergischer Kunstverein, Stuttgart

Biography

Fig. 1 Nuremberg, Germanisches Nationalmuseum, Deutsches Kunstarchiv, NL Grote, Ludwig, AMK 9, 0017a, no. 47
Fig. 2 Photo: unknown, Nuremberg, Germanisches Nationalmuseum, Deutsches Kunstarchiv, NL Grote, Ludwig, AFS 1
Fig. 3 Nuremberg, Germanisches Nationalmuseum, Deutsches Kunstarchiv, NL Grote, Ludwig, AFS 1, no. 12
Fig. 4 Photo: unknown, Nuremberg, Germanisches Nationalmuseum, Deutsches Kunstarchiv, NL Grote, Ludwig, AMK 9, 0022a, no. 062
Fig. 5 Nuremberg, Germanisches Nationalmuseum, Deutsches Kunstarchiv, NL Grote, Ludwig, 1367, © (Ludwig Mies van der Rohe) VG Bild-Kunst, Bonn 2020
Fig. 6 Nuremberg, Germanisches Nationalmuseum, Deutsches Kunstarchiv, NL Grote, Ludwig, AMK 9, no. 054
Fig. 7 Nuremberg, Germanisches Nationalmuseum, Deutsches Kunstarchiv, NL Grote, Ludwig, AMK 9, no. 053
Fig. 8 Nuremberg, Germanisches Nationalmuseum, Deutsches Kunstarchiv, NL Grote, Ludwig, AFS 1, no. 0027
Figs. 9, 10 Nuremberg, Germanisches Nationalmuseum, Deutsches Kunstarchiv, NL Grote, Ludwig, AMK 9, no. 041
Fig. 11 Nuremberg, Germanisches Nationalmuseum, Deutsches Kunstarchiv, NL Grote, Ludwig, AMK 9, no. 024
Fig. 12 Photo: Gabriele Gräfin von Arnim, Münchner Stadtmuseum, Sammlung Fotografie, Arnim Archive, Nuremberg, Germanisches Nationalmuseum, Deutsches Kunstarchiv, NL Grote, Ludwig, AMK 9, 0014a, no. 039

Front cover: Ludwig Grote with a painting by Franz Marc (*Bild mit Rindern 1* [Picture with Cattle 1], 1913) during the preparations for the exhibition *Der Blaue Reiter* (The Blue Rider) at the Haus der Kunst, Munich, 1949. Photo: Johannes Felbermeyer (?), Nuremberg, Germanisches Nationalmuseum, Deutsches Kunstarchiv, NL Grote, Ludwig, AFS 2, no. 0004

Back cover: Ludwig Grote in Marcel Breuer's B3 club chair, 1950, Nuremberg, Germanisches Nationalmuseum, Deutsches Kunstarchiv, NL Grote, Ludwig, AMK 9, no. 49

Abbreviations:
SBD: Stiftung Bauhaus Dessau (Bauhaus Dessau Foundation)
DKA: Deutsches Kunstarchiv, Germanisches Nationalmuseum, Nuremberg
NL: Nachlass (Papers)

Colophon

Stiftung Bauhaus Dessau
Edition Bauhaus 53

Edited for the Bauhaus Dessau Foundation by Peter Bernhard and Torsten Blume

Directorate: Regina Bittner
Director and CEO a. i. of the Bauhaus Dessau Foundation
Gropiusallee 38
06846 Dessau-Rosslau

Coordination, concept, and management: Caroline Jansky
Research: Marian Wild, Thomas Altmann
Design: Hannes Drißner, based on a preliminary concept by Katharina Köhler
Translation: Steven Lindberg
Copy-editing: Keonaona Peterson
Printed by: Gutenberg Beuys Feindruckerei GmbH

This publication is indexed in the Deutsche Nationalbibliografie of the German National Library; detailed bibliographic information is available online at www.dnb.de

Published by:
Spector Books
Harkortstrasse 10
04107 Leipzig
Germany
www.spectorbooks.com

Distribution:
Germany, Austria: GVA, Gemeinsame Verlagsauslieferung Göttingen GmbH&Co. KG, www.gva-verlage.de
Switzerland: AVA Verlagsauslieferung AG, www.ava.ch
France, Belgium: Interart Paris, www.interart.fr
UK: Central Books Ltd, www.centralbooks.com
USA, Canada, Central and South America, Africa: ARTBOOK/ D.A.P., www.artbook.com
Japan: twelvebooks, www.twelvebooks.com
South Korea: The Book Society, www.thebooksociety.org
Australia, New Zealand: Perimeter Distribution, www.perimeterdistribution.com

ISBN 978-3-95905-280-1

First edition
Printed in Germany

Die deutsche Ausgabe von *Ludwig Grote und die Bauhaus-Idee* erscheint bei Spector Books unter der folgenden ISBN: 978-3-95905-279-5

The Bauhaus Dessau Foundation is a nonprofit foundation under public law. It is institutionally funded by the German Federal Commissioner for Culture and the Media, the State of Saxony-Anhalt, and the City of Dessau-Rosslau. The Publication *Ludwig Grote and the Bauhaus Idea* is generously funded by:

EvS
ERNST VON SIEMENS KUNSTSTIFTUNG

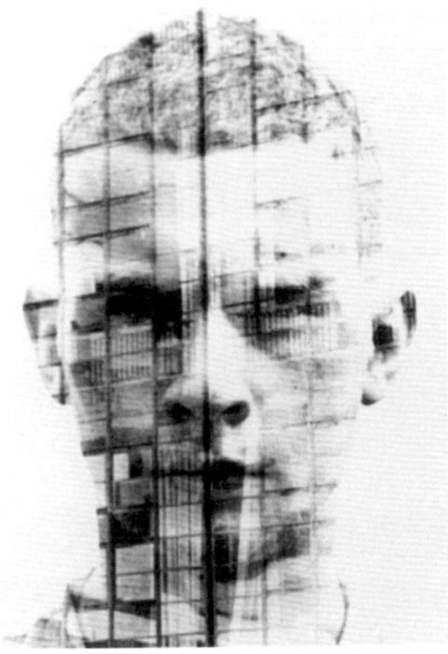

The Progressive Heritage of the Bauhaus

On the Origins of an East German Bauhaus Collection

Wolfgang Thöner and Christin Müller-Wenzel

The collection of the Bauhaus Dessau Foundation currently includes more than 50,000 objects and documents relating to the history of the Bauhaus from 1919 to 1933 as well as to the history of how that institution was received, particularly in East Germany from 1945 to 1989. The collection of the Bauhaus Dessau Foundation has its origins in the 1970s, although this was the result of much earlier developments. This publication revisits those early years of "Bauhaus collecting": it describes and analyzes the content-related institutional mechanisms in the German Democratic Republic that preceded and rationalized the collection, as well as the actual processes of collecting — none of which would have been possible without the interaction of various personal networks.

ISBN 978-3-95905-278-8
112 pp. / 20.00 € / 90 color- and bw-illustrations

Recently published by Spector Books in the series *Edition Bauhaus*

Edition Bauhaus 35
Kurt Kranz
schwarz : weiß/weiß : schwarz
ISBN: 978-3-940064-21-9
80 pp. / 35.00€

Edition Bauhaus 38
Human – Space – Machine
Stage experiments at the Bauhaus
ISBN: 978-3-944669-22-9
252 pp. / 36.00€

Edition Bauhaus 39
László Moholy-Nagy
Sehen in Bewegung
ISBN: 978-3-944669-32-8
376 pp. / 42.00€

Edition Bauhaus 46
The New Masters' Houses in Dessau
ISBN: 978-3-944669-73-1
176 pp. / 40.00€

Edition Bauhaus 49
In Reserve:
The Household! Historic Models and
Contemporary Positions from the Bauhaus
ISBN: 978-3-95905-091-3
270 pp. / 32.00€

Edition Bauhaus 54
The Progressive Heritage of the Bauhaus.
On the Origins of an East German Bauhaus
Collection
ISBN: 978-3-95905-278-8
296 pp. / 20.00€

Edition Bauhaus 57
Design Rehearsals.
Conversations about Bauhaus Lessons
ISBN: 978-3-95905-270-2
180 pp. / 36.00€